ANIMERICA EXTRA GRAPHIC NOVEL

REVOLUTIONARY GIRL
UTENA™

VOL. 3: To Sprout

Manga by
CHIHO SAITO

Story by
BE PAPAS

ONE DAY, THE TRUTH COMES CRASHING DOWN ON A LITTLE GIRL — HER PARENTS AREN'T AWAY ON A TRIP, THEY'VE DIED. THE GRADE-SCHOOL-AGE GIRL WANDERS THE RAIN-SOAKED STREETS OF HER HOMETOWN WITH NO DISTINCT PURPOSE. DRENCHED IN RAINWATER AND TEARS, SHE FINDS HERSELF BY A RIVER, AND WITHOUT KNOWING WHAT SHE IS DOING, SHE THROWS HERSELF INTO THE ROARING FLOOD.

SUDDENLY, A MAN APPEARS. HE IS HER PRINCE AND HE LEAPS TO HER RESCUE. BANISHING HER TEARS, HE GIVES HER A RING WITH A MYSTERIOUS ROSE-ENGRAVED CREST AND TELLS HER TO GROW UP INTO A STRONG, NOBLE WOMAN. SAVED AND SMITTEN, THE GIRL MAKES A PROMISE TO HERSELF: FROM THAT DAY FORWARD SHE'LL STRIVE, NOT TO BECOME A PRINCESS, BUT RATHER TO GROW UP TO BE A PRINCE JUST LIKE HIM!

UTENA TENJOU BEGINS RECEIVING ANNUAL LETTERS FROM HER PRINCE, AND AFTER SEVEN YEARS, A DISPATCH ARRIVES WITH GOOD NEWS. FINALLY, AFTER ALL THIS TIME, SHE AND HER PRINCE WOULD BE REUNITED. DEDUCING THAT HE IS WAITING FOR HER AT AN ELITE BOARDING SCHOOL CALLED OHTORI ACADEMY, SHE PACKS HER BAGS AND WALKS HEADFIRST TOWARDS HER DESTINY.

DESPITE ENROLLING AT THE ACADEMY, UTENA HAS YET TO DETERMINE THE IDENTITY OF HER EVER-ELUSIVE PRINCE. SHE HAS, HOWEVER, BECOME INTIMATELY INVOLVED WITH VARIOUS MEMBERS OF THE ACADEMY'S STUDENT COUNCIL.

BY PARTICIPATING IN THE COUNCIL'S BIZARRE, RITUALISTIC SWORD FIGHTS, UTENA FINDS HERSELF ENGAGED TO AN EXOTIC-LOOKING ODDBALL NAMED ANTHY HIMEMIYA, ALSO KNOWN AS THE ROSE BRIDE.

WITHOUT A DOUBT, THE COUNCIL AND THE ROSE BRIDE HOLD THE KEY TO UTENA'S FUTURE. BUT ALONG THE WAY, SHE MUST DETERMINE WHO SHE CAN TRUST AND WHO SHE CAN'T. IF SHE'S NOT CAREFUL, UTENA'S TRUSTING NATURE MIGHT BE HER ULTIMATE DOWNFALL.

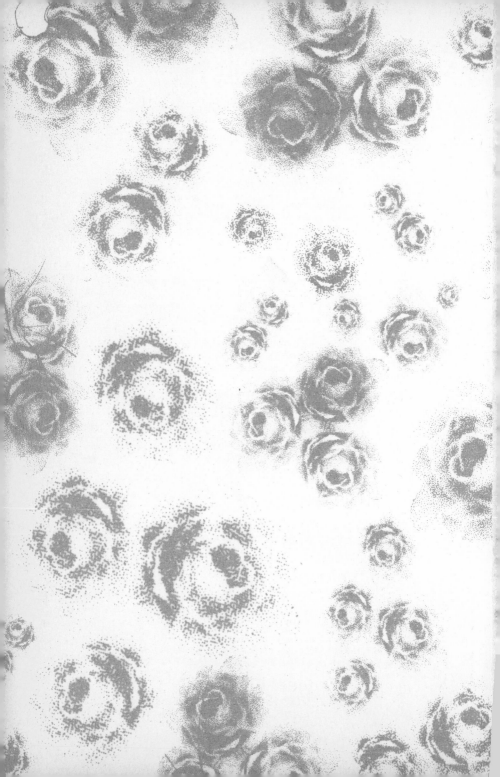

REVOLUTIONARY GIRL UTENA
VOL. 3: TO SPROUT

This volume contains the Revolutionary Girl Utena installments from
Animerica Extra Vol. 5 , No. 5 through Vol. 5 , No. 11 in their entirety.

Manga by
CHIHO SAITO

Story by
BE PAPAS

English Adaptation by
Fred Burke

Translator/Lillian Olsen
Touch-up & Lettering/Steve Dutro
Cover Design/Hidemi Sahara
Graphic Design/Carolina Ugalde
Editor/William Flanagan
Graphic Novel Editor/Eric Searleman

Managing Editor/Annette Roman
Editor-in-Chief/William Flanagan
Director of Licensing and Acquisitions/Rika Inouye
Sr. VP of Sales & Marketing/Rick Bauer
Sr. VP of Editorial/Hyoe Narita
Publisher/Seiji Horibuchi

Printed in Canada.

Published by VIZ, LLC
P.O. Box 77010
San Francisco, CA 94107

10 9 8 7 6 5 4 3 2 1
First printing, May 2003

store.viz.com

www.viz.com

ANIMERICA EXTRA GRAPHIC NOVEL

REVOLUTIONARY GIRL

UTENA™

VOL. 3: To Sprout

CONTENTS

PRONUNCIATION GUIDE:
THE "OU" SOUND IN UTENA'S LAST NAME TENJOU AND
TOUGA'S NAME IS PRONOUNCED "OH" (RHYMES WITH "SNOW").

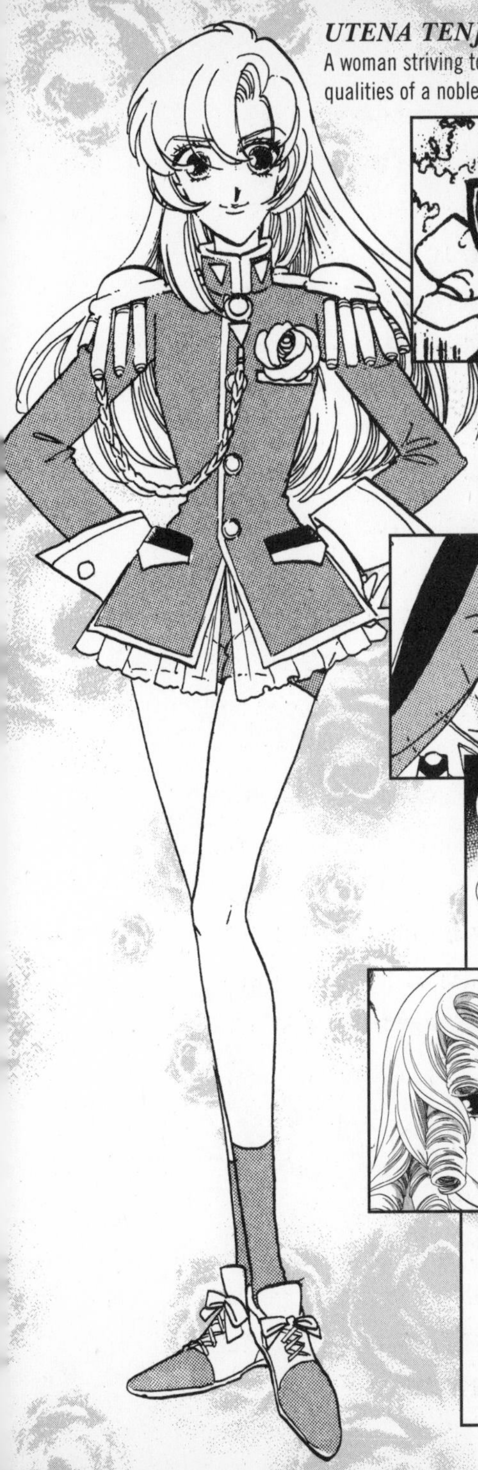

UTENA TENJOU:
A woman striving to possess all the qualities of a noble prince.

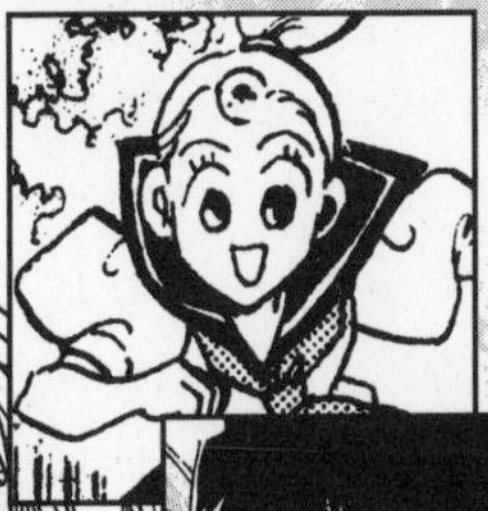

WAKABA:
Utena's manic first roommate has been her best friend since Utena first enrolled.

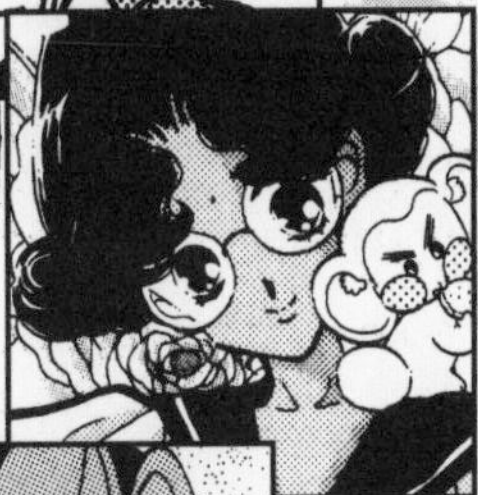

ANTHY HIMEMIYA:
The mysterious "Rose Bride" is now Utena's roommate and fiancé.

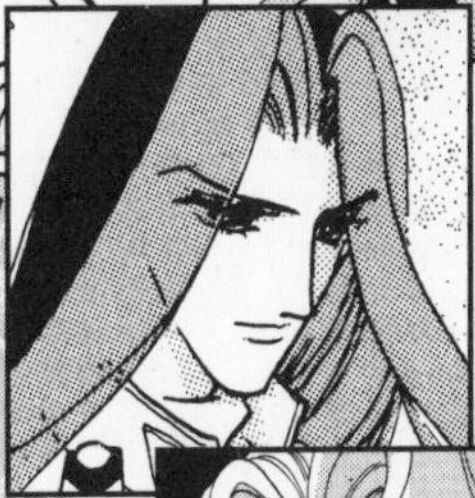

TOUGA KIRYUU:
The Student Council President is also the playboy leader of the duelists.

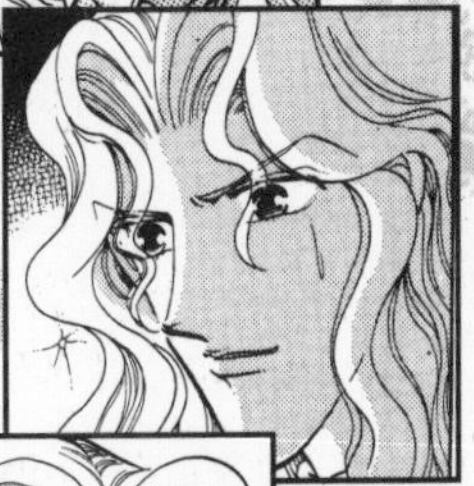

KYOUICHI SAIONJI:
The Student Council Vice President is romantically attached to Anthy, although it seems one-sided.

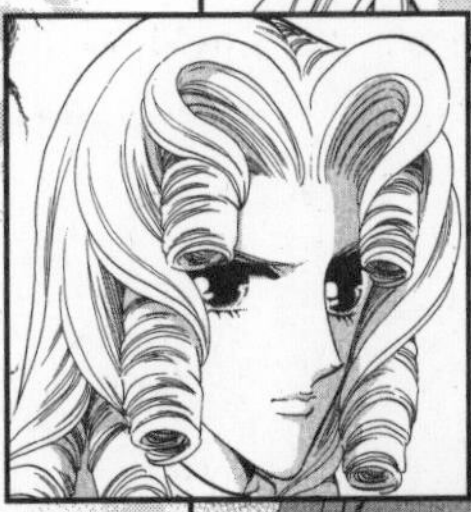

JURI ARISUGAWA:
This fierce Student Council member is in love with playboy Touga Kiryuu.

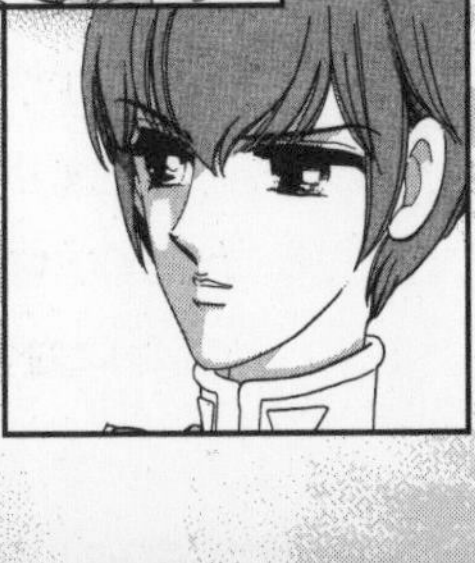

MIKI KAORU:
This mild-mannered Student Council member is the youngest of the duelists.

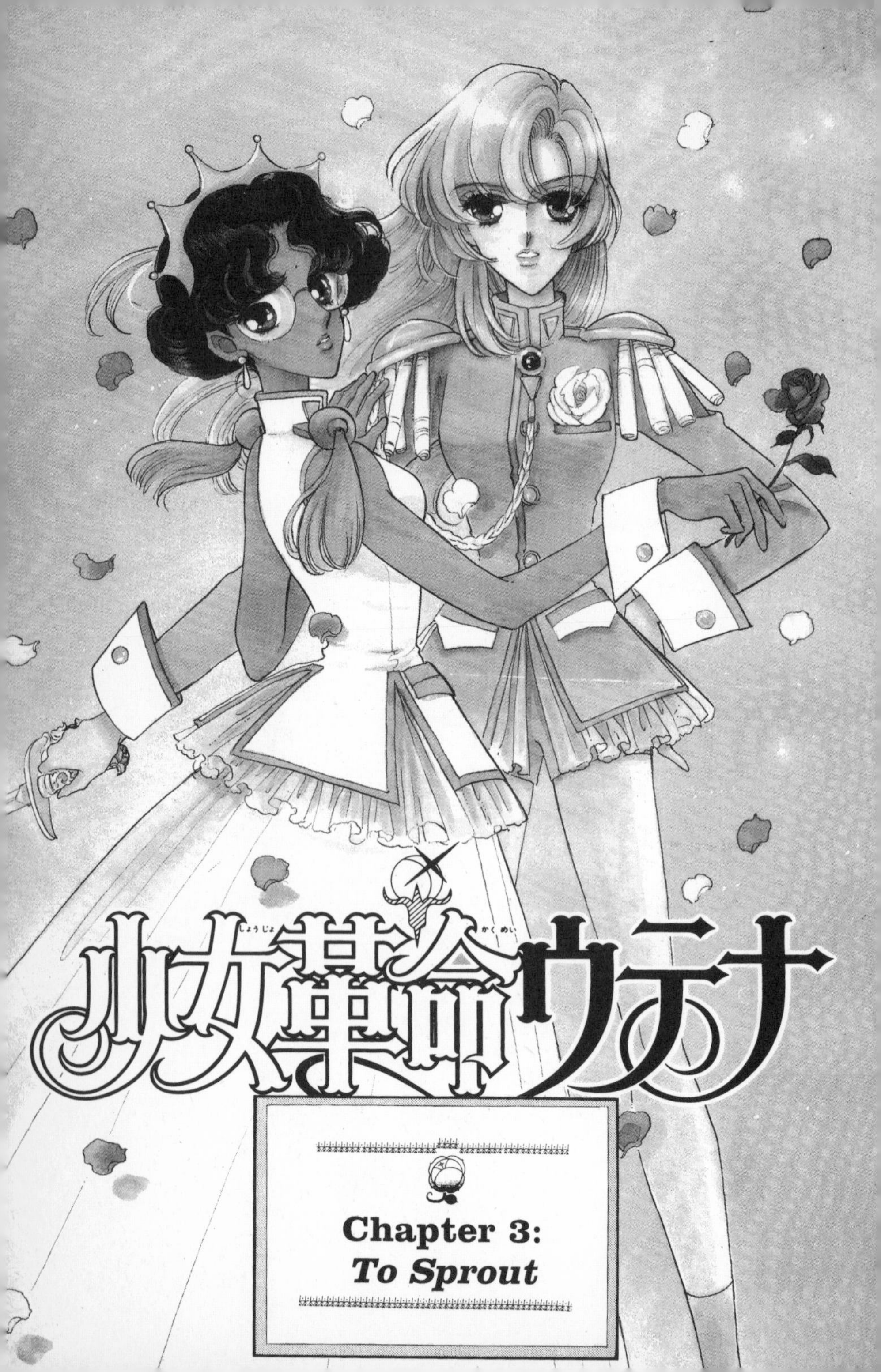
少女革命ウテナ
Chapter 3:
To Sprout

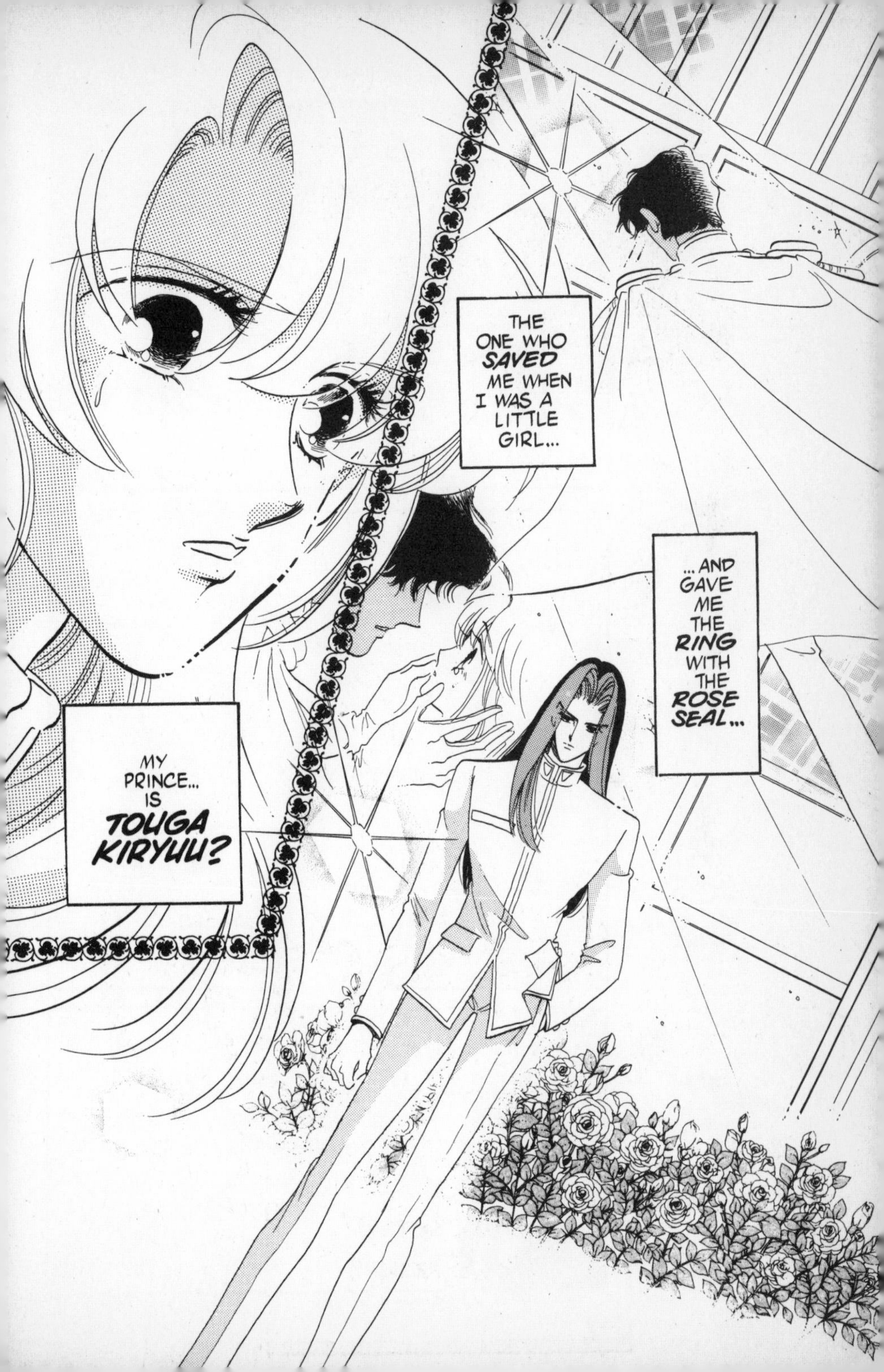
THE ONE WHO SAVED ME WHEN I WAS A LITTLE GIRL...
...AND GAVE ME THE RING WITH THE ROSE SEAL...
MY PRINCE... IS TOUGA KIRYUU?

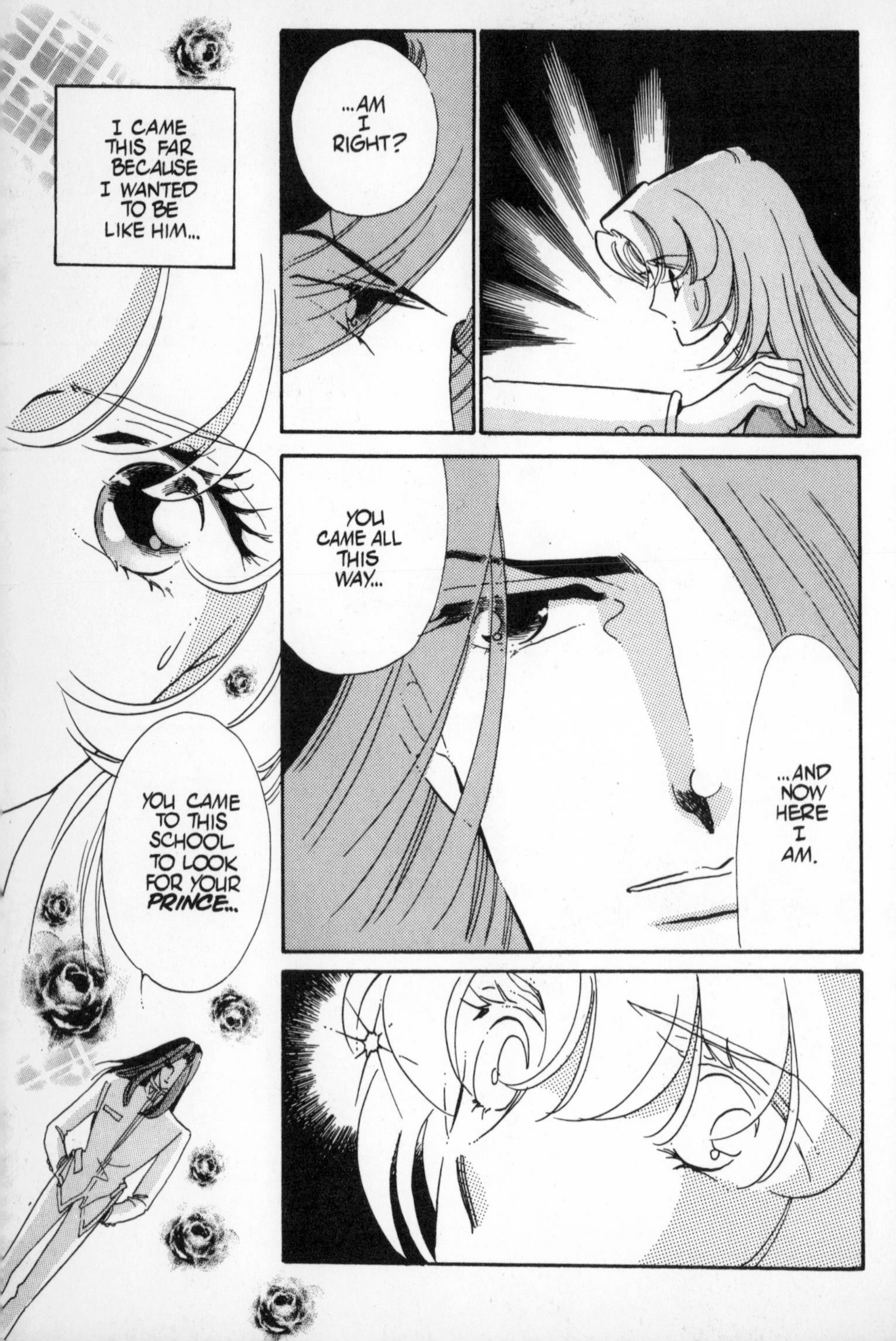
I CAME THIS FAR BECAUSE I WANTED TO BE LIKE HIM...
YOU CAME TO THIS SCHOOL TO LOOK FOR YOUR **PRINCE**...
...AM I RIGHT?
YOU CAME ALL THIS WAY...
...AND NOW HERE I AM.

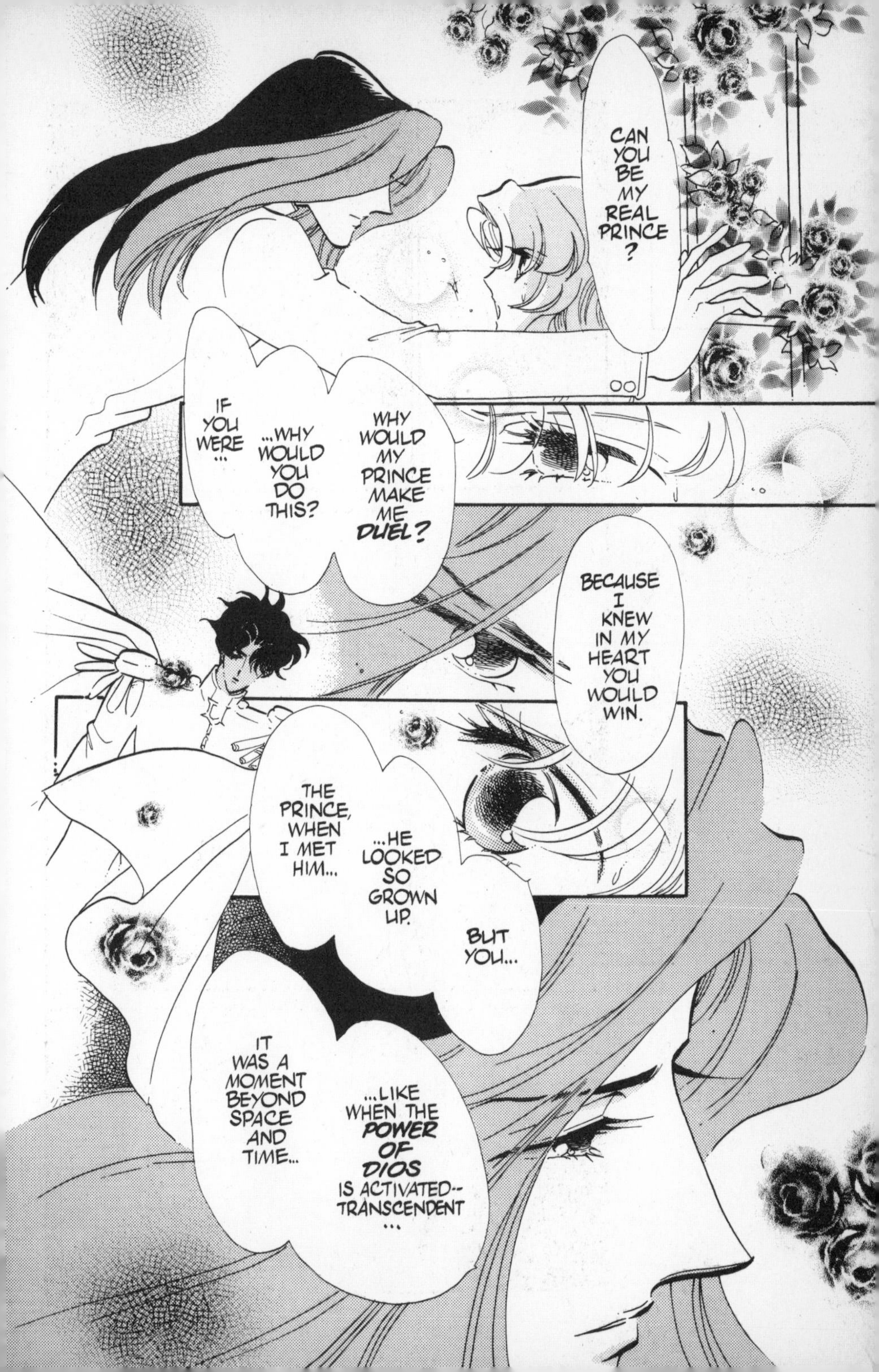
CAN YOU BE MY REAL PRINCE?
IF YOU WERE...
...WHY WOULD YOU DO THIS?
WHY WOULD MY PRINCE MAKE ME DUEL?
BECAUSE I KNEW IN MY HEART YOU WOULD WIN.
THE PRINCE, WHEN I MET HIM...
...HE LOOKED SO GROWN UP.
BUT YOU...
IT WAS A MOMENT BEYOND SPACE AND TIME...
...LIKE WHEN THE POWER OF DIOS IS ACTIVATED--TRANSCENDENT...

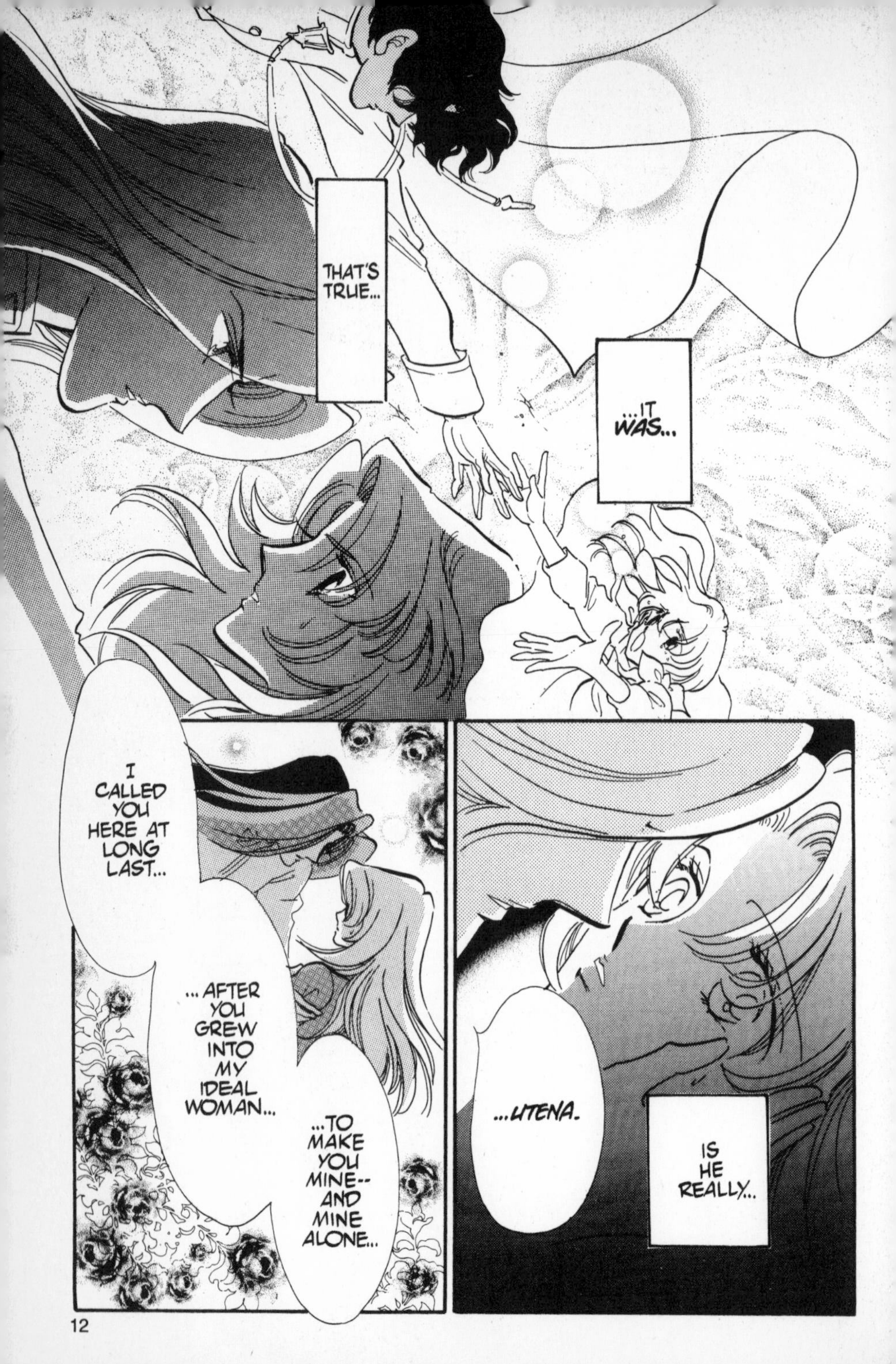
THAT'S TRUE...
...IT WAS...
I CALLED YOU HERE AT LONG LAST...
...AFTER YOU GREW INTO MY IDEAL WOMAN...
...TO MAKE YOU MINE-- AND MINE ALONE...
...UTENA.
IS HE REALLY...

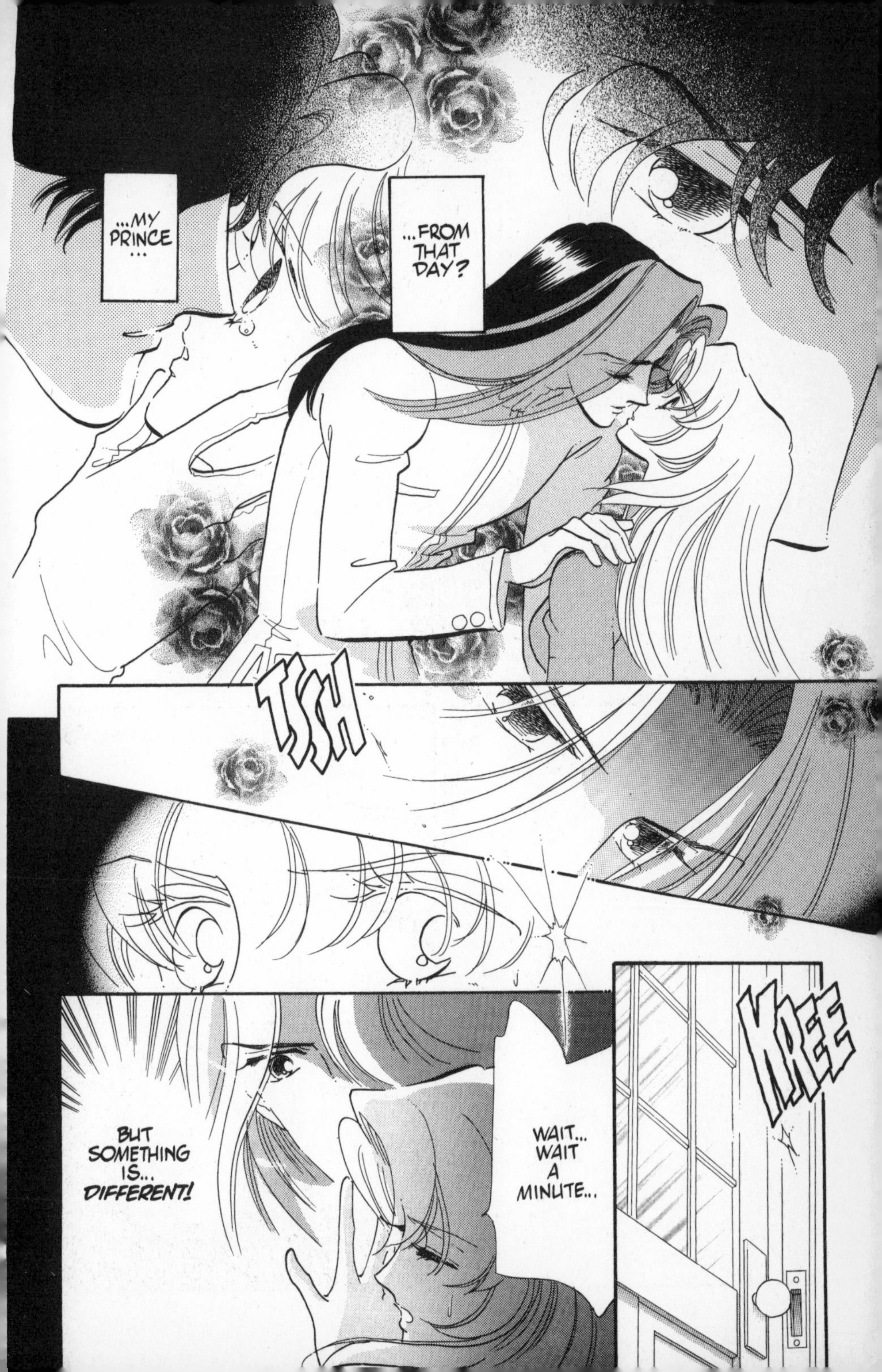
...MY PRINCE ...
...FROM THAT DAY?
TSH
KREE
BUT SOMETHING IS... DIFFERENT!
WAIT... WAIT A MINUTE...

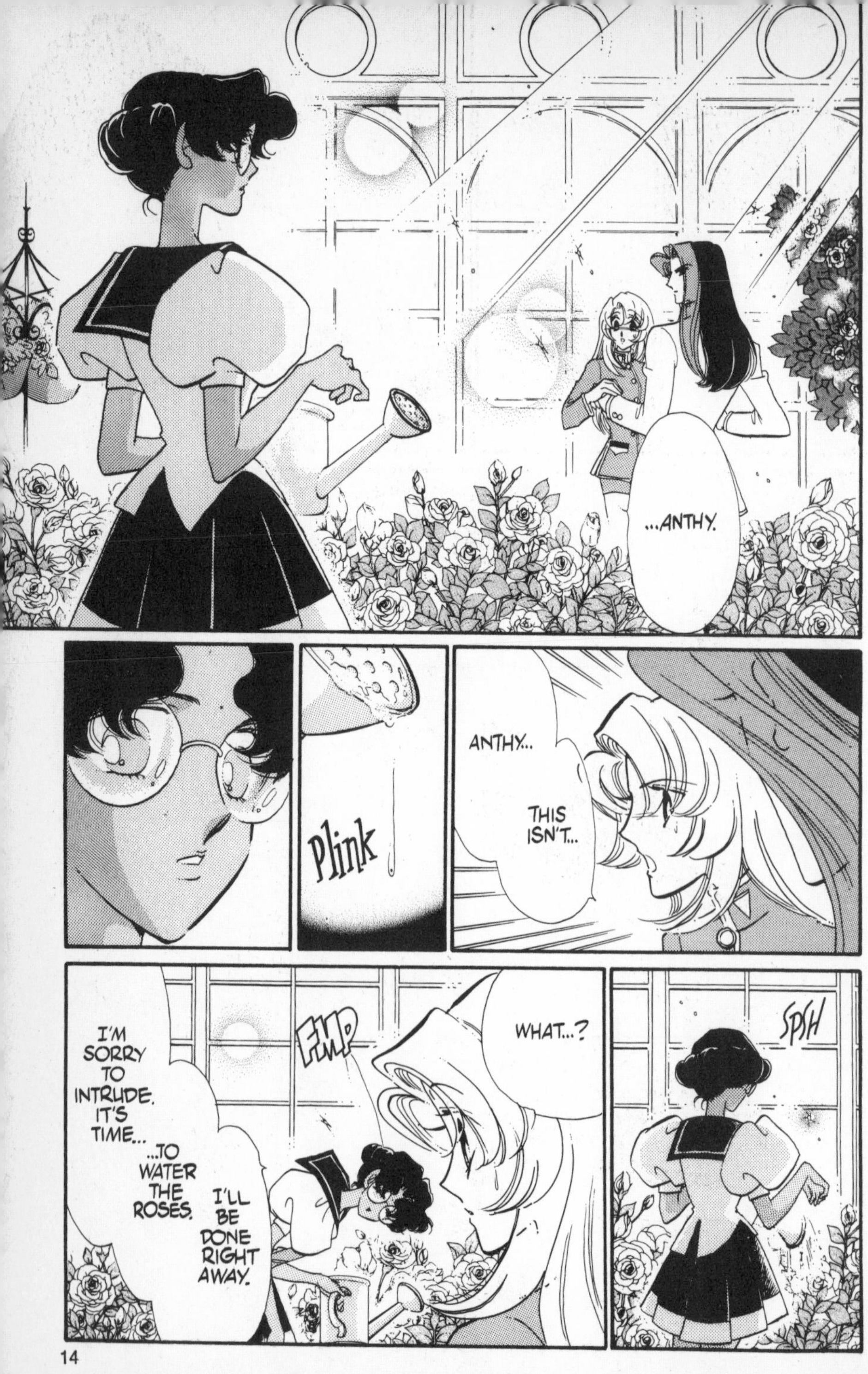
...ANTHY.
Plink
ANTHY...
THIS ISN'T...
I'M SORRY TO INTRUDE. IT'S TIME...
...TO WATER THE ROSES.
I'LL BE DONE RIGHT AWAY.
FMP
WHAT...?
SPSH

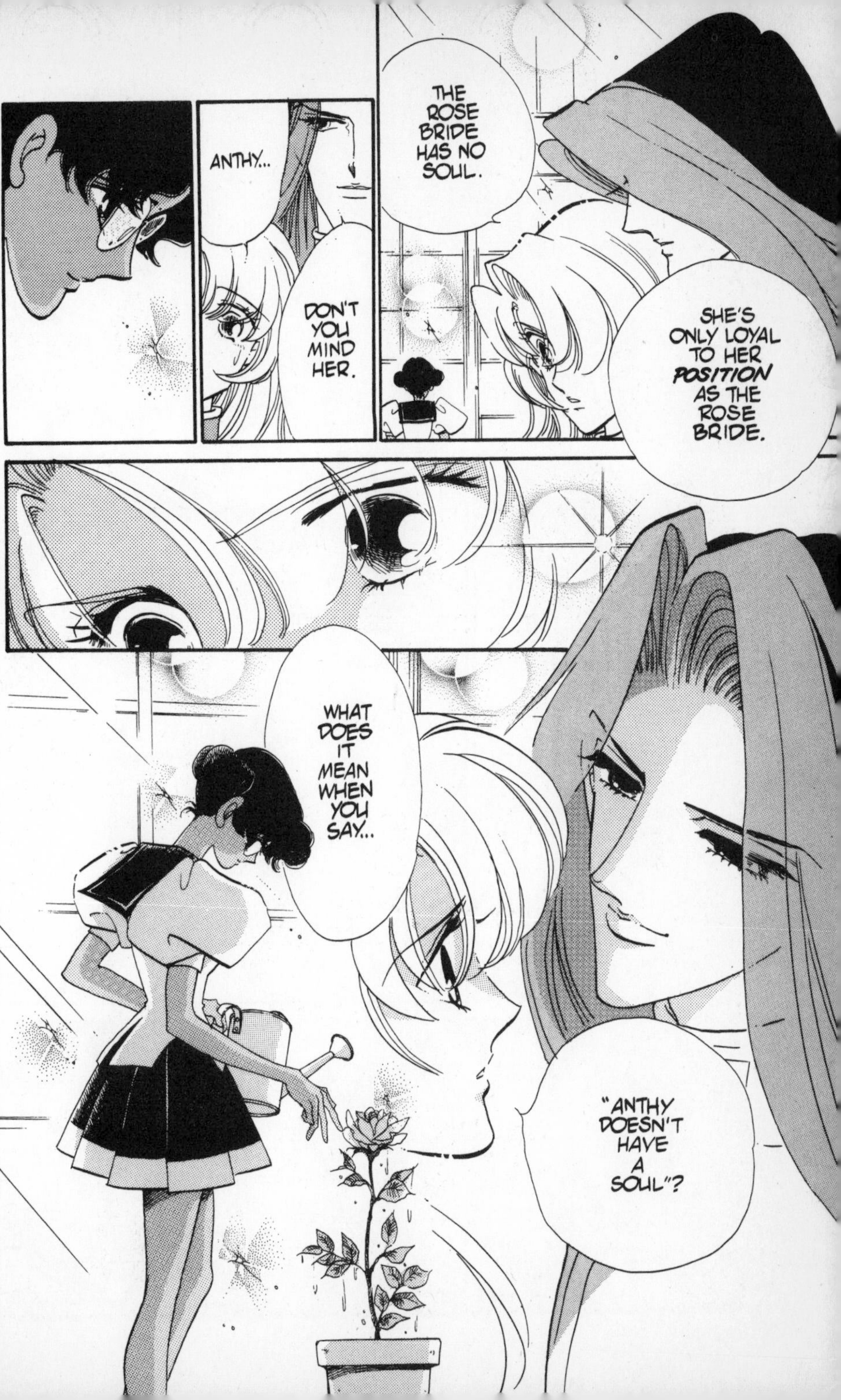
ANTHY...
DON'T YOU MIND HER.
THE ROSE BRIDE HAS NO SOUL.
SHE'S ONLY LOYAL TO HER *POSITION* AS THE ROSE BRIDE.
WHAT DOES IT MEAN WHEN YOU SAY...
"ANTHY DOESN'T HAVE A SOUL"?

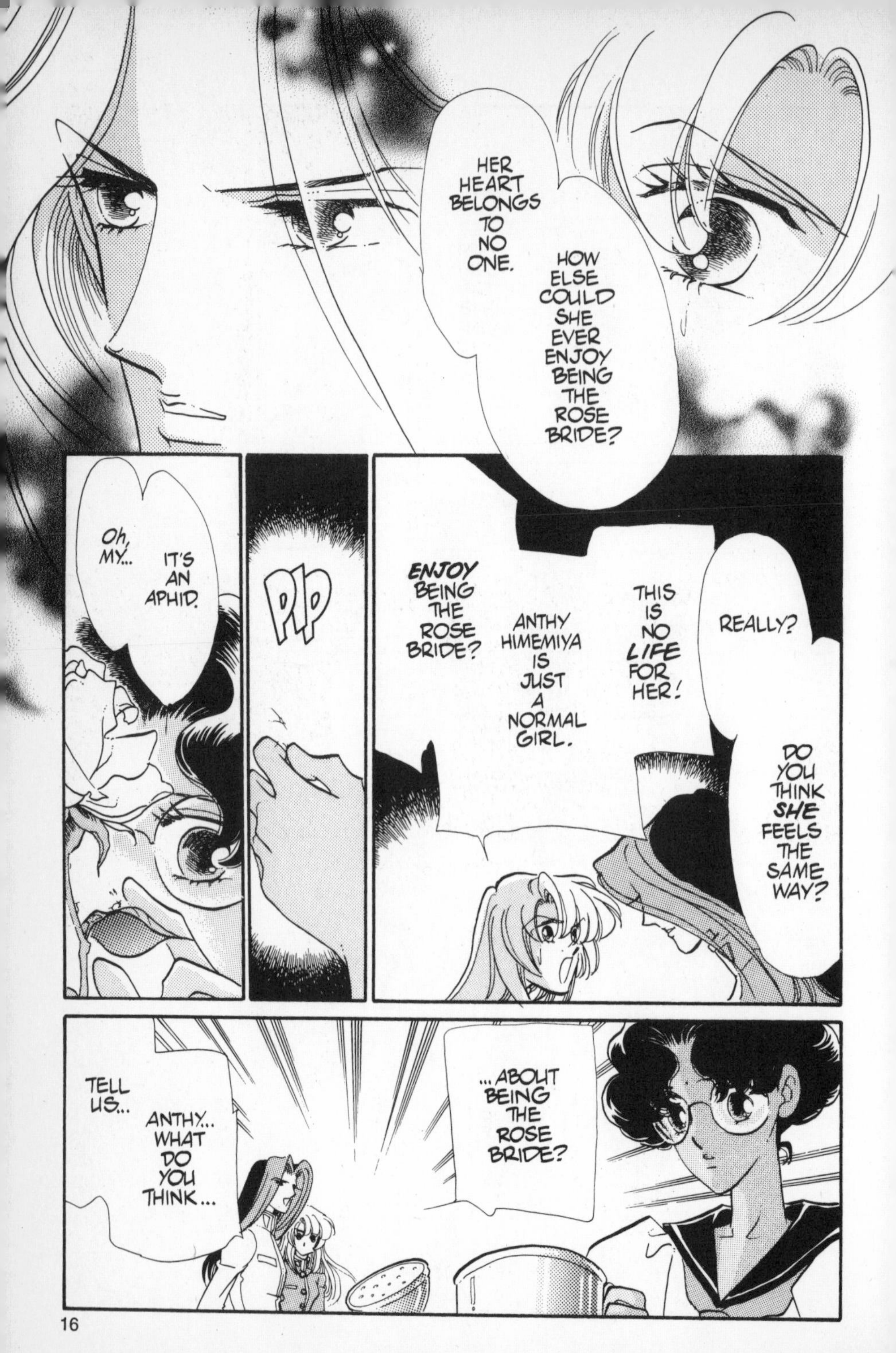
HER HEART BELONGS TO NO ONE.
HOW ELSE COULD SHE EVER ENJOY BEING THE ROSE BRIDE?
Oh, MY... IT'S AN APHID.
PIP
ENJOY BEING THE ROSE BRIDE?
ANTHY HIMEMIYA IS JUST A NORMAL GIRL.
THIS IS NO LIFE FOR HER!
REALLY?
DO YOU THINK SHE FEELS THE SAME WAY?
TELL US...
ANTHY... WHAT DO YOU THINK...
...ABOUT BEING THE ROSE BRIDE?

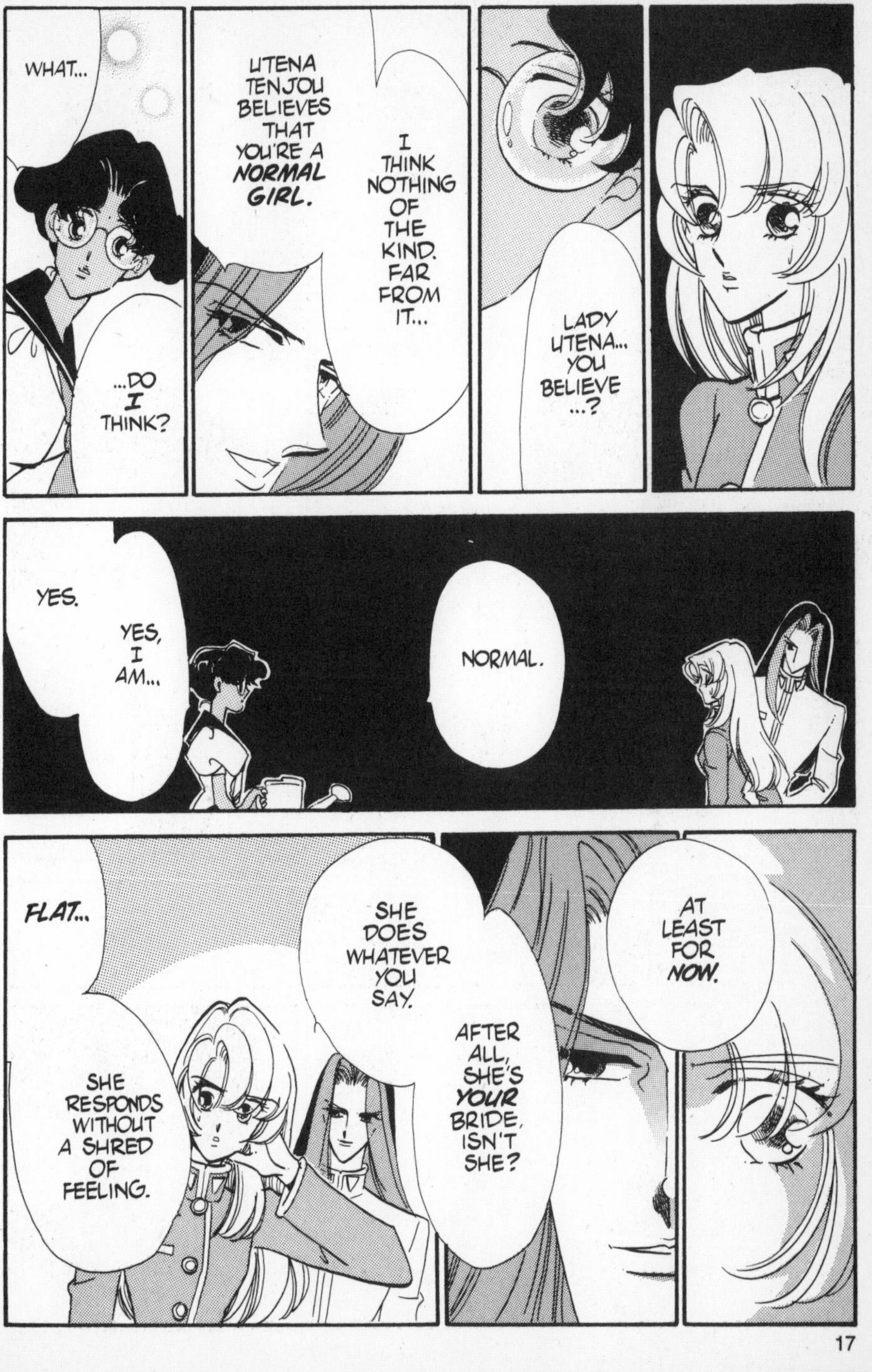
WHAT...
...DO I THINK?
UTENA TENJOU BELIEVES THAT YOU'RE A NORMAL GIRL.
I THINK NOTHING OF THE KIND. FAR FROM IT...
LADY UTENA... YOU BELIEVE ...?
YES.
YES, I AM...
NORMAL.
FLAT...
SHE RESPONDS WITHOUT A SHRED OF FEELING.
SHE DOES WHATEVER YOU SAY.
AFTER ALL, SHE'S YOUR BRIDE, ISN'T SHE?
AT LEAST FOR NOW.

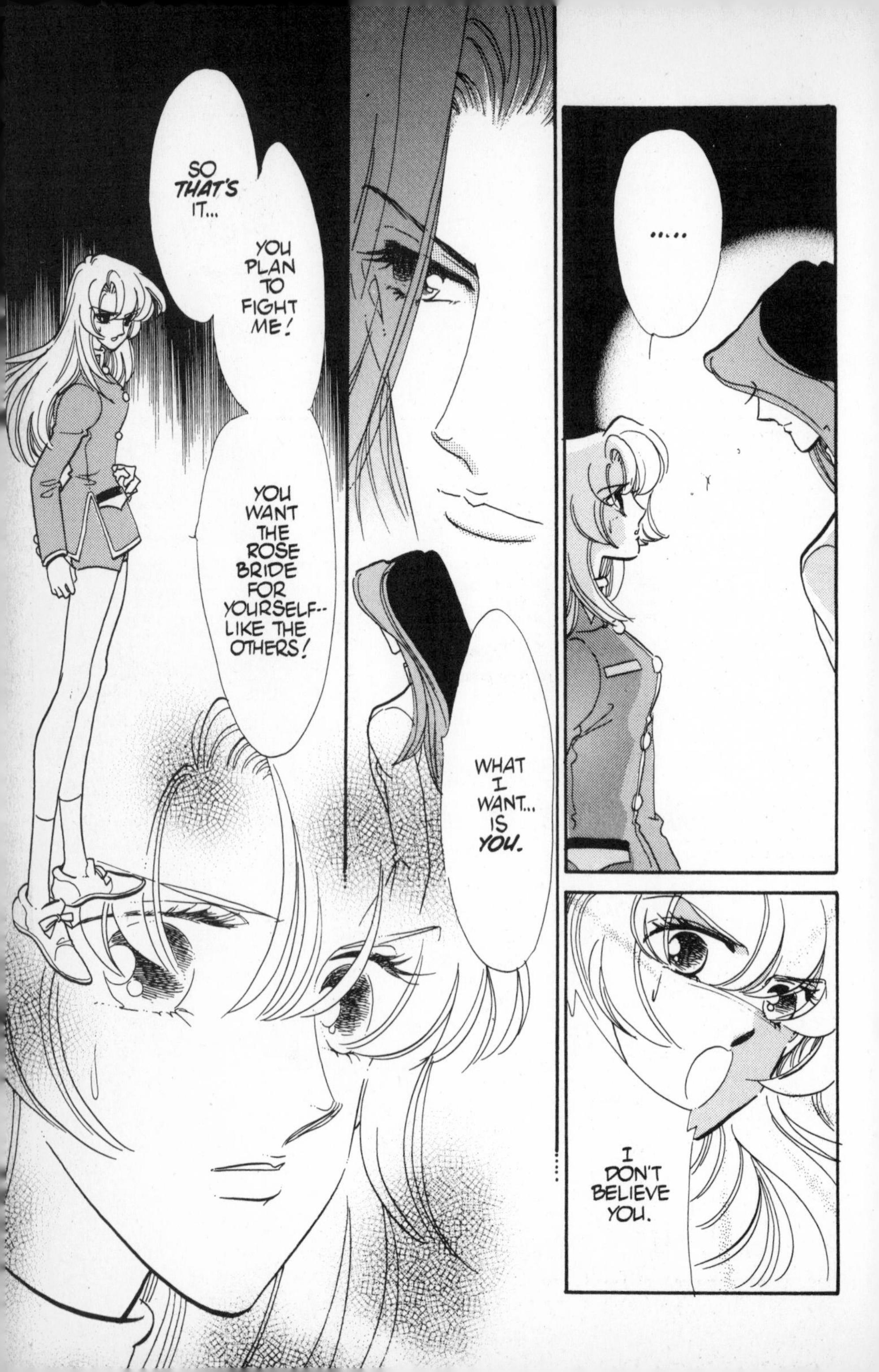
SO *THAT'S* IT...
YOU PLAN TO FIGHT ME!
YOU WANT THE ROSE BRIDE FOR YOURSELF-- LIKE THE OTHERS!
WHAT I WANT... IS *YOU*.
.....
I DON'T BELIEVE YOU.

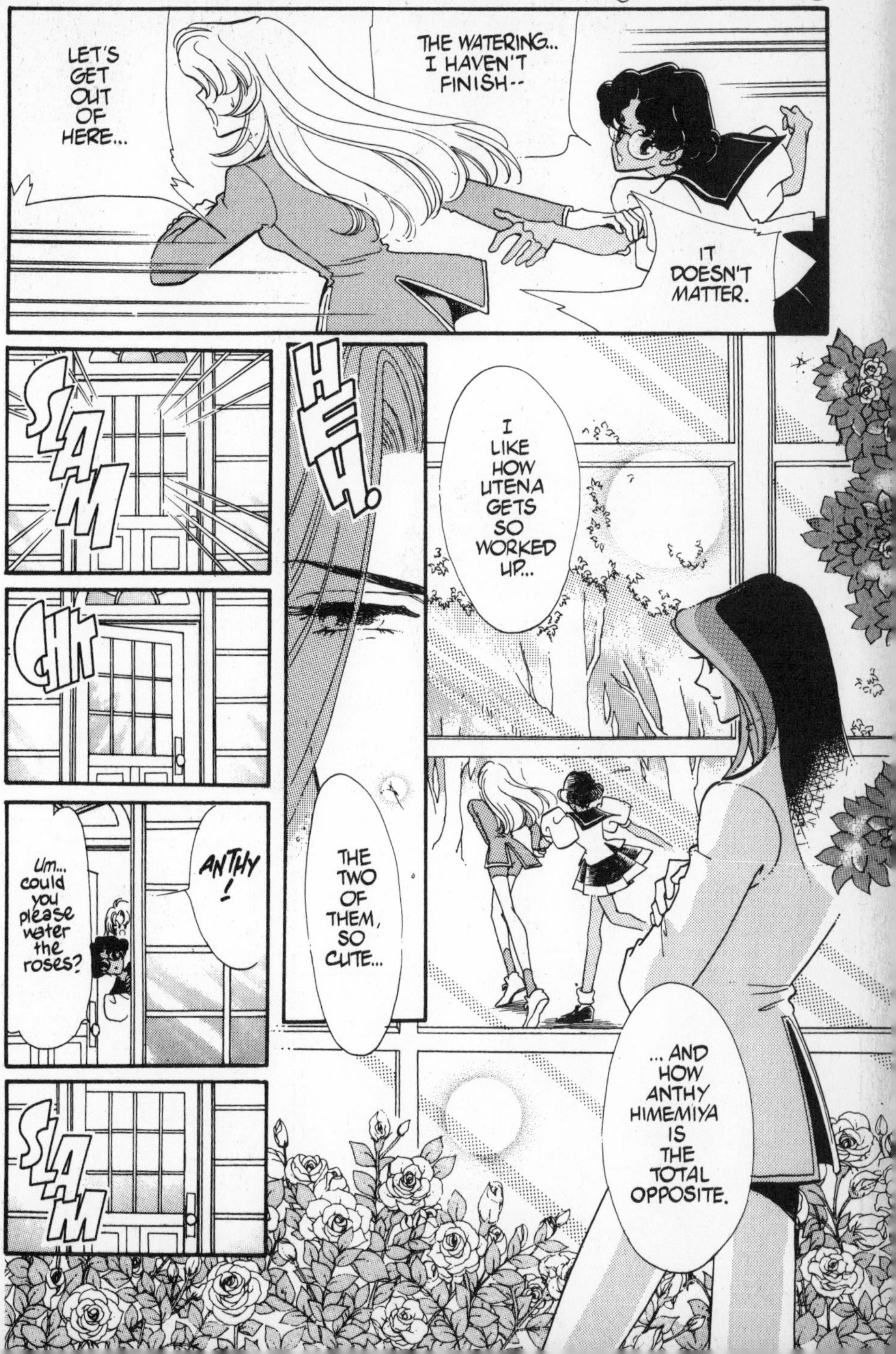
LET'S GET OUT OF HERE...
THE WATERING... I HAVEN'T FINISH--
IT DOESN'T MATTER.
SLAM
CHK
Um... could you please water the roses?
ANTHY!
SLAM
HEH!
THE TWO OF THEM, SO CUTE...
I LIKE HOW UTENA GETS SO WORKED UP...
... AND HOW ANTHY HIMEMIYA IS THE TOTAL OPPOSITE.

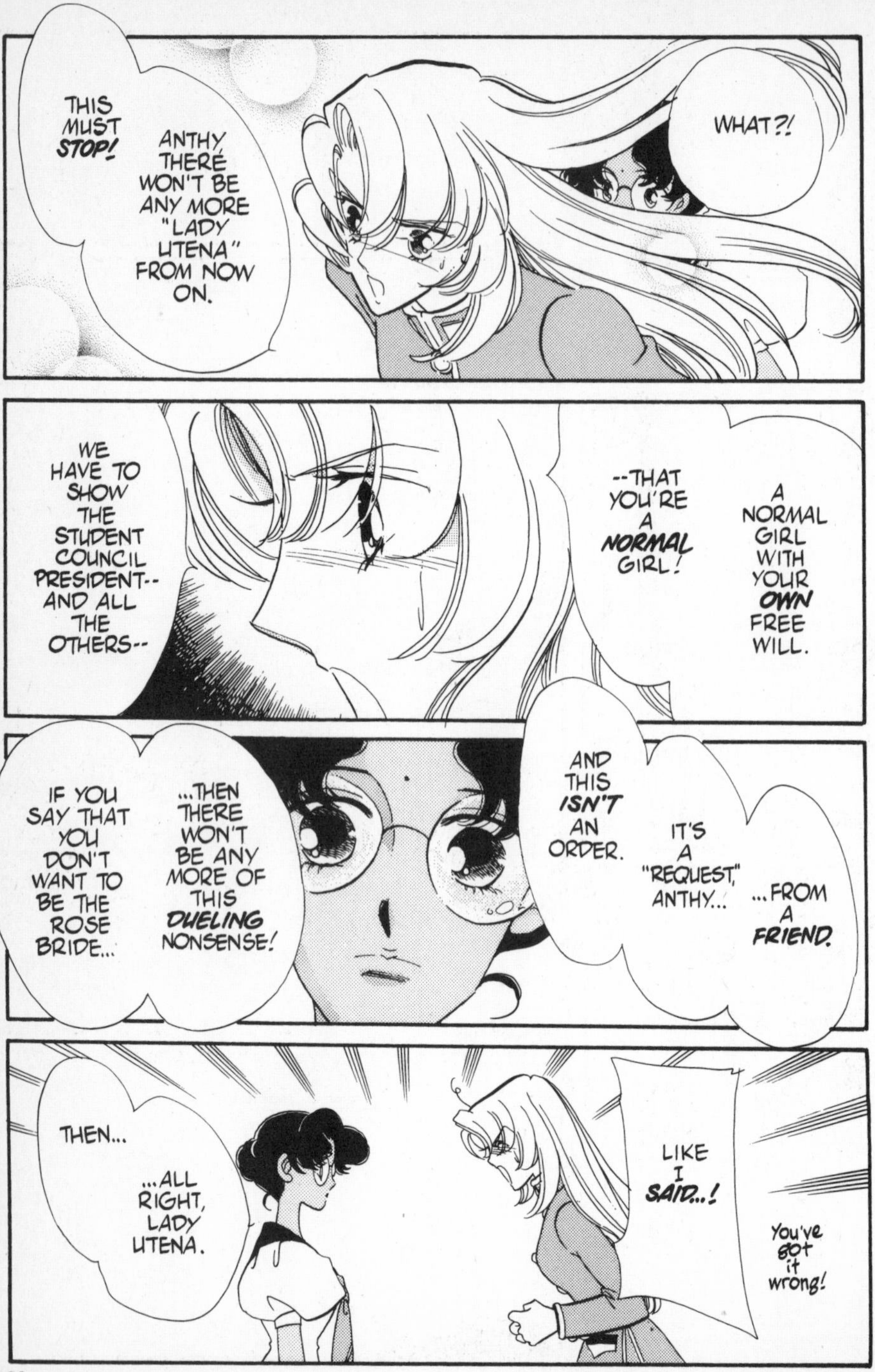
THIS MUST STOP!
ANTHY, THERE WON'T BE ANY MORE "LADY UTENA" FROM NOW ON.
WHAT?!
WE HAVE TO SHOW THE STUDENT COUNCIL PRESIDENT-- AND ALL THE OTHERS--
--THAT YOU'RE A NORMAL GIRL!
A NORMAL GIRL WITH YOUR OWN FREE WILL.
IF YOU SAY THAT YOU DON'T WANT TO BE THE ROSE BRIDE...
...THEN THERE WON'T BE ANY MORE OF THIS DUELING NONSENSE!
AND THIS ISN'T AN ORDER.
IT'S A "REQUEST," ANTHY...
...FROM A FRIEND.
THEN...
...ALL RIGHT, LADY UTENA.
LIKE I SAID...!
You've got it wrong!

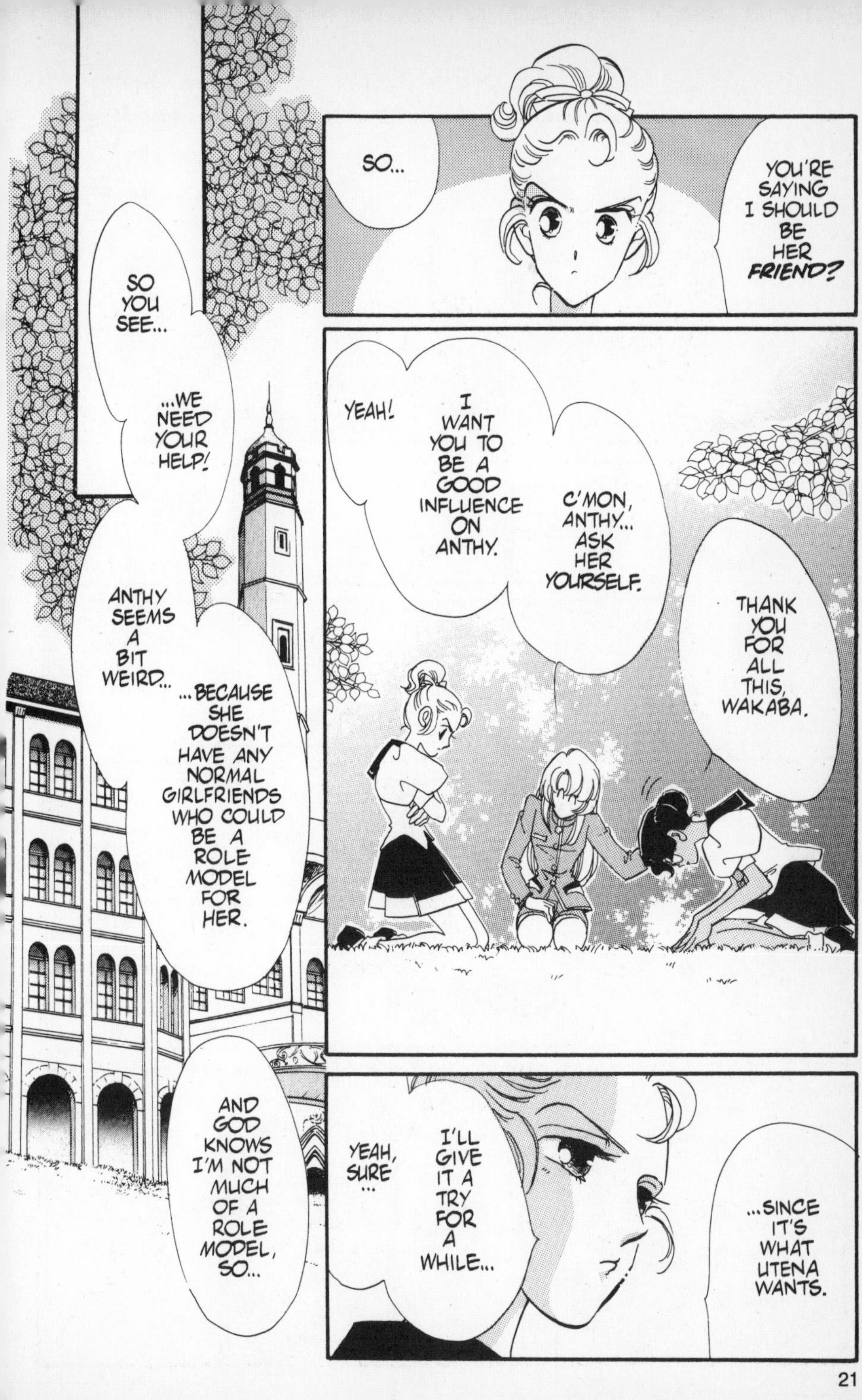
SO YOU SEE...
...WE NEED YOUR HELP!
ANTHY SEEMS A BIT WEIRD...
...BECAUSE SHE DOESN'T HAVE ANY NORMAL GIRLFRIENDS WHO COULD BE A ROLE MODEL FOR HER.
AND GOD KNOWS I'M NOT MUCH OF A ROLE MODEL, SO...
SO...
YOU'RE SAYING I SHOULD BE HER FRIEND?
YEAH!
I WANT YOU TO BE A GOOD INFLUENCE ON ANTHY.
C'MON, ANTHY... ASK HER YOURSELF.
THANK YOU FOR ALL THIS, WAKABA.
YEAH, SURE...
I'LL GIVE IT A TRY FOR A WHILE...
...SINCE IT'S WHAT UTENA WANTS.

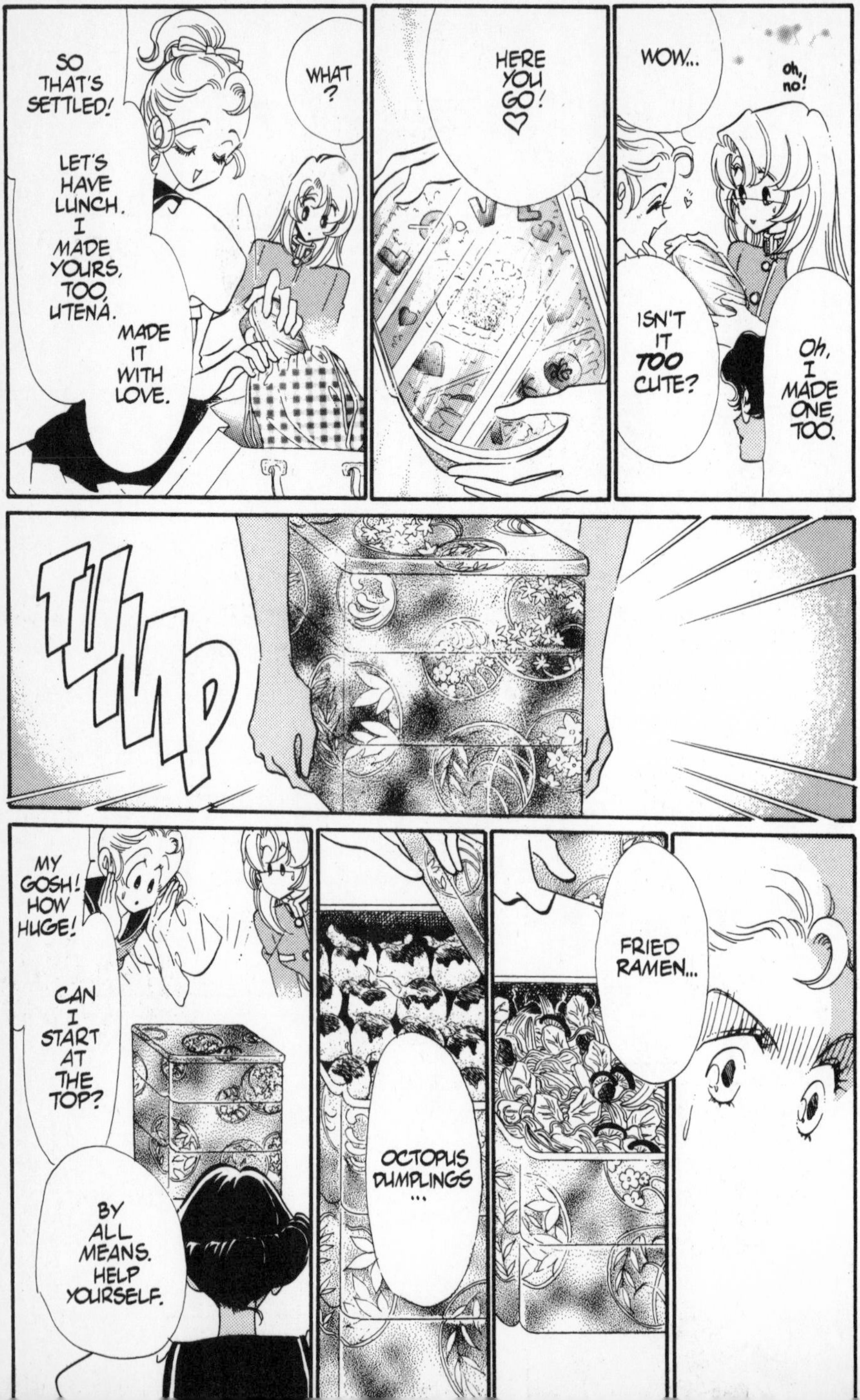
SO THAT'S SETTLED!
LET'S HAVE LUNCH. I MADE YOURS, TOO, UTENA.
MADE IT WITH LOVE.
WHAT?
HERE YOU GO! ♡
WOW...
Oh, no!
ISN'T IT TOO CUTE?
Oh, I MADE ONE, TOO.
THUMP
MY GOSH! HOW HUGE!
CAN I START AT THE TOP?
BY ALL MEANS. HELP YOURSELF.
OCTOPUS DUMPLINGS...
FRIED RAMEN...

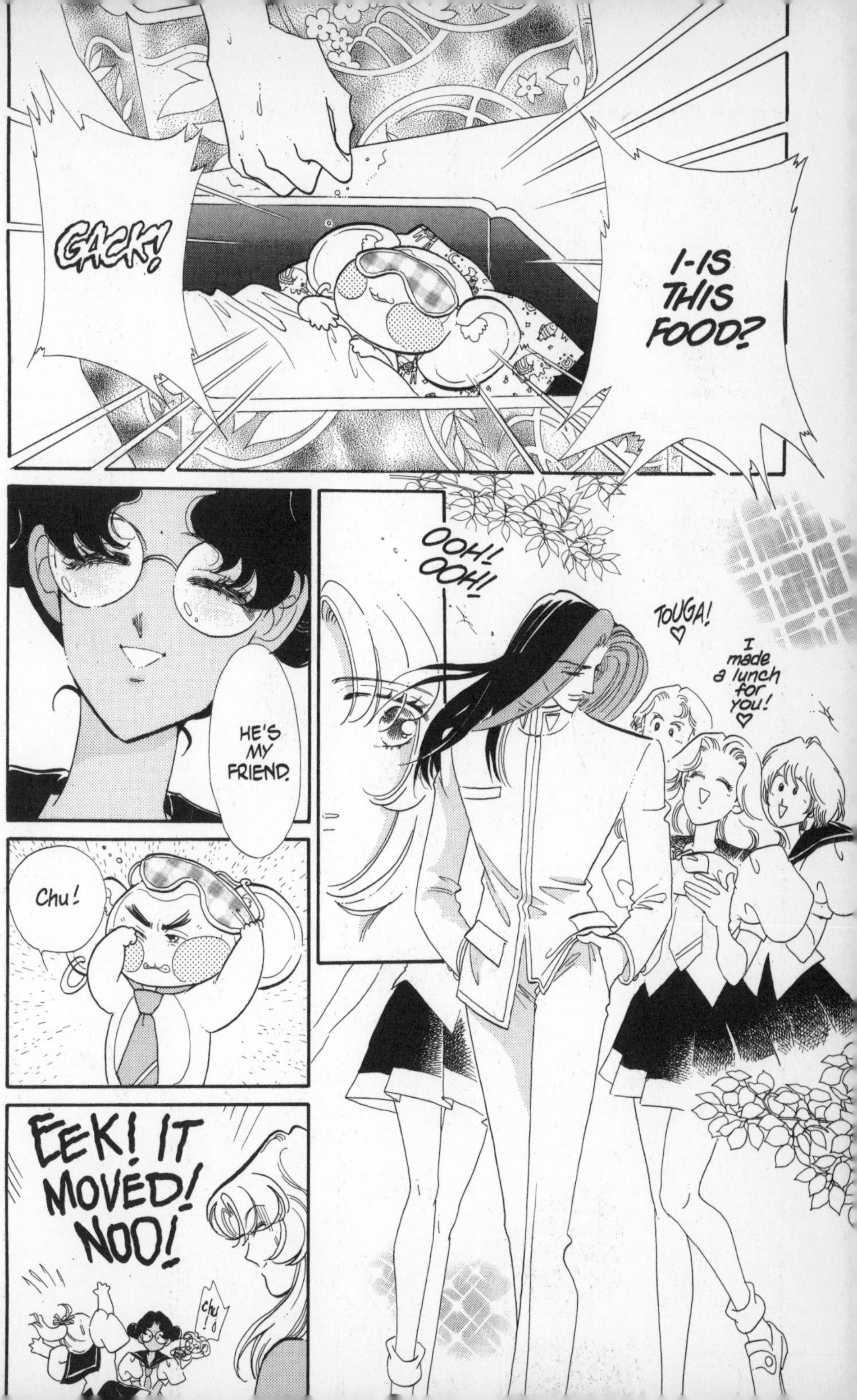
GACK!
I-IS THIS FOOD?
HE'S MY FRIEND.
Chu!
EEK! IT MOVED! NOO!
Chu!
OOH! OOH!
TOUGA! ♡
I made a lunch for you! ♡

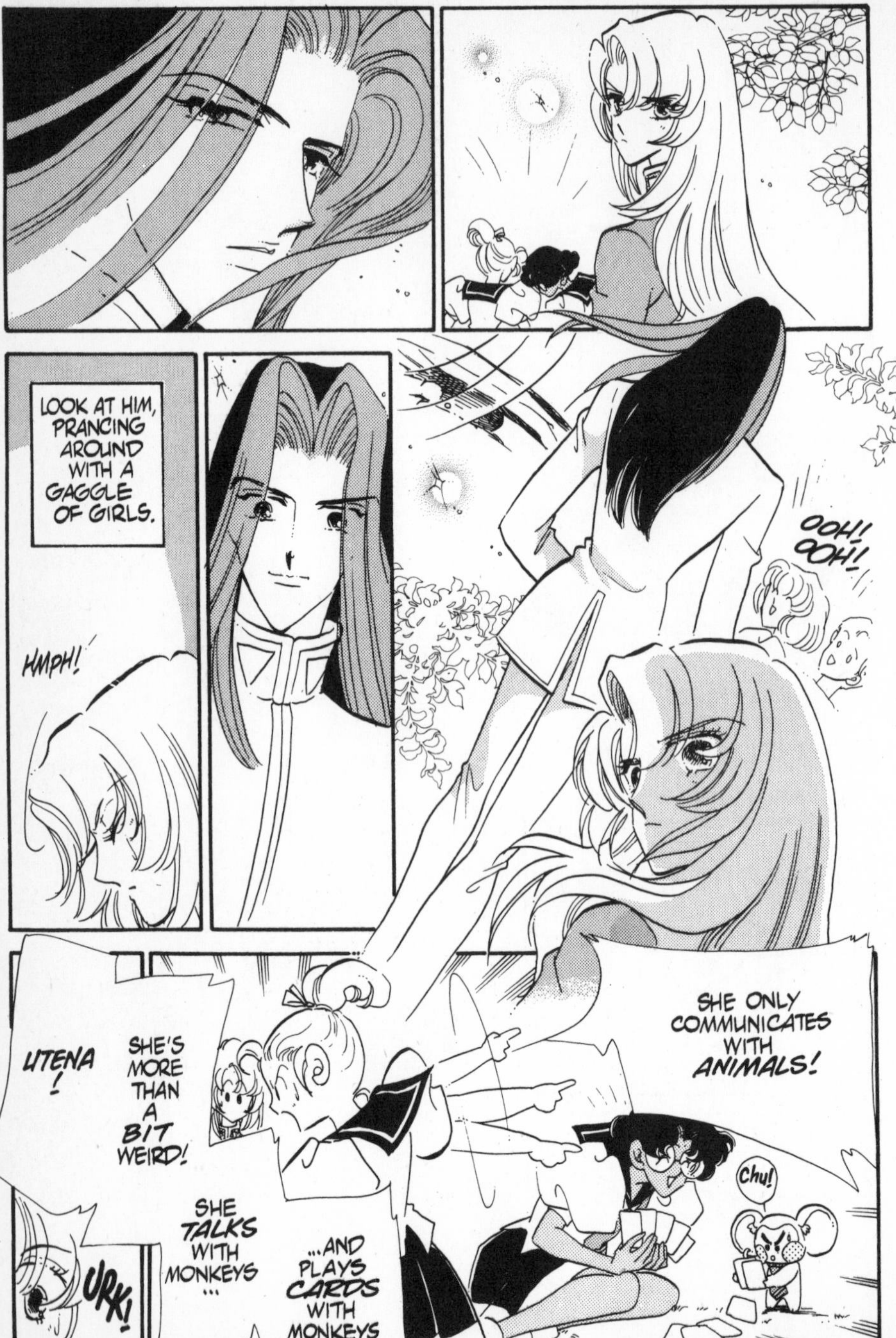
LOOK AT HIM, PRANCING AROUND WITH A GAGGLE OF GIRLS.
HMPH!
OOH! OOH!
UTENA!
SHE'S MORE THAN A BIT WEIRD!
SHE ONLY COMMUNICATES WITH ANIMALS!
Chu!
URK!
SHE TALKS WITH MONKEYS...
...AND PLAYS CARDS WITH MONKEYS!

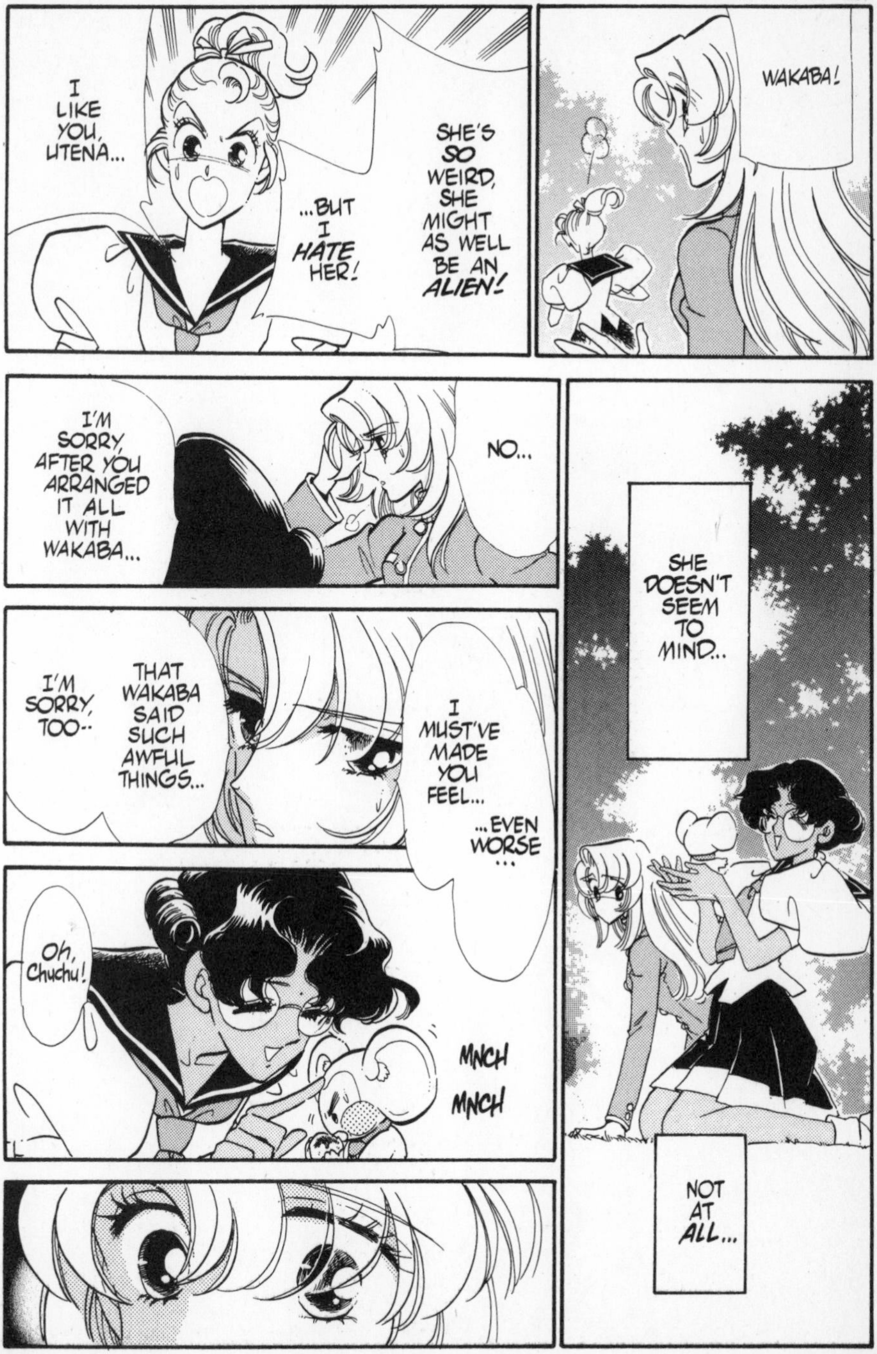
I LIKE YOU, UTENA...
...BUT I *HATE* HER!
SHE'S *SO* WEIRD, SHE MIGHT AS WELL BE AN *ALIEN!*
WAKABA!
I'M SORRY, AFTER YOU ARRANGED IT ALL WITH WAKABA...
NO...
I'M SORRY, TOO--
THAT WAKABA SAID SUCH AWFUL THINGS...
I MUST'VE MADE YOU FEEL...
...EVEN WORSE...
Oh, Chuchu!
MNCH
MNCH
SHE DOESN'T SEEM TO MIND...
NOT AT *ALL*...

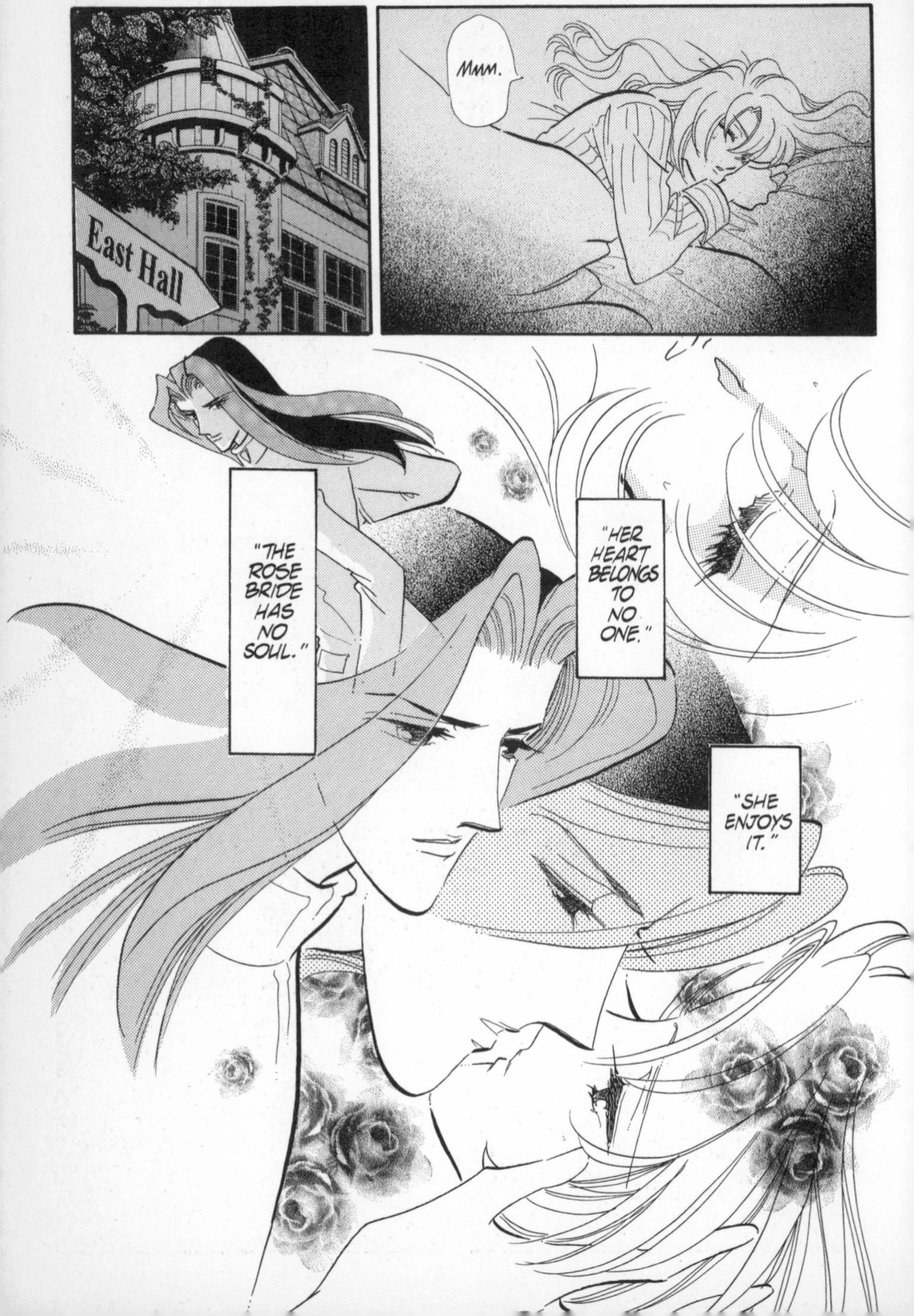
East Hall
MMM.
"THE ROSE BRIDE HAS NO SOUL."
"HER HEART BELONGS TO NO ONE."
"SHE ENJOYS IT."

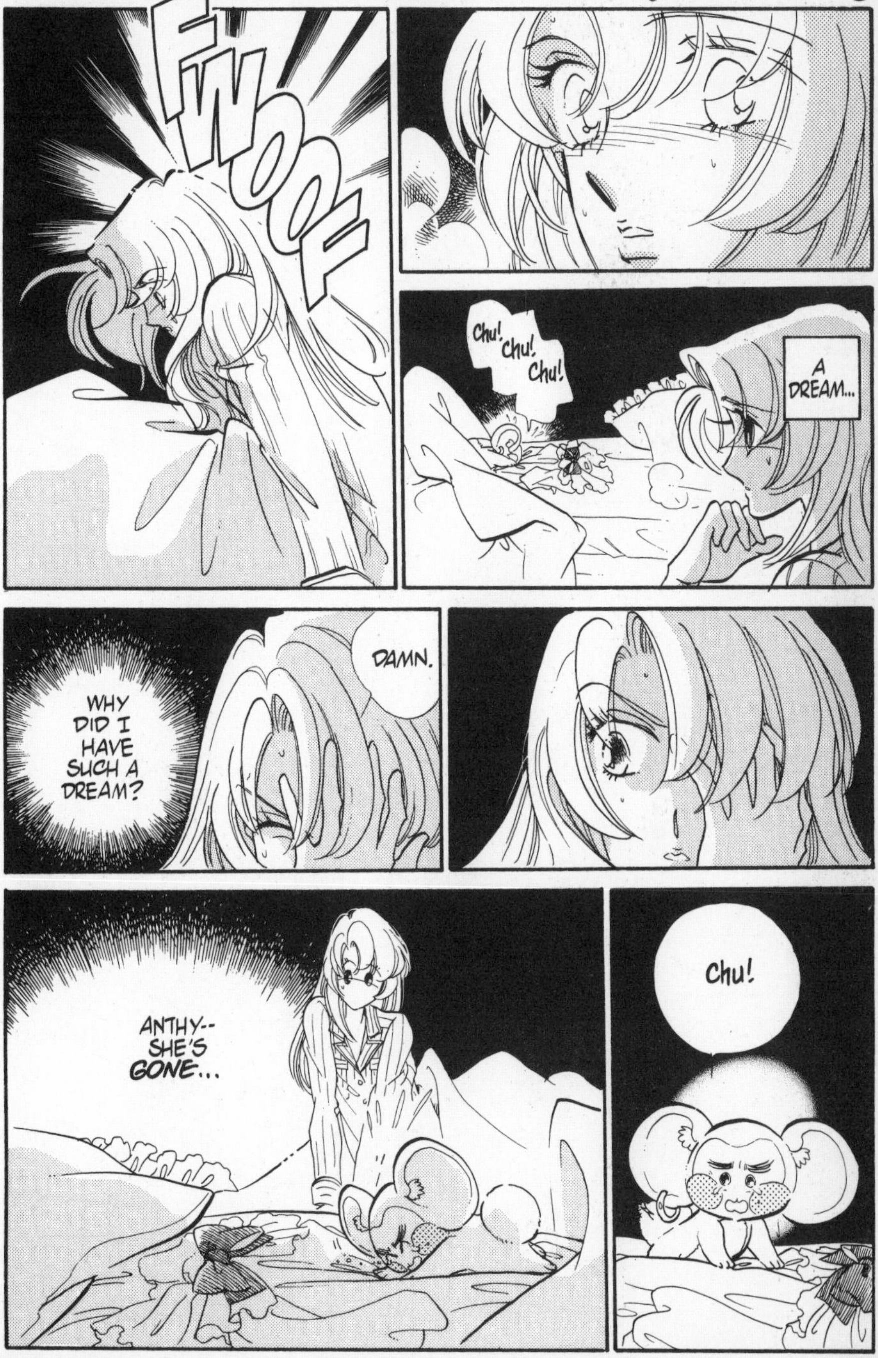
FWOOOF
Chu! Chu! Chu!
A DREAM...
WHY DID I HAVE SUCH A DREAM?
DAMN.
ANTHY-- SHE'S GONE...
Chu!

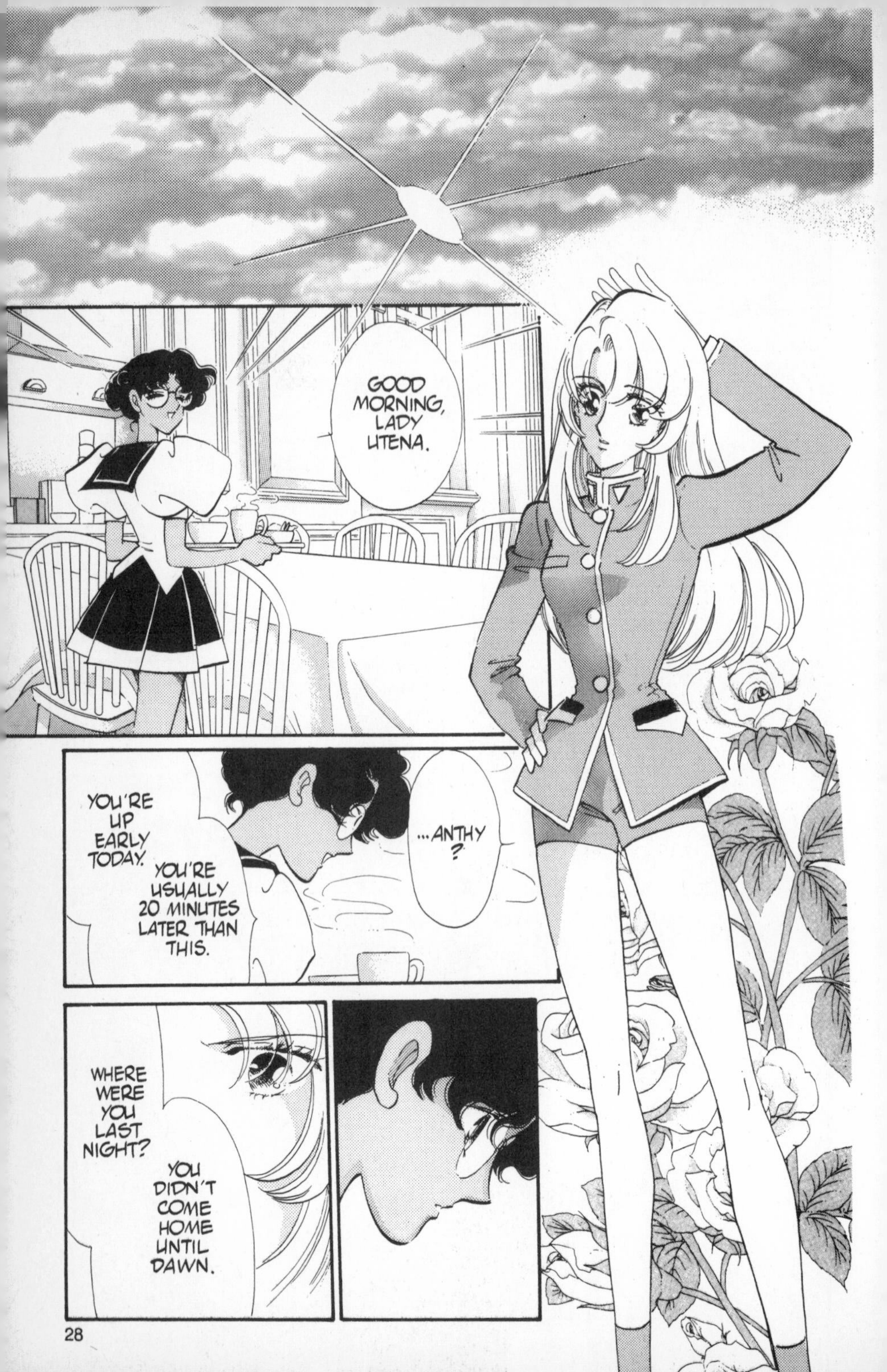
GOOD MORNING, LADY UTENA.
YOU'RE UP EARLY TODAY.
YOU'RE USUALLY 20 MINUTES LATER THAN THIS.
...ANTHY?
WHERE WERE YOU LAST NIGHT?
YOU DIDN'T COME HOME UNTIL DAWN.

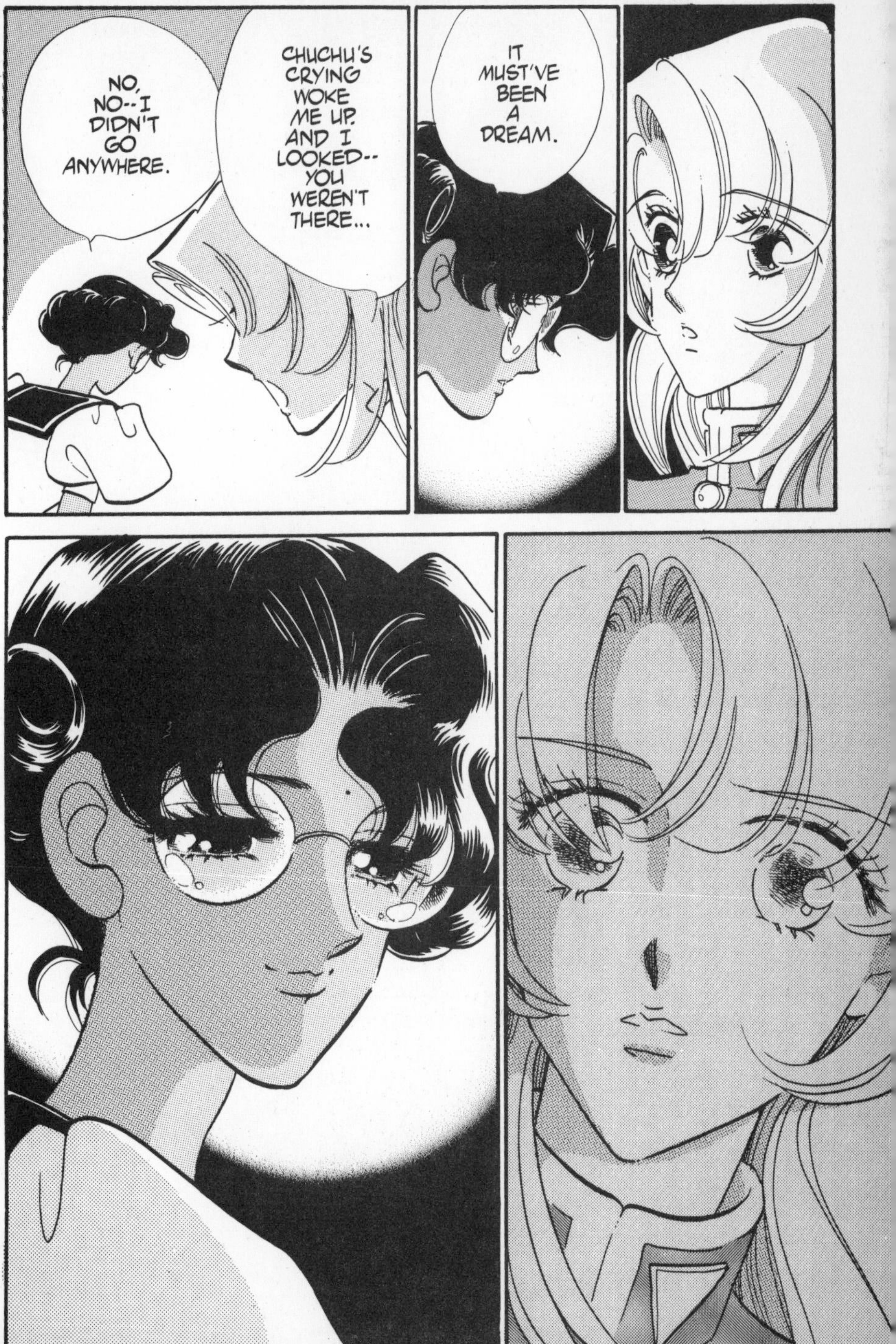
NO, NO--I DIDN'T GO ANYWHERE.
CHUCHU'S CRYING WOKE ME UP. AND I LOOKED--YOU WEREN'T THERE...
IT MUST'VE BEEN A DREAM.

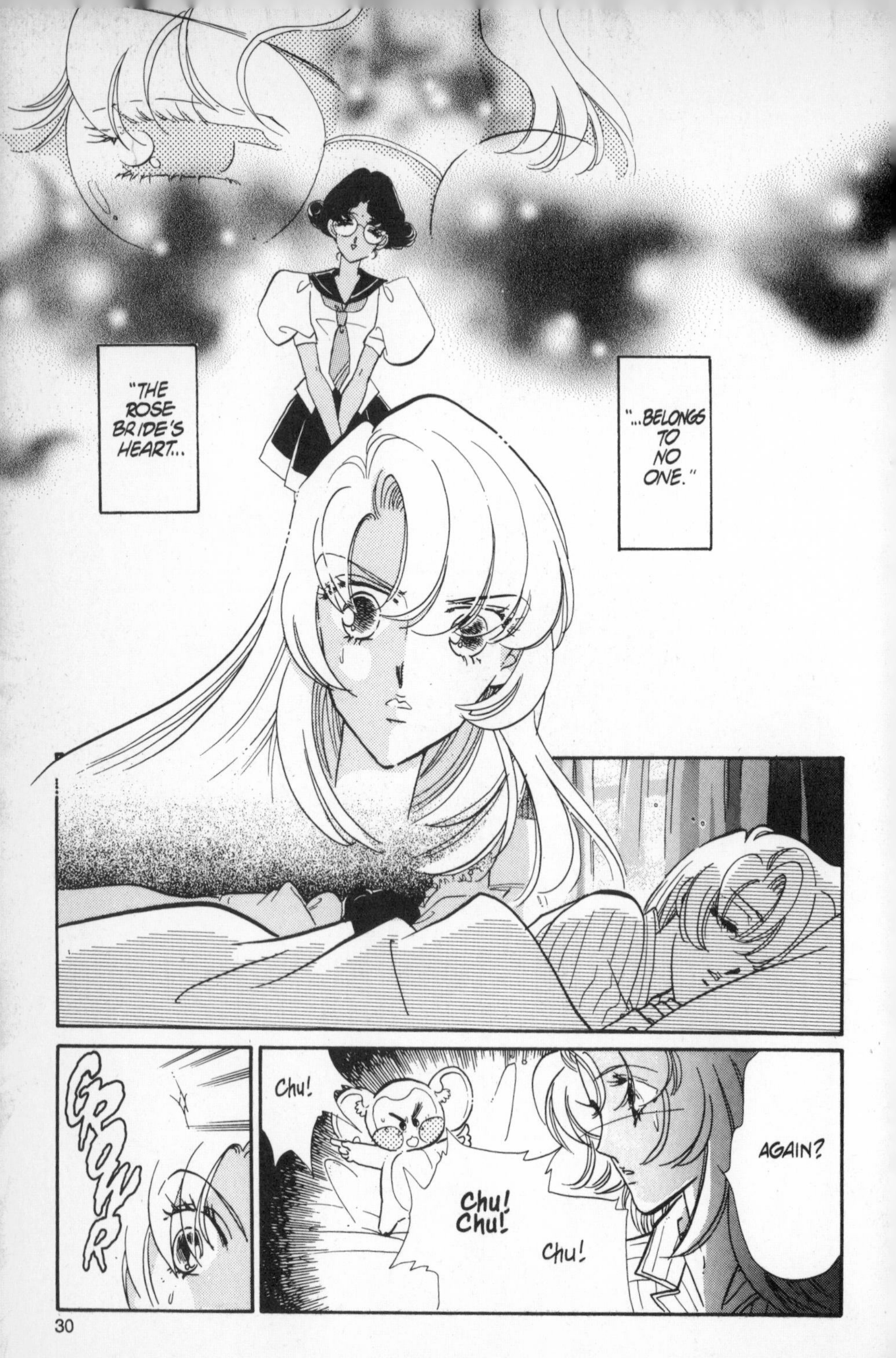
"THE ROSE BRIDE'S HEART...
"...BELONGS TO NO ONE."
GROWR
Chu!
Chu! Chu!
Chu!
AGAIN?

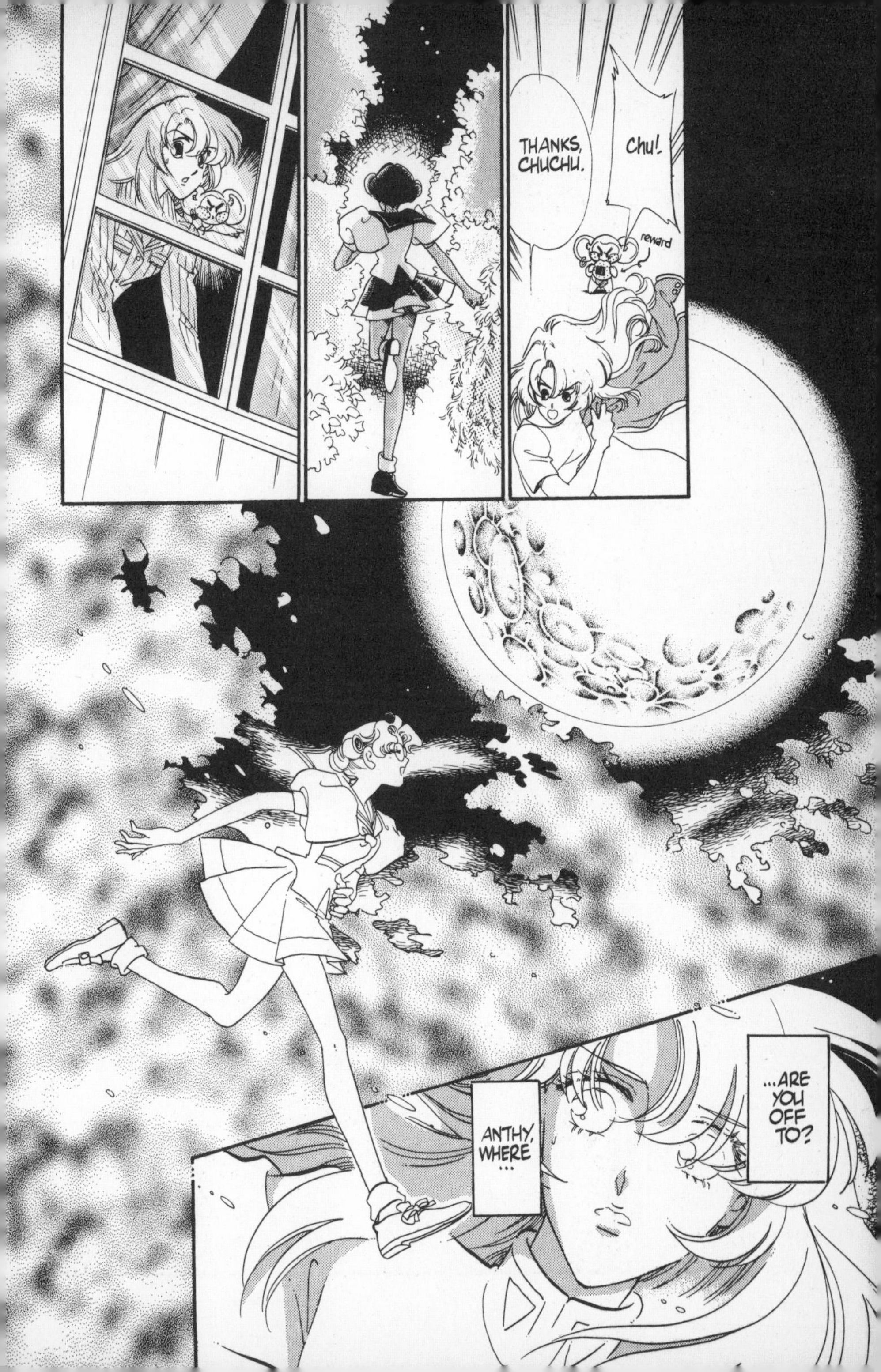
THANKS, CHUCHU.
Chu!
reward
ANTHY, WHERE ...
...ARE YOU OFF TO?

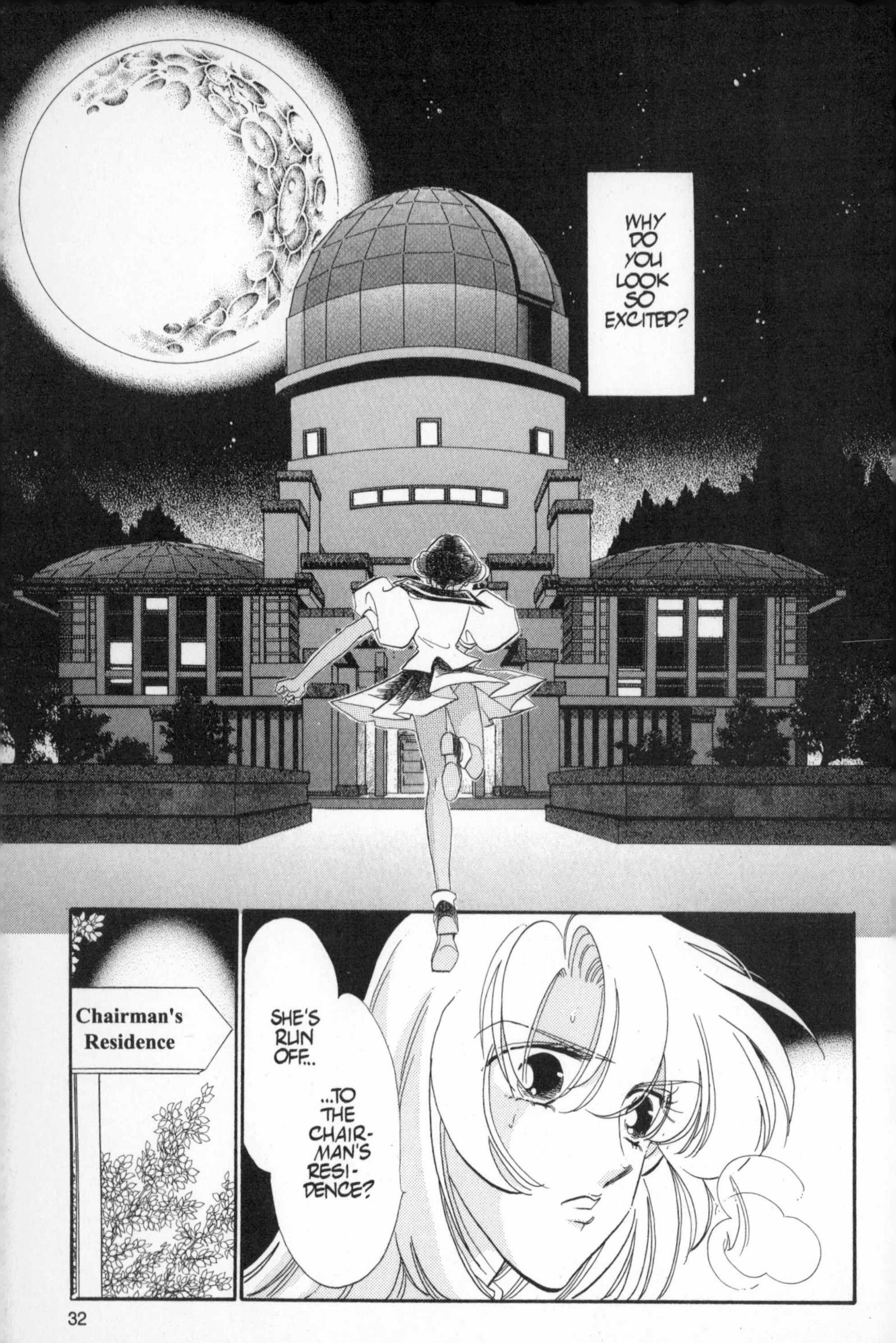
WHY DO YOU LOOK SO EXCITED?
Chairman's Residence
SHE'S RUN OFF...
...TO THE CHAIR-MAN'S RESI-DENCE?

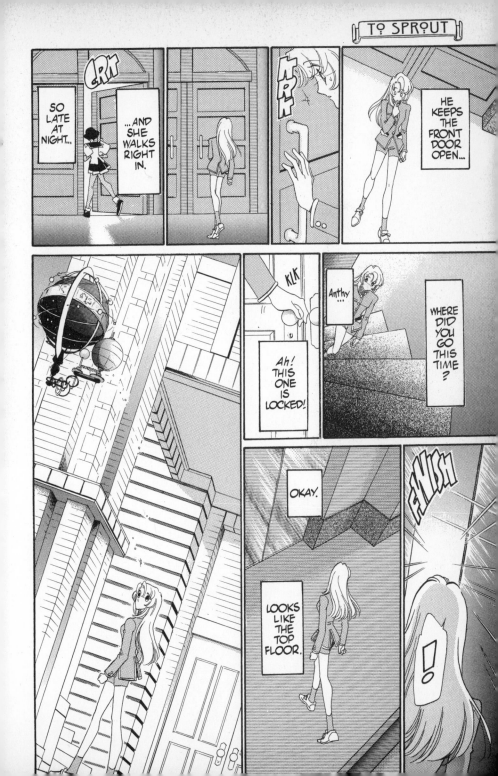

CRK

SO LATE AT NIGHT...

...AND SHE WALKS RIGHT IN.

CRK

HE KEEPS THE FRONT DOOR OPEN...

KLK

Ah! THIS ONE IS LOCKED!

Anthy...

WHERE DID YOU GO THIS TIME?

OKAY.

LOOKS LIKE THE TOP FLOOR.

FINISH

!

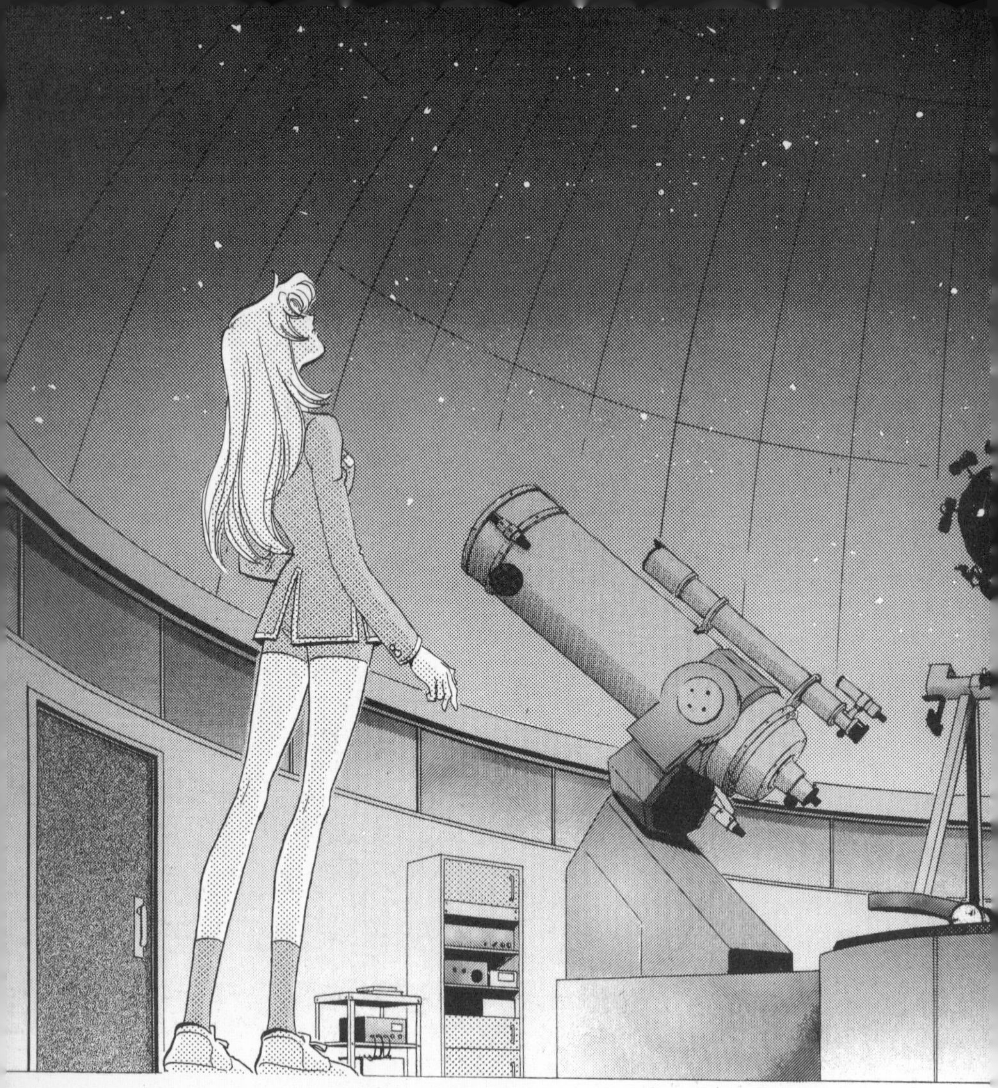
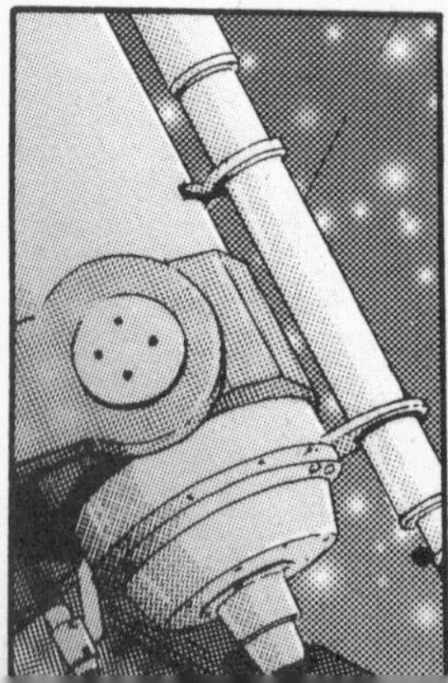
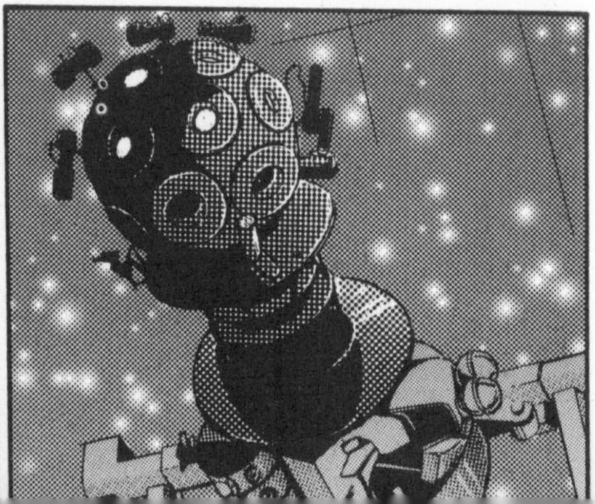

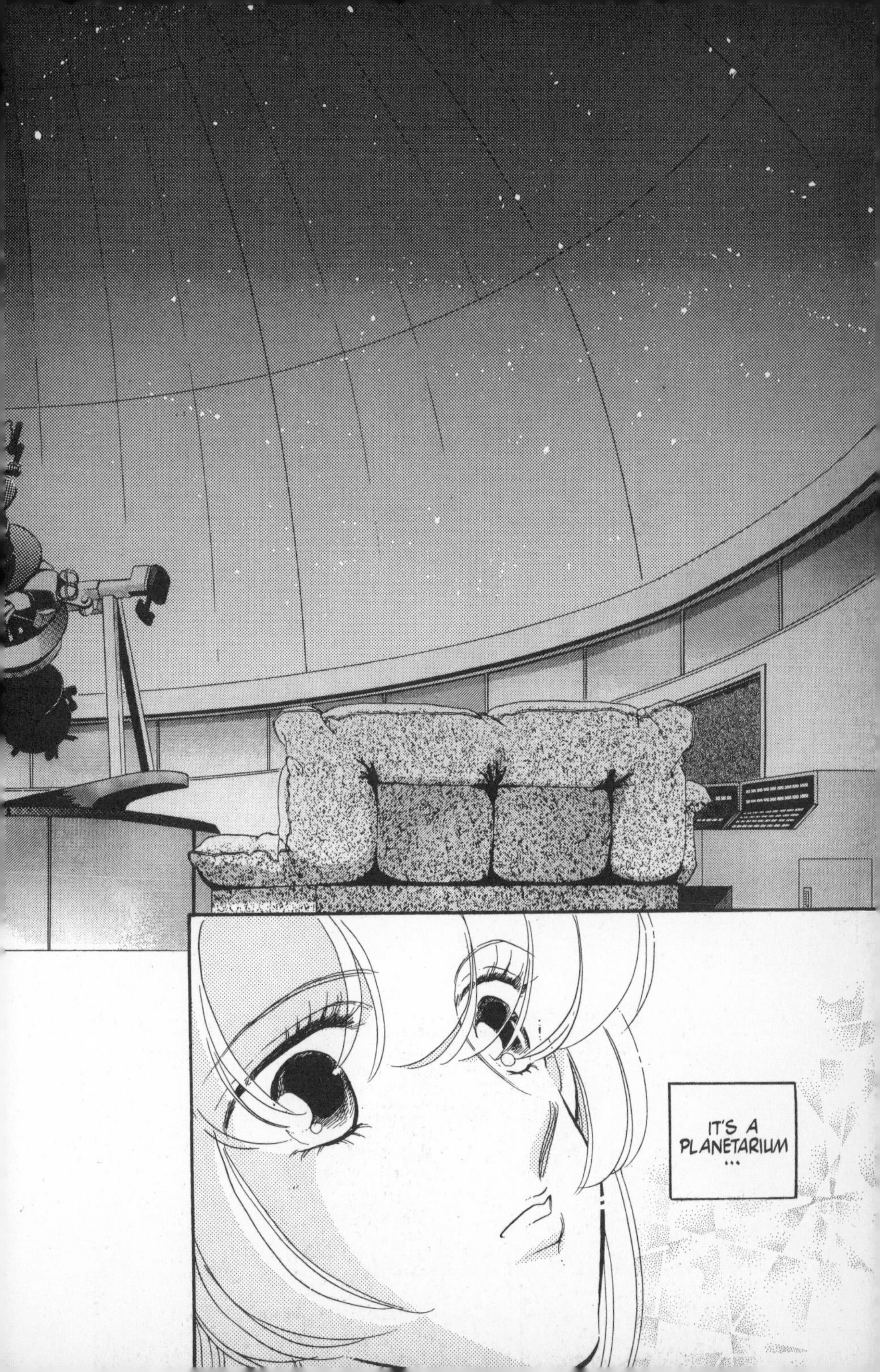
IT'S A PLANETARIUM ...

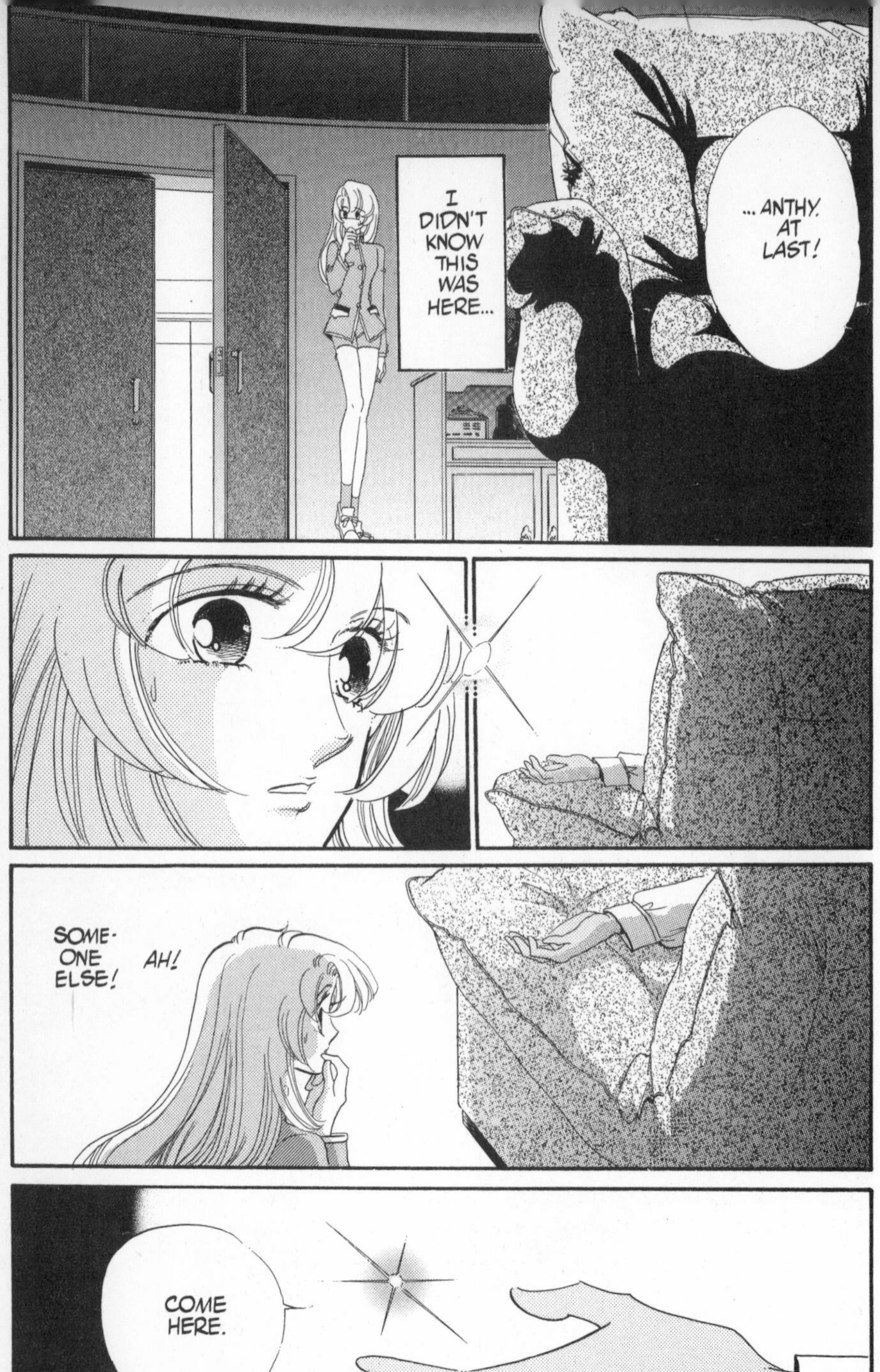
I DIDN'T KNOW THIS WAS HERE...
... ANTHY. AT LAST!
SOME-ONE ELSE!
AH!
COME HERE.

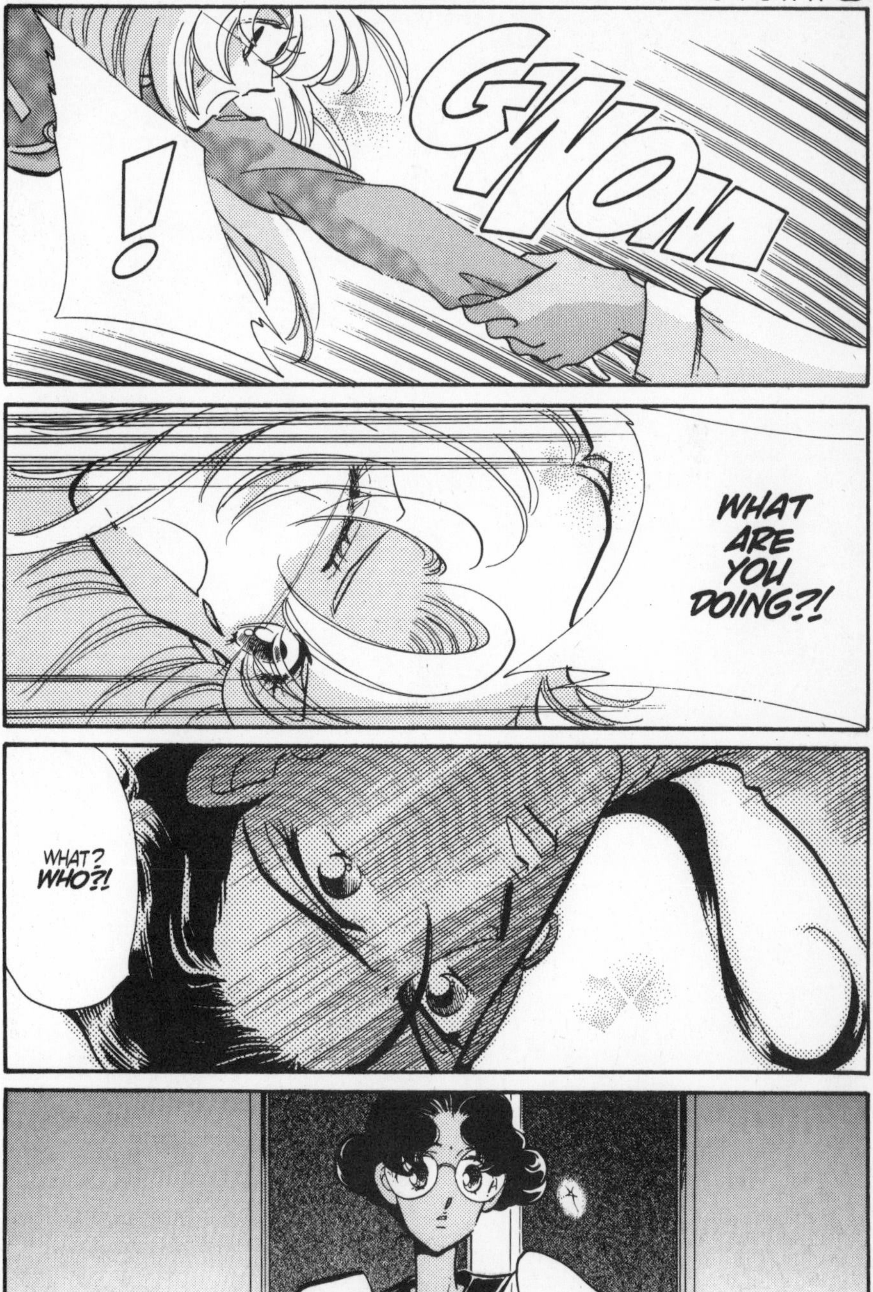
GWOM
!
WHAT ARE YOU DOING?!
WHAT? WHO?!

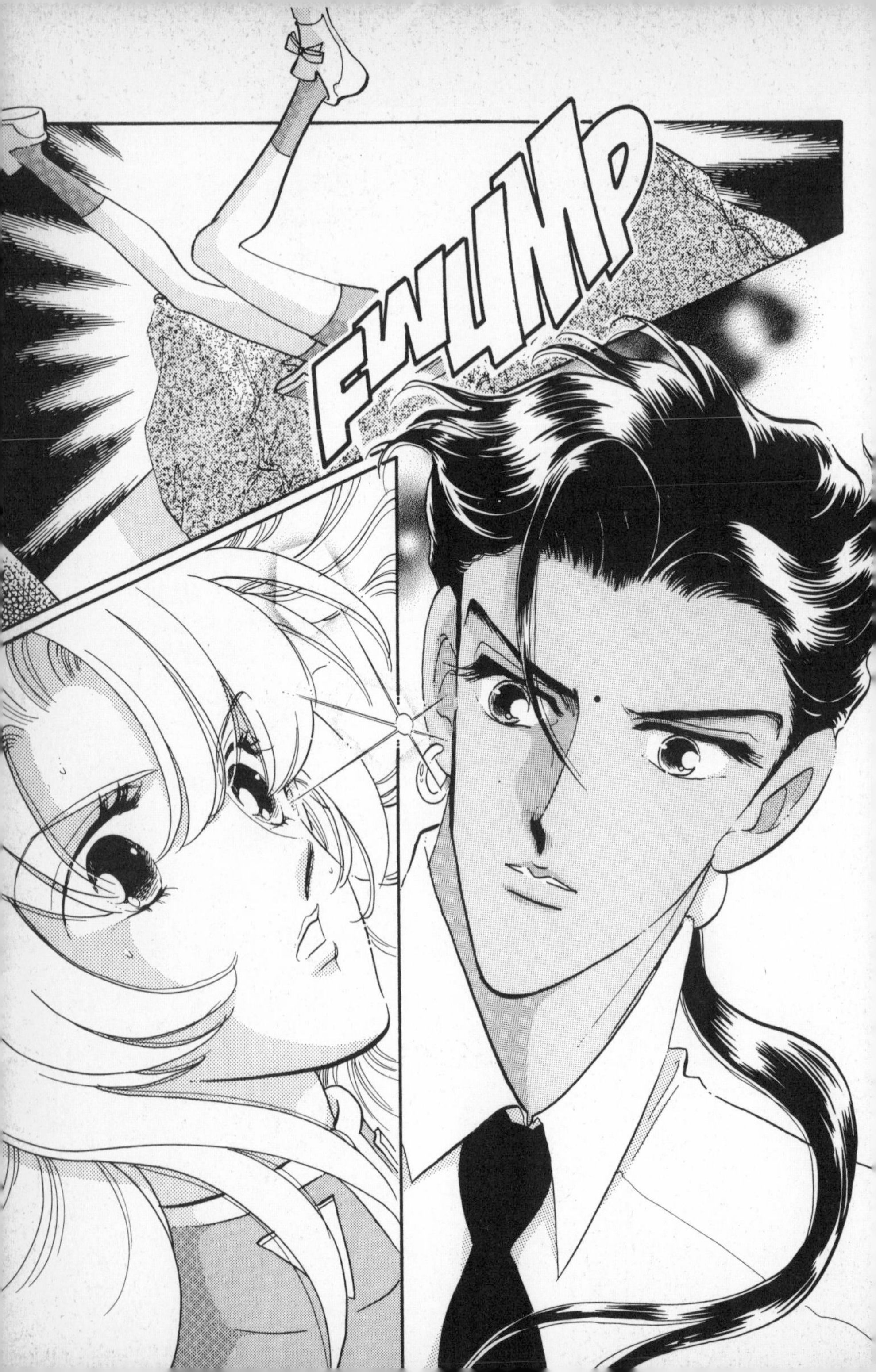
FWUMP

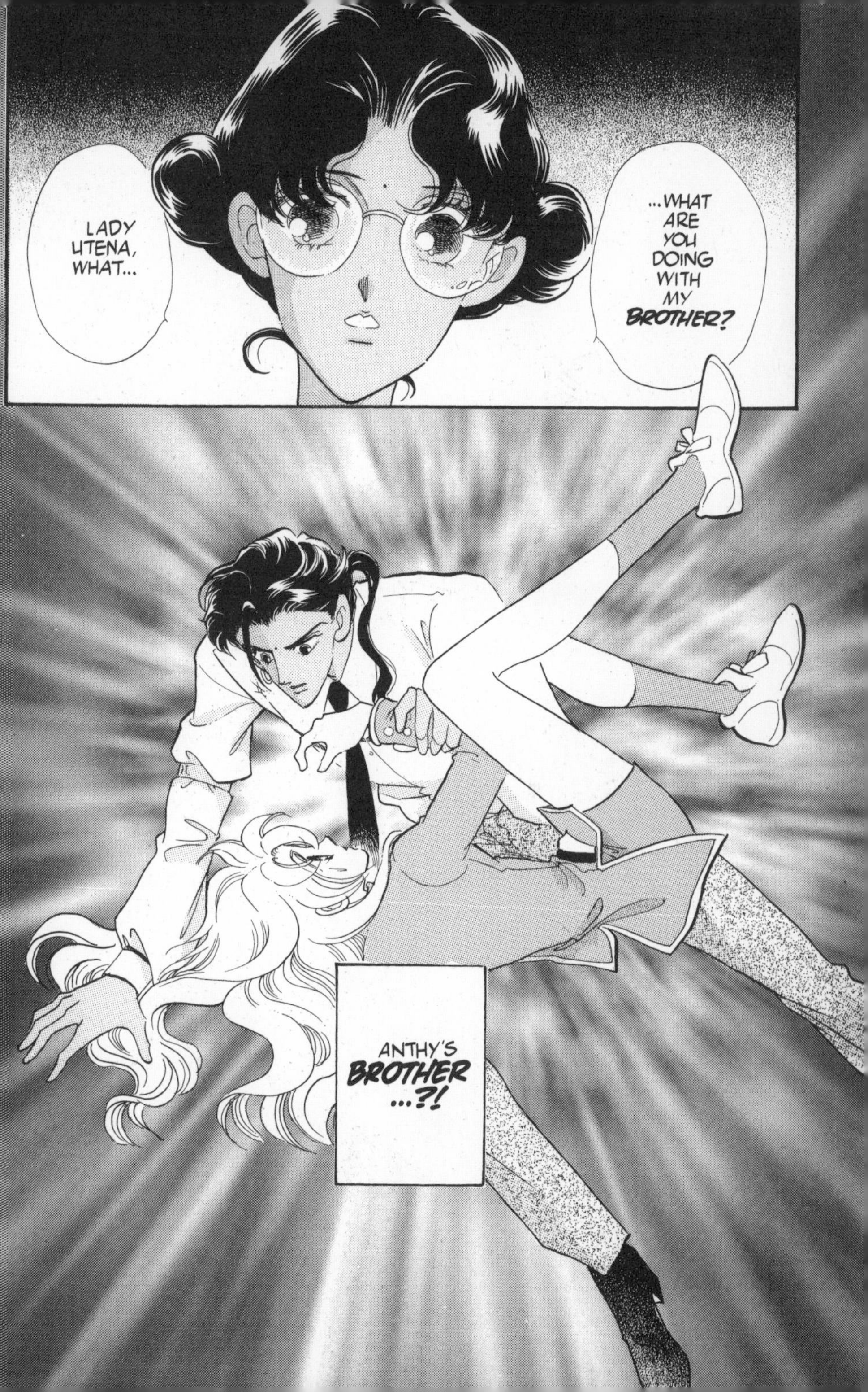
LADY UTENA, WHAT...
...WHAT ARE YOU DOING WITH MY BROTHER?
ANTHY'S BROTHER ...?!

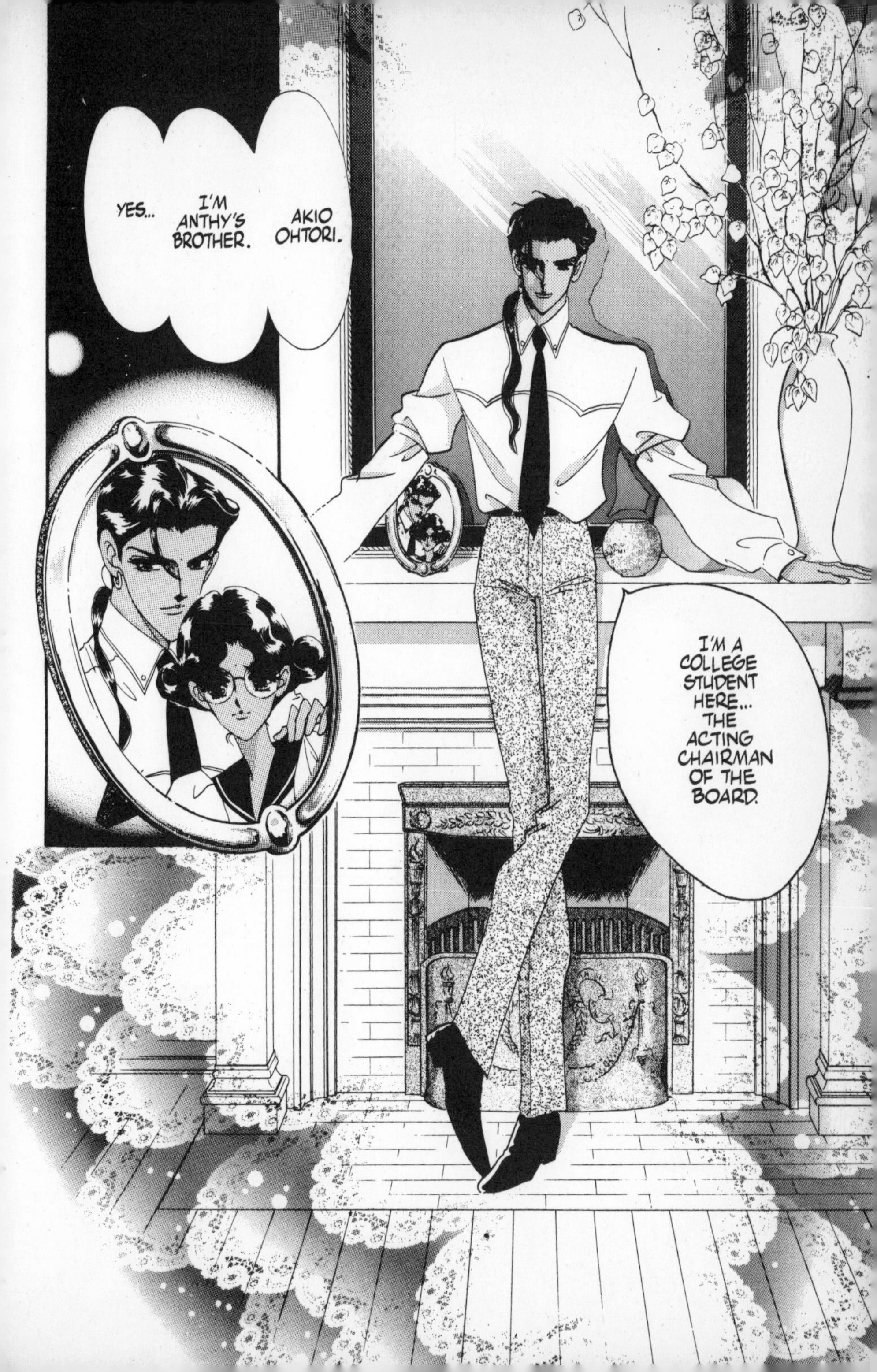
YES...
I'M ANTHY'S BROTHER.
AKIO OHTORI.
I'M A COLLEGE STUDENT HERE... THE ACTING CHAIRMAN OF THE BOARD.

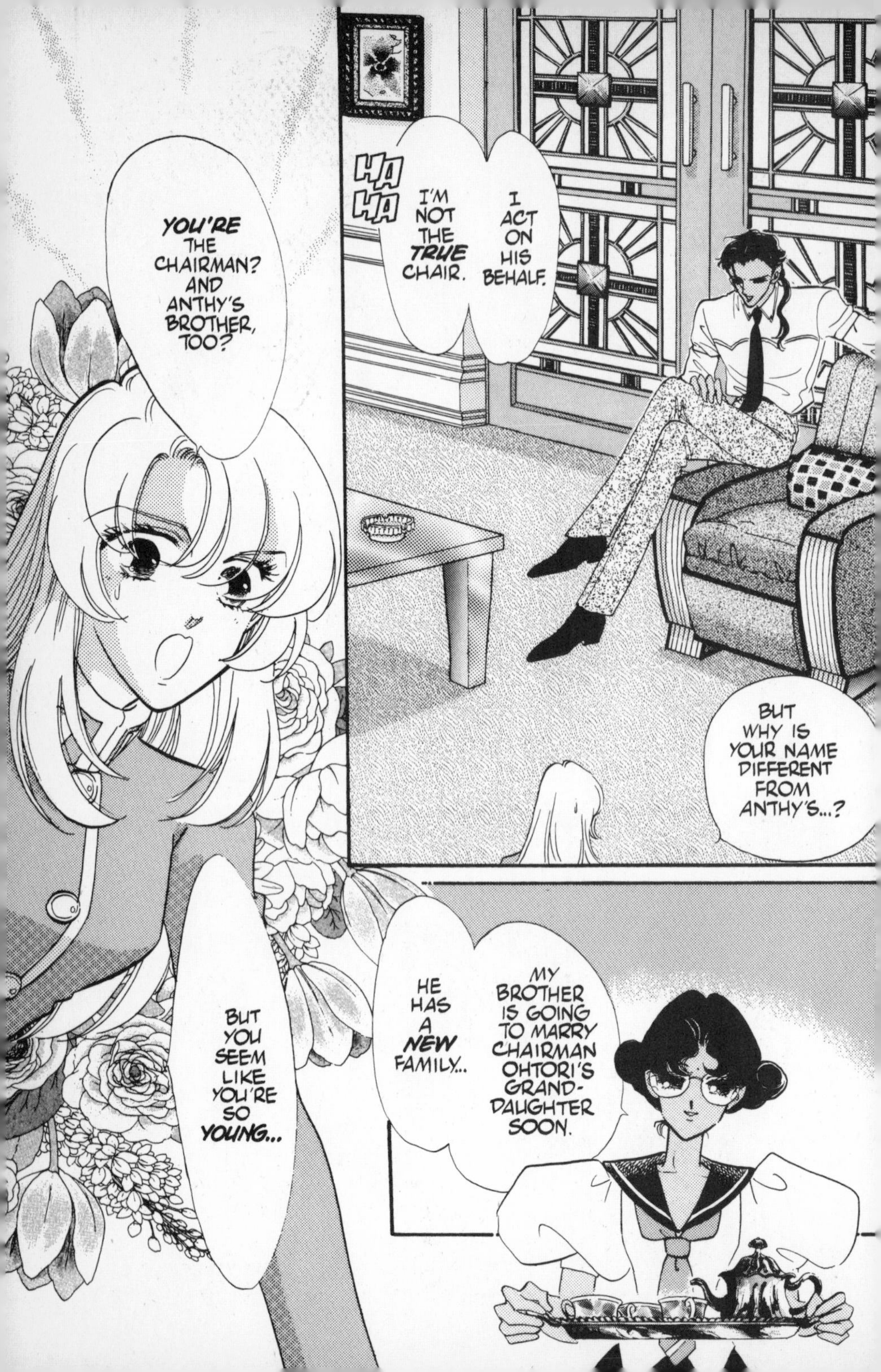
YOU'RE THE CHAIRMAN? AND ANTHY'S BROTHER, TOO?
BUT YOU SEEM LIKE YOU'RE SO YOUNG...
HA HA
I'M NOT THE TRUE CHAIR.
I ACT ON HIS BEHALF.
BUT WHY IS YOUR NAME DIFFERENT FROM ANTHY'S...?
HE HAS A NEW FAMILY...
MY BROTHER IS GOING TO MARRY CHAIRMAN OHTORI'S GRAND-DAUGHTER SOON.

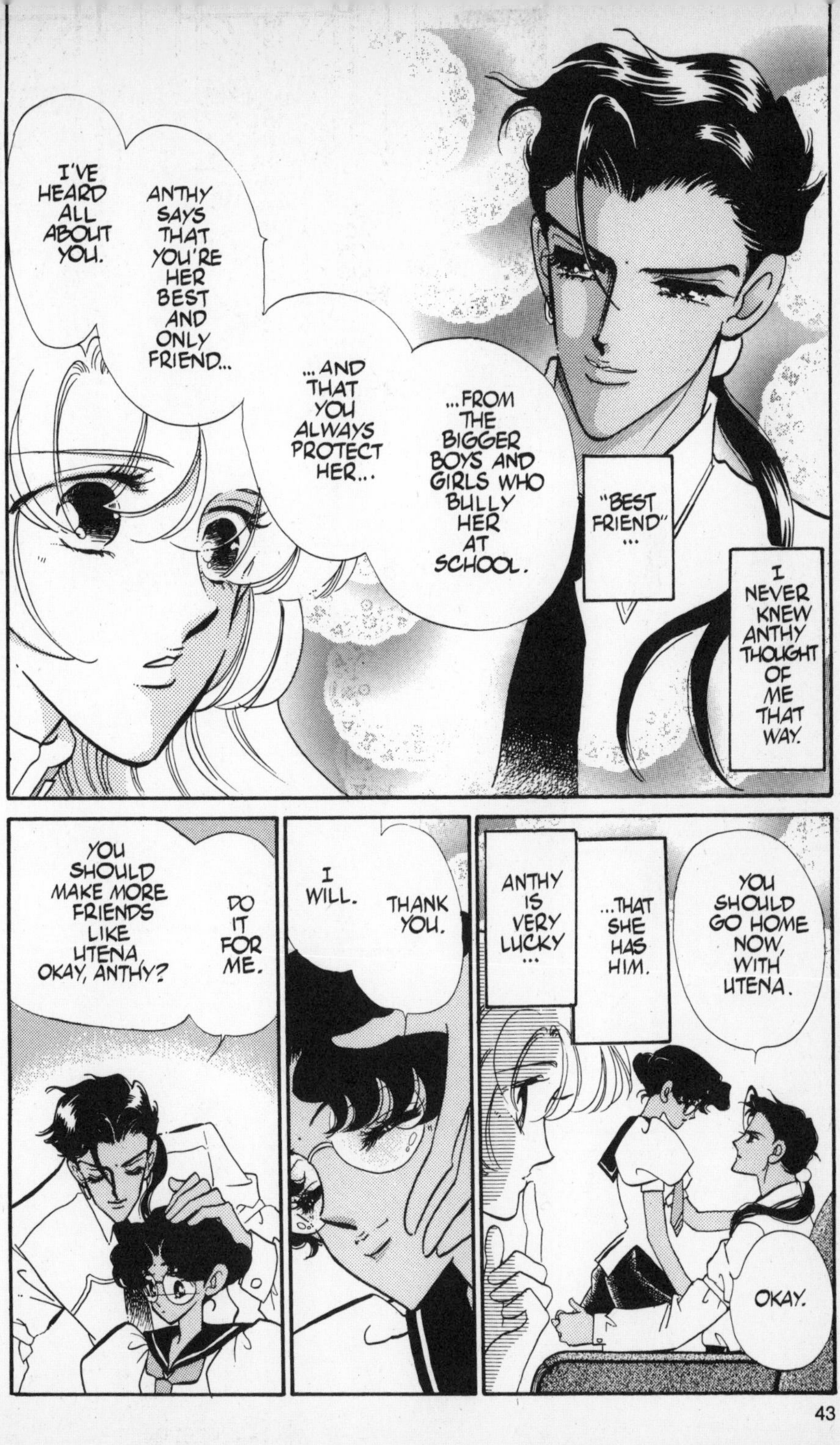
I'VE HEARD ALL ABOUT YOU.
ANTHY SAYS THAT YOU'RE HER BEST AND ONLY FRIEND...
...AND THAT YOU ALWAYS PROTECT HER...
...FROM THE BIGGER BOYS AND GIRLS WHO BULLY HER AT SCHOOL.
"BEST FRIEND"...
I NEVER KNEW ANTHY THOUGHT OF ME THAT WAY.
YOU SHOULD MAKE MORE FRIENDS LIKE UTENA OKAY, ANTHY?
DO IT FOR ME.
I WILL.
THANK YOU.
ANTHY IS VERY LUCKY...
...THAT SHE HAS HIM.
YOU SHOULD GO HOME NOW, WITH UTENA.
OKAY.

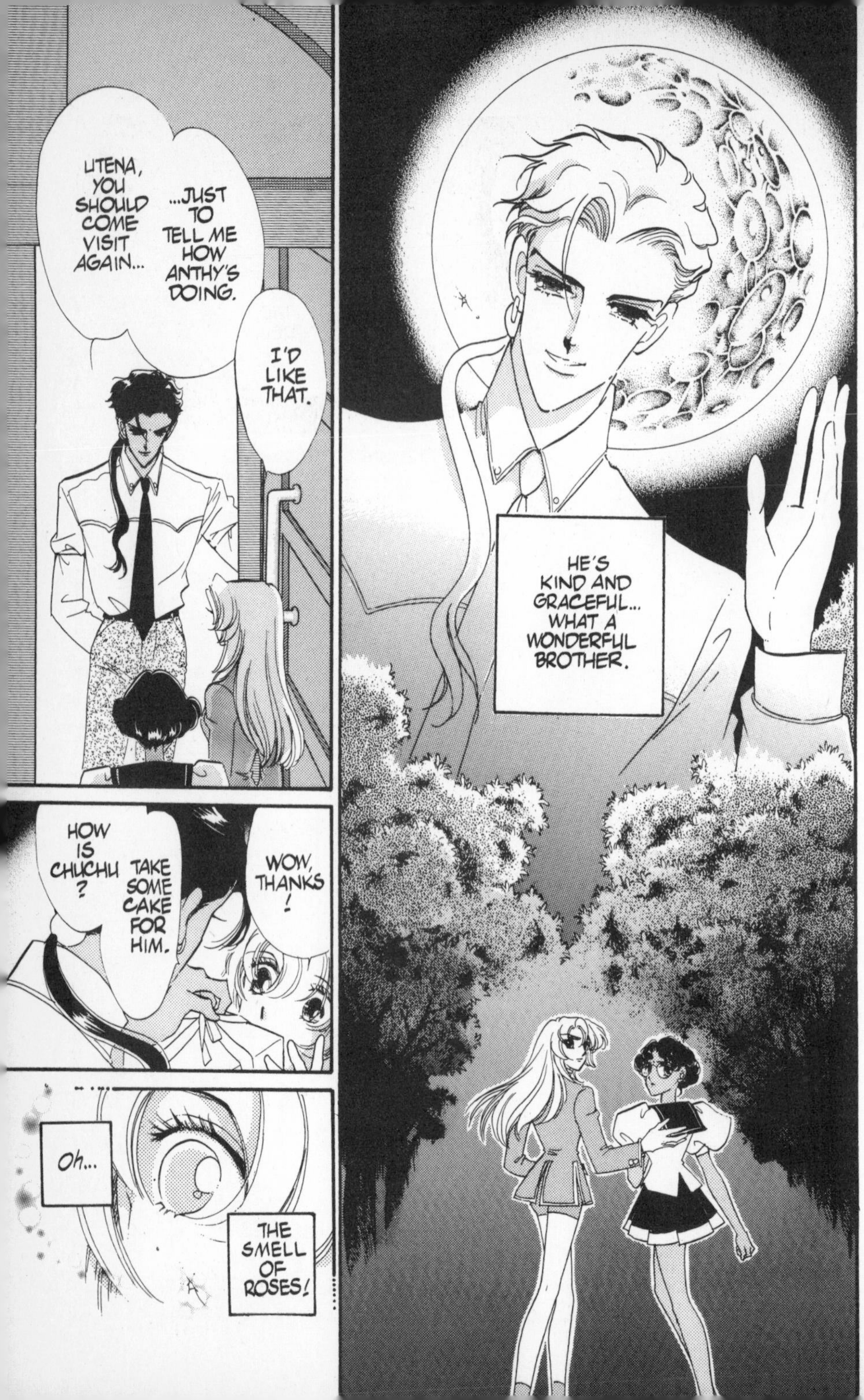
UTENA, YOU SHOULD COME VISIT AGAIN...
...JUST TO TELL ME HOW ANTHY'S DOING.
I'D LIKE THAT.
HOW IS CHUCHU?
TAKE SOME CAKE FOR HIM.
WOW, THANKS!
Oh...
THE SMELL OF ROSES!
HE'S KIND AND GRACEFUL... WHAT A WONDERFUL BROTHER.

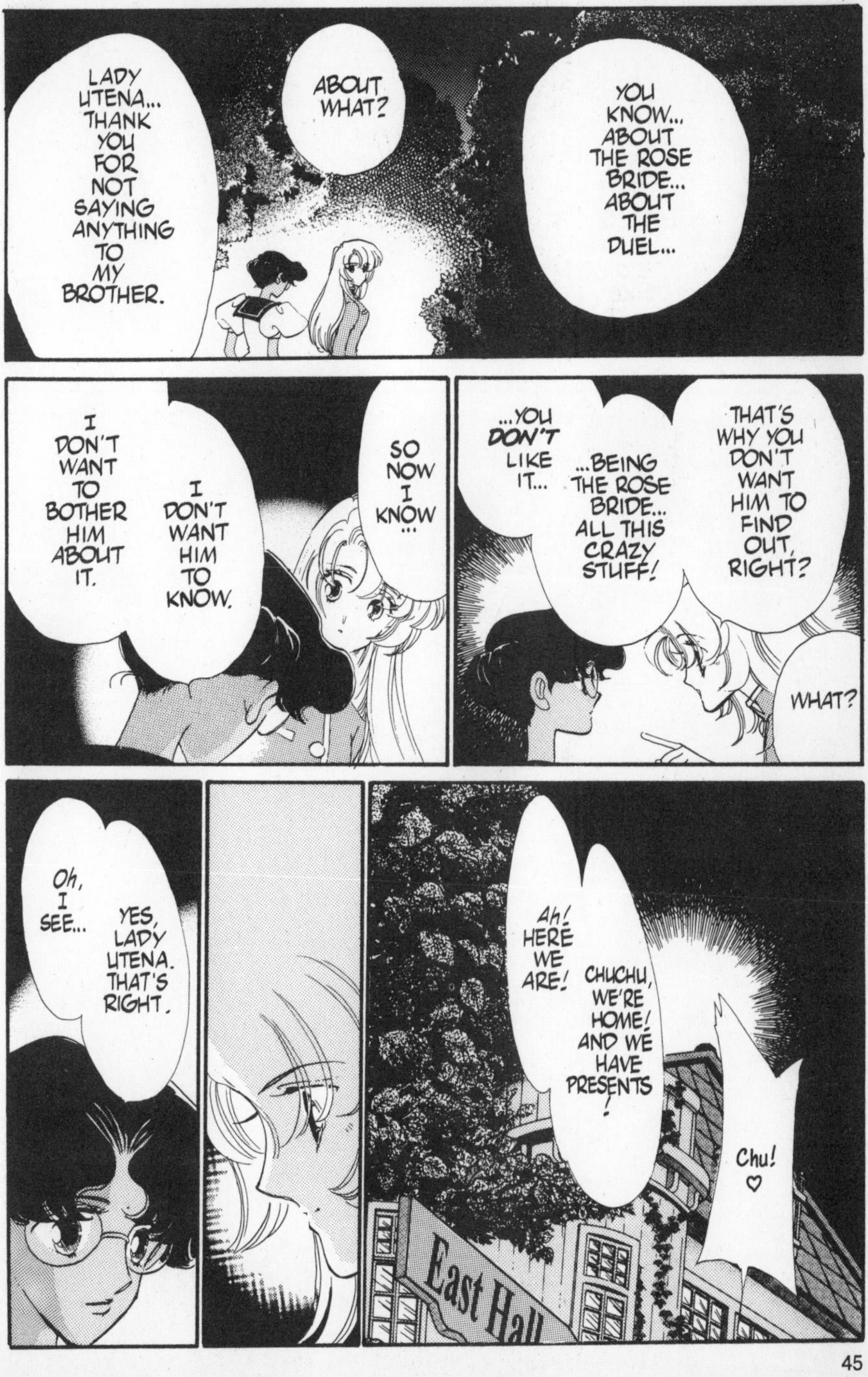
LADY UTENA... THANK YOU FOR NOT SAYING ANYTHING TO MY BROTHER.
ABOUT WHAT?
YOU KNOW... ABOUT THE ROSE BRIDE... ABOUT THE DUEL...
I DON'T WANT TO BOTHER HIM ABOUT IT.
I DON'T WANT HIM TO KNOW.
SO NOW I KNOW...
...YOU **DON'T** LIKE IT...
...BEING THE ROSE BRIDE... ALL THIS CRAZY STUFF!
THAT'S WHY YOU DON'T WANT HIM TO FIND OUT, RIGHT?
WHAT?
Oh, I SEE...
YES, LADY UTENA. THAT'S RIGHT.
Ah! HERE WE ARE!
CHUCHU, WE'RE HOME! AND WE HAVE PRESENTS!
Chu! ♡
East Hall

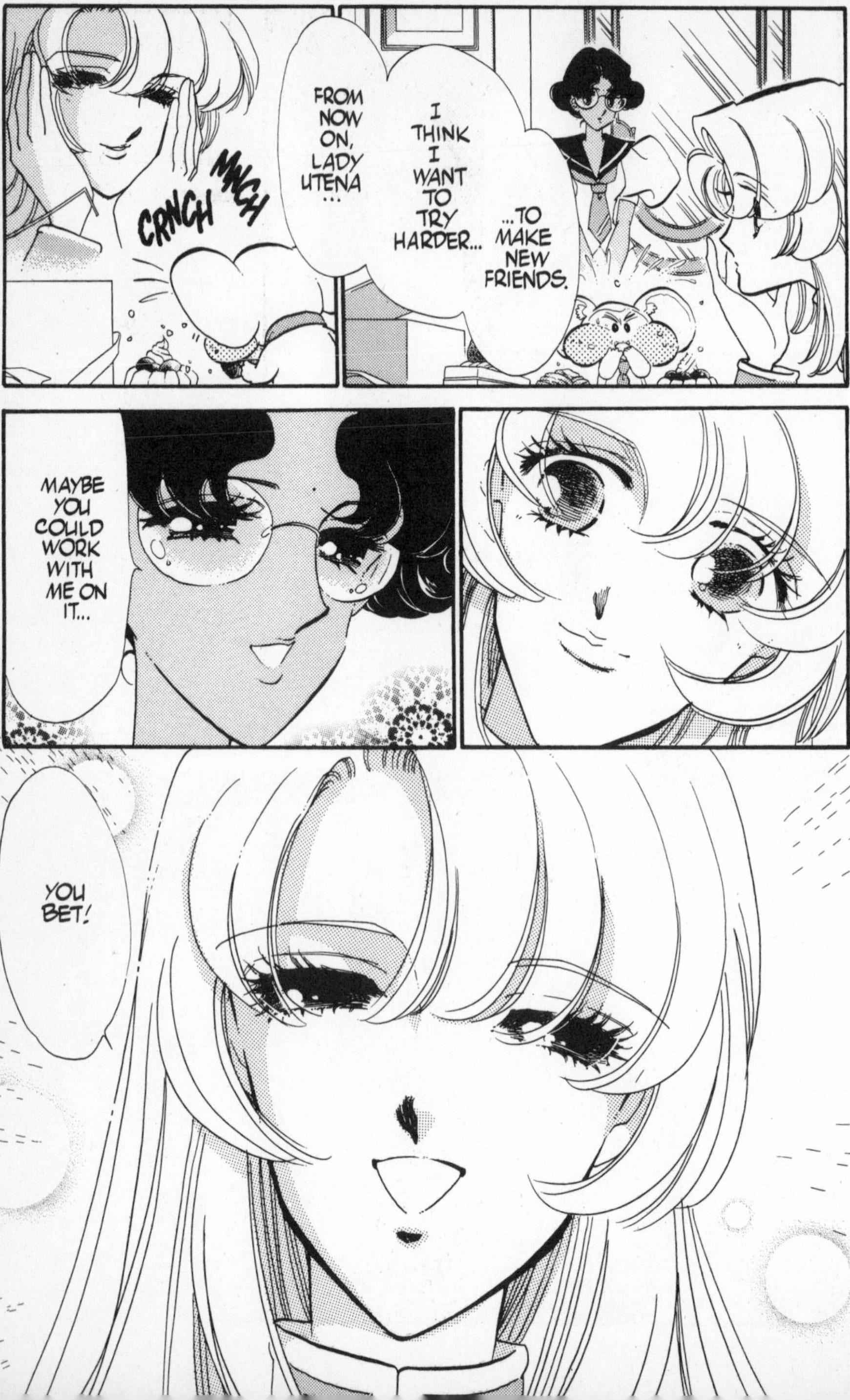
CRNCH
MNCH
FROM NOW ON, LADY UTENA...
I THINK I WANT TO TRY HARDER...
...TO MAKE NEW FRIENDS.
MAYBE YOU COULD WORK WITH ME ON IT...
YOU BET!

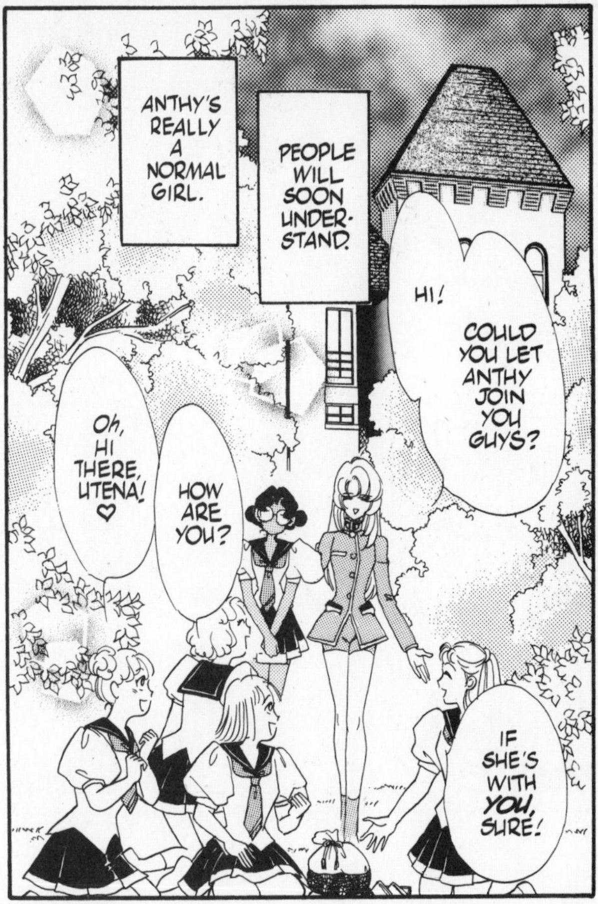
ANTHY'S REALLY A NORMAL GIRL.
PEOPLE WILL SOON UNDERSTAND.
HI!
COULD YOU LET ANTHY JOIN YOU GUYS?
Oh, HI THERE, UTENA! ♡
HOW ARE YOU?
IF SHE'S WITH YOU, SURE!

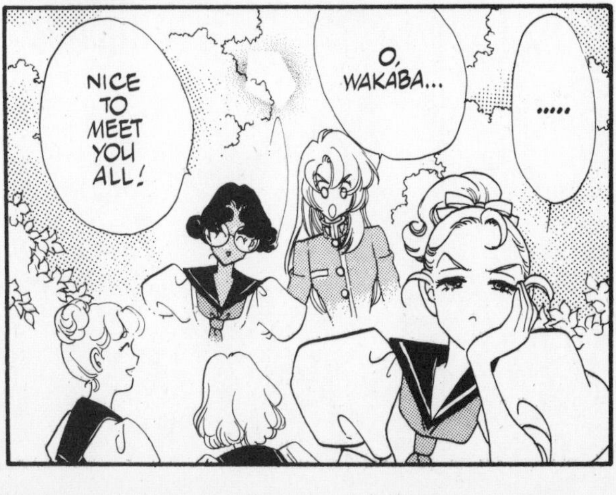
NICE TO MEET YOU ALL!
O, WAKABA...
.....

Team Utena Member No. 3

Juri Arisugawa

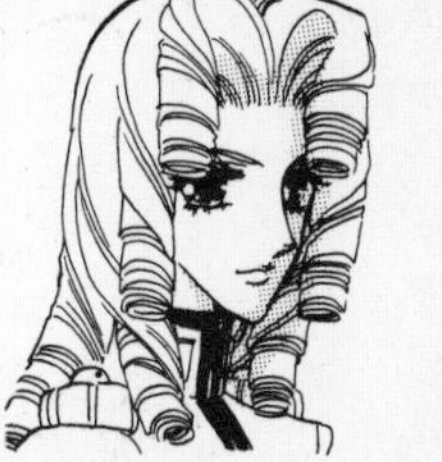

AGE: 16
BIRTHDAY: December 1
SIGN: Sagittarius
BLOOD TYPE: A
HEIGHT: 167cm (5'6")
NICKNAME: Beautiful Leopard
TALENTS: Fencing
Prior Modeling Experience
FAVORITE THINGS: Lilies
Designer Products
MOTTO: "Beautiful lifestyle, beautiful attire, beautiful life."
WEAK POINT: Too many secrets

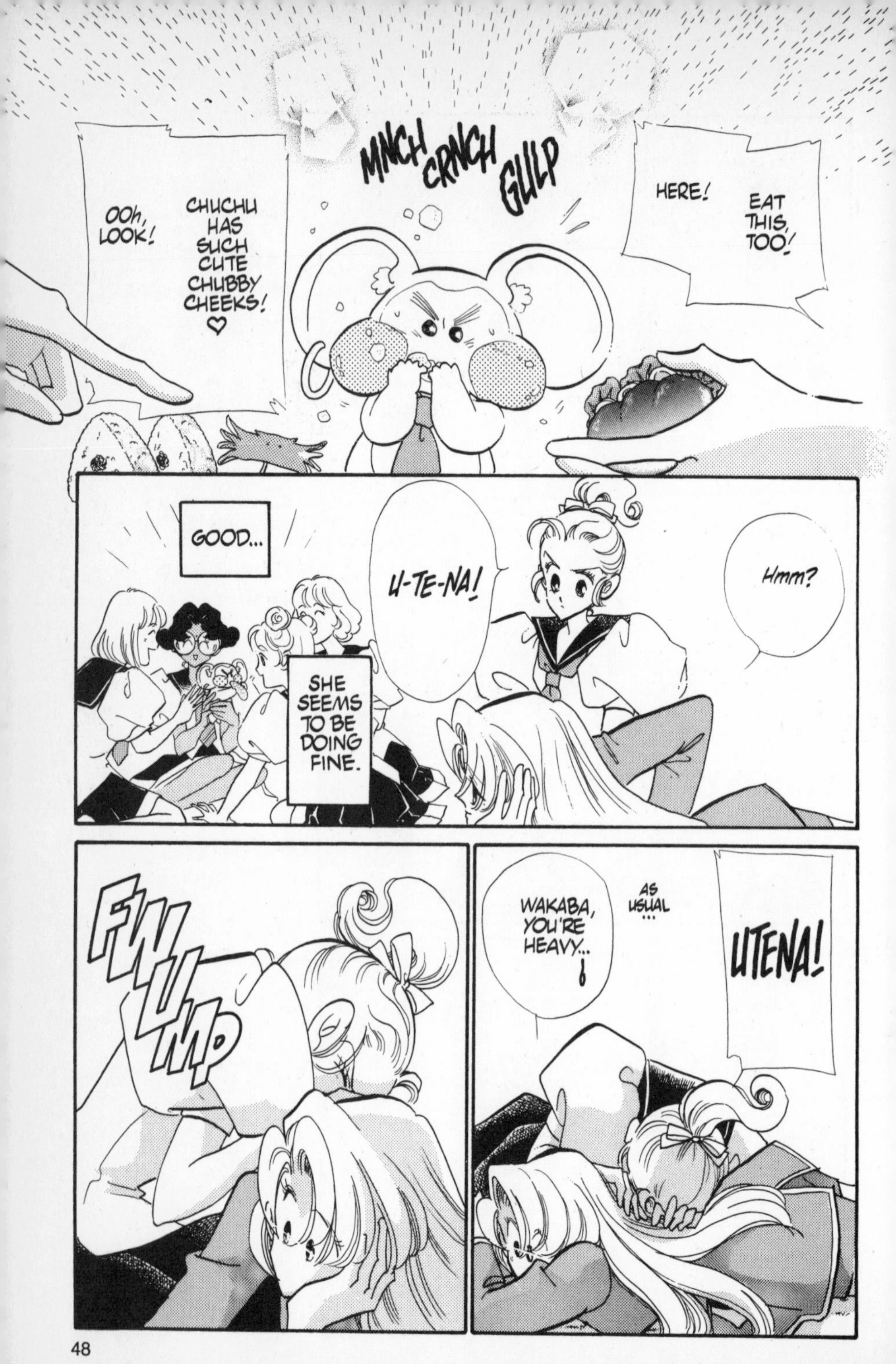
OOH, LOOK!
CHUCHU HAS SUCH CUTE CHUBBY CHEEKS! ♡
MNCH CRNCH GULP
HERE!
EAT THIS, TOO!
GOOD...
SHE SEEMS TO BE DOING FINE.
U-TE-NA!
Hmm?
FWUMP
UTENA!
WAKABA, YOU'RE HEAVY...
AS USUAL...

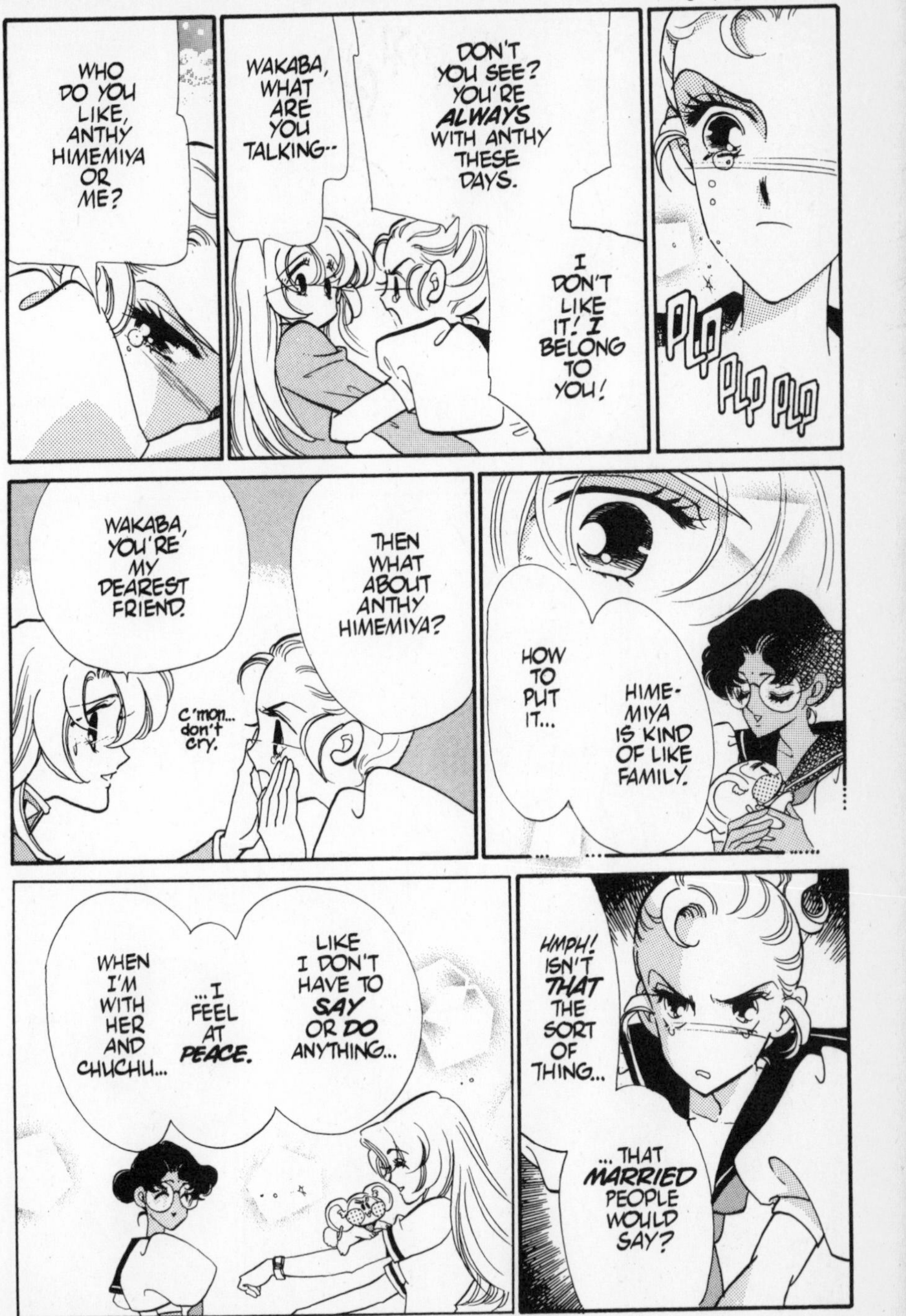
WHO DO YOU LIKE, ANTHY HIMEMIYA OR ME?
WAKABA, WHAT ARE YOU TALKING..
DON'T YOU SEE? YOU'RE ALWAYS WITH ANTHY THESE DAYS.
I DON'T LIKE IT! I BELONG TO YOU!
PLP PLP PLP
WAKABA, YOU'RE MY DEAREST FRIEND.
THEN WHAT ABOUT ANTHY HIMEMIYA?
C'mon... don't cry.
HOW TO PUT IT...
HIME-MIYA IS KIND OF LIKE FAMILY.
WHEN I'M WITH HER AND CHUCHU...
...I FEEL AT PEACE.
LIKE I DON'T HAVE TO SAY OR DO ANYTHING...
HMPH! ISN'T THAT THE SORT OF THING...
...THAT MARRIED PEOPLE WOULD SAY?

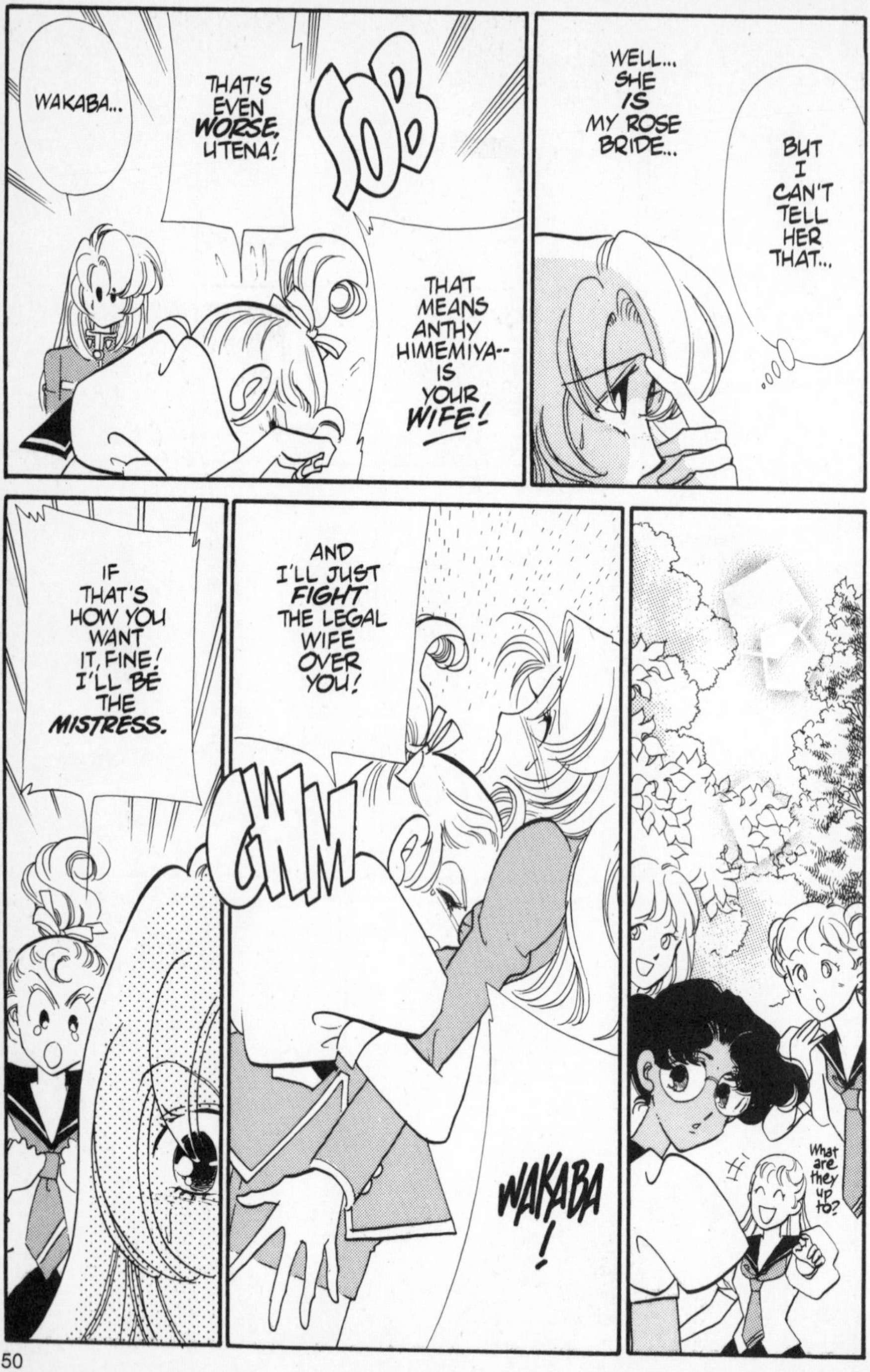
WAKABA...
THAT'S EVEN WORSE, UTENA!
SOB
THAT MEANS ANTHY HIMEMIYA-- IS YOUR WIFE!
WELL... SHE IS MY ROSE BRIDE...
BUT I CAN'T TELL HER THAT...
IF THAT'S HOW YOU WANT IT, FINE! I'LL BE THE MISTRESS.
AND I'LL JUST FIGHT THE LEGAL WIFE OVER YOU!
GLMP
WAKABA!
What are they up to?

Kendo Team

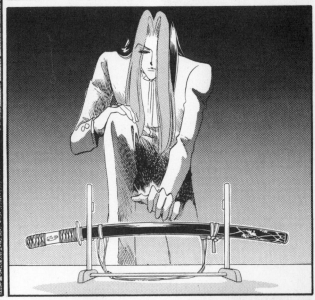

SO... ARE YOU... *FINALLY GOING TO DUEL WITH UTENA TENJOU?*

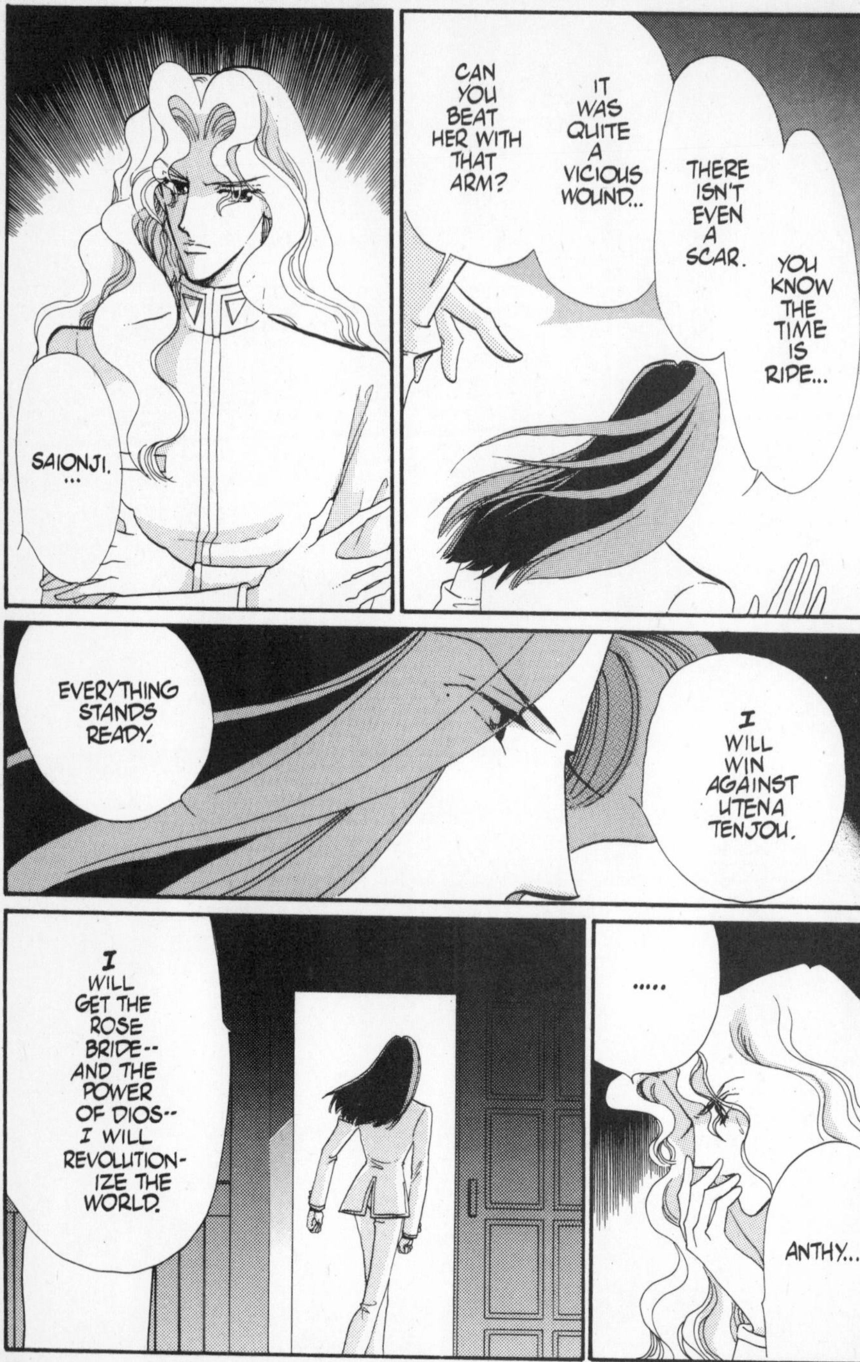
SAIONJI. ...
CAN YOU BEAT HER WITH THAT ARM?
IT WAS QUITE A VICIOUS WOUND...
THERE ISN'T EVEN A SCAR.
YOU KNOW THE TIME IS RIPE...
EVERYTHING STANDS READY.
I WILL WIN AGAINST UTENA TENJOU.
I WILL GET THE ROSE BRIDE-- AND THE POWER OF DIOS-- I WILL REVOLUTION-IZE THE WORLD.
.....
ANTHY...

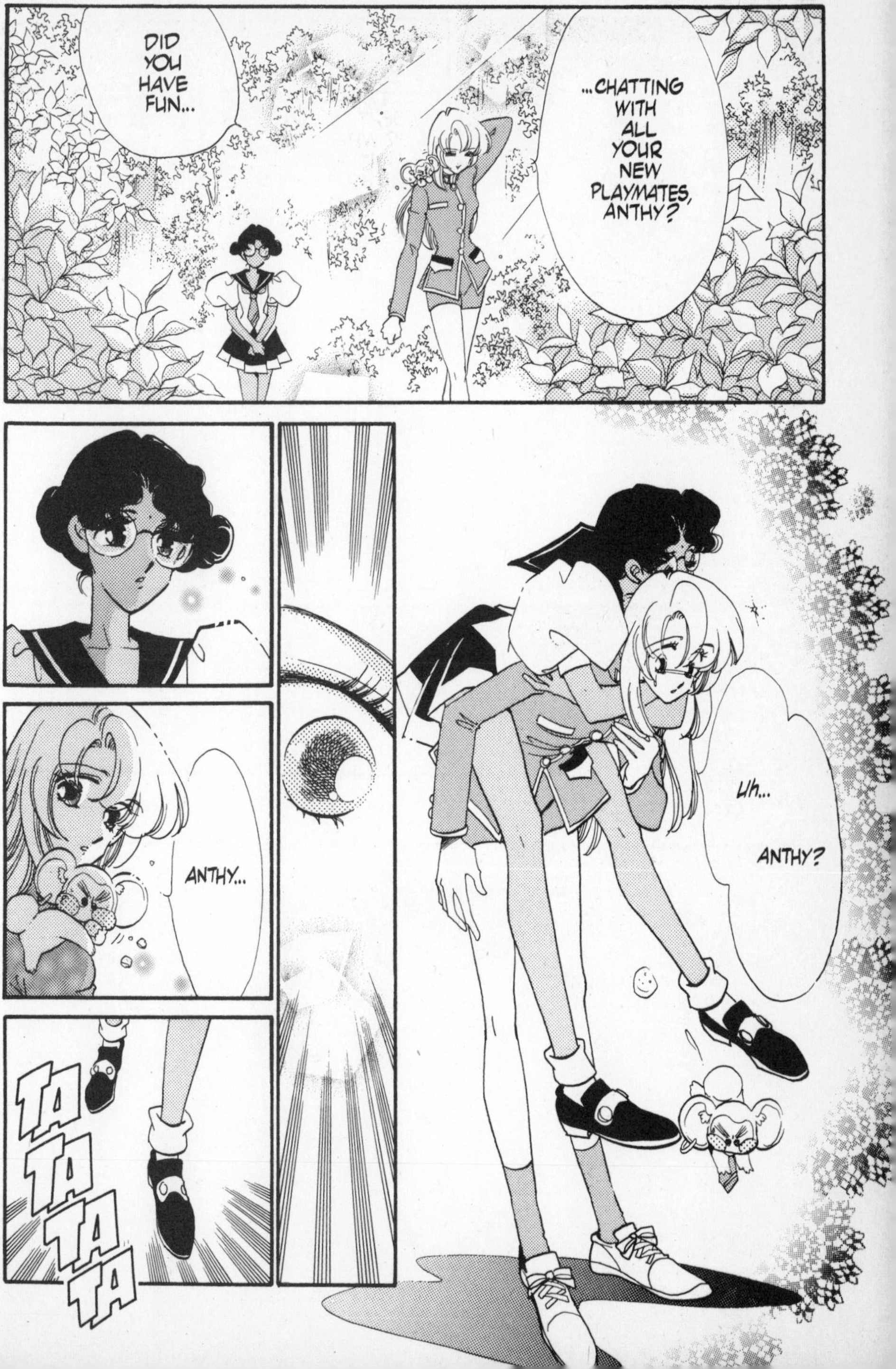
DID YOU HAVE FUN...
...CHATTING WITH ALL YOUR NEW PLAYMATES, ANTHY?
ANTHY...
TA TA TA TA TA
Uh... ANTHY?

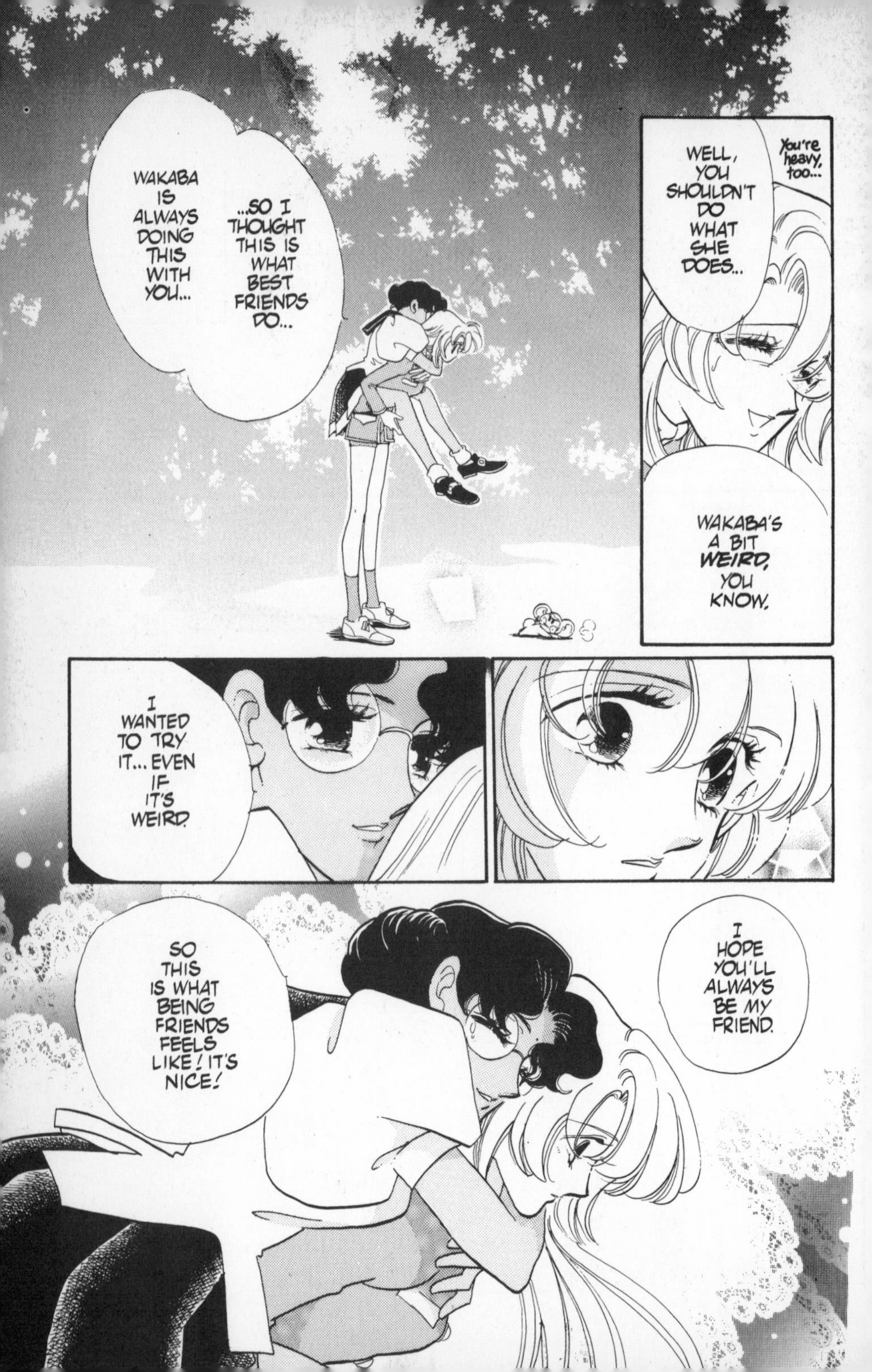
WAKABA IS ALWAYS DOING THIS WITH YOU...
...SO I THOUGHT THIS IS WHAT BEST FRIENDS DO...
WELL, YOU SHOULDN'T DO WHAT SHE DOES...
You're heavy, too...
WAKABA'S A BIT *WEIRD,* YOU KNOW.
I WANTED TO TRY IT... EVEN IF IT'S WEIRD.
SO THIS IS WHAT BEING FRIENDS FEELS LIKE! IT'S NICE!
I HOPE YOU'LL ALWAYS BE MY FRIEND.

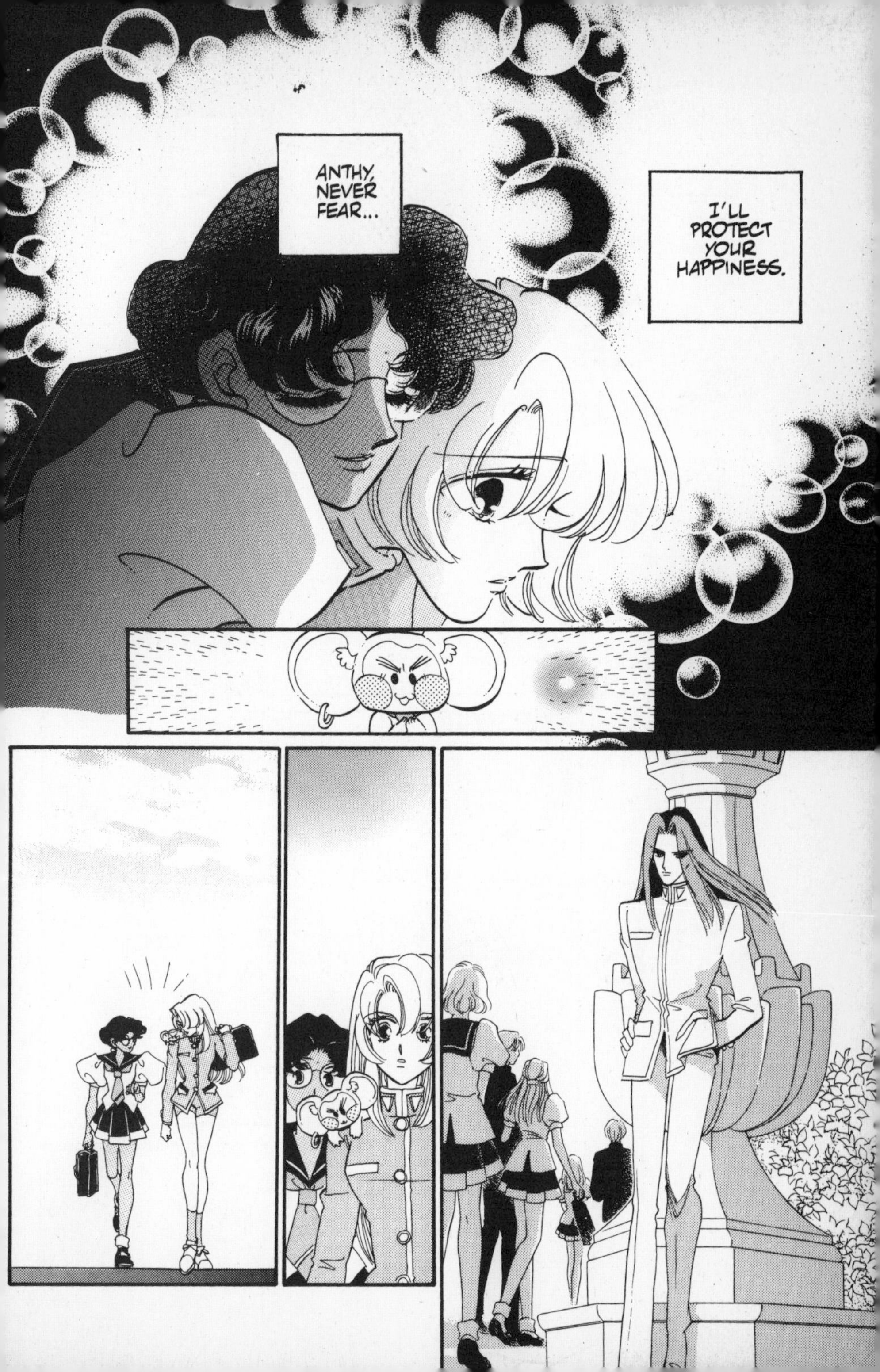
ANTHY, NEVER FEAR...
I'LL PROTECT YOUR HAPPINESS.

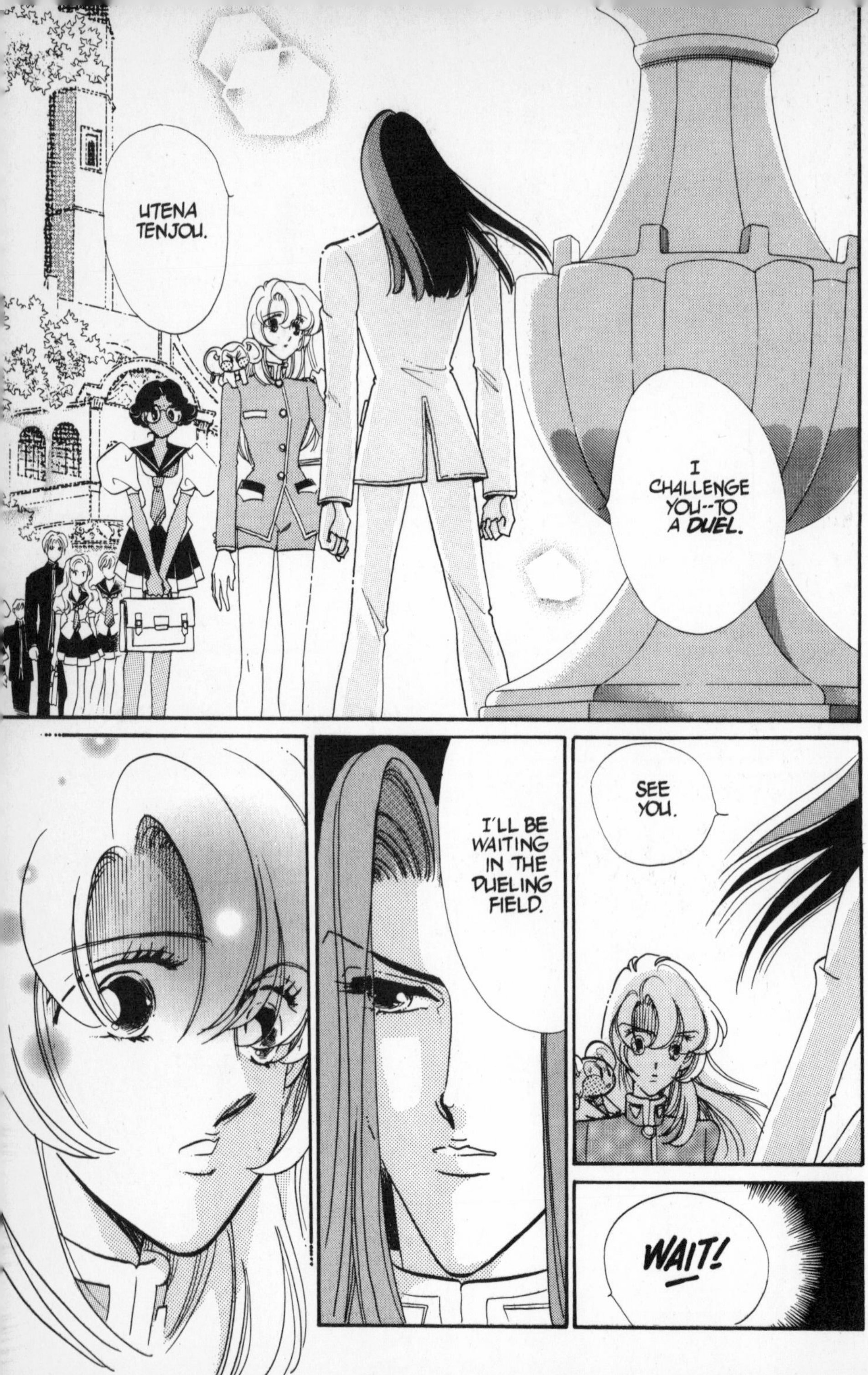
UTENA TENJOU.
I CHALLENGE YOU--TO A DUEL.
I'LL BE WAITING IN THE DUELING FIELD.
SEE YOU.
WAIT!

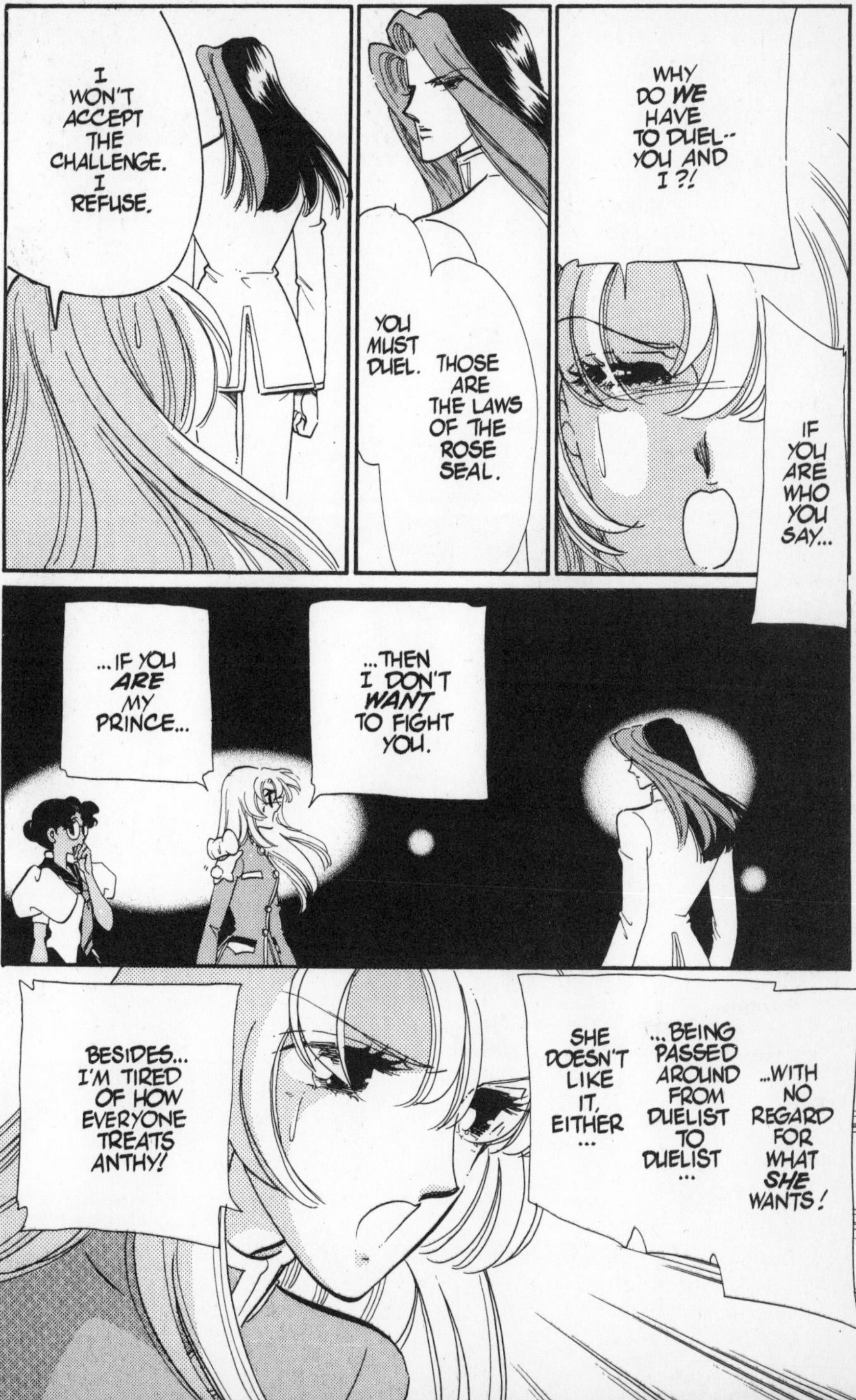
I WON'T ACCEPT THE CHALLENGE. I REFUSE.
YOU MUST DUEL.
THOSE ARE THE LAWS OF THE ROSE SEAL.
WHY DO *WE* HAVE TO DUEL-- YOU AND I ?!
IF YOU ARE WHO YOU SAY...
...IF YOU *ARE* MY PRINCE...
...THEN I DON'T *WANT* TO FIGHT YOU.
BESIDES... I'M TIRED OF HOW EVERYONE TREATS ANTHY!
SHE DOESN'T LIKE IT, EITHER ...
...BEING PASSED AROUND FROM DUELIST TO DUELIST ...
...WITH NO REGARD FOR WHAT *SHE* WANTS!

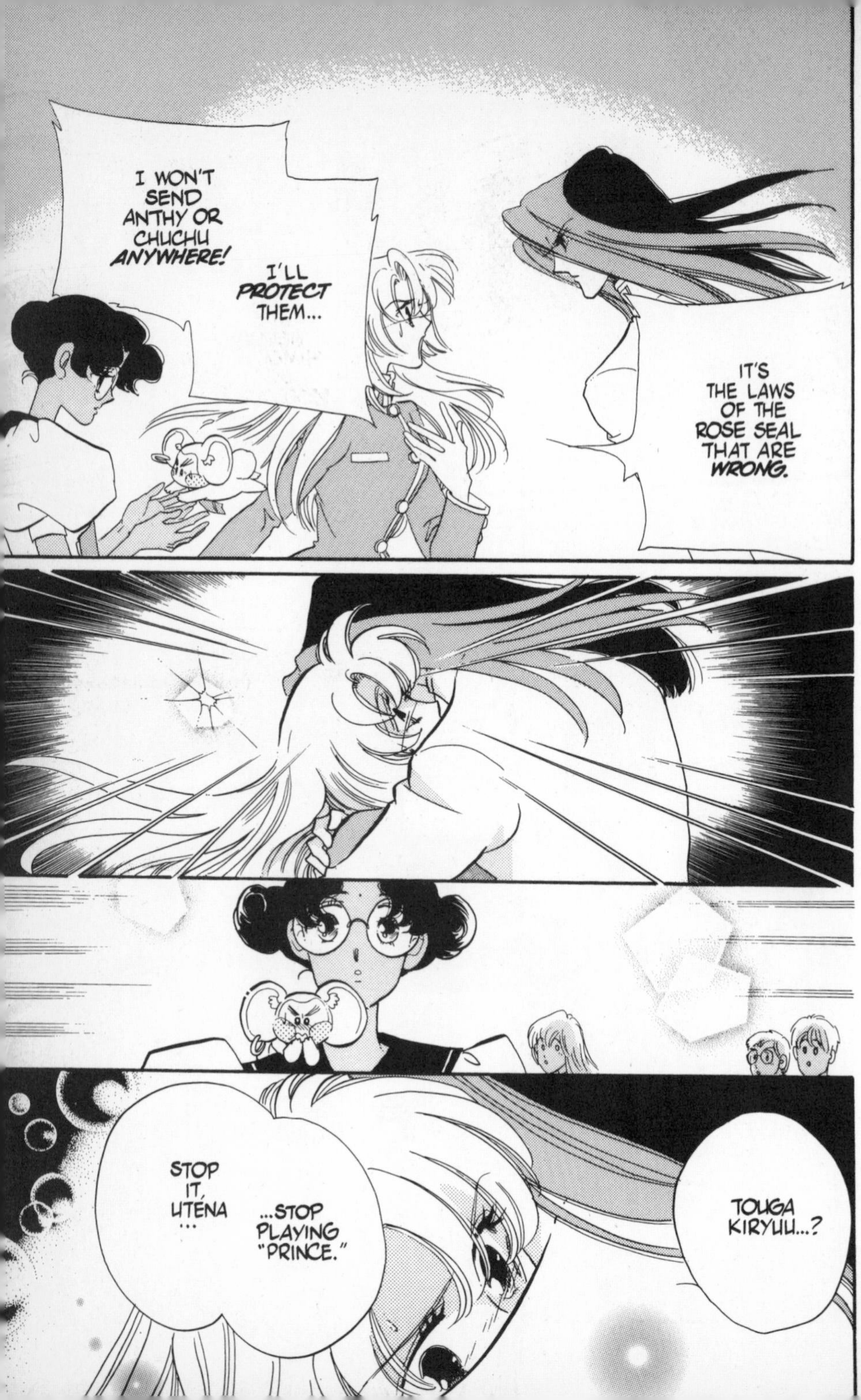
I WON'T SEND ANTHY OR CHUCHU ANYWHERE!
I'LL PROTECT THEM...
IT'S THE LAWS OF THE ROSE SEAL THAT ARE WRONG.
STOP IT, UTENA...
...STOP PLAYING "PRINCE."
TOUGA KIRYUU...?

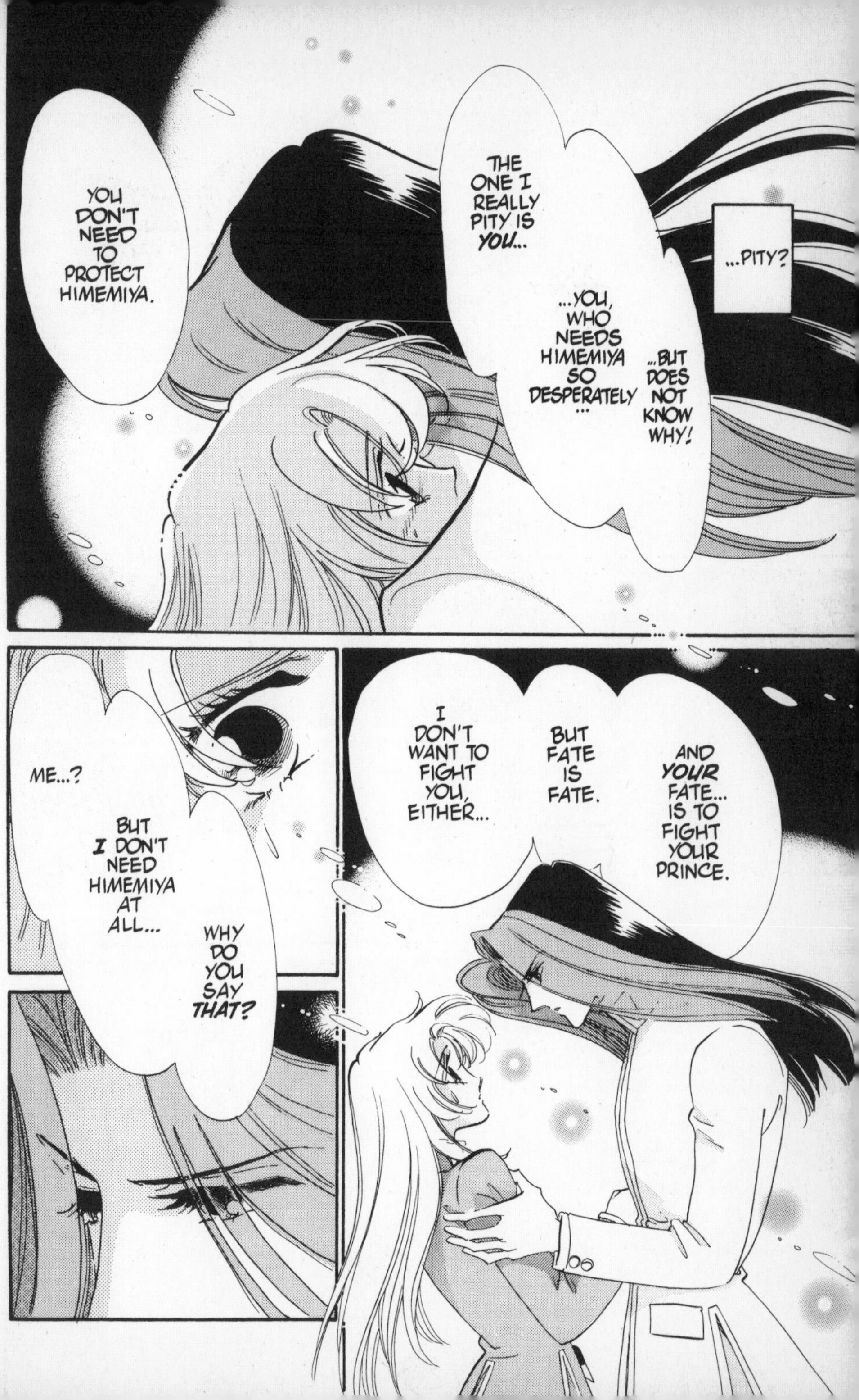
YOU DON'T NEED TO PROTECT HIMEMIYA.
THE ONE I REALLY PITY IS *YOU*...
...YOU, WHO NEEDS HIMEMIYA SO DESPERATELY...
...BUT DOES NOT KNOW WHY!
...PITY?
ME...?
BUT *I* DON'T NEED HIMEMIYA AT ALL...
WHY DO YOU SAY *THAT*?
I DON'T WANT TO FIGHT YOU, EITHER...
BUT FATE IS FATE.
AND *YOUR* FATE... IS TO FIGHT YOUR PRINCE.

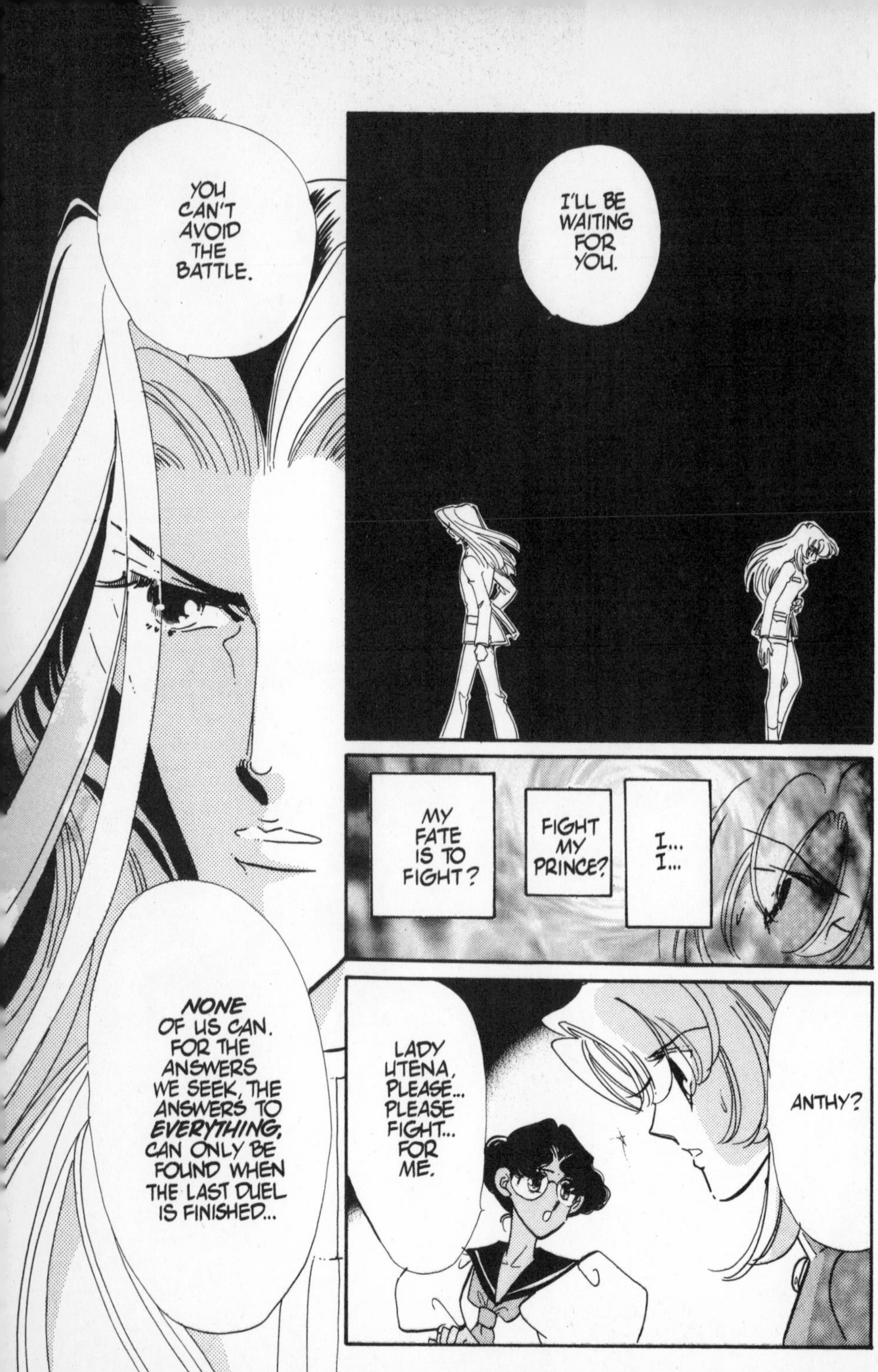
YOU CAN'T AVOID THE BATTLE.
NONE OF US CAN. FOR THE ANSWERS WE SEEK, THE ANSWERS TO *EVERYTHING*, CAN ONLY BE FOUND WHEN THE LAST DUEL IS FINISHED...
I'LL BE WAITING FOR YOU.
MY FATE IS TO FIGHT?
FIGHT MY PRINCE?
I... I...
LADY UTENA, PLEASE... PLEASE FIGHT... FOR ME.
ANTHY?

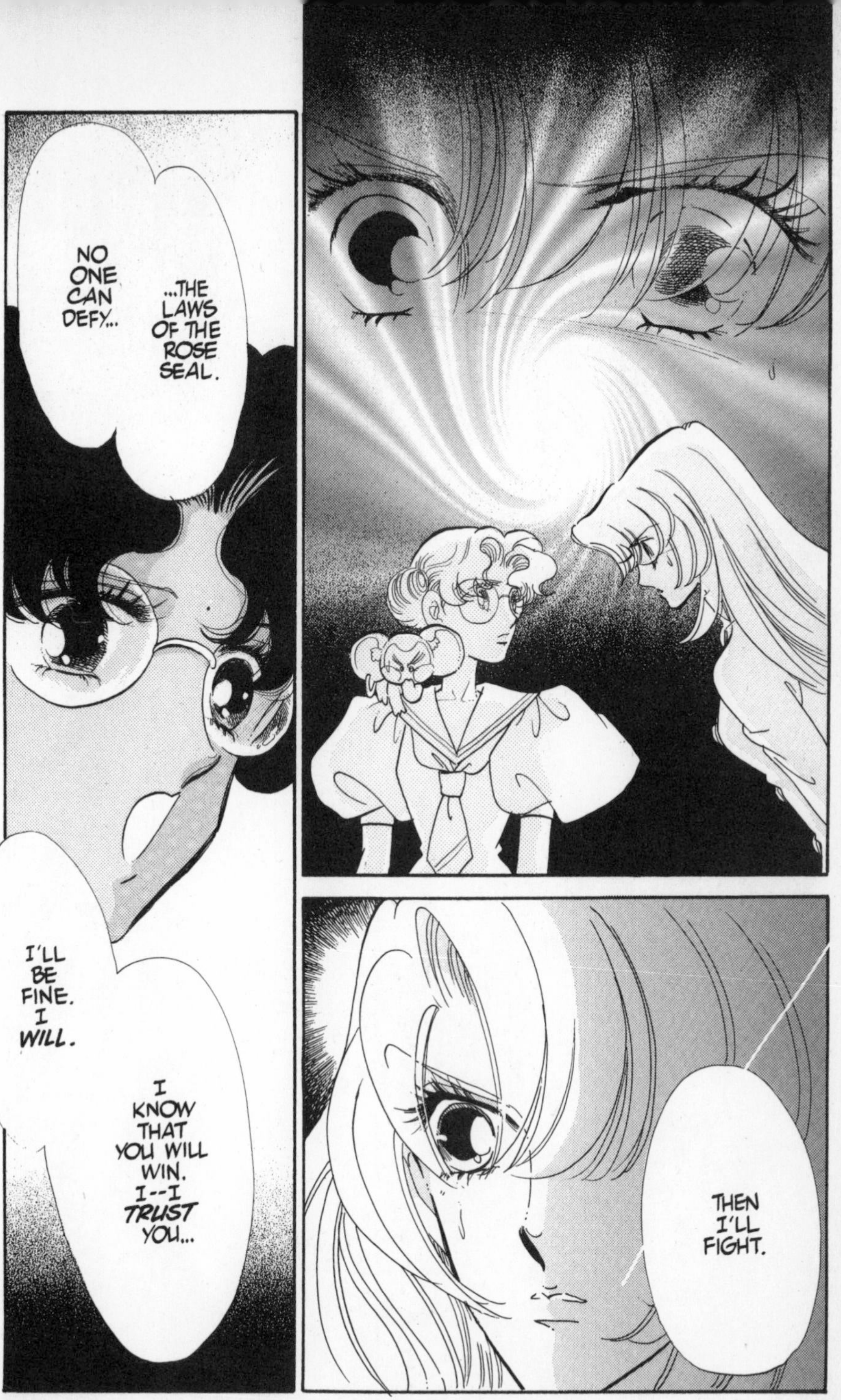
NO ONE CAN DEFY... ...THE LAWS OF THE ROSE SEAL.
I'LL BE FINE. I *WILL*.
I KNOW THAT YOU WILL WIN. I--I *TRUST* YOU...
THEN I'LL FIGHT.

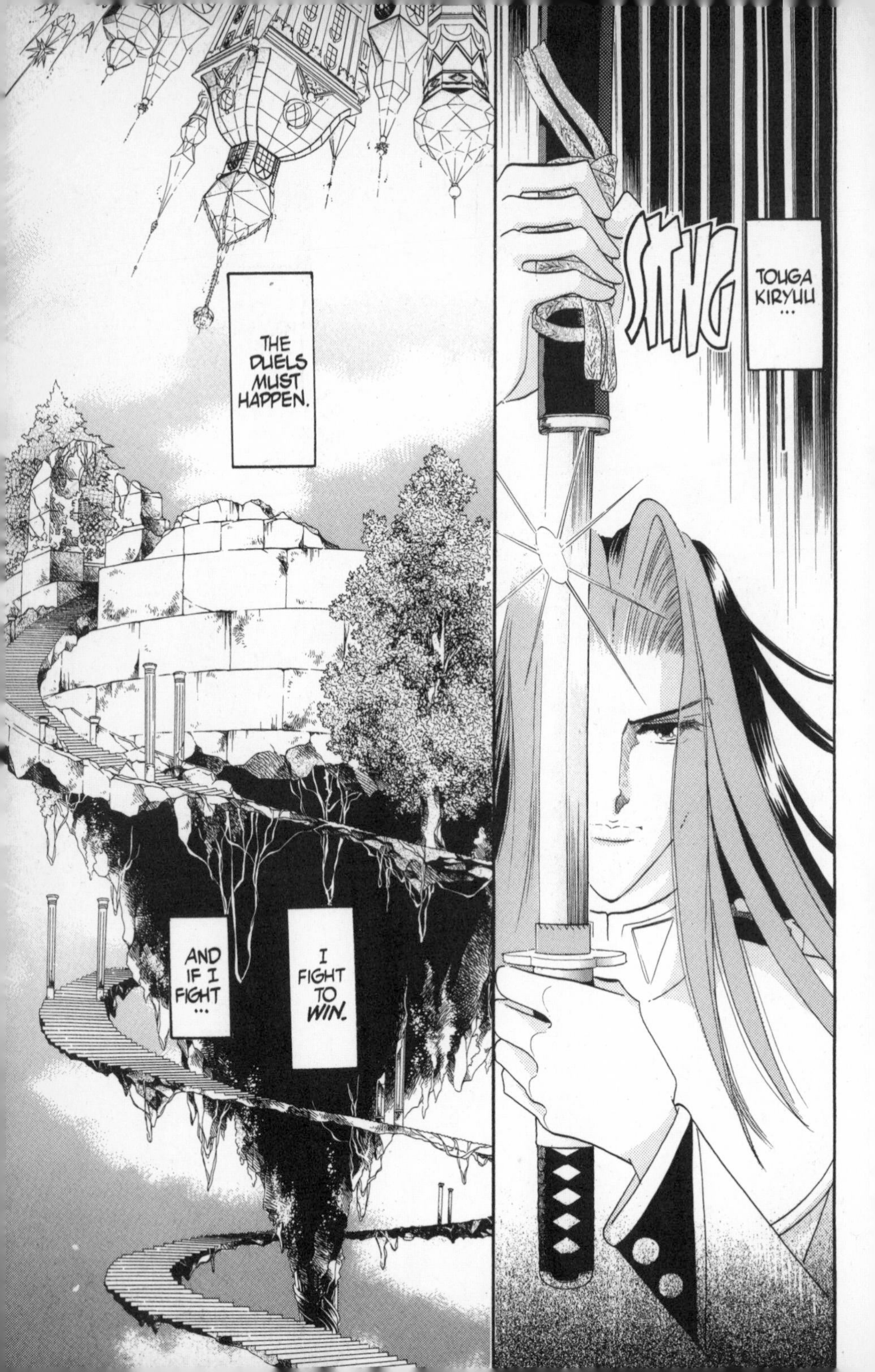
THE DUELS MUST HAPPEN.
AND IF I FIGHT ...
I FIGHT TO WIN.
SHING
TOUGA KIRYUU ...

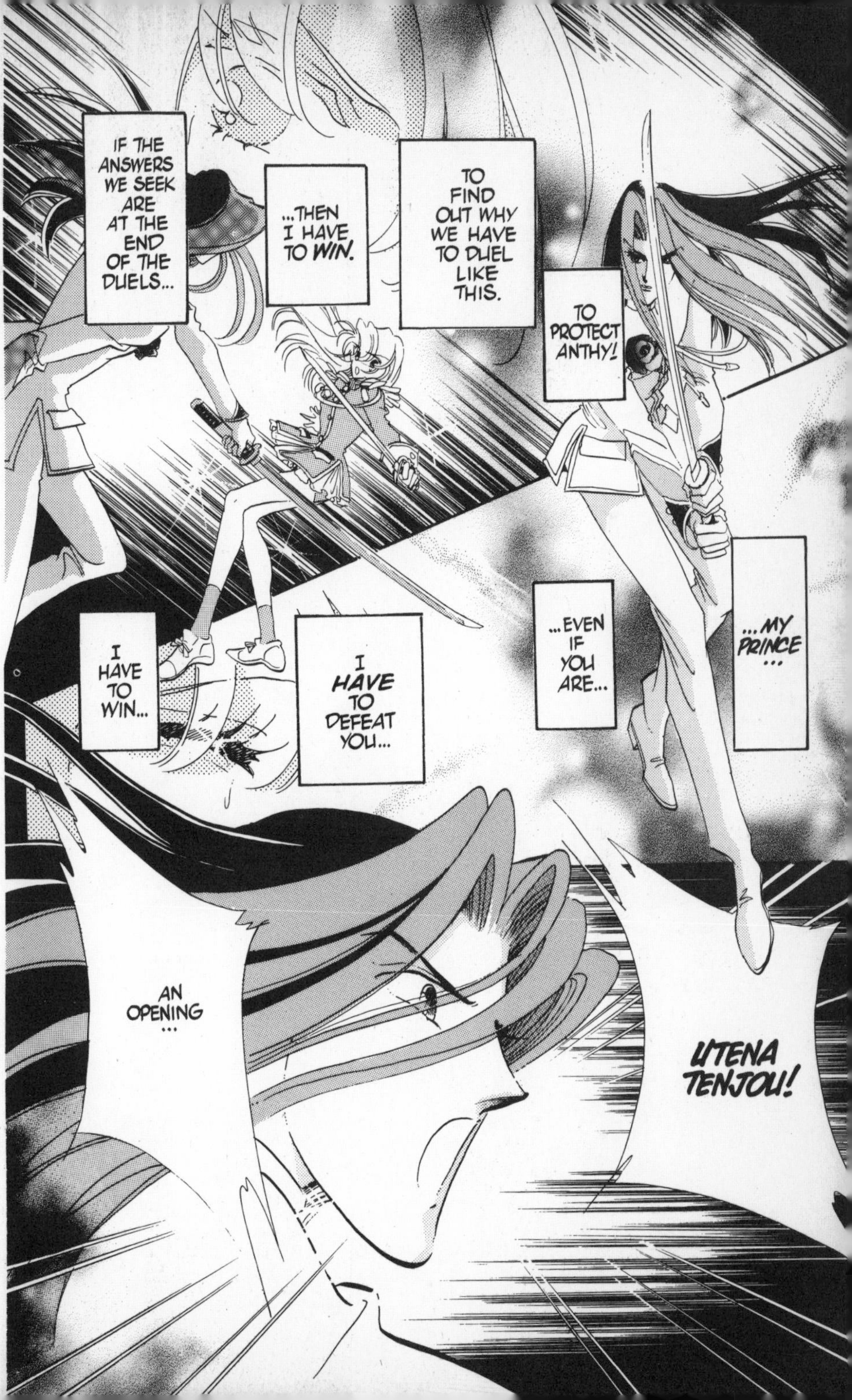
IF THE ANSWERS WE SEEK ARE AT THE END OF THE DUELS...
...THEN I HAVE TO *WIN.*
TO FIND OUT WHY WE HAVE TO DUEL LIKE THIS.
TO PROTECT ANTHY!
I HAVE TO WIN...
I *HAVE* TO DEFEAT YOU...
...EVEN IF YOU ARE...
...MY PRINCE...
AN OPENING...
UTENA TENJOU!

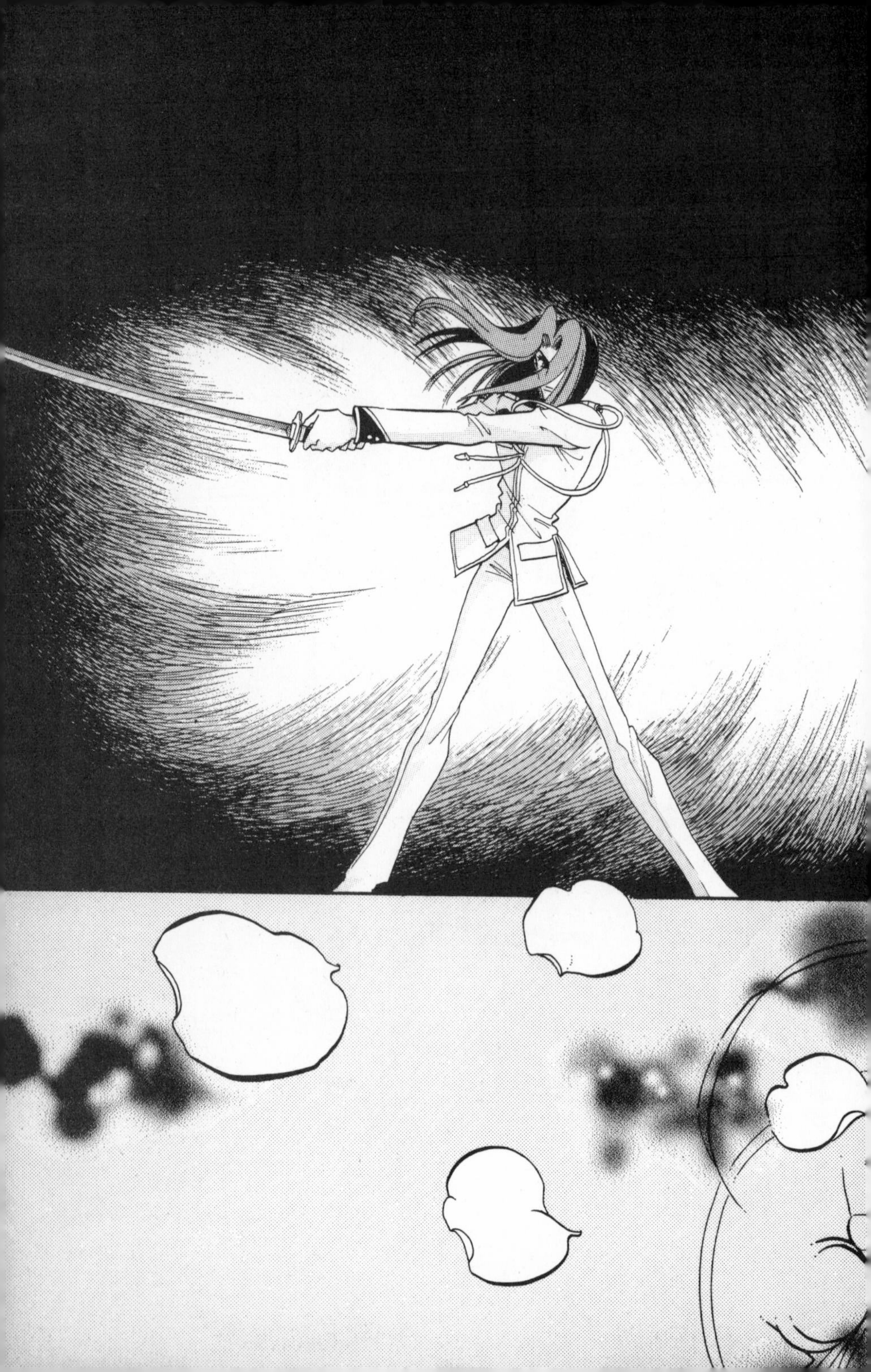

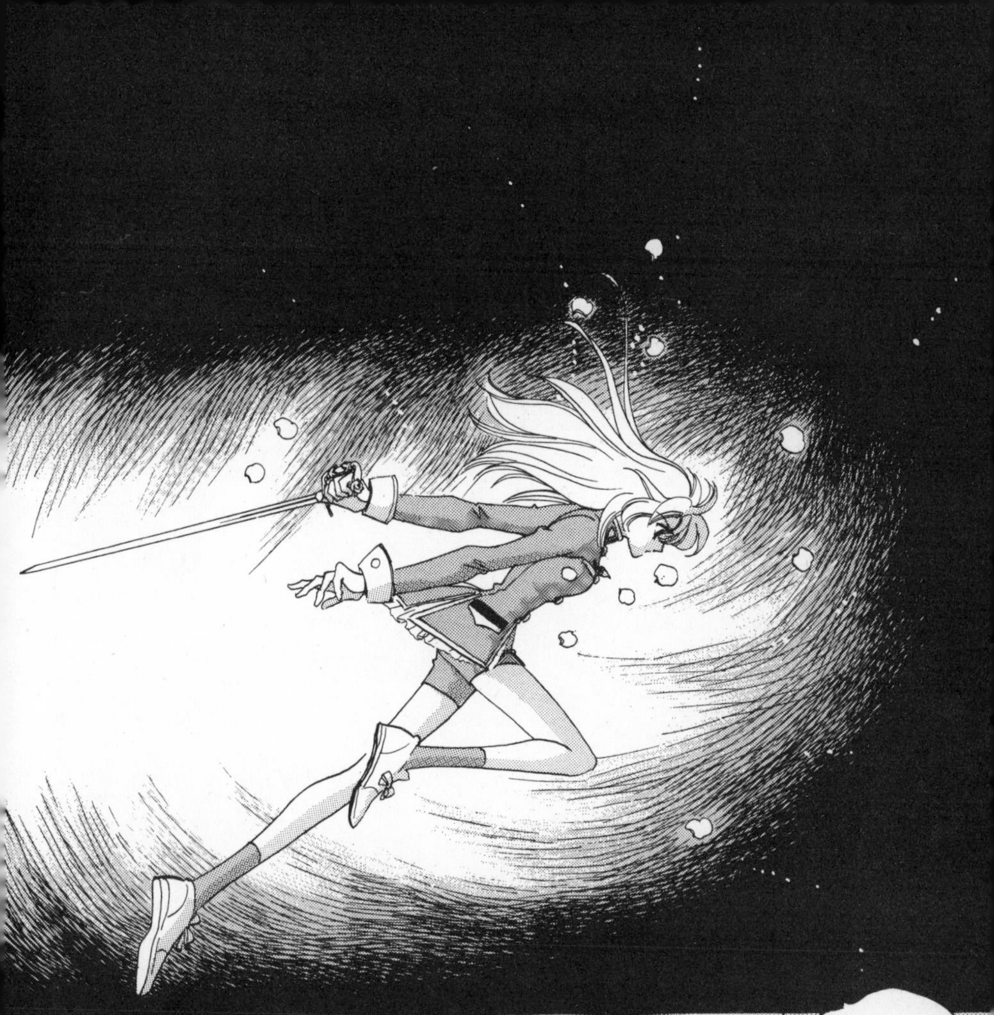
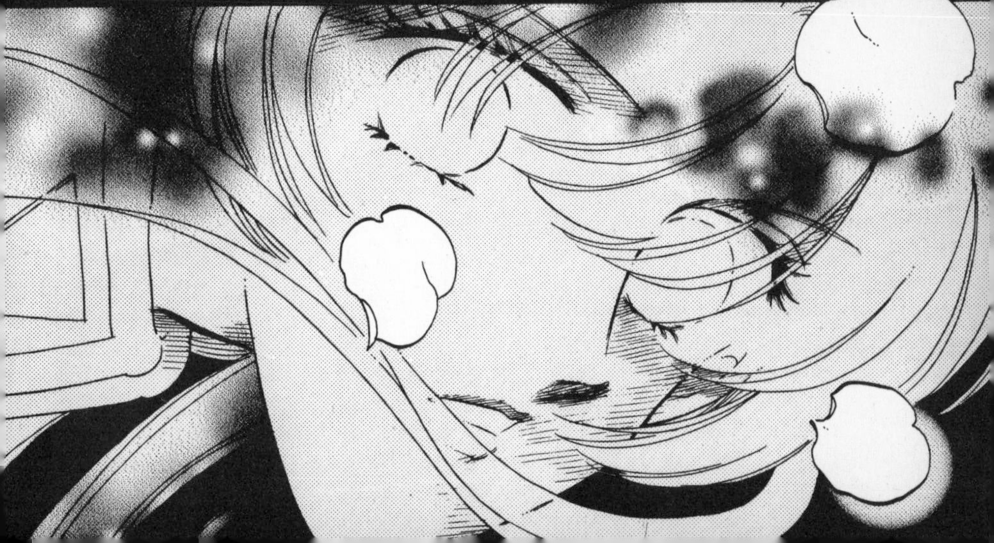

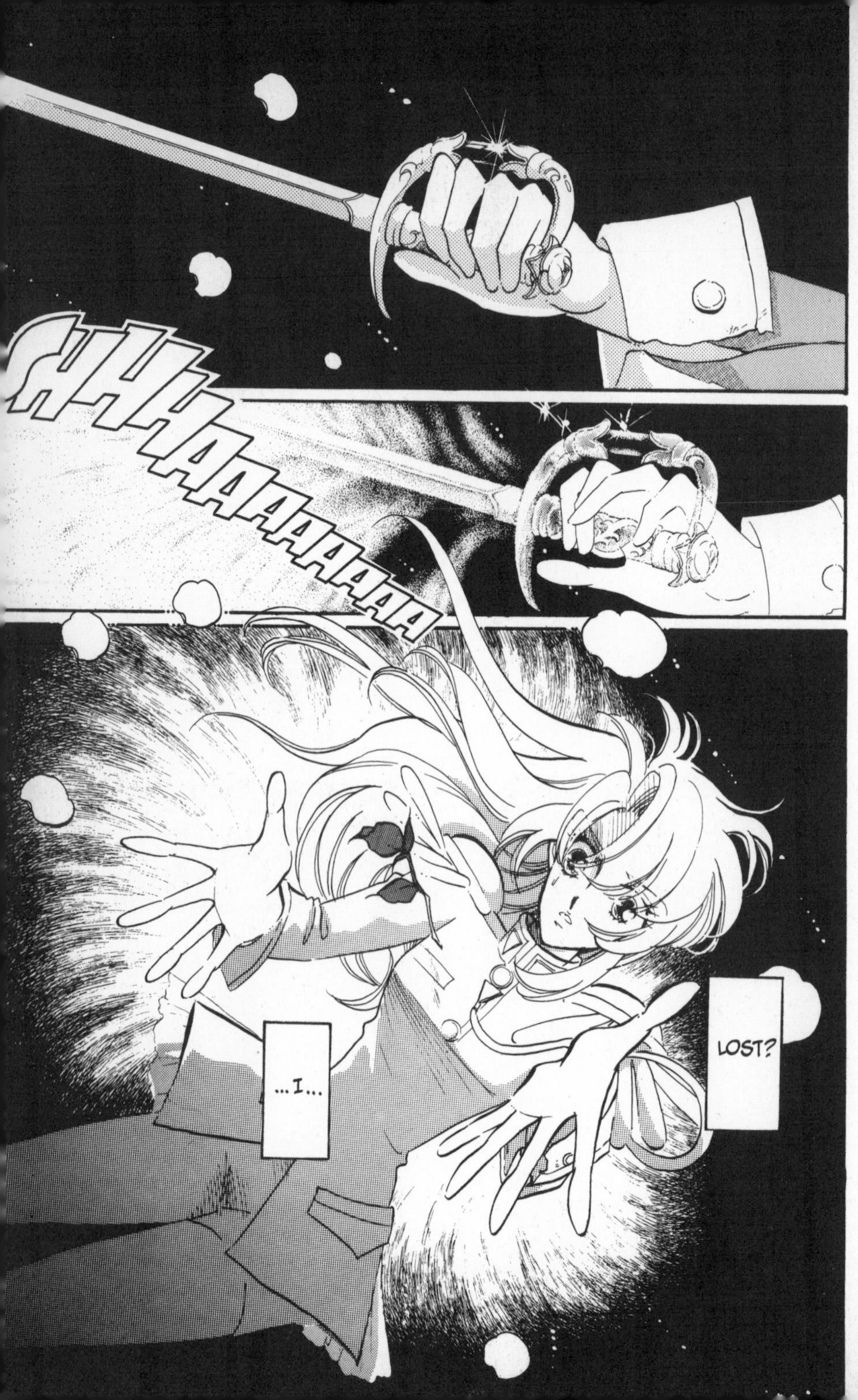
SHHAAAAAAAA
...I...
LOST?

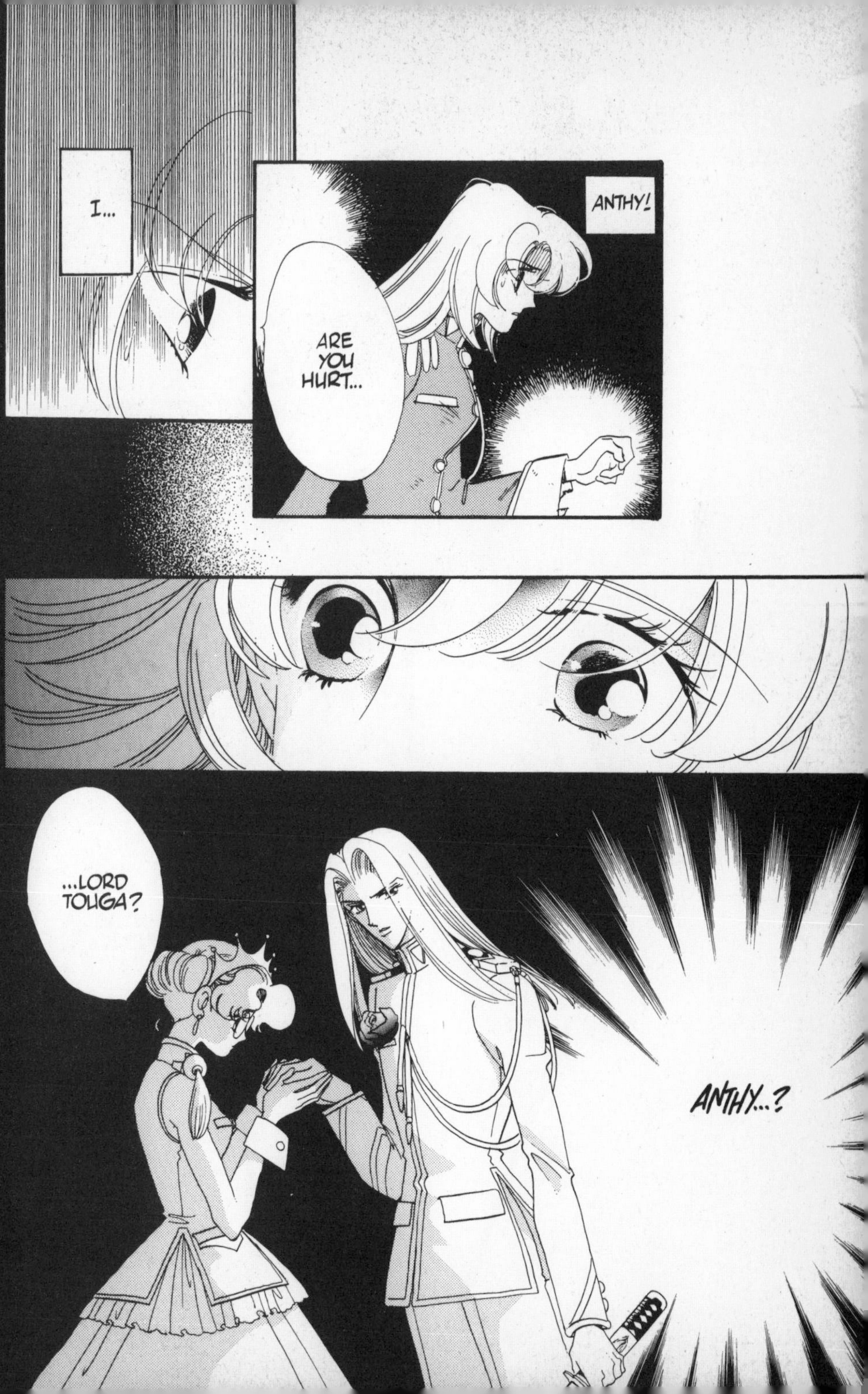
I...
ANTHY!
ARE YOU HURT...
...LORD TOUGA?
ANTHY...?

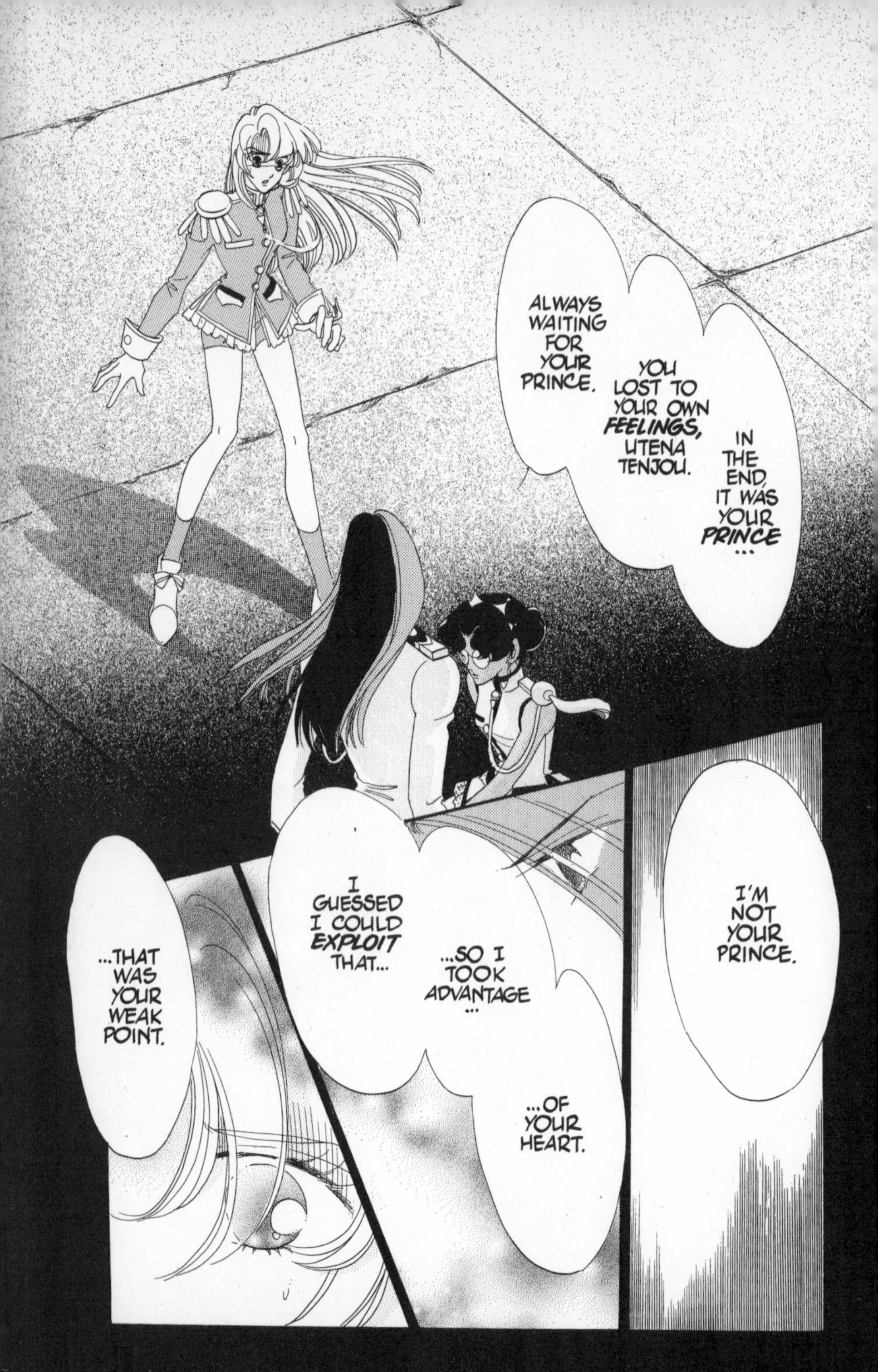
ALWAYS WAITING FOR YOUR PRINCE.
YOU LOST TO YOUR OWN *FEELINGS,* UTENA TENJOU.
IN THE END, IT WAS YOUR *PRINCE*...
...THAT WAS YOUR WEAK POINT.
I GUESSED I COULD *EXPLOIT* THAT...
...SO I TOOK ADVANTAGE...
...OF YOUR HEART.
I'M NOT YOUR PRINCE.

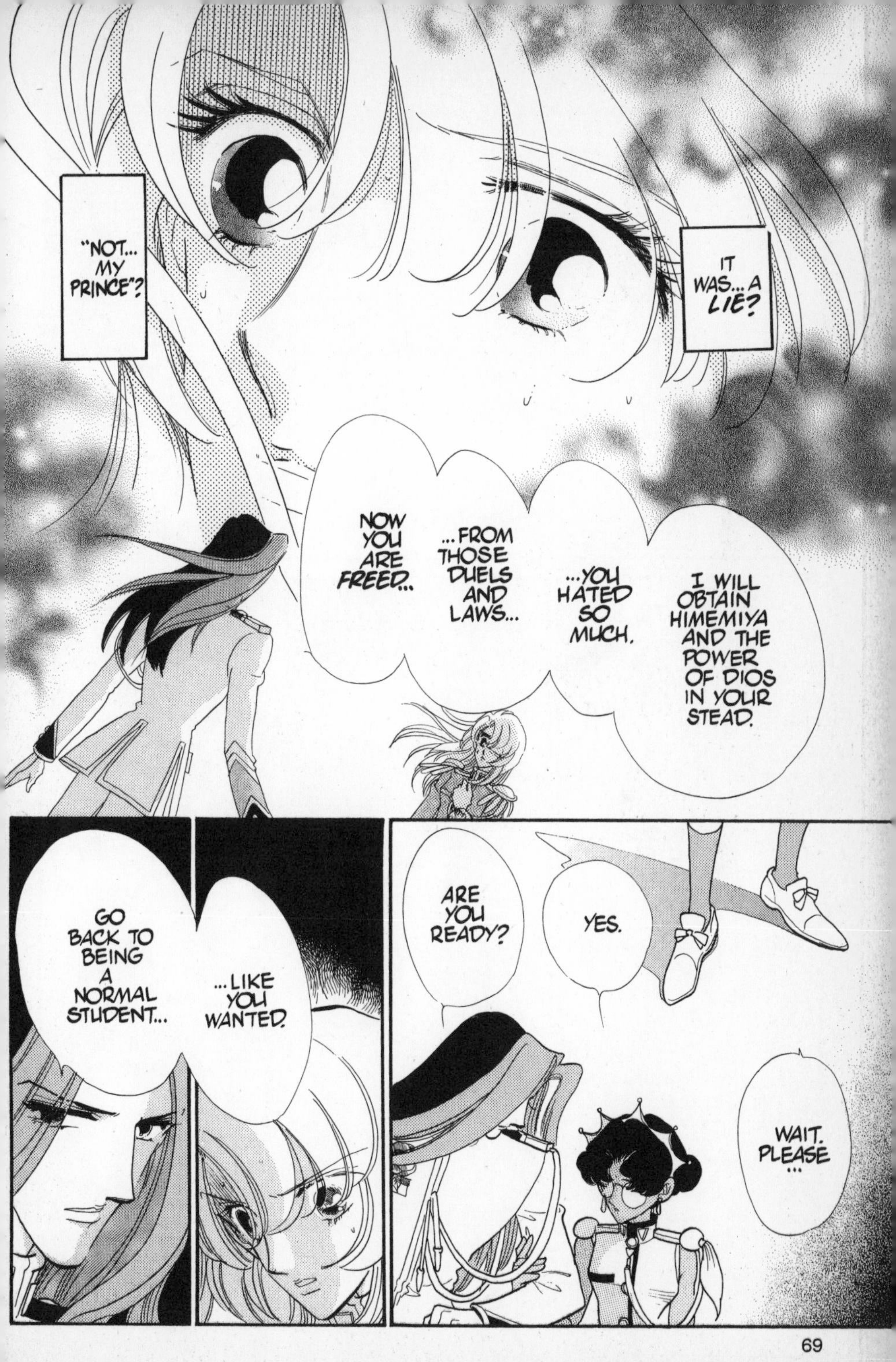
"NOT... MY PRINCE"?
IT WAS... A LIE?
NOW YOU ARE FREED...
...FROM THOSE DUELS AND LAWS...
...YOU HATED SO MUCH.
I WILL OBTAIN HIMEMIYA AND THE POWER OF DIOS IN YOUR STEAD.
GO BACK TO BEING A NORMAL STUDENT...
...LIKE YOU WANTED.
ARE YOU READY?
YES.
WAIT. PLEASE ...

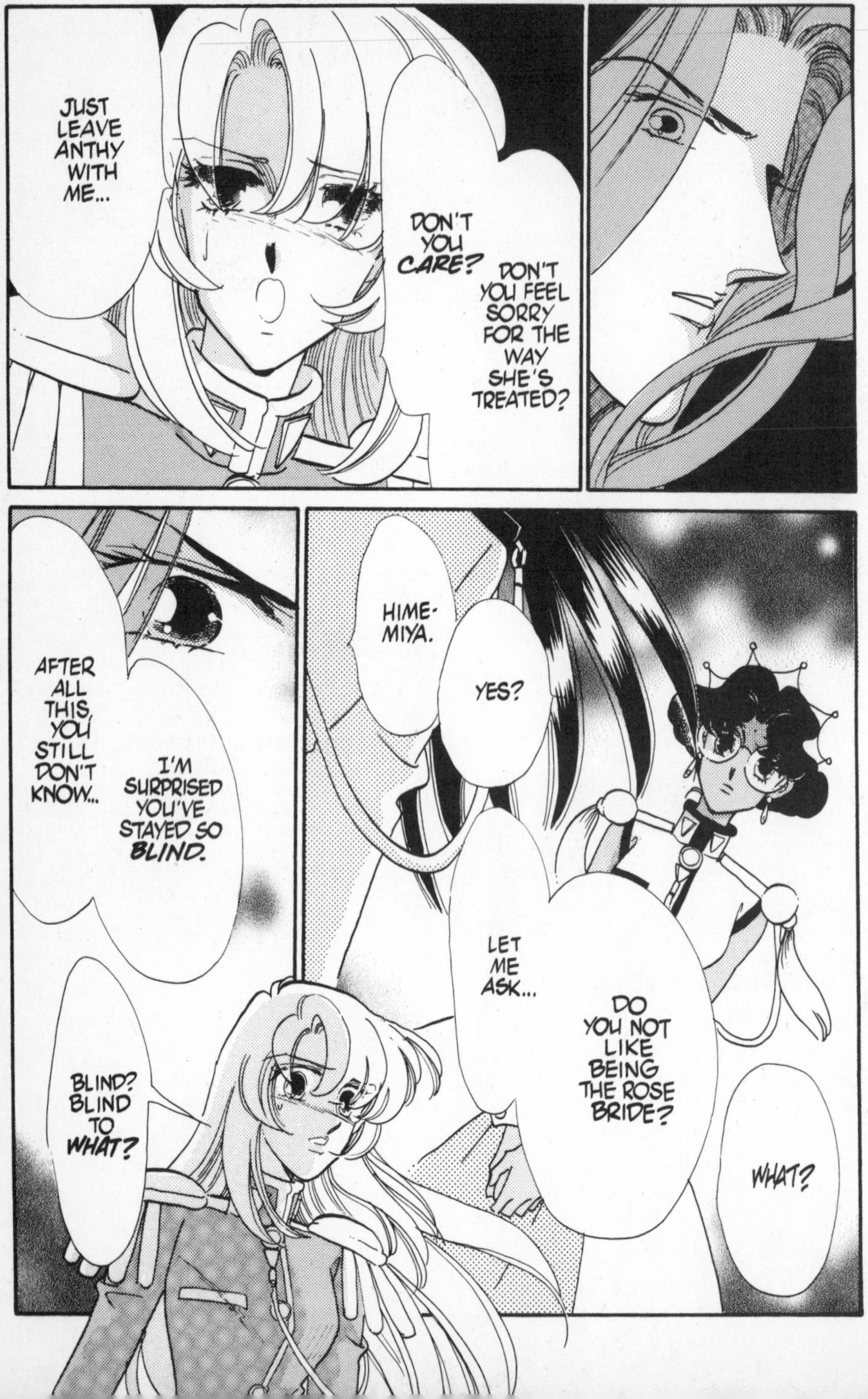
JUST LEAVE ANTHY WITH ME...
DON'T YOU CARE?
DON'T YOU FEEL SORRY FOR THE WAY SHE'S TREATED?
AFTER ALL THIS, YOU STILL DON'T KNOW...
I'M SURPRISED YOU'VE STAYED SO BLIND.
HIME-MIYA.
YES?
LET ME ASK...
DO YOU NOT LIKE BEING THE ROSE BRIDE?
WHAT?
BLIND? BLIND TO WHAT?

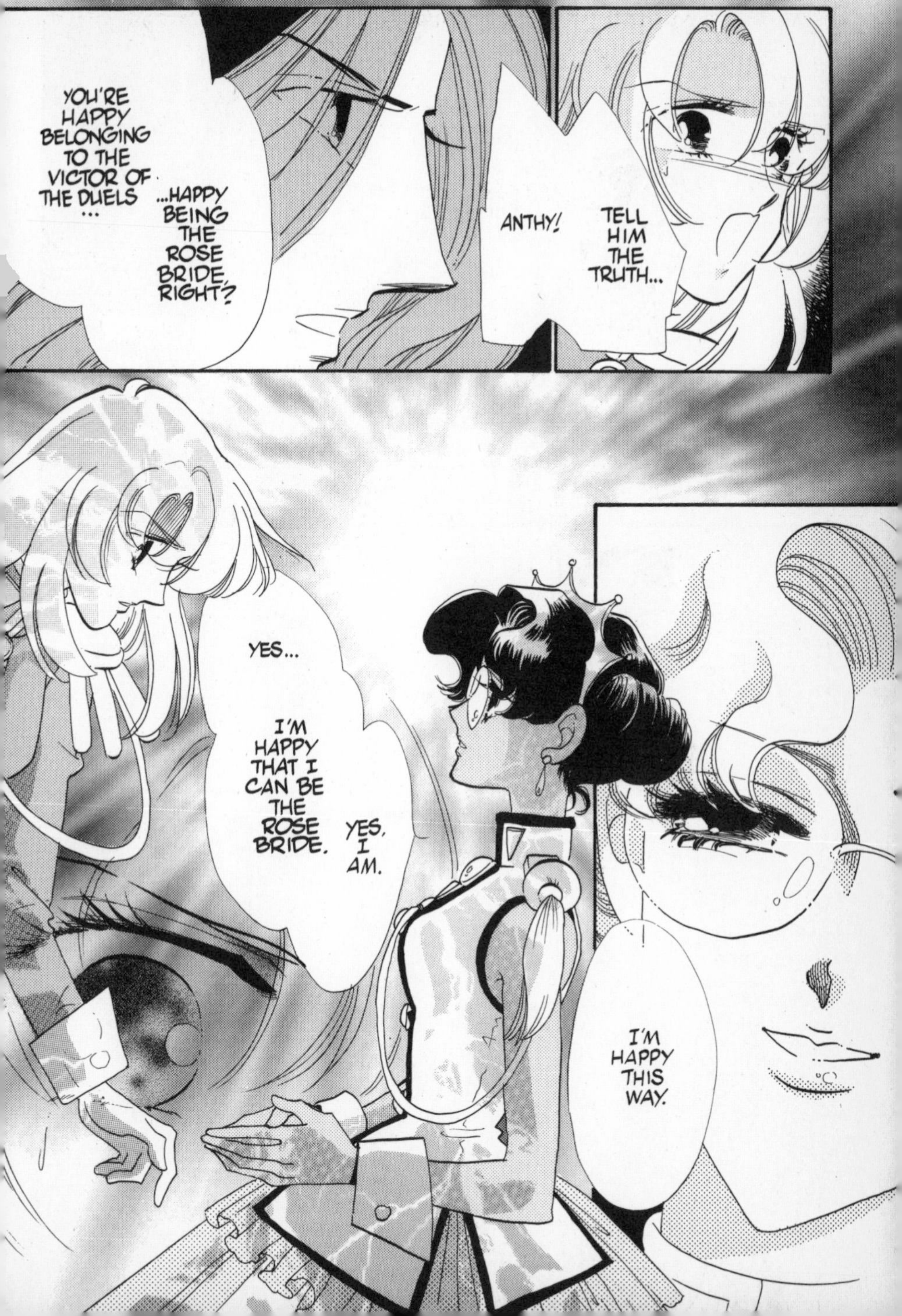
YOU'RE HAPPY BELONGING TO THE VICTOR OF THE DUELS ...
...HAPPY BEING THE ROSE BRIDE, RIGHT?
ANTHY!
TELL HIM THE TRUTH...
YES...
I'M HAPPY THAT I CAN BE THE ROSE BRIDE.
YES, I AM.
!
I'M HAPPY THIS WAY.

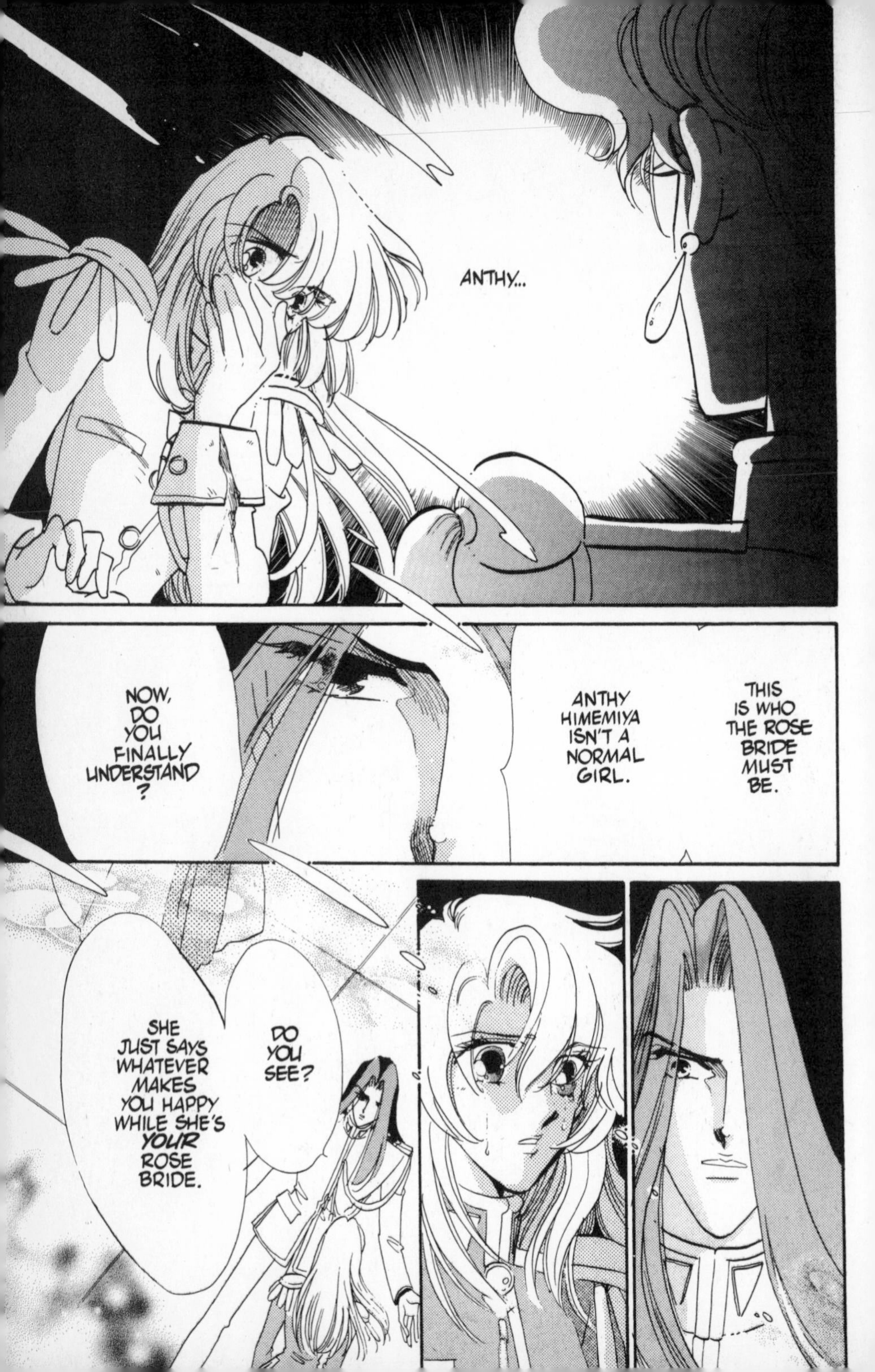
ANTHY...
NOW, DO YOU FINALLY UNDERSTAND?
ANTHY HIMEMIYA ISN'T A NORMAL GIRL.
THIS IS WHO THE ROSE BRIDE MUST BE.
SHE JUST SAYS WHATEVER MAKES YOU HAPPY WHILE SHE'S ***YOUR*** ROSE BRIDE.
DO YOU SEE?

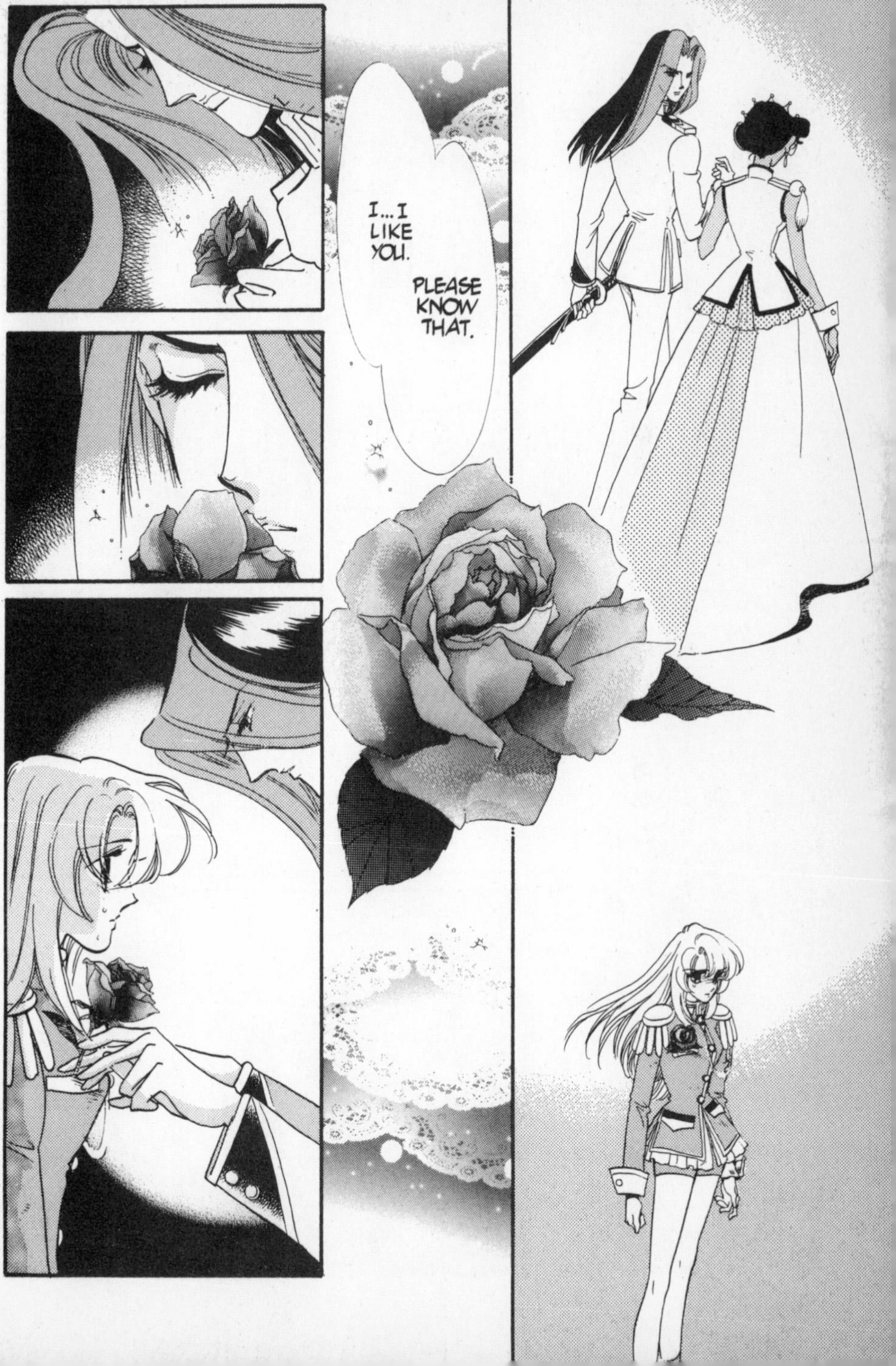
I... I LIKE YOU.
PLEASE KNOW THAT.

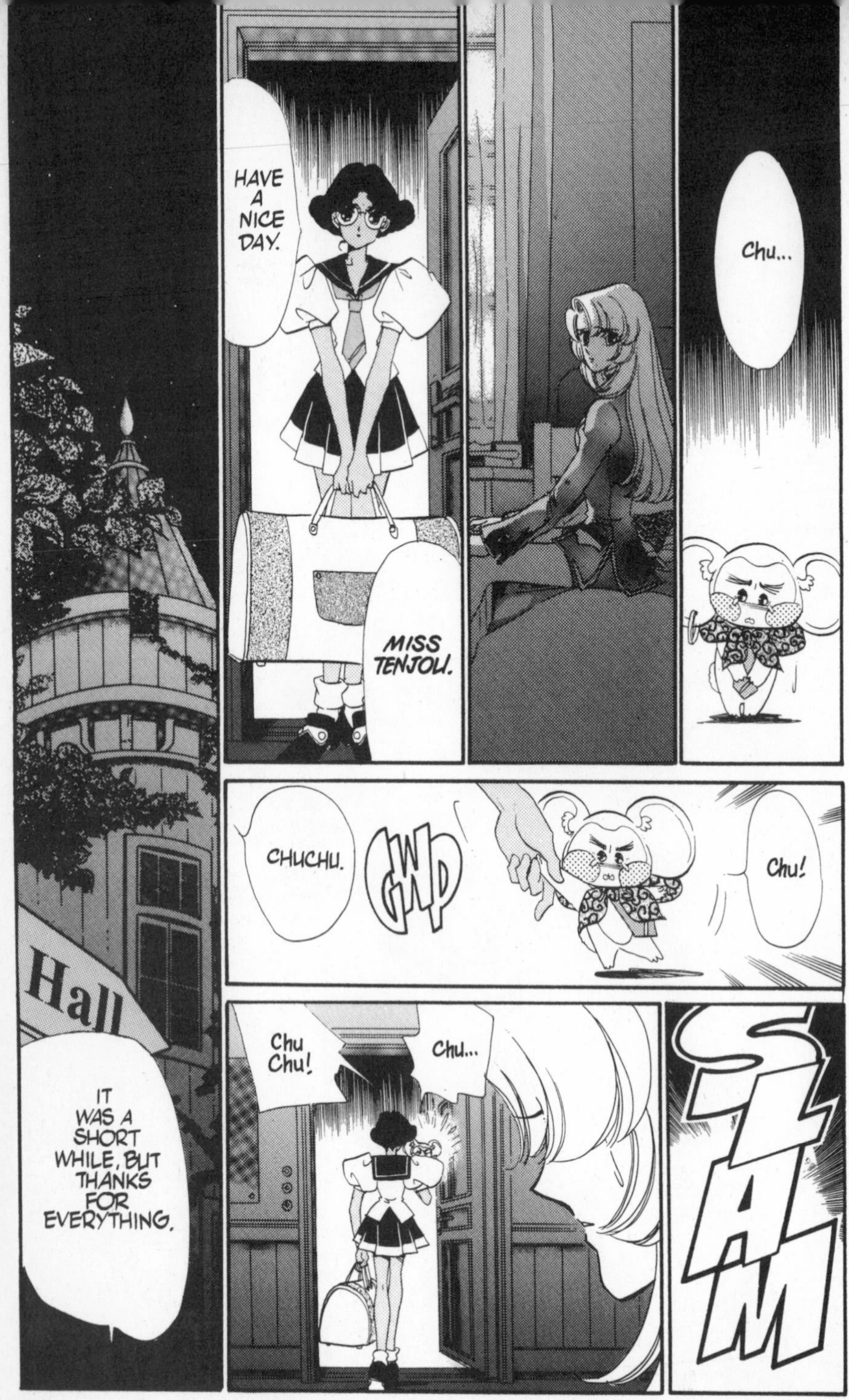
Hall
IT WAS A SHORT WHILE, BUT THANKS FOR EVERYTHING.
HAVE A NICE DAY.
MISS TENJOU.
Chu...
CHUCHU.
GWP
Chu!
Chu Chu!
Chu...
SLAM

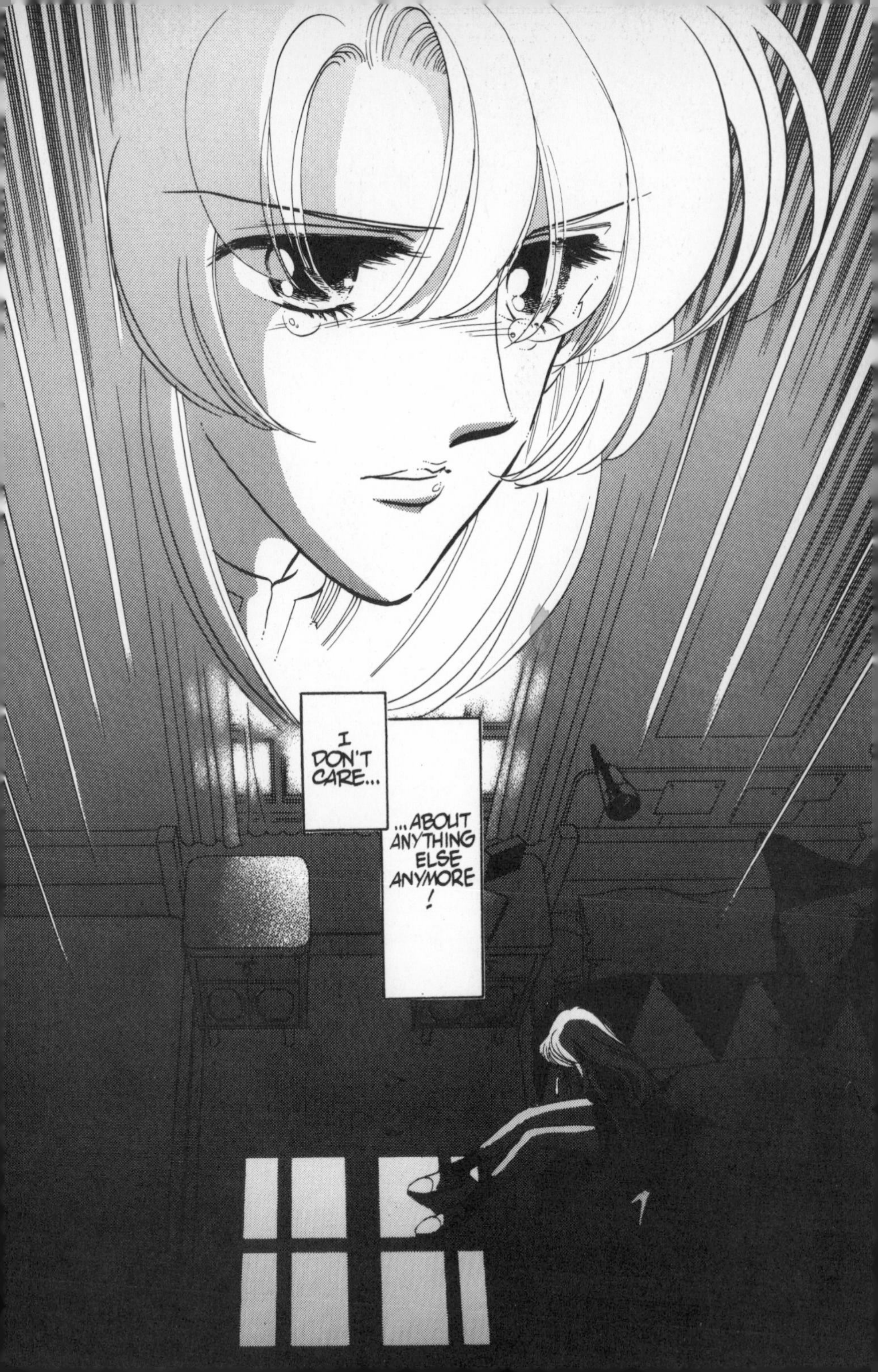
I DON'T CARE...
...ABOUT ANYTHING ELSE ANYMORE!

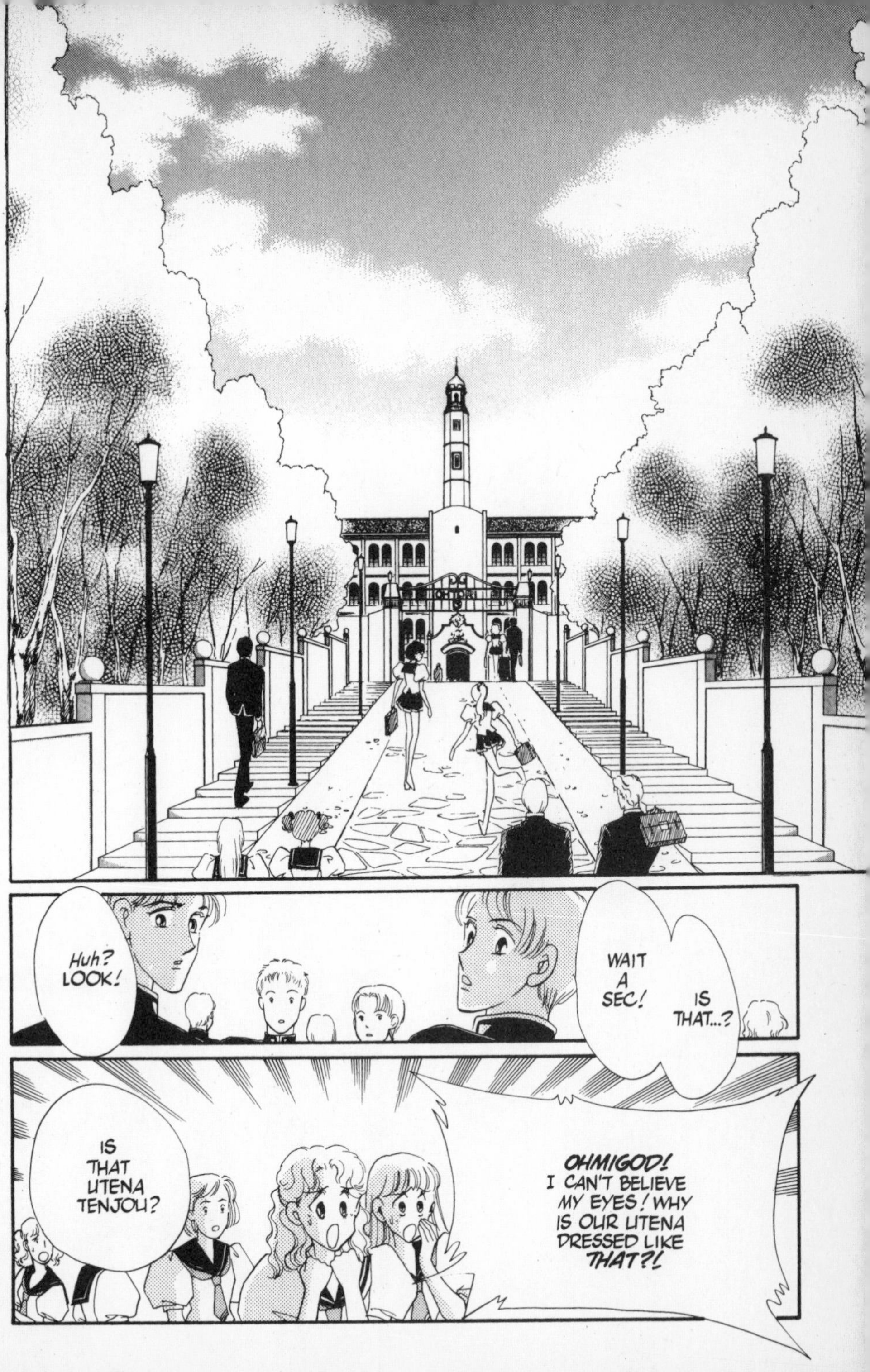
Huh? LOOK!
WAIT A SEC!
IS THAT...?
IS THAT UTENA TENJOU?
OHMIGOD! I CAN'T BELIEVE MY EYES! WHY IS OUR UTENA DRESSED LIKE THAT?!

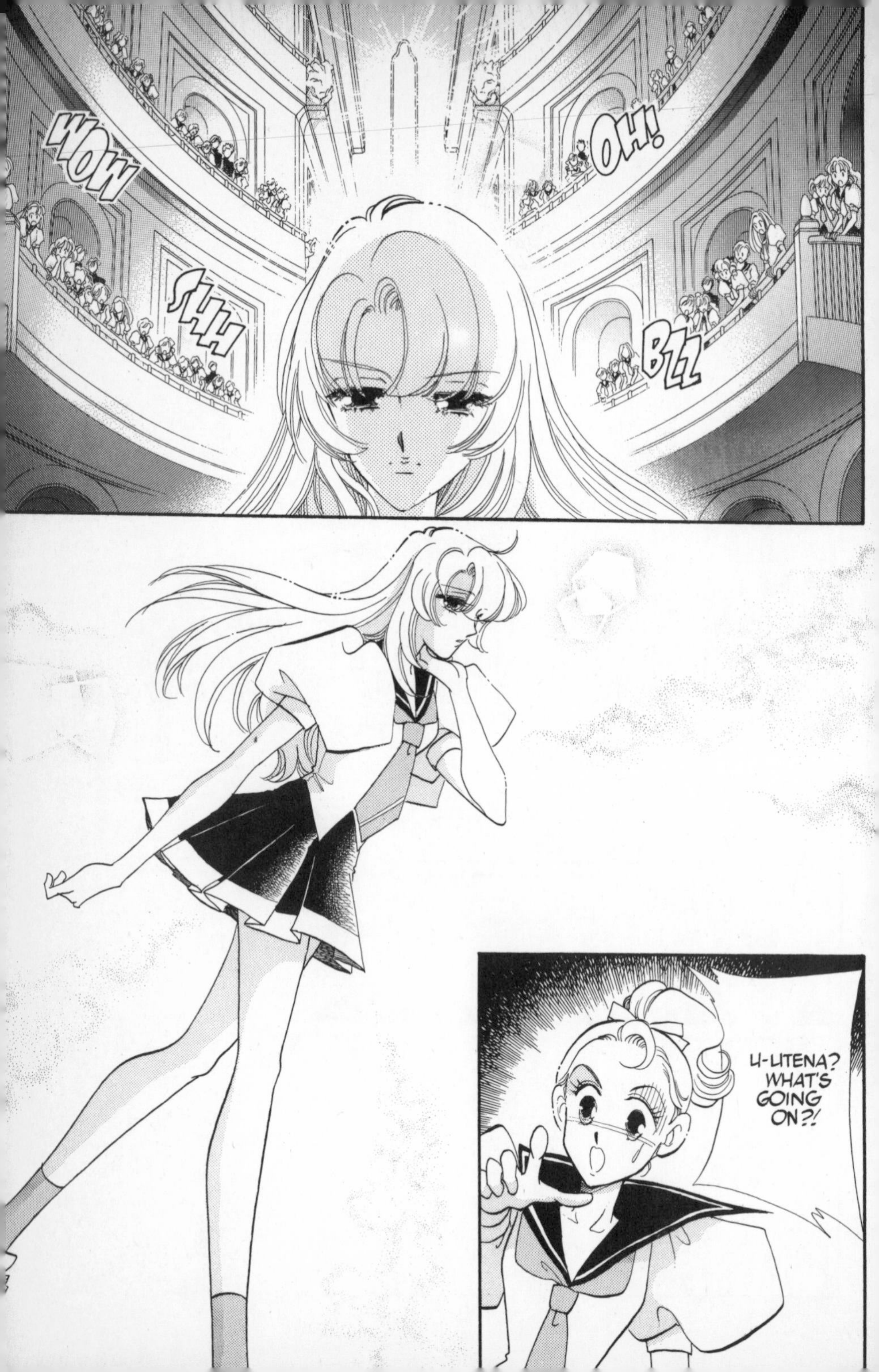
WOW
OH!
SHH
BZZ
U-UTENA? WHAT'S GOING ON?!

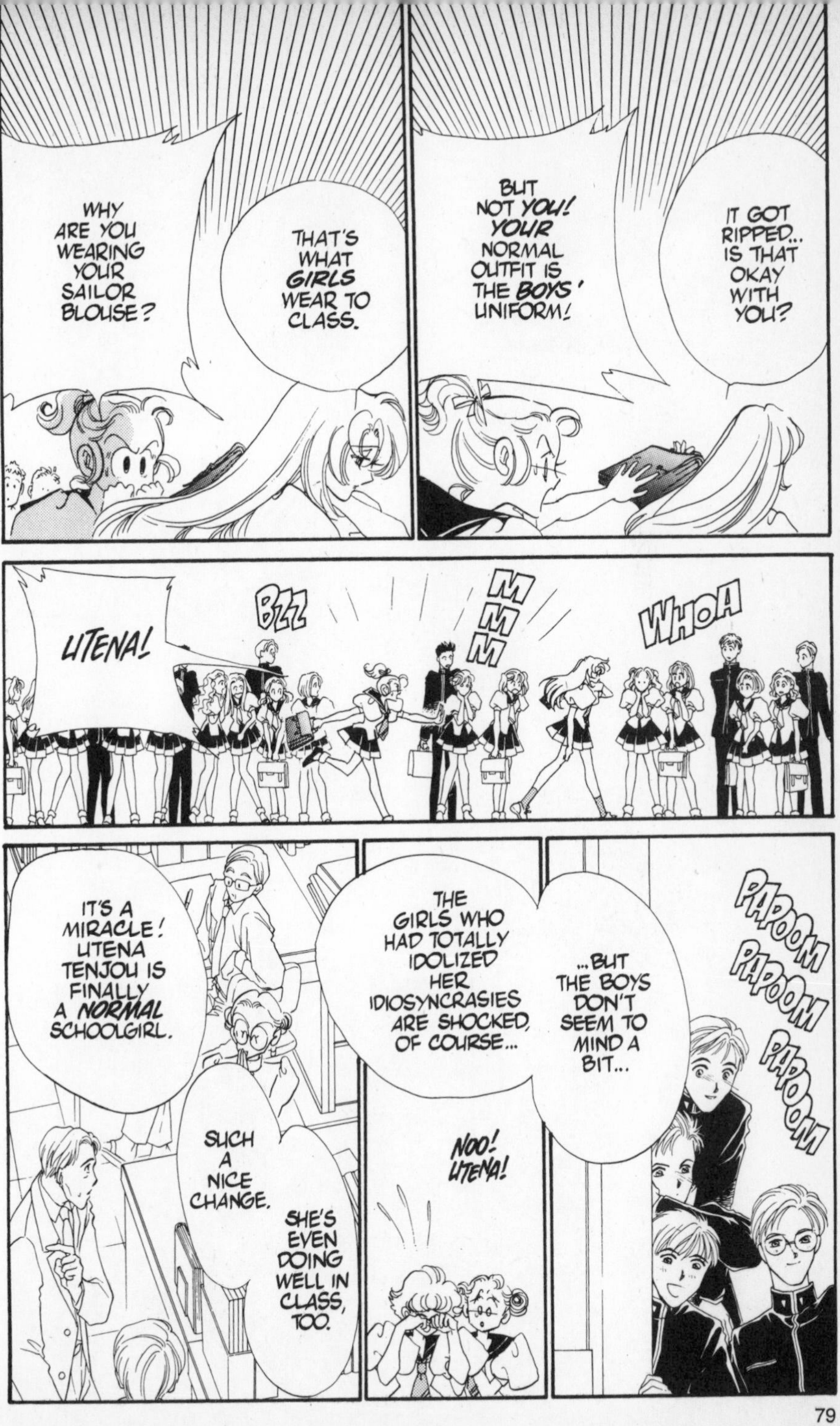
WHY ARE YOU WEARING YOUR SAILOR BLOUSE?
THAT'S WHAT GIRLS WEAR TO CLASS.
BUT NOT YOU! YOUR NORMAL OUTFIT IS THE BOYS' UNIFORM!
IT GOT RIPPED... IS THAT OKAY WITH YOU?
UTENA!
BZZ
MMM
WHOA
IT'S A MIRACLE! UTENA TENJOU IS FINALLY A NORMAL SCHOOLGIRL.
SUCH A NICE CHANGE.
SHE'S EVEN DOING WELL IN CLASS, TOO.
THE GIRLS WHO HAD TOTALLY IDOLIZED HER IDIOSYNCRASIES ARE SHOCKED, OF COURSE...
NOO! UTENA!
...BUT THE BOYS DON'T SEEM TO MIND A BIT...
PAPOOM
PAPOOM
PAPOOM

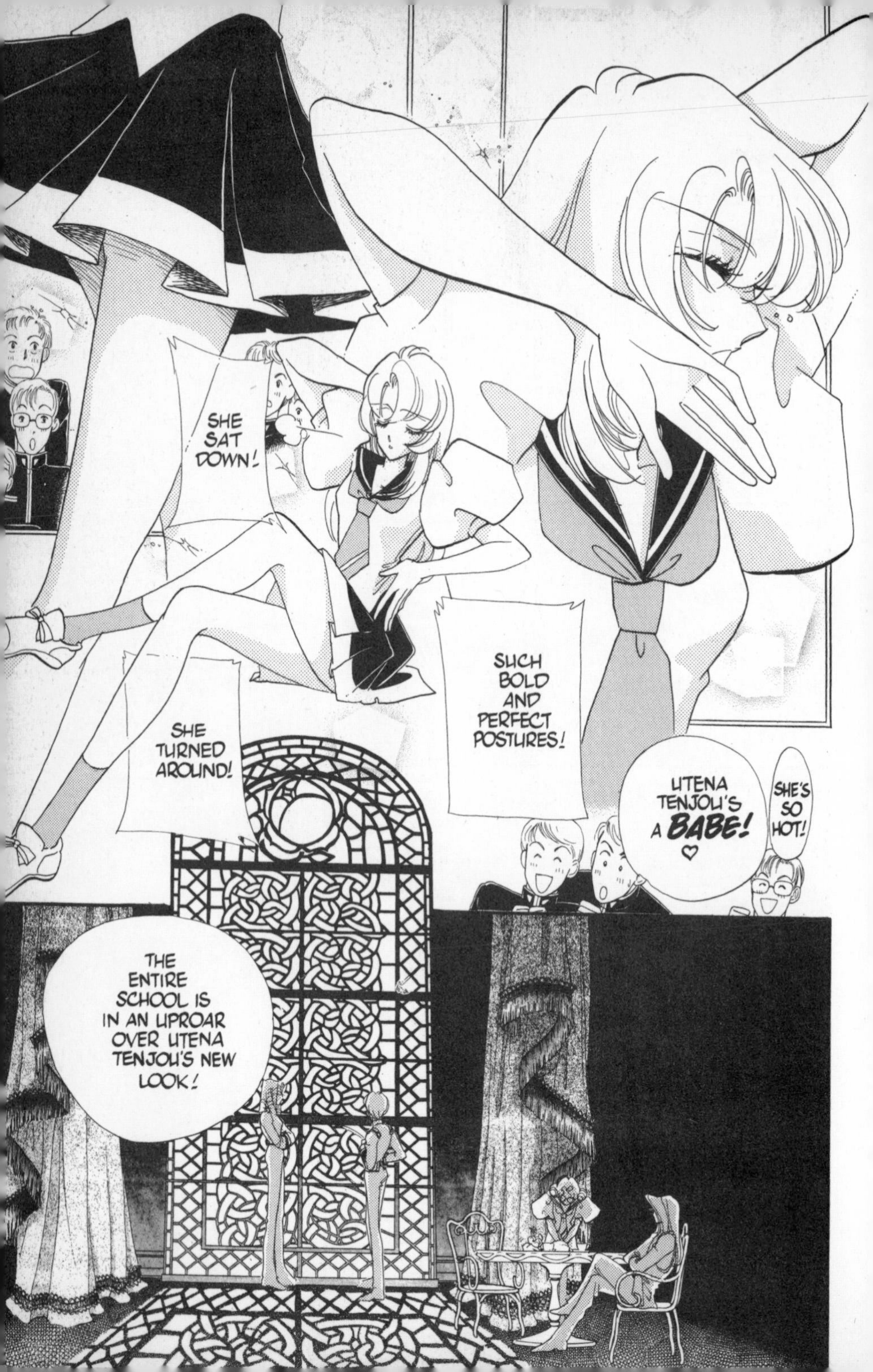
SHE SAT DOWN!
SUCH BOLD AND PERFECT POSTURES!
SHE TURNED AROUND!
SHE'S SO HOT!
UTENA TENJOU'S A **BABE!** ♡
THE ENTIRE SCHOOL IS IN AN UPROAR OVER UTENA TENJOU'S NEW LOOK!

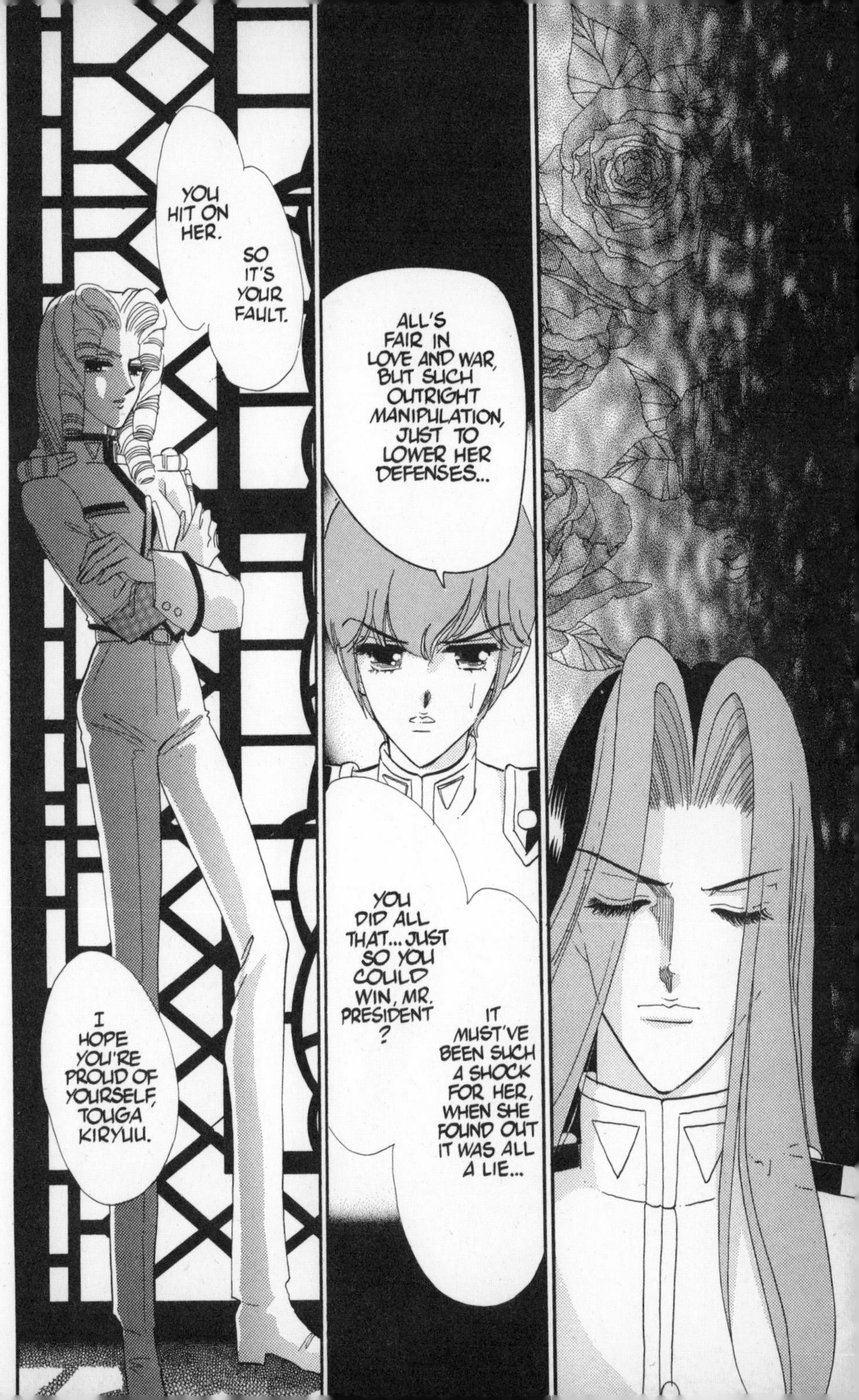
YOU HIT ON HER.
SO IT'S YOUR FAULT.
I HOPE YOU'RE PROUD OF YOURSELF, TOUGA KIRYUU.
ALL'S FAIR IN LOVE AND WAR, BUT SUCH OUTRIGHT MANIPULATION, JUST TO LOWER HER DEFENSES...
YOU DID ALL THAT... JUST SO YOU COULD WIN, MR. PRESIDENT?
IT MUST'VE BEEN SUCH A SHOCK FOR HER, WHEN SHE FOUND OUT IT WAS ALL A LIE...

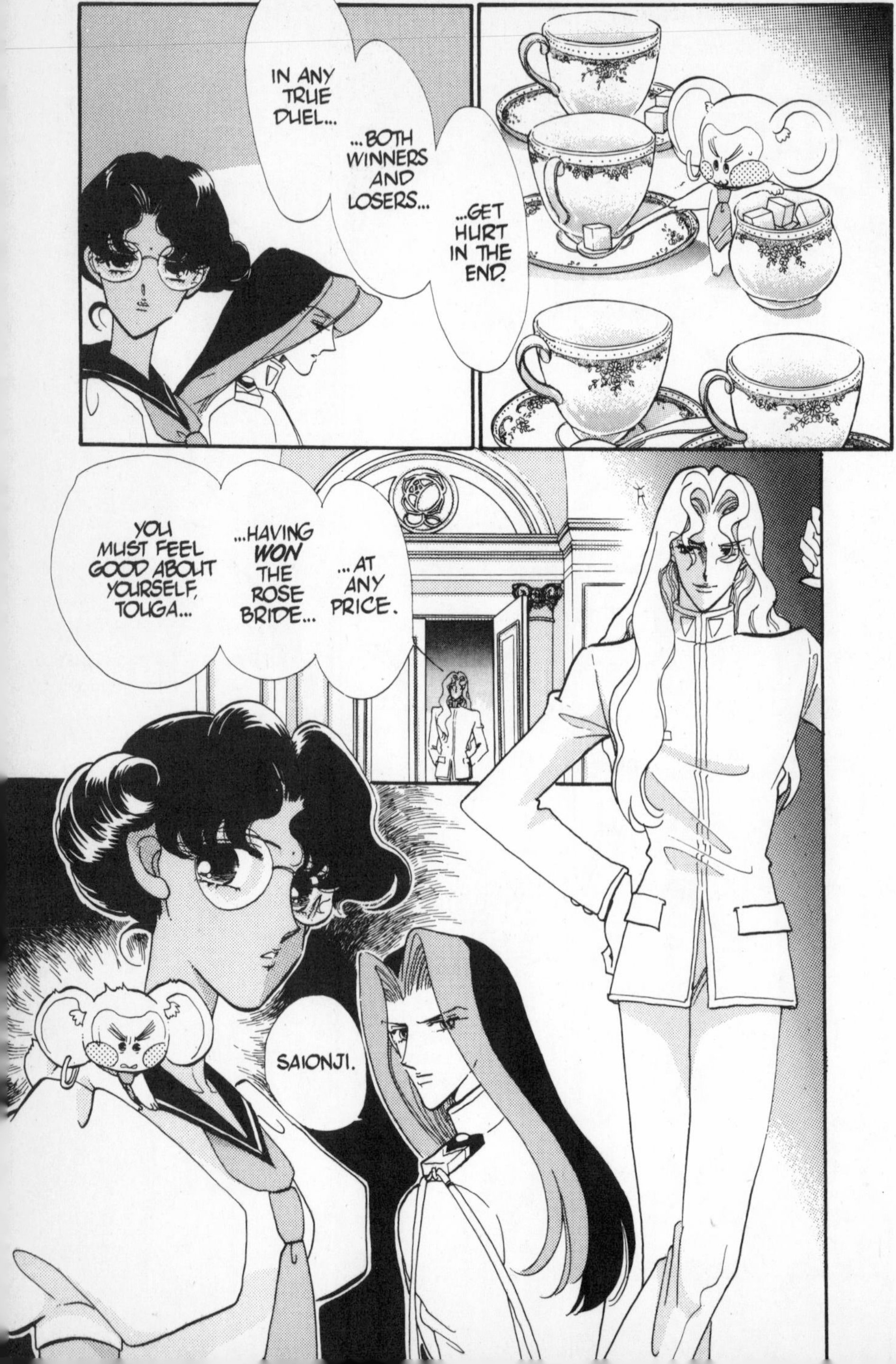
IN ANY TRUE DUEL...
...BOTH WINNERS AND LOSERS...
...GET HURT IN THE END.
YOU MUST FEEL GOOD ABOUT YOURSELF, TOUGA...
...HAVING **WON** THE ROSE BRIDE...
...AT ANY PRICE.
SAIONJI.

DON'T YOU CARE AT ALL?

THAT YOU HURT PEOPLE'S FEELINGS... THAT YOU HURT UTENA?

MIKI, CALM DOWN. THIS IS JUST OUR REGULAR STUDENT COUNCIL TEA...

Chu!

IT'S NOT THE PLACE FOR THIS.

I KNOW. BUT I FEEL SORRY... SORRY FOR UTENA.

Chu.

I AGREE. YOU DISGUST ME, TOUGA.

Clink Tink

Chu! Chu!

Team Utena
Member Number 4

Miki Karou

✦✧✦✧✦✧✦✧

Age:	13
Birthday:	May 28
Sign:	Gemini
Blood Type:	O
Height:	5'5"
Nickname:	Mickey
Talents:	Fencing, piano, composing
Likes:	Milkshakes
Motto:	"A Life with Order"
Vulnera-bilities:	Twin sister Being too unguarded

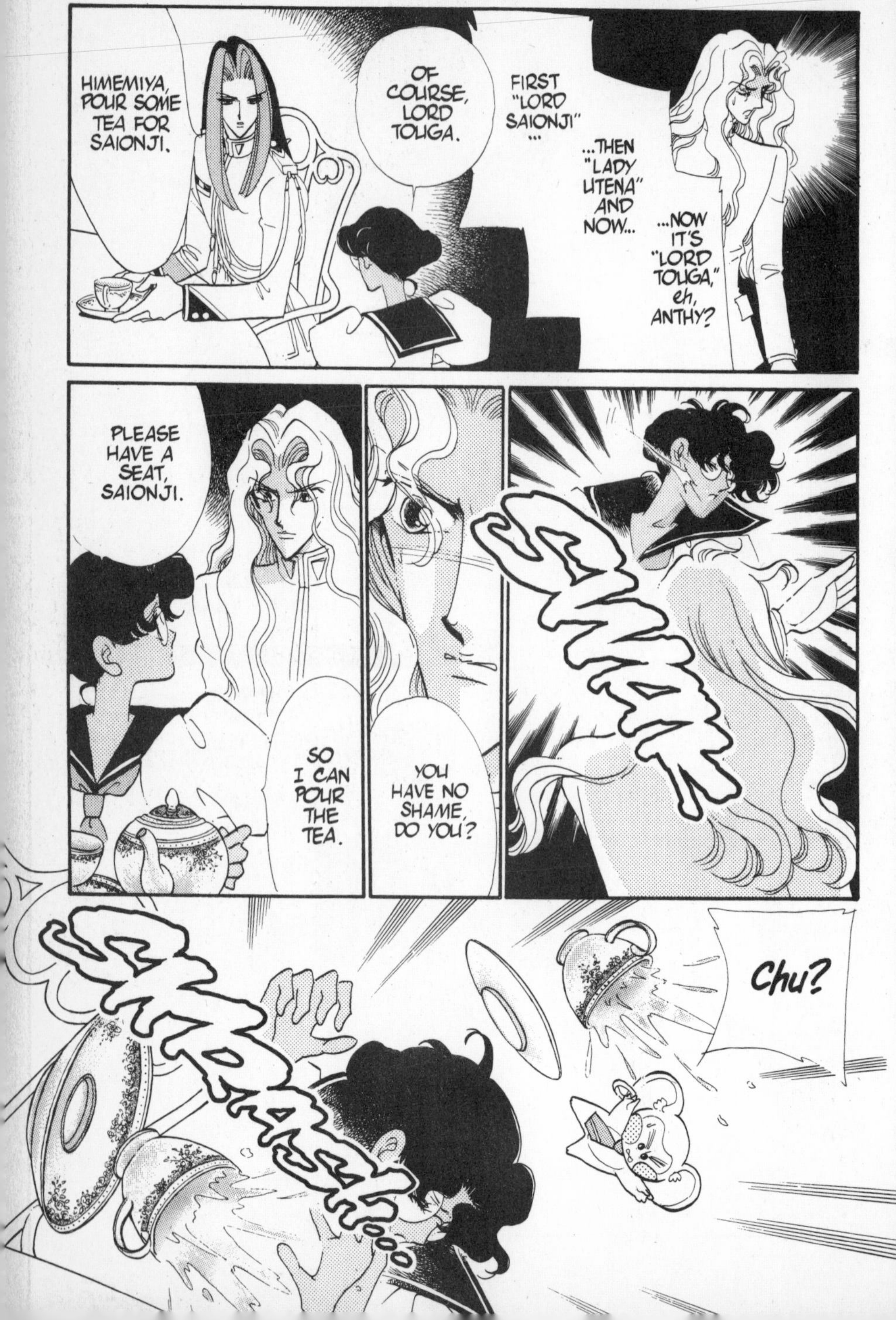
HIMEMIYA, POUR SOME TEA FOR SAIONJI.
OF COURSE, LORD TOUGA.
FIRST "LORD SAIONJI" ...
...THEN "LADY UTENA" AND NOW...
...NOW IT'S "LORD TOUGA," eh, ANTHY?
PLEASE HAVE A SEAT, SAIONJI.
SO I CAN POUR THE TEA.
YOU HAVE NO SHAME, DO YOU?
Chu?

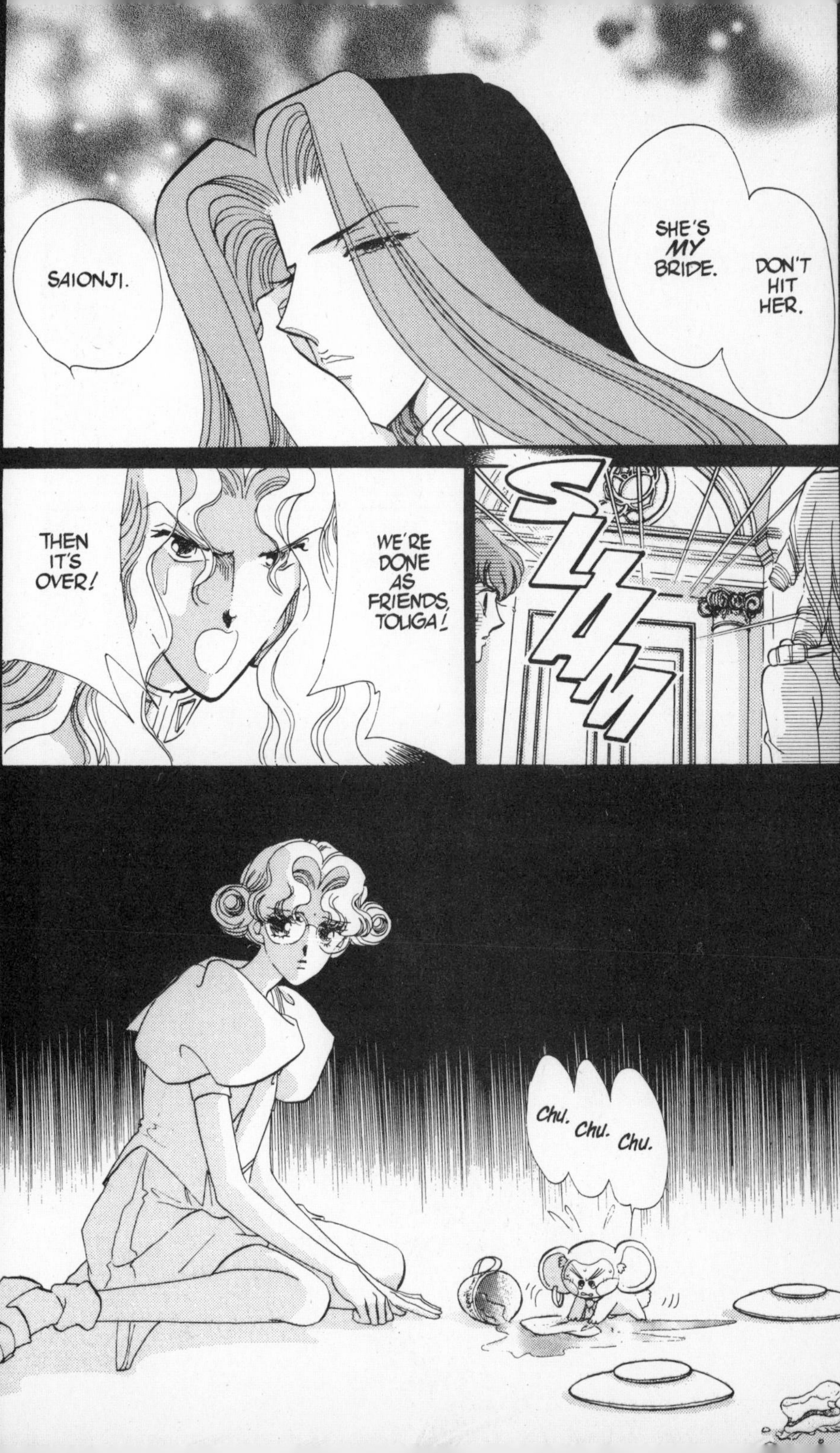

SAIONJI.
SHE'S MY BRIDE.
DON'T HIT HER.
THEN IT'S OVER!
WE'RE DONE AS FRIENDS, TOUGA!
SLAM
Chu. Chu. Chu.

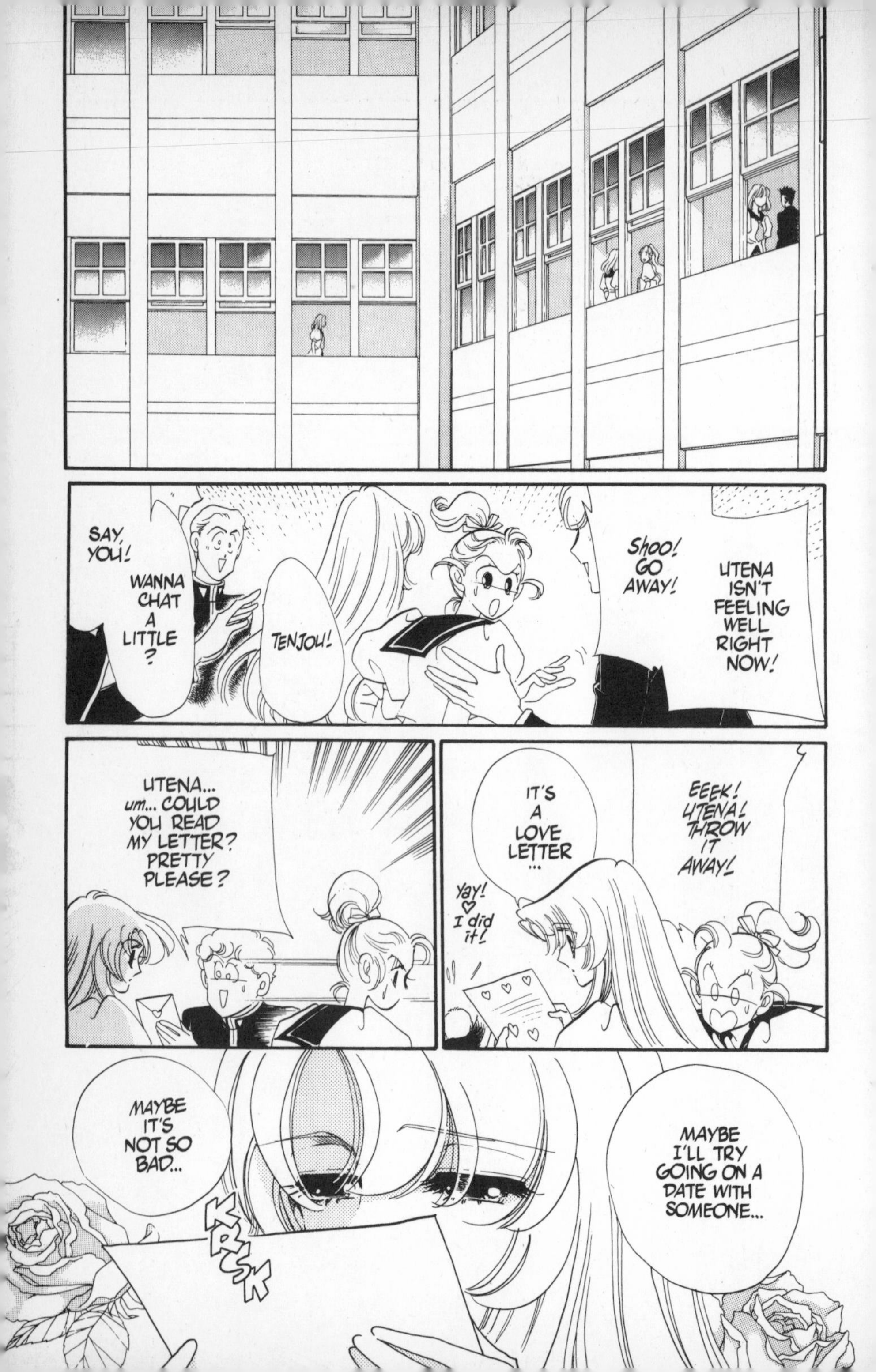
SAY, YOU! WANNA CHAT A LITTLE?
TENJOU!
Shoo! GO AWAY!
UTENA ISN'T FEELING WELL RIGHT NOW!
UTENA... um... COULD YOU READ MY LETTER? PRETTY PLEASE?
IT'S A LOVE LETTER...
Yay! ♡ I did it!
EEEK! UTENA! THROW IT AWAY!
MAYBE IT'S NOT SO BAD...
KRSK
MAYBE I'LL TRY GOING ON A DATE WITH SOMEONE...

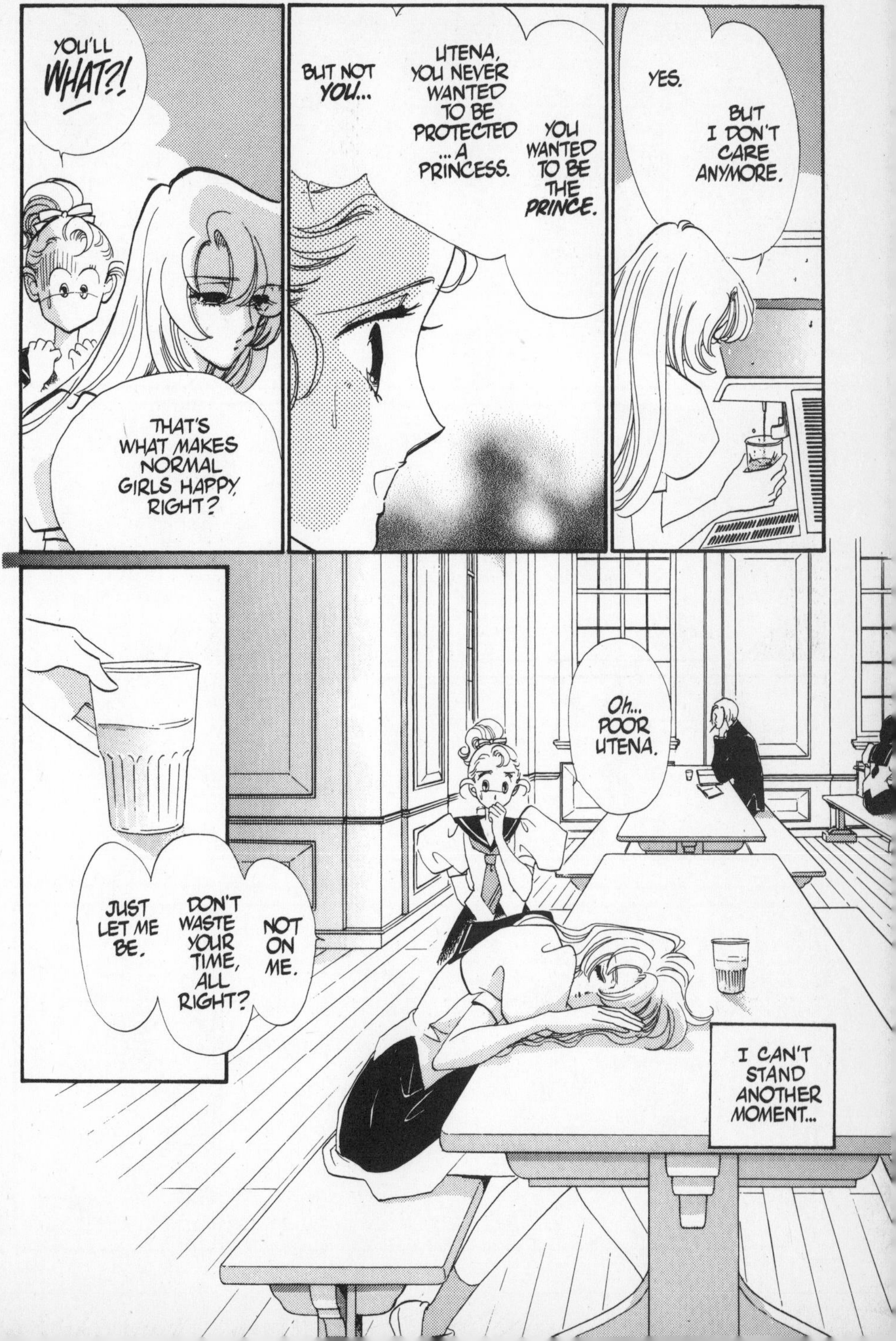
YOU'LL WHAT?!
THAT'S WHAT MAKES NORMAL GIRLS HAPPY, RIGHT?
BUT NOT YOU...
UTENA, YOU NEVER WANTED TO BE PROTECTED ... A PRINCESS.
YOU WANTED TO BE THE PRINCE.
YES.
BUT I DON'T CARE ANYMORE.
JUST LET ME BE.
DON'T WASTE YOUR TIME, ALL RIGHT?
NOT ON ME.
Oh... POOR UTENA.
I CAN'T STAND ANOTHER MOMENT...

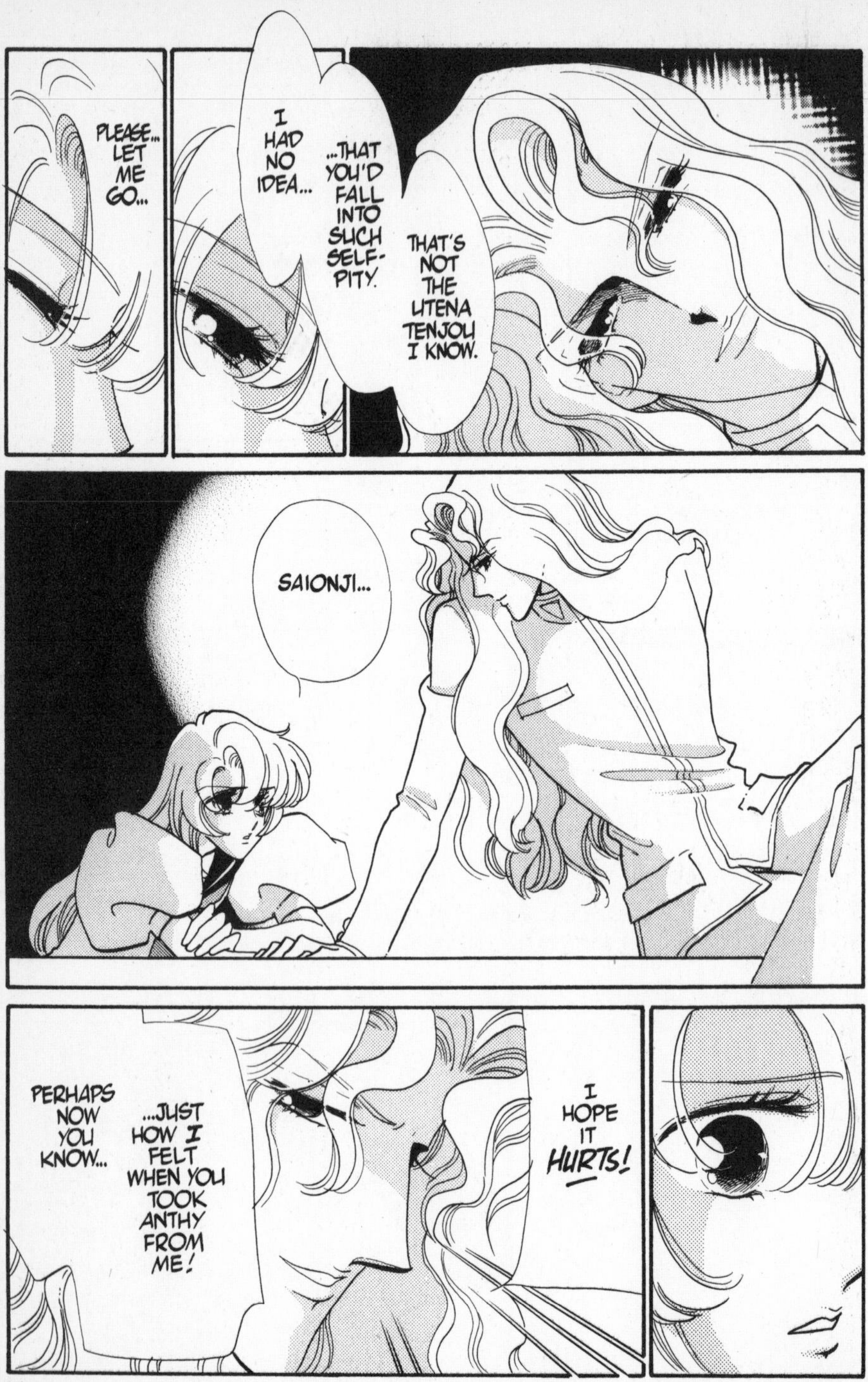
PLEASE... LET ME GO...
I HAD NO IDEA...
...THAT YOU'D FALL INTO SUCH SELF-PITY.
THAT'S NOT THE UTENA TENJOU I KNOW.
SAIONJI...
PERHAPS NOW YOU KNOW...
...JUST HOW I FELT WHEN YOU TOOK ANTHY FROM ME!
I HOPE IT HURTS!

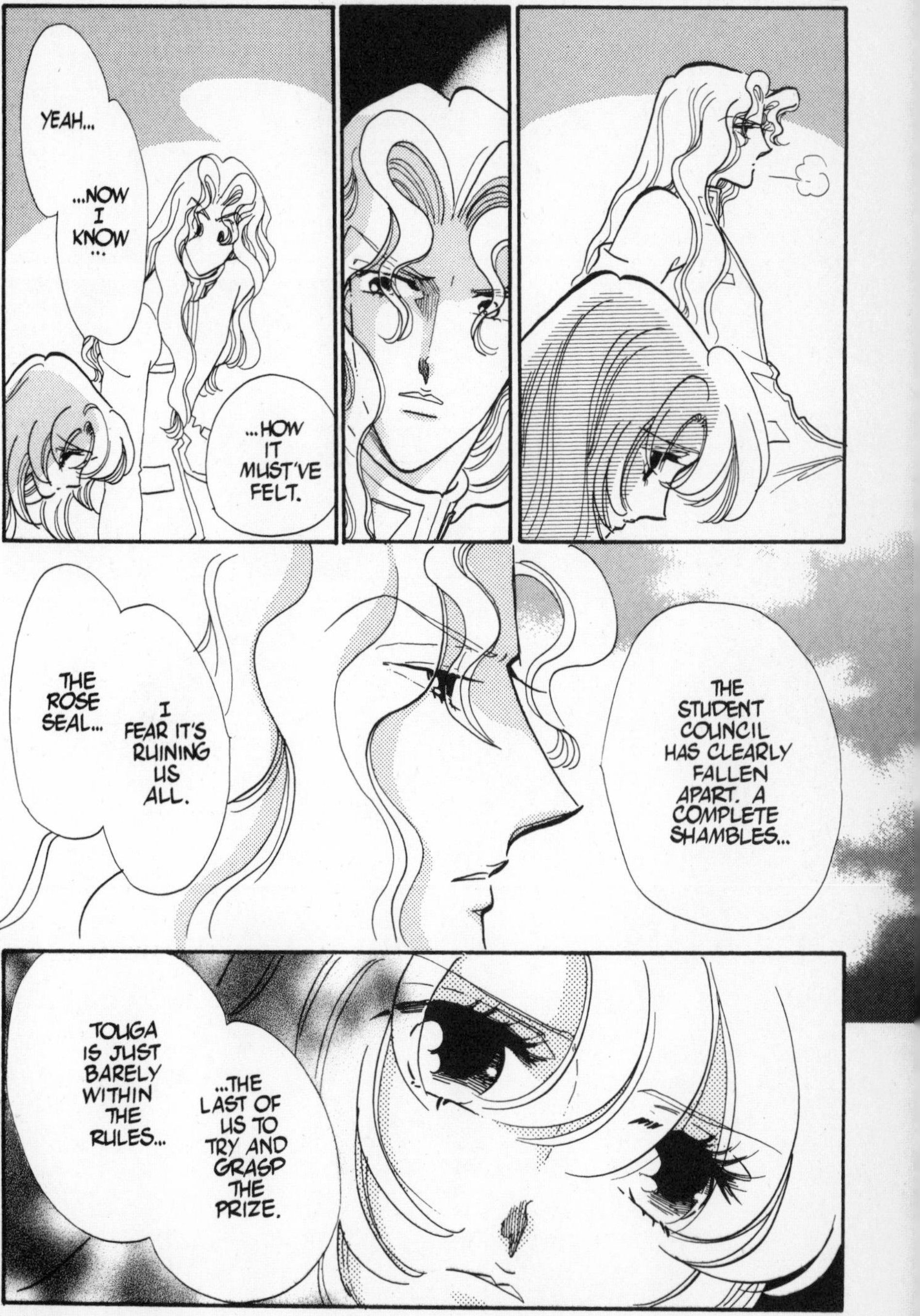
YEAH...
...NOW I KNOW...
...HOW IT MUST'VE FELT.
THE ROSE SEAL...
I FEAR IT'S RUINING US ALL.
THE STUDENT COUNCIL HAS CLEARLY FALLEN APART. A COMPLETE SHAMBLES...
TOUGA IS JUST BARELY WITHIN THE RULES...
...THE LAST OF US TO TRY AND GRASP THE PRIZE.

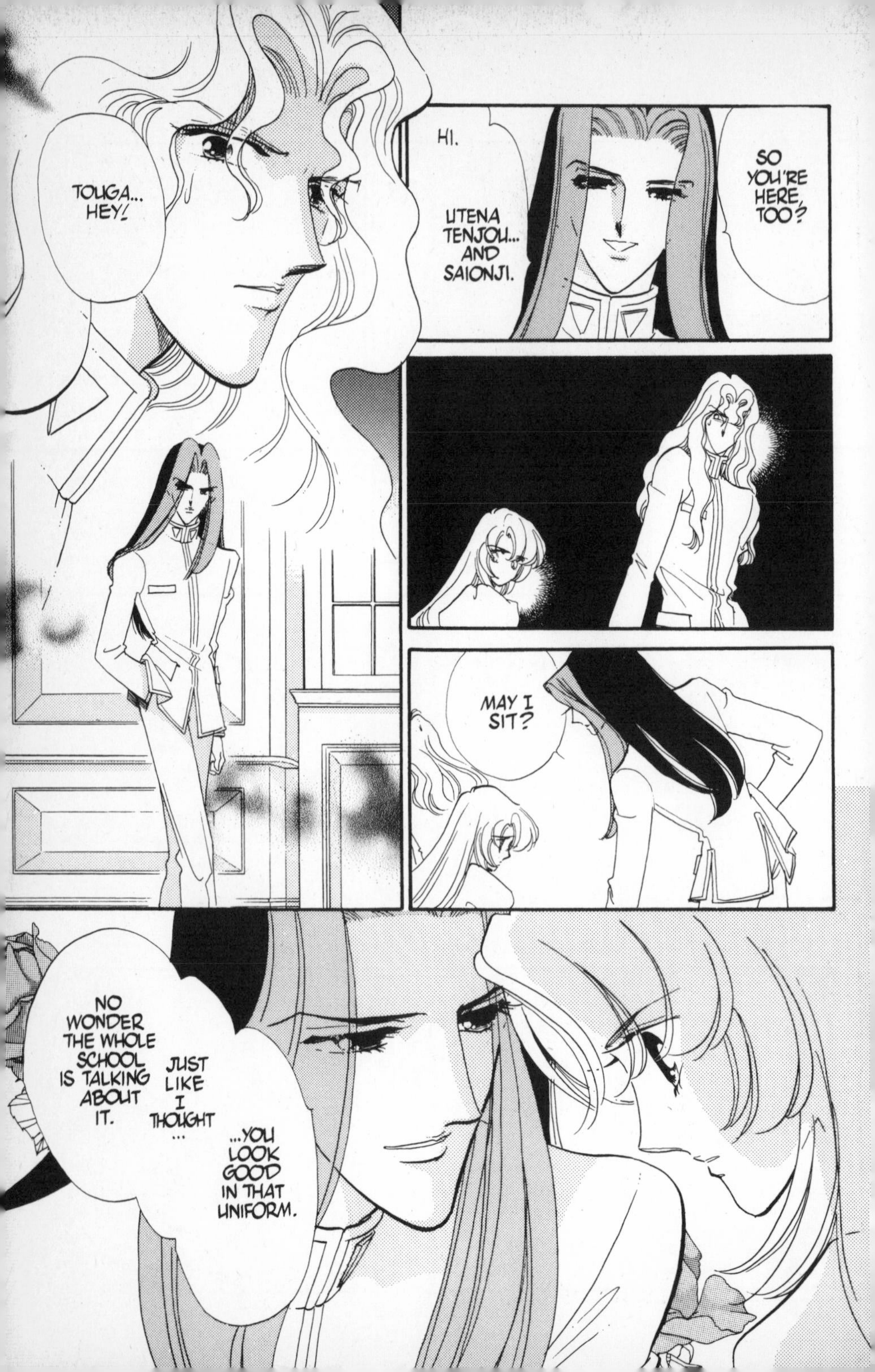
TOUGA... HEY!
HI.
UTENA TENJOU... AND SAIONJI.
SO YOU'RE HERE, TOO?
MAY I SIT?
NO WONDER THE WHOLE SCHOOL IS TALKING ABOUT IT.
JUST LIKE I THOUGHT...
...YOU LOOK GOOD IN THAT UNIFORM.

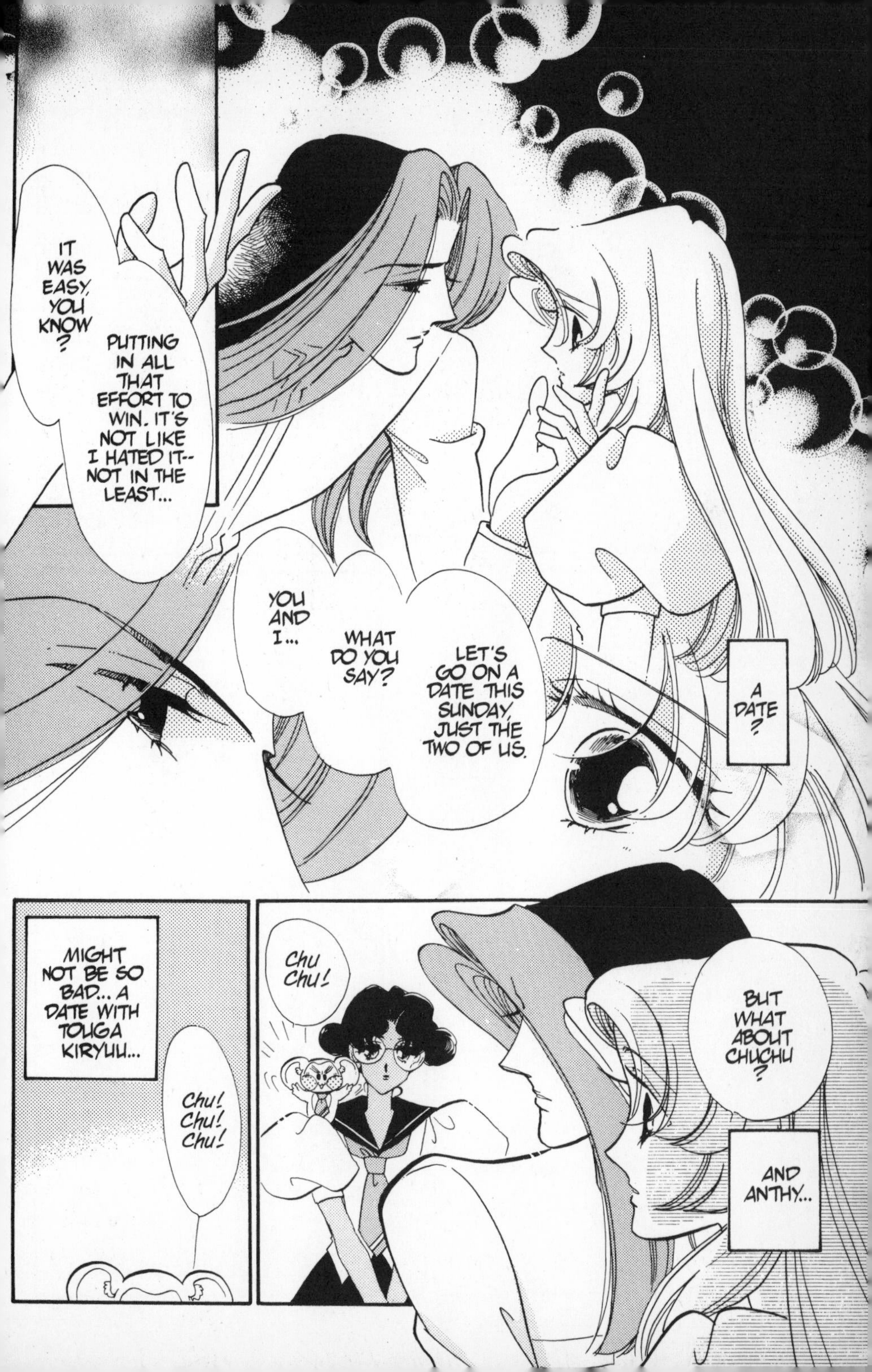
IT WAS EASY, YOU KNOW?
PUTTING IN ALL THAT EFFORT TO WIN. IT'S NOT LIKE I HATED IT--NOT IN THE LEAST...
YOU AND I...
WHAT DO YOU SAY?
LET'S GO ON A DATE THIS SUNDAY, JUST THE TWO OF US.
A DATE?
MIGHT NOT BE SO BAD... A DATE WITH TOUGA KIRYUU...
Chu! Chu! Chu!
Chu Chu!
BUT WHAT ABOUT CHUCHU?
AND ANTHY...

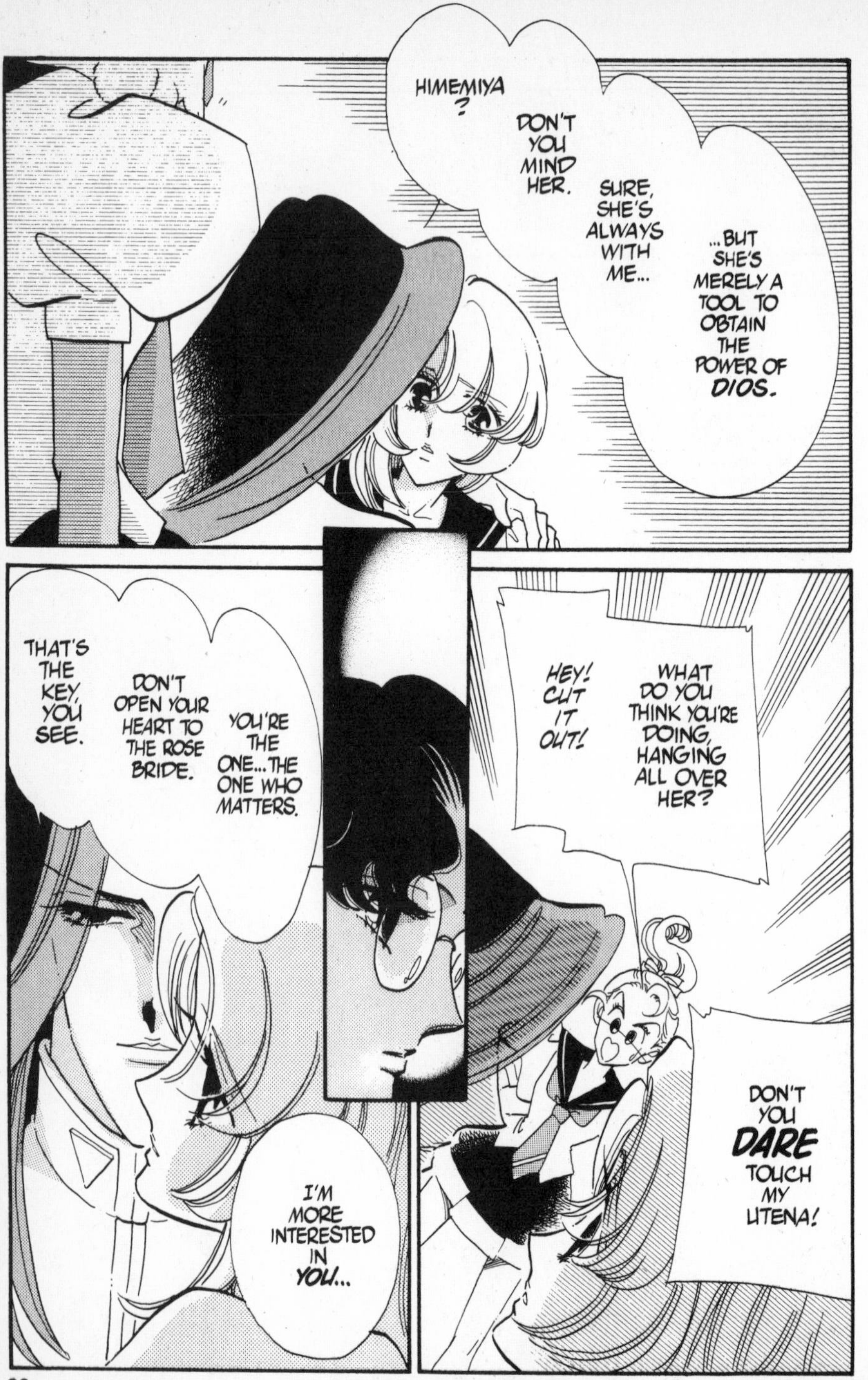
HIMEMIYA?
DON'T YOU MIND HER.
SURE, SHE'S ALWAYS WITH ME...
...BUT SHE'S MERELY A TOOL TO OBTAIN THE POWER OF DIOS.
THAT'S THE KEY, YOU SEE.
DON'T OPEN YOUR HEART TO THE ROSE BRIDE.
YOU'RE THE ONE...THE ONE WHO MATTERS.
I'M MORE INTERESTED IN YOU...
HEY! CUT IT OUT!
WHAT DO YOU THINK YOU'RE DOING, HANGING ALL OVER HER?
DON'T YOU DARE TOUCH MY UTENA!

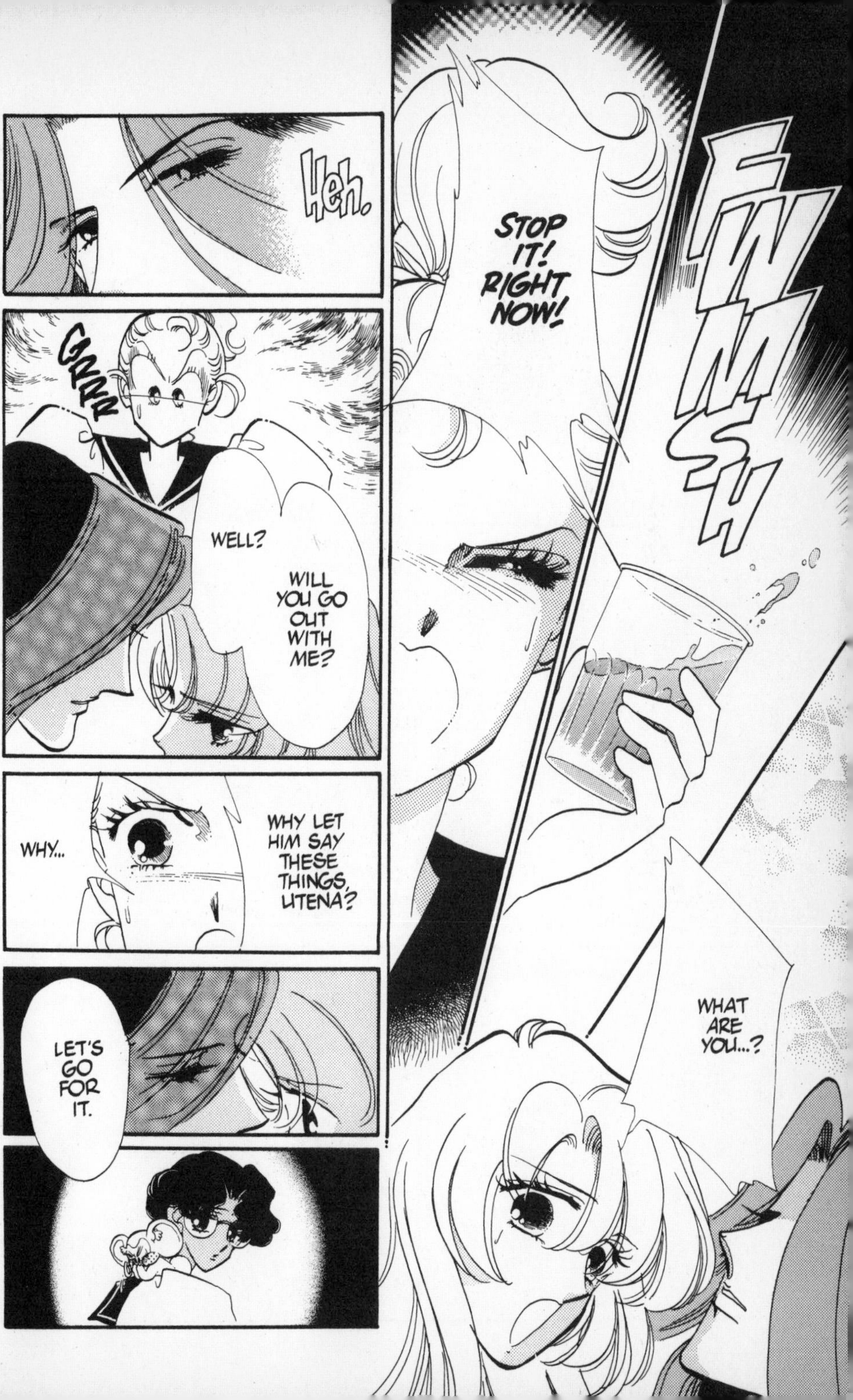
Heh.
GRRR
WELL?
WILL YOU GO OUT WITH ME?
WHY...
WHY LET HIM SAY THESE THINGS, UTENA?
LET'S GO FOR IT.
STOP IT! RIGHT NOW!
FWASH
WHAT ARE YOU...?

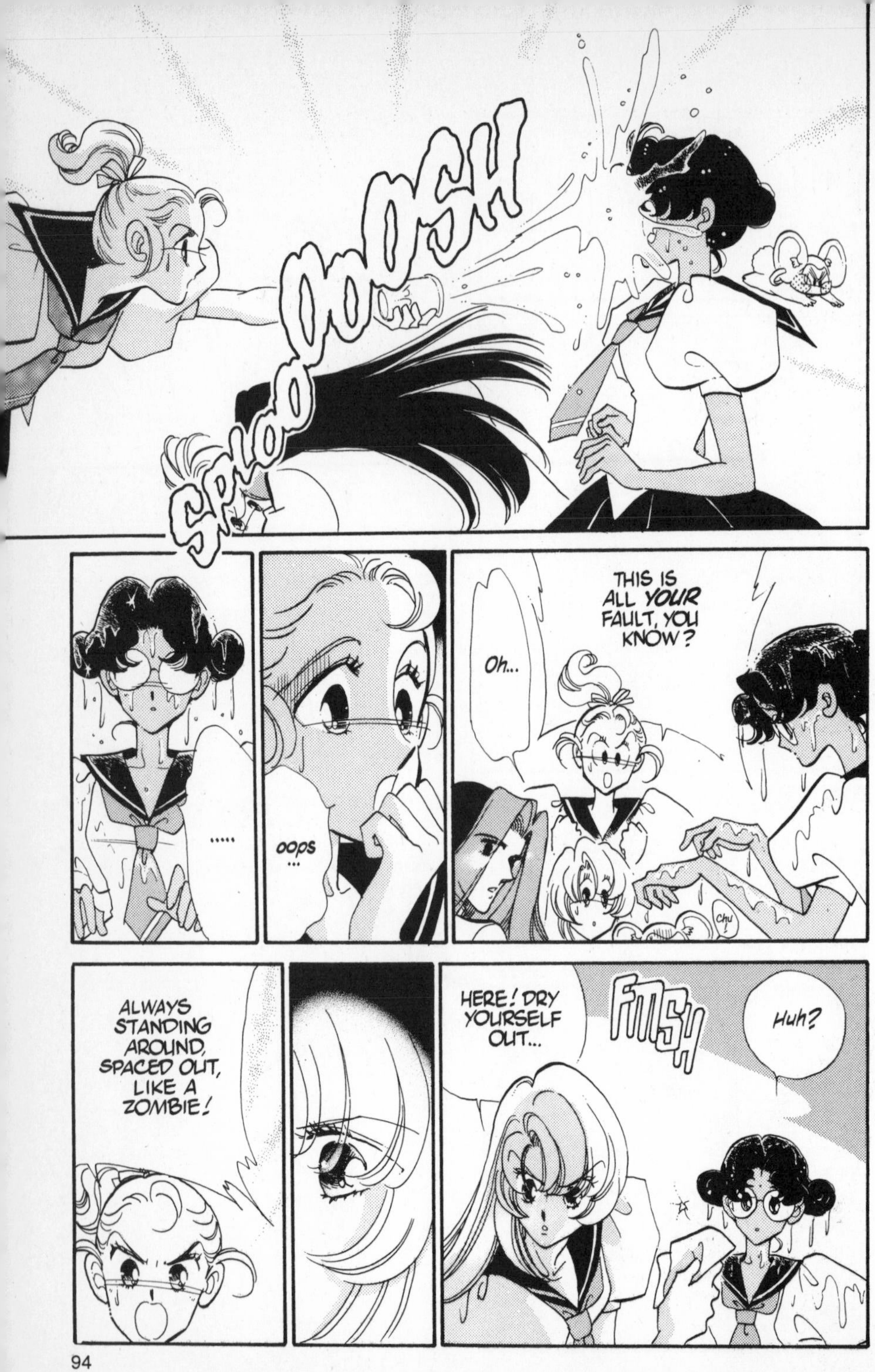
SPLOOOOOSH
.....
oops ...
Oh...
THIS IS ALL YOUR FAULT, YOU KNOW?
Chu
ALWAYS STANDING AROUND, SPACED OUT, LIKE A ZOMBIE!
HERE! DRY YOURSELF OUT...
FWSH
Huh?

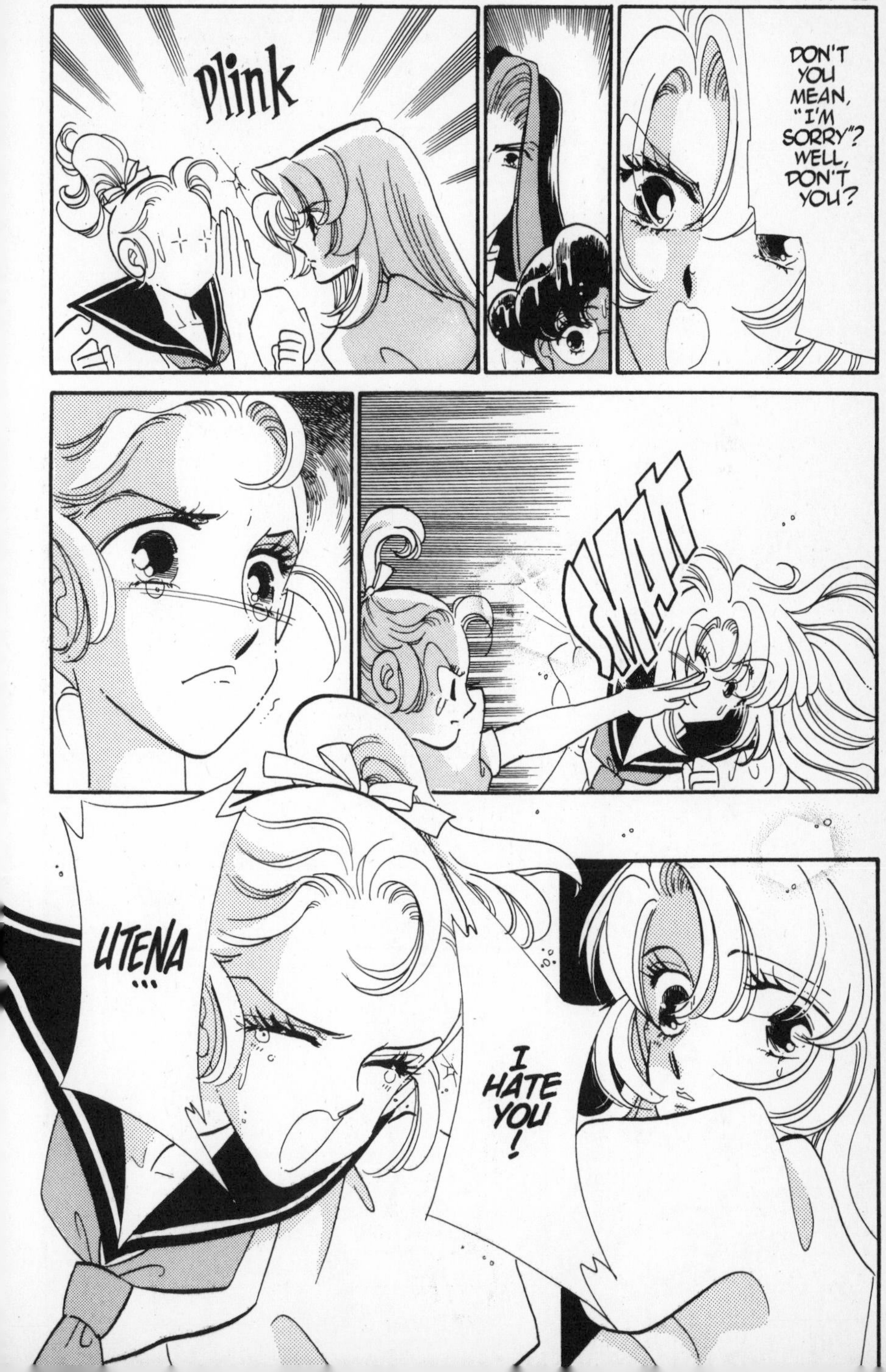
Plink
DON'T YOU MEAN, "I'M SORRY"? WELL, DON'T YOU?
SMAK
UTENA ...
I HATE YOU!

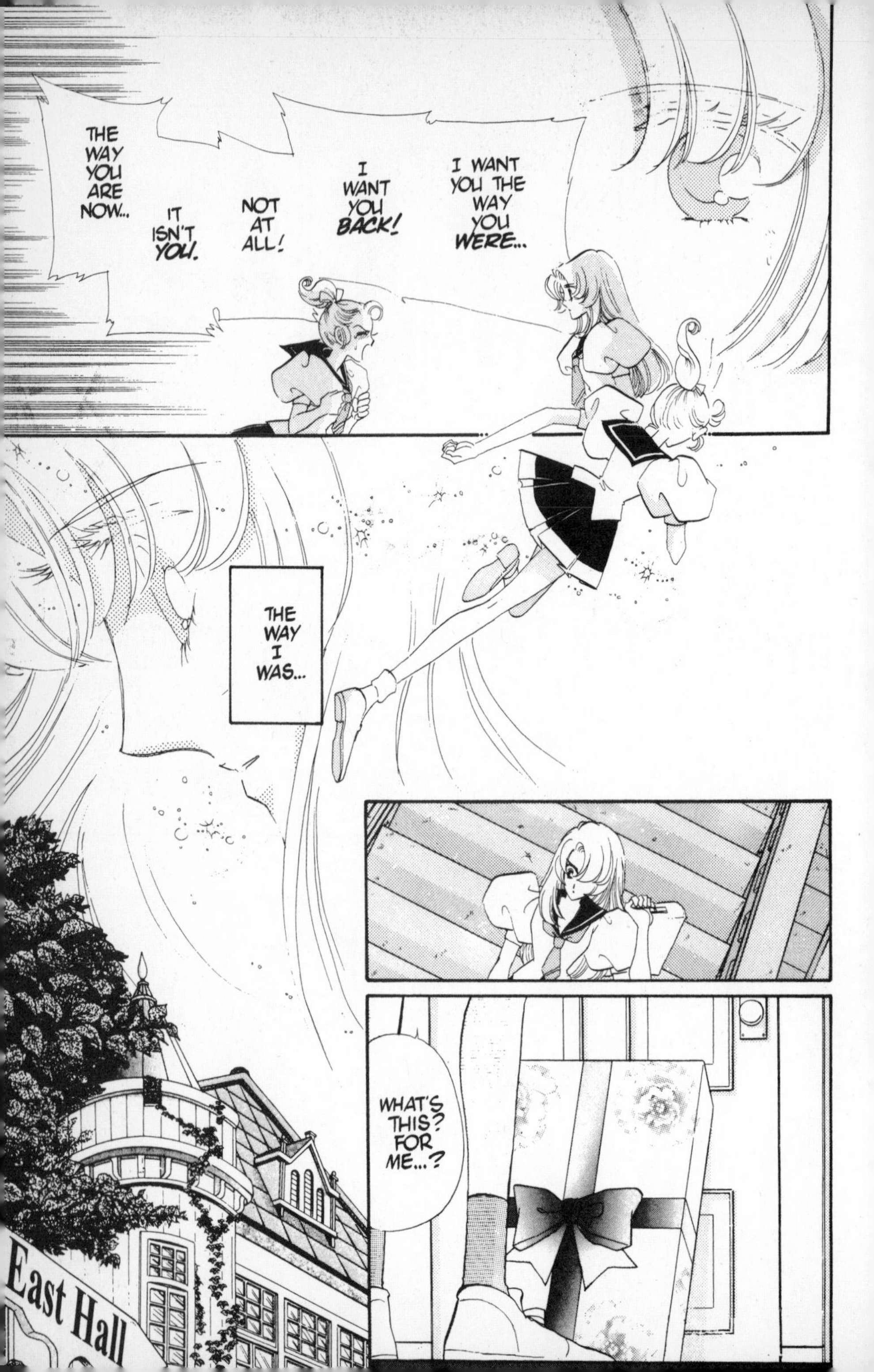
THE WAY YOU ARE NOW...
IT ISN'T *YOU*.
NOT AT ALL!
I WANT YOU *BACK!*
I WANT YOU THE WAY YOU *WERE*...
THE WAY I WAS...
East Hall
WHAT'S THIS? FOR ME...?

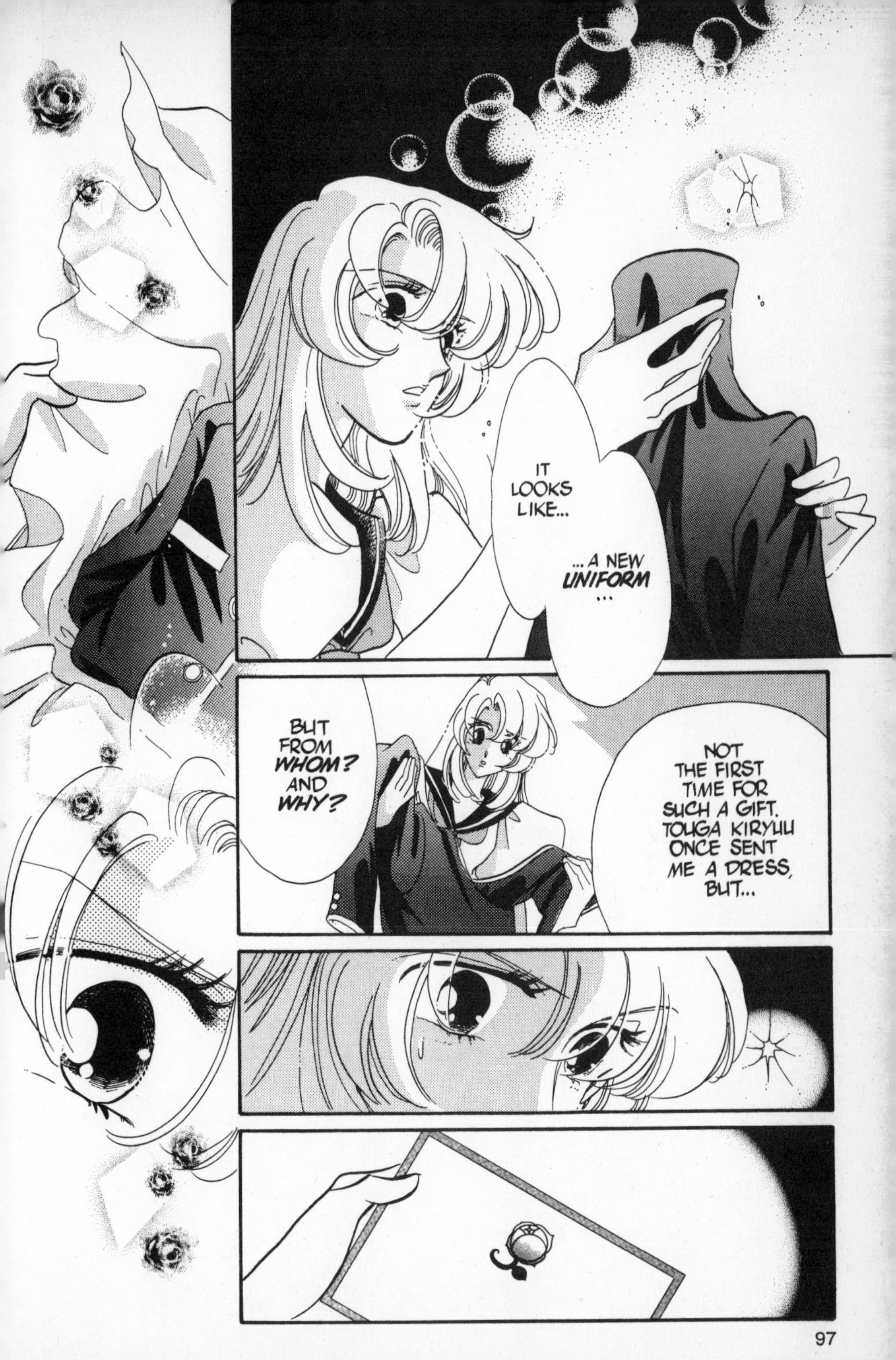
IT LOOKS LIKE...
...A NEW **UNIFORM** ...
BUT FROM **WHOM?** AND **WHY?**
NOT THE FIRST TIME FOR SUCH A GIFT. TOUGA KIRYUU ONCE SENT ME A DRESS, BUT...

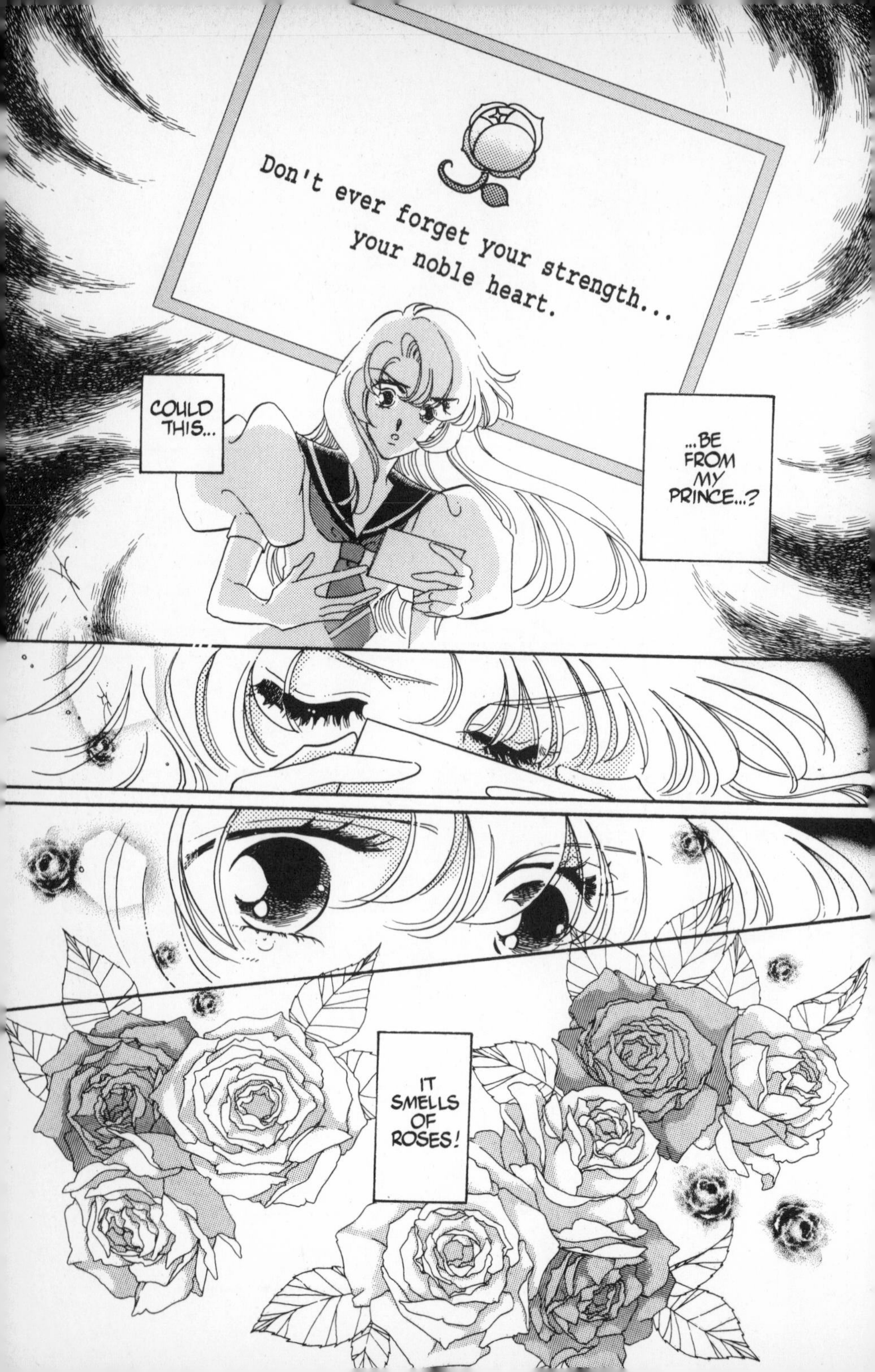
Don't ever forget your strength... your noble heart.
COULD THIS...
...BE FROM MY PRINCE...?
IT SMELLS OF ROSES!

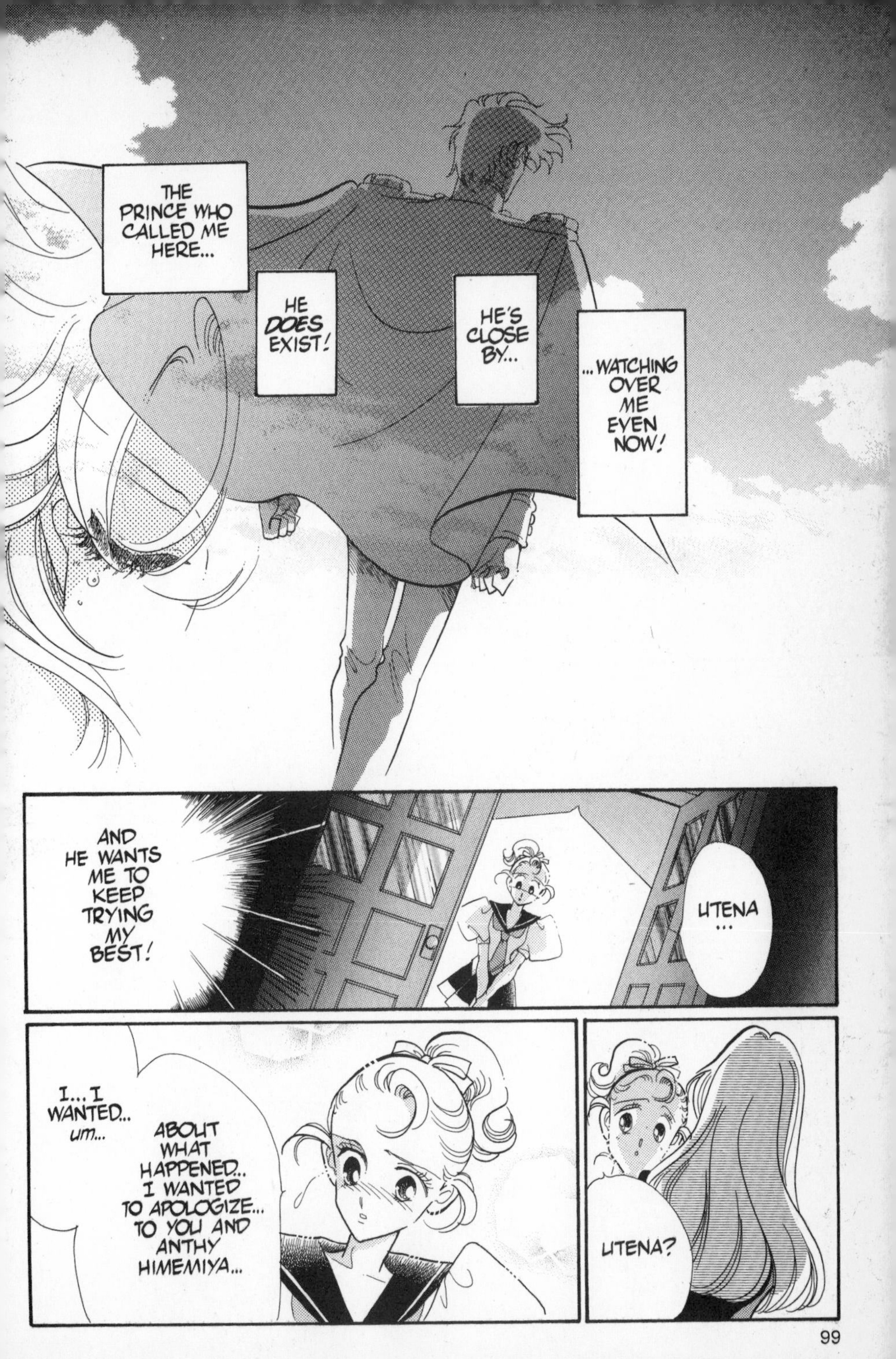
THE PRINCE WHO CALLED ME HERE...
HE DOES EXIST!
HE'S CLOSE BY...
...WATCHING OVER ME EVEN NOW!
AND HE WANTS ME TO KEEP TRYING MY BEST!
UTENA ...
I... I WANTED... um...
ABOUT WHAT HAPPENED... I WANTED TO APOLOGIZE... TO YOU AND ANTHY HIMEMIYA...
UTENA?

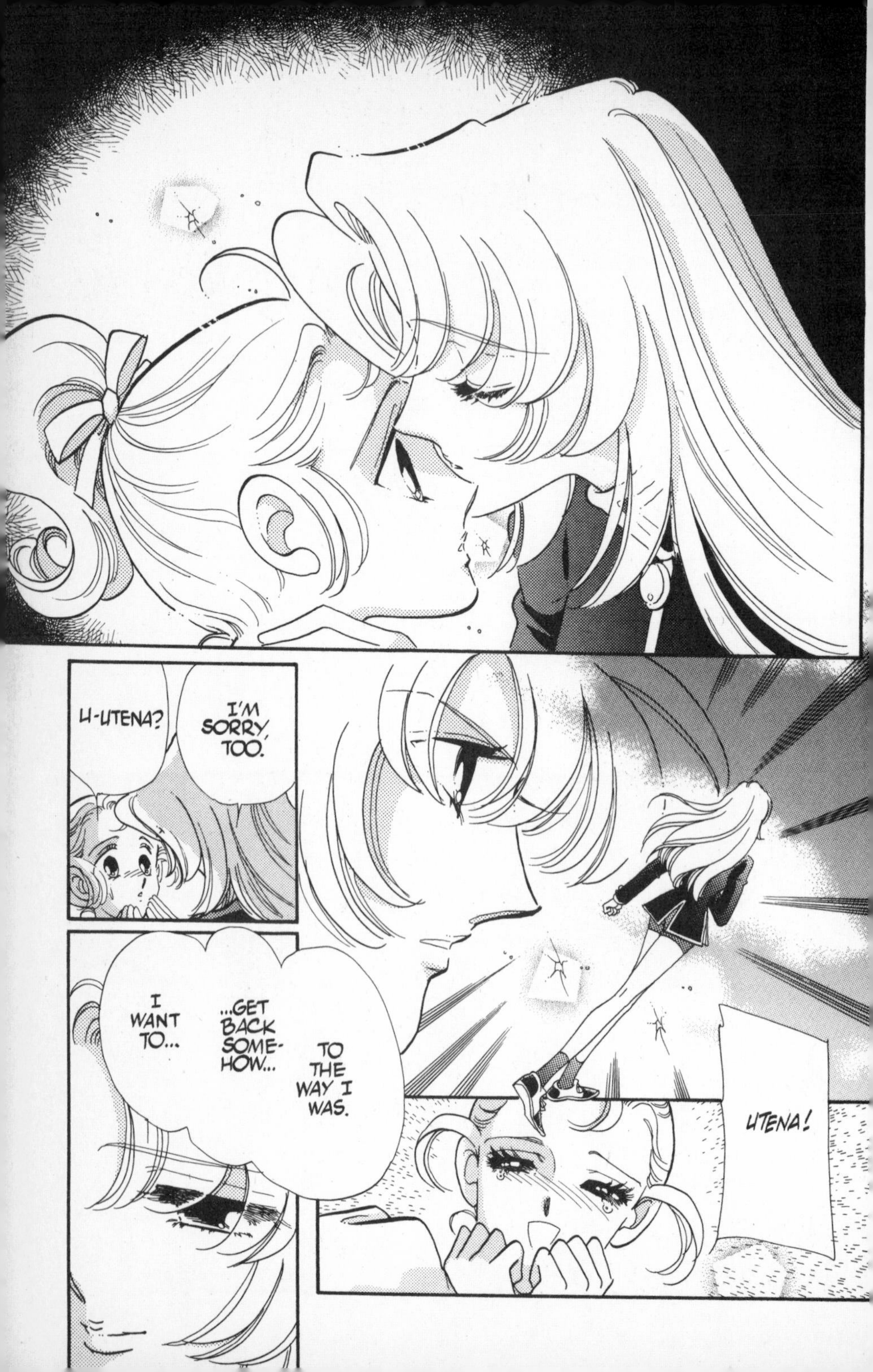
I'M SORRY, TOO.
U-UTENA?
I WANT TO...
...GET BACK SOMEHOW...
TO THE WAY I WAS.
UTENA!

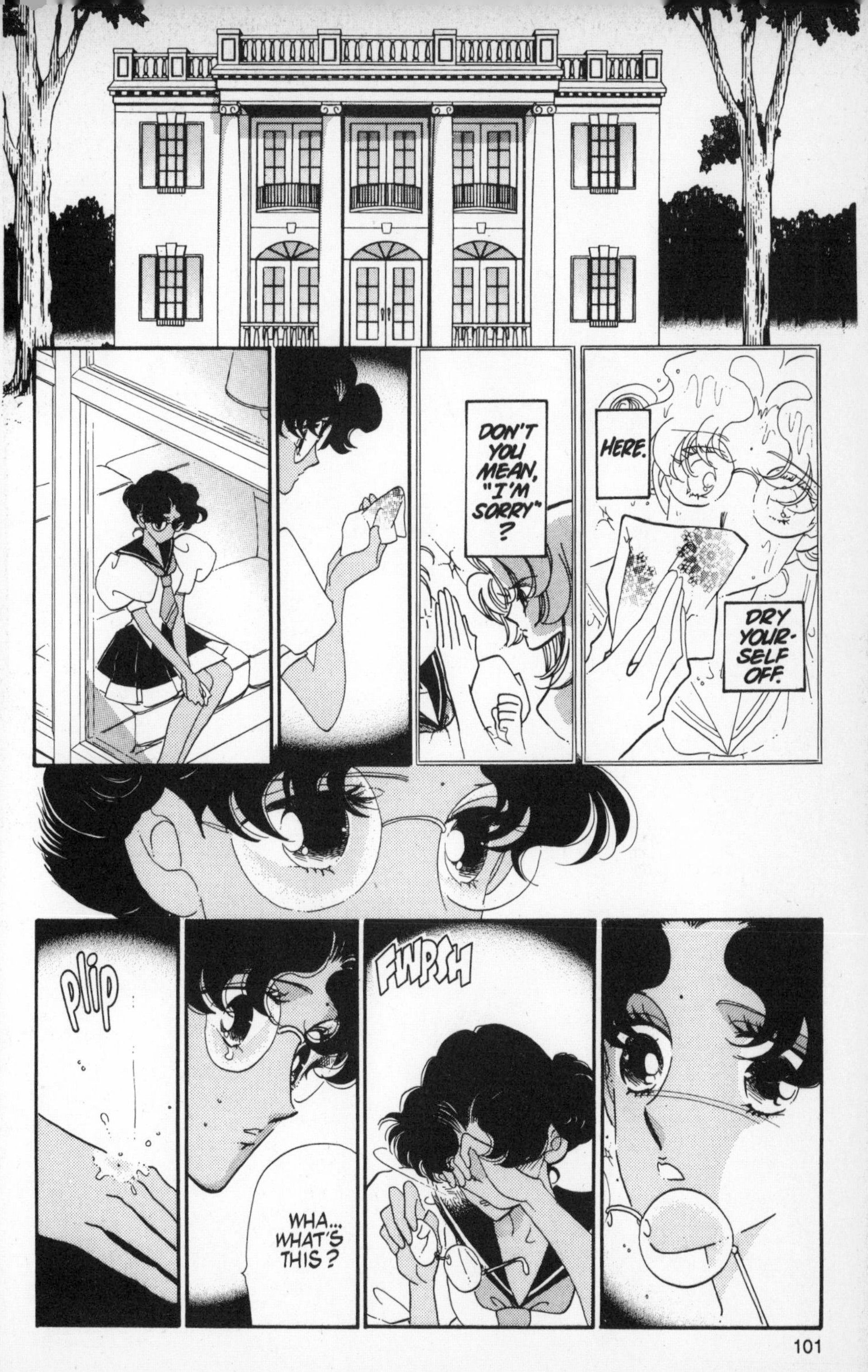
DON'T YOU MEAN, "I'M SORRY"?
HERE.
DRY YOURSELF OFF.
plip
WHA... WHAT'S THIS?
FWPSH

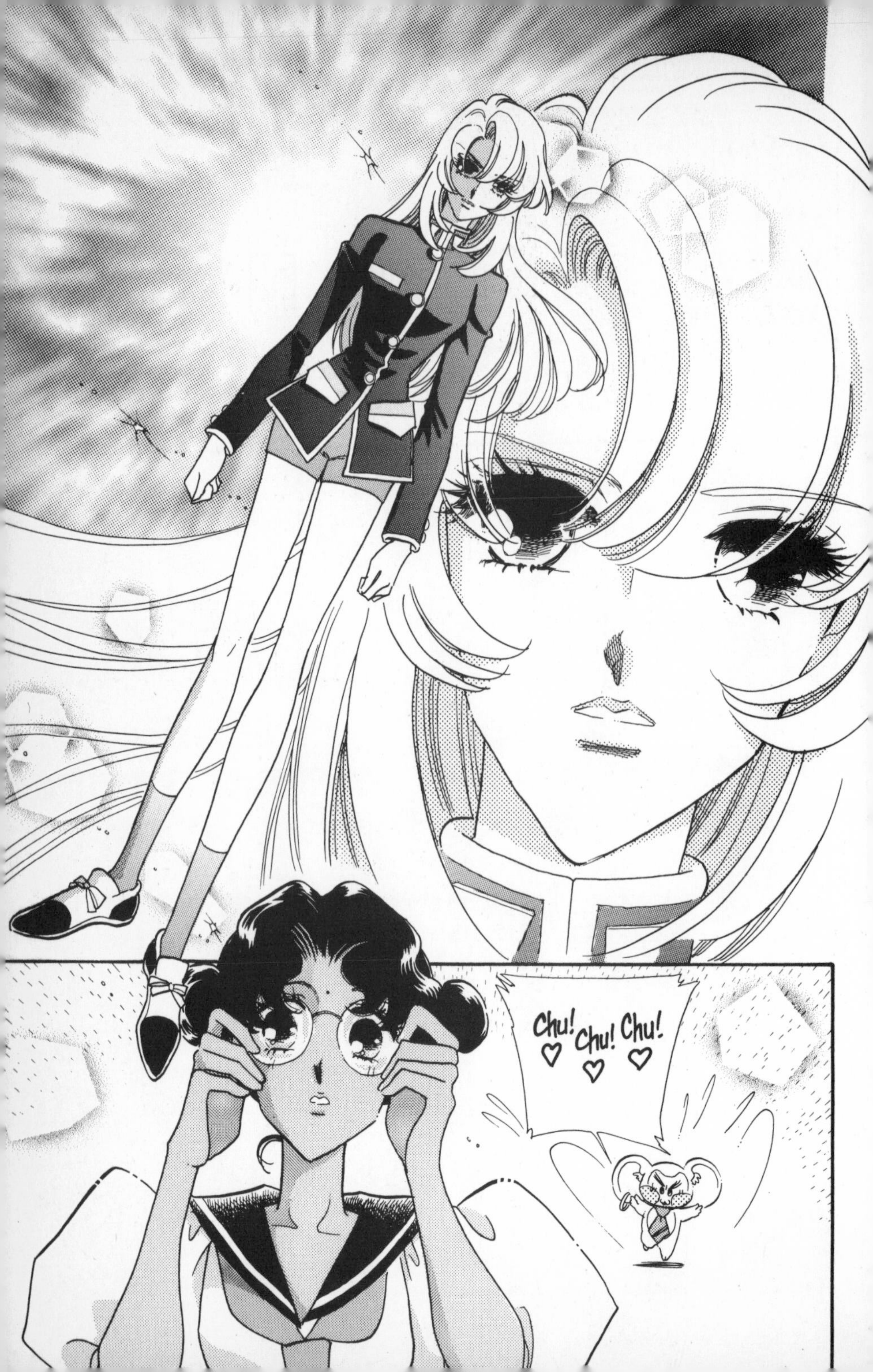
Chu! ♡ Chu! ♡ Chu! ♡

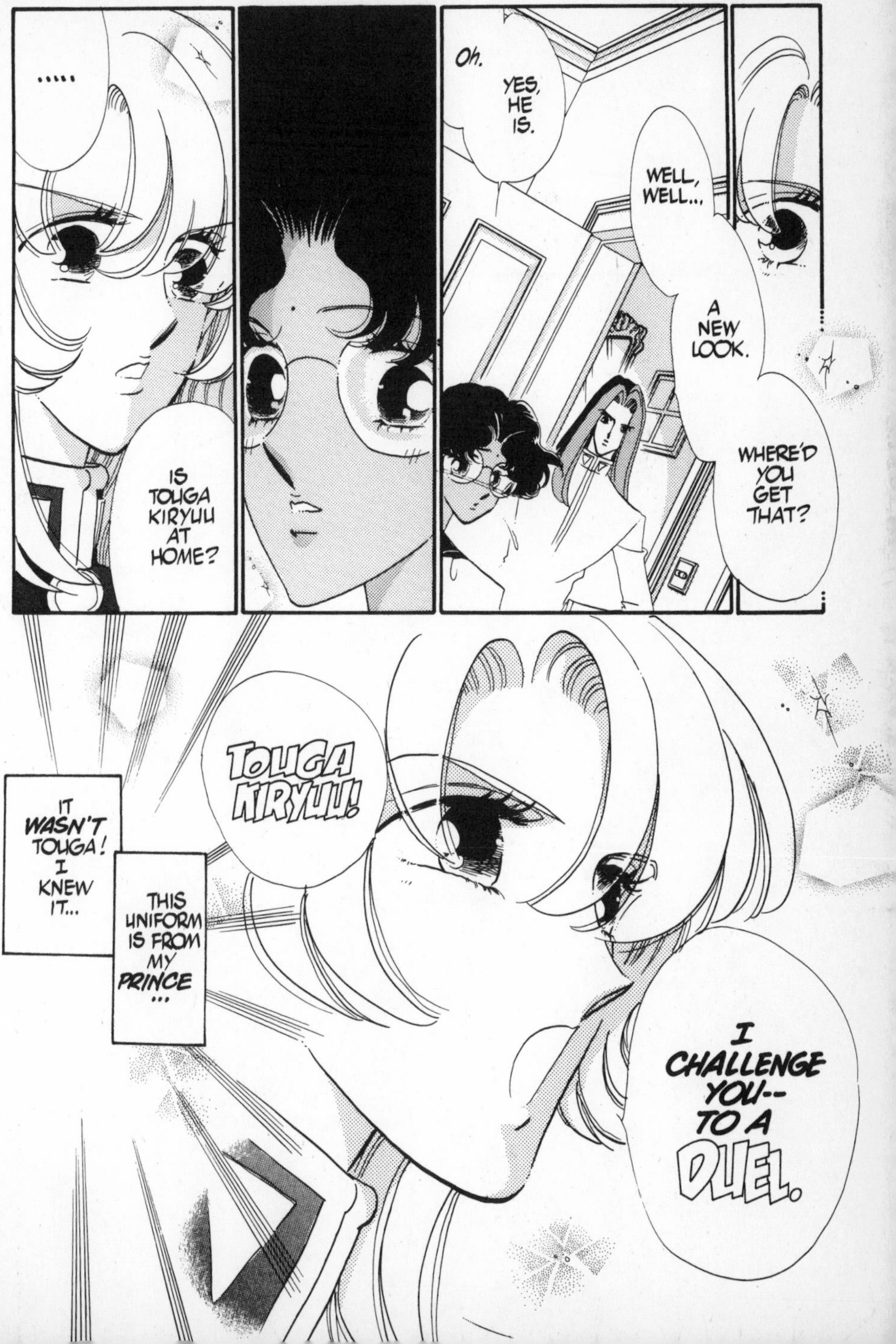
.....
IS TOUGA KIRYUU AT HOME?
Oh.
YES, HE IS.
WELL, WELL...
A NEW LOOK.
WHERE'D YOU GET THAT?
IT WASN'T TOUGA! I KNEW IT...
THIS UNIFORM IS FROM MY PRINCE...
TOUGA KIRYUU!
I CHALLENGE YOU-- TO A DUEL.

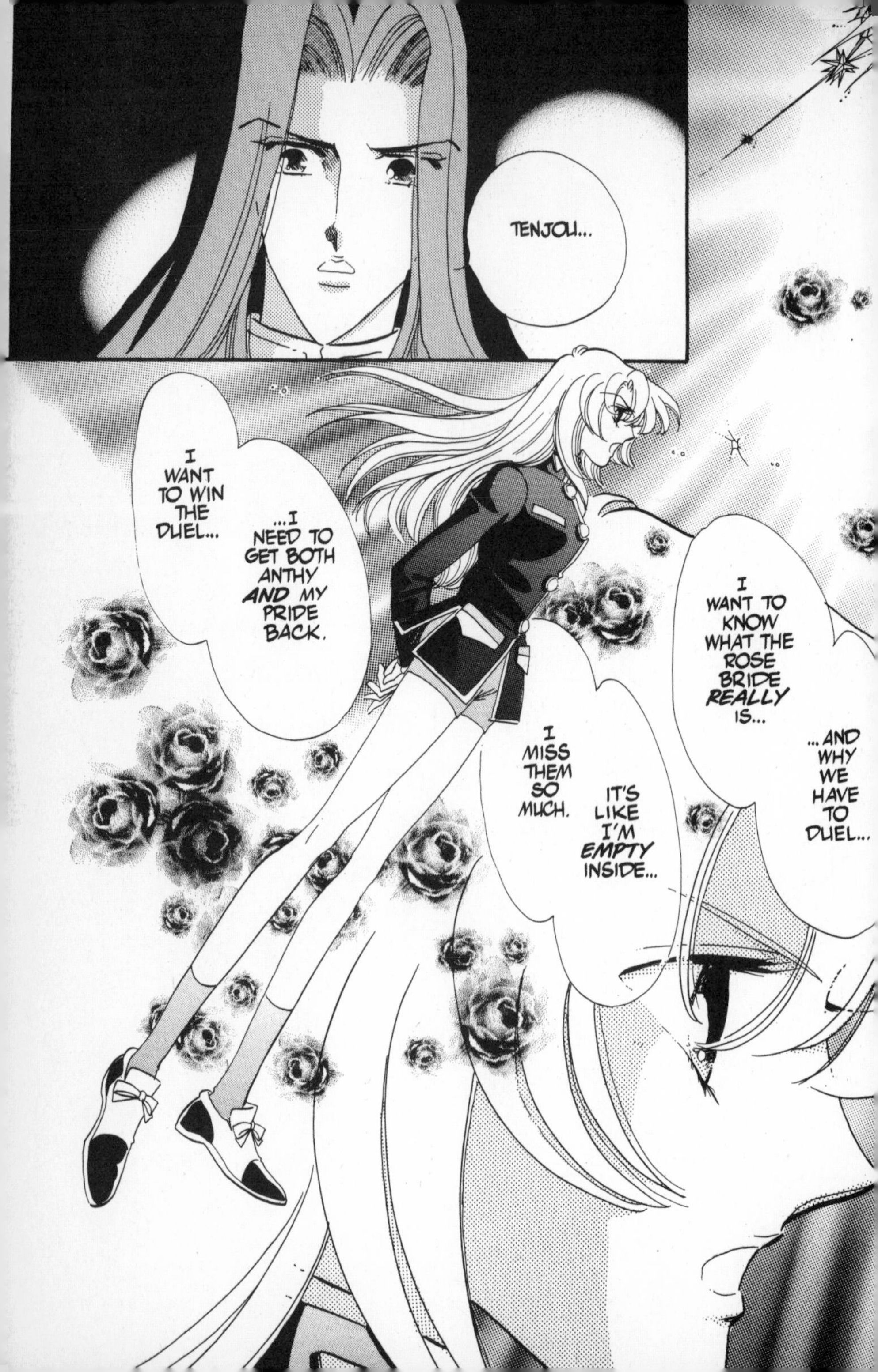
TENJOU...
I WANT TO WIN THE DUEL...
...I NEED TO GET BOTH ANTHY AND MY PRIDE BACK.
I WANT TO KNOW WHAT THE ROSE BRIDE REALLY IS...
...AND WHY WE HAVE TO DUEL...
I MISS THEM SO MUCH.
IT'S LIKE I'M EMPTY INSIDE...

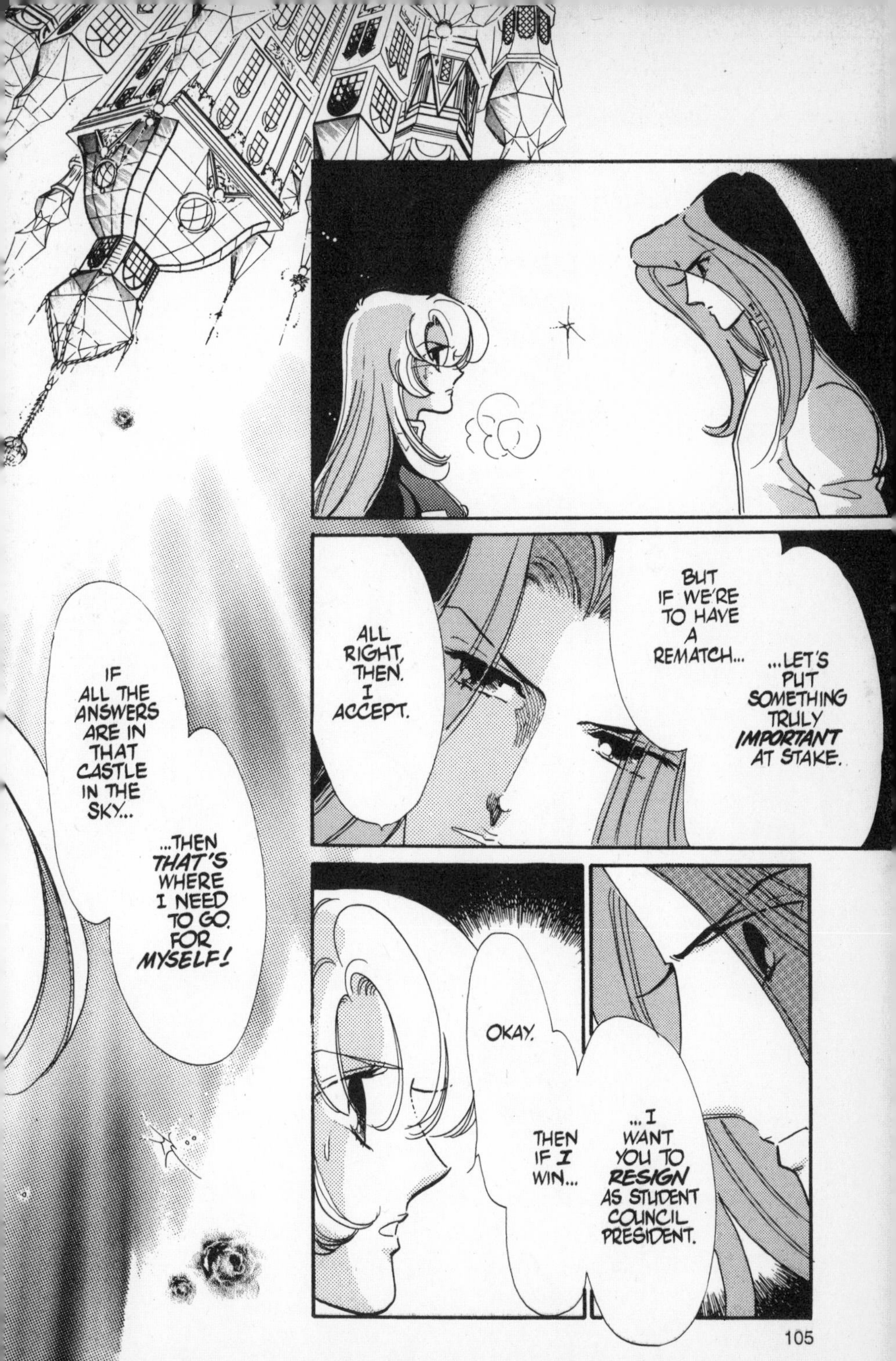
IF ALL THE ANSWERS ARE IN THAT CASTLE IN THE SKY...
...THEN THAT'S WHERE I NEED TO GO. FOR MYSELF!
ALL RIGHT, THEN. I ACCEPT.
BUT IF WE'RE TO HAVE A REMATCH...
...LET'S PUT SOMETHING TRULY IMPORTANT AT STAKE.
OKAY.
THEN IF I WIN...
...I WANT YOU TO RESIGN AS STUDENT COUNCIL PRESIDENT.

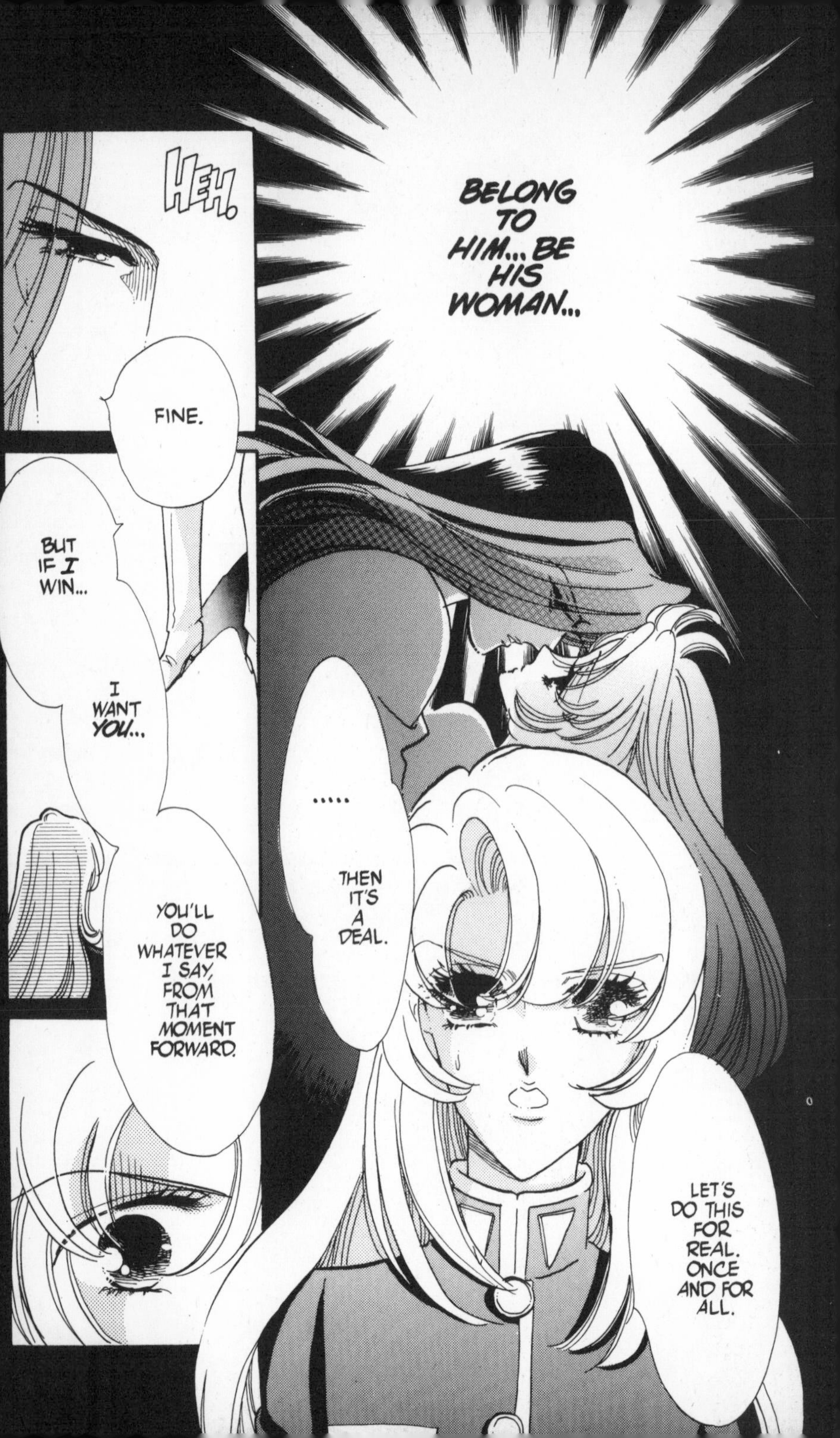
HEH.
FINE.
BUT IF I WIN...
I WANT YOU...
YOU'LL DO WHATEVER I SAY, FROM THAT MOMENT FORWARD.
BELONG TO HIM... BE HIS WOMAN...
.....
THEN IT'S A DEAL.
LET'S DO THIS FOR REAL. ONCE AND FOR ALL.

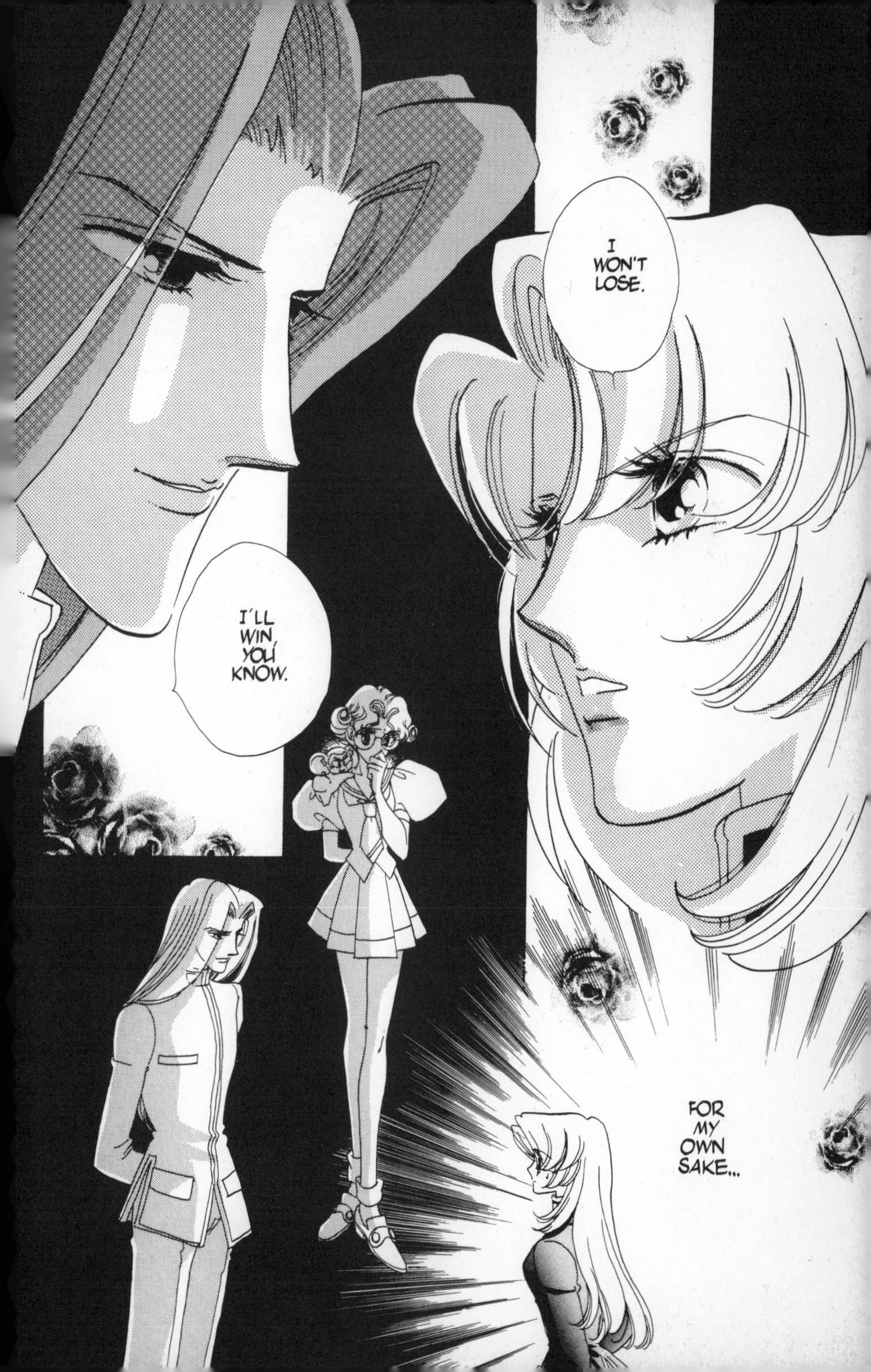
I'LL WIN, YOU KNOW.
I WON'T LOSE.
FOR MY OWN SAKE...

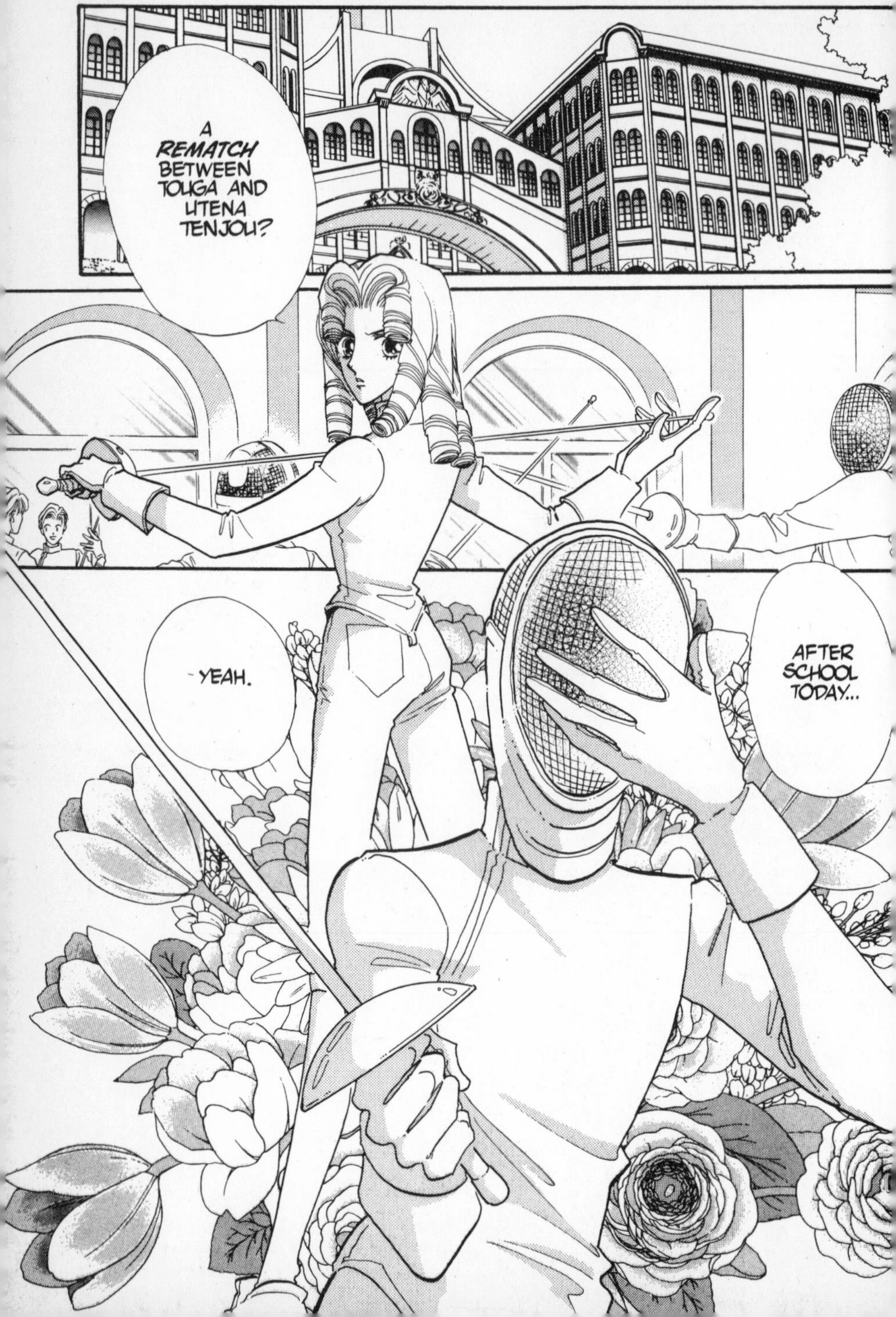
A *REMATCH* BETWEEN TOUGA AND UTENA TENJOU?
-YEAH.
AFTER SCHOOL TODAY...

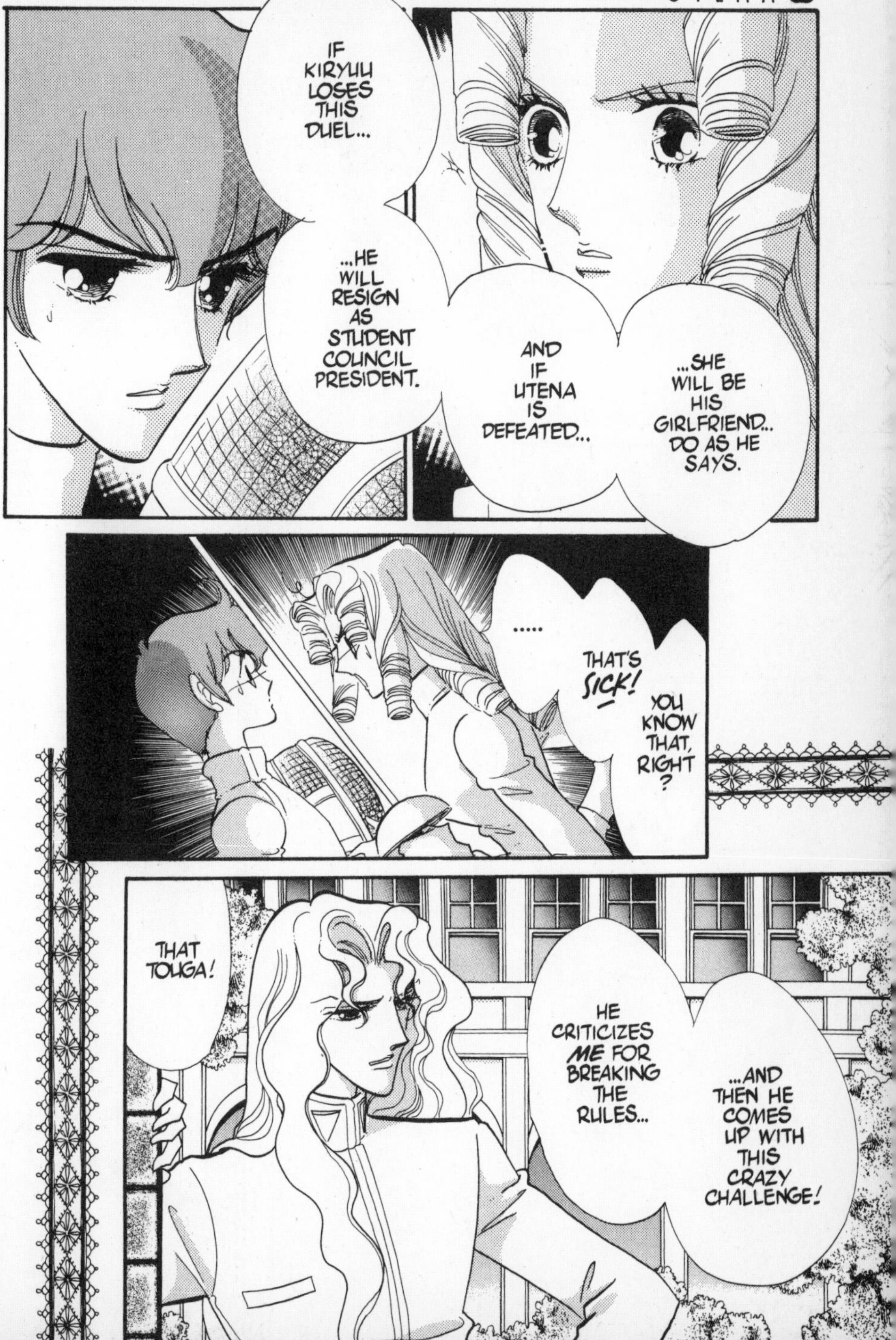
IF KIRYUU LOSES THIS DUEL...
...HE WILL RESIGN AS STUDENT COUNCIL PRESIDENT.
AND IF UTENA IS DEFEATED...
...SHE WILL BE HIS GIRLFRIEND.. DO AS HE SAYS.
.....
THAT'S SICK!
YOU KNOW THAT, RIGHT?
THAT TOUGA!
HE CRITICIZES ME FOR BREAKING THE RULES...
...AND THEN HE COMES UP WITH THIS CRAZY CHALLENGE!

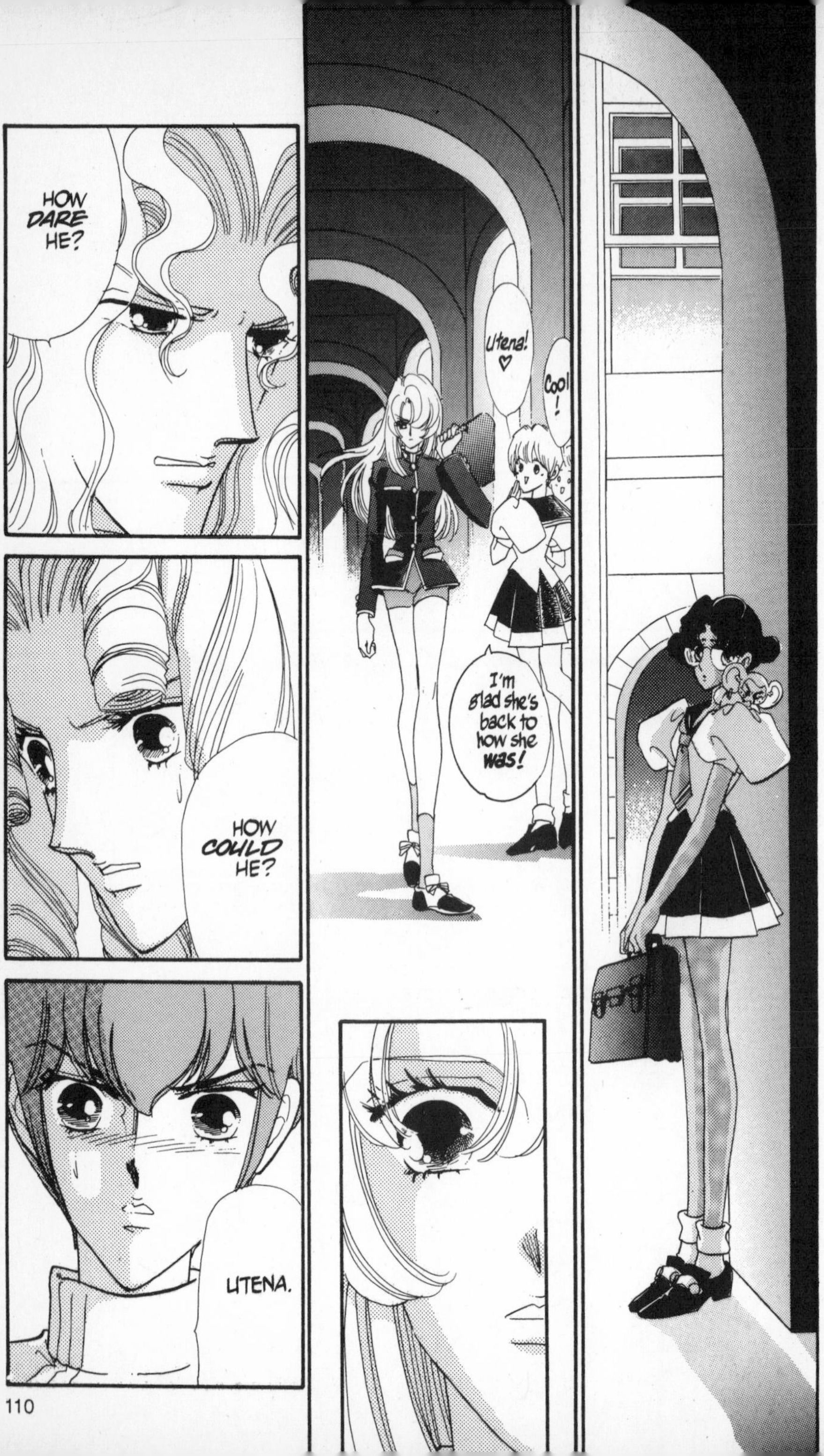
HOW DARE HE?
HOW COULD HE?
UTENA.
Utena! ♡
Cool!
I'm glad she's back to how she was!

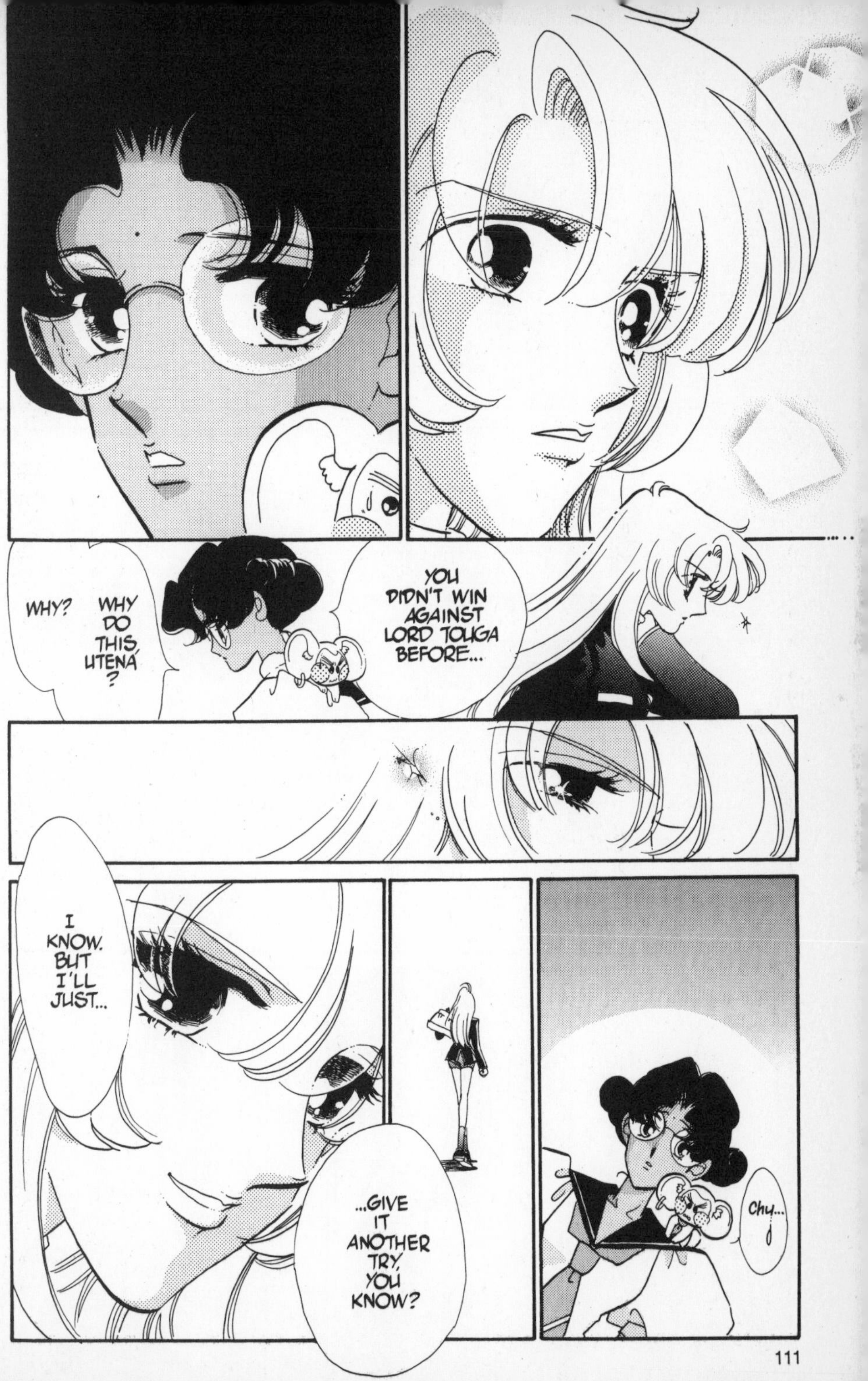
.....
WHY?
WHY DO THIS, UTENA?
YOU DIDN'T WIN AGAINST LORD TOUGA BEFORE...
I KNOW. BUT I'LL JUST...
...GIVE IT ANOTHER TRY, YOU KNOW?
Chy...

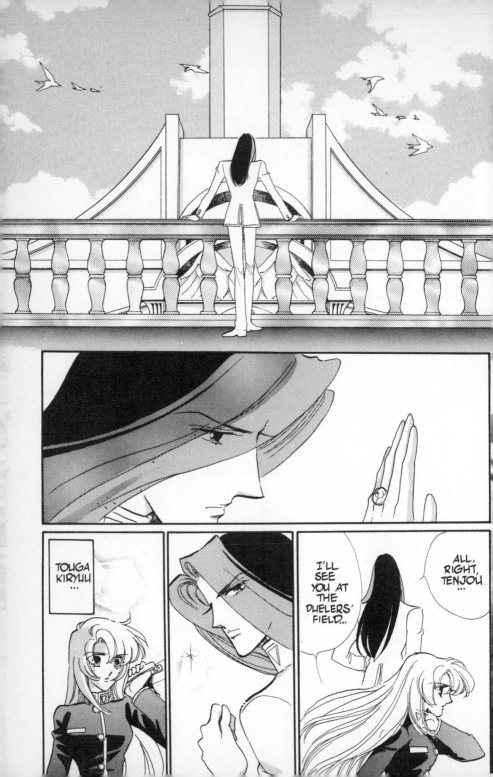

TOUGA KIRYUU...

I'LL SEE YOU AT THE DUELERS' FIELD...

ALL, RIGHT, TENJOU...

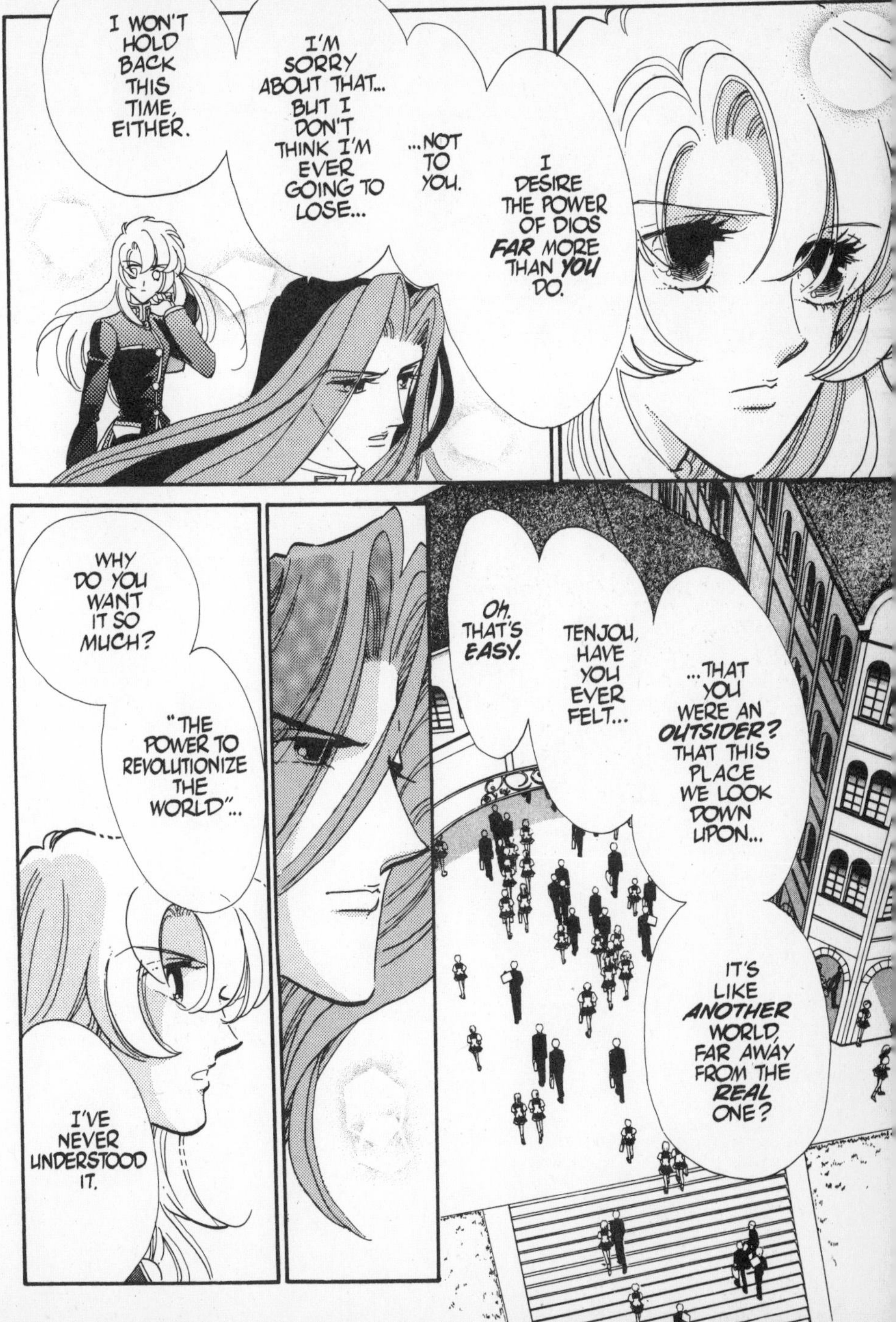
I WON'T HOLD BACK THIS TIME, EITHER.
I'M SORRY ABOUT THAT... BUT I DON'T THINK I'M EVER GOING TO LOSE...
...NOT TO YOU.
I DESIRE THE POWER OF DIOS FAR MORE THAN YOU DO.
WHY DO YOU WANT IT SO MUCH?
"THE POWER TO REVOLUTIONIZE THE WORLD"...
I'VE NEVER UNDERSTOOD IT.
Oh. THAT'S EASY.
TENJOU, HAVE YOU EVER FELT...
...THAT YOU WERE AN OUTSIDER? THAT THIS PLACE WE LOOK DOWN UPON...
IT'S LIKE ANOTHER WORLD, FAR AWAY FROM THE REAL ONE?

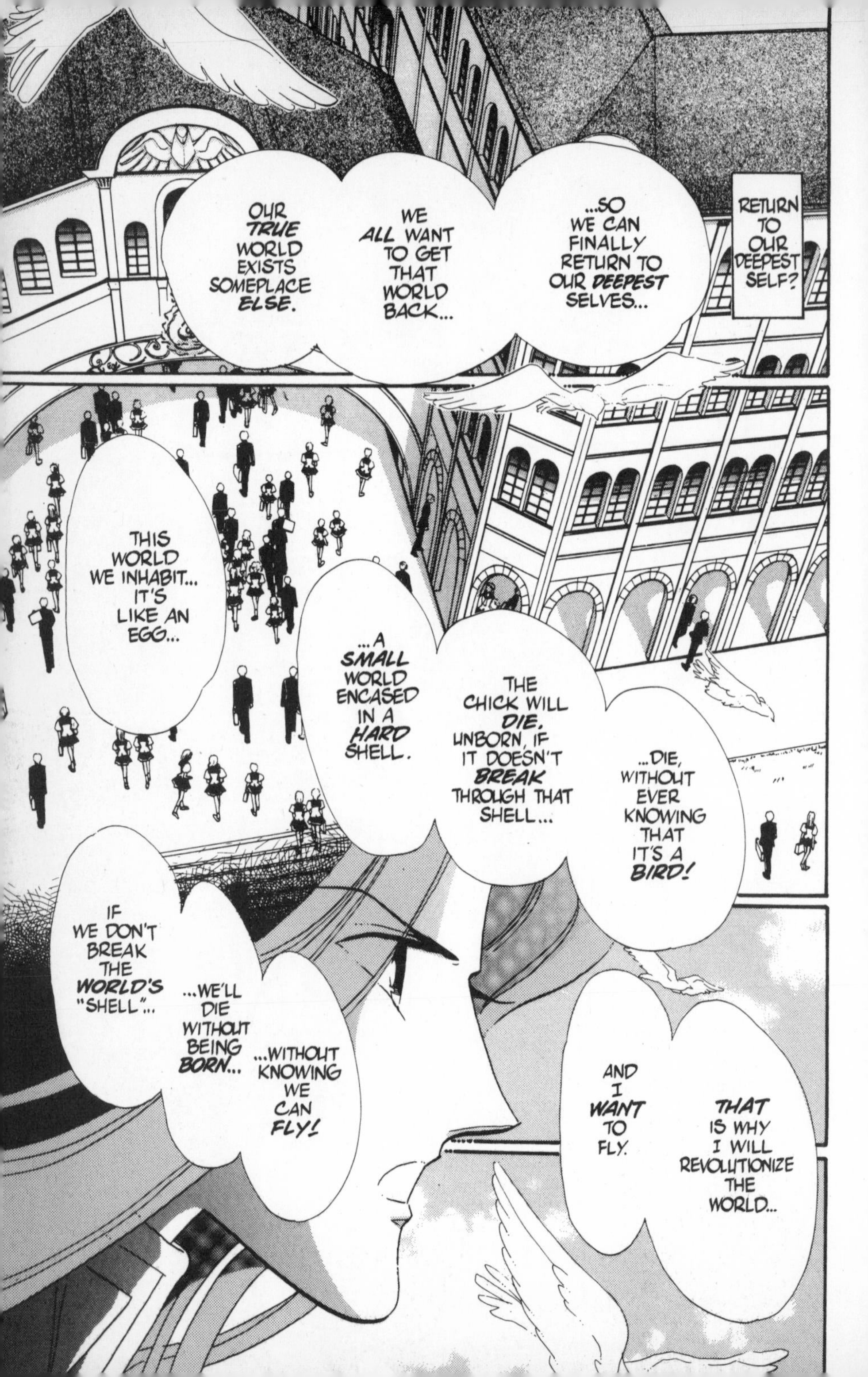
OUR TRUE WORLD EXISTS SOMEPLACE ELSE.
WE ALL WANT TO GET THAT WORLD BACK...
...SO WE CAN FINALLY RETURN TO OUR DEEPEST SELVES...
RETURN TO OUR DEEPEST SELF?
THIS WORLD WE INHABIT... IT'S LIKE AN EGG...
...A SMALL WORLD ENCASED IN A HARD SHELL.
THE CHICK WILL DIE, UNBORN, IF IT DOESN'T BREAK THROUGH THAT SHELL...
...DIE, WITHOUT EVER KNOWING THAT IT'S A BIRD!
IF WE DON'T BREAK THE WORLD'S "SHELL"...
...WE'LL DIE WITHOUT BEING BORN...
...WITHOUT KNOWING WE CAN FLY!
AND I WANT TO FLY.
THAT IS WHY I WILL REVOLUTIONIZE THE WORLD...

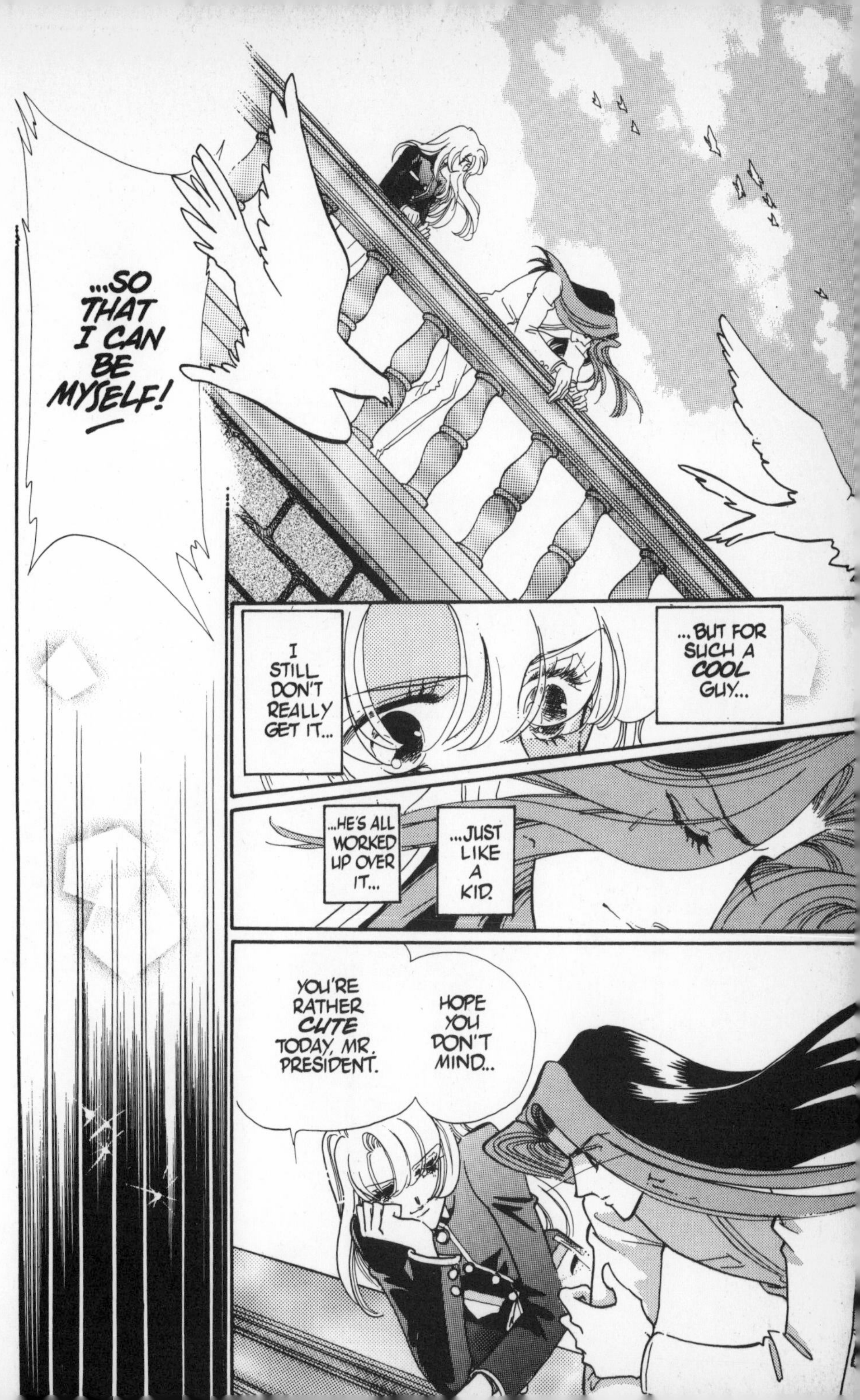
...SO THAT I CAN BE MYSELF!
I STILL DON'T REALLY GET IT...
...BUT FOR SUCH A COOL GUY...
...HE'S ALL WORKED UP OVER IT...
...JUST LIKE A KID.
YOU'RE RATHER CUTE TODAY, MR. PRESIDENT.
HOPE YOU DON'T MIND...

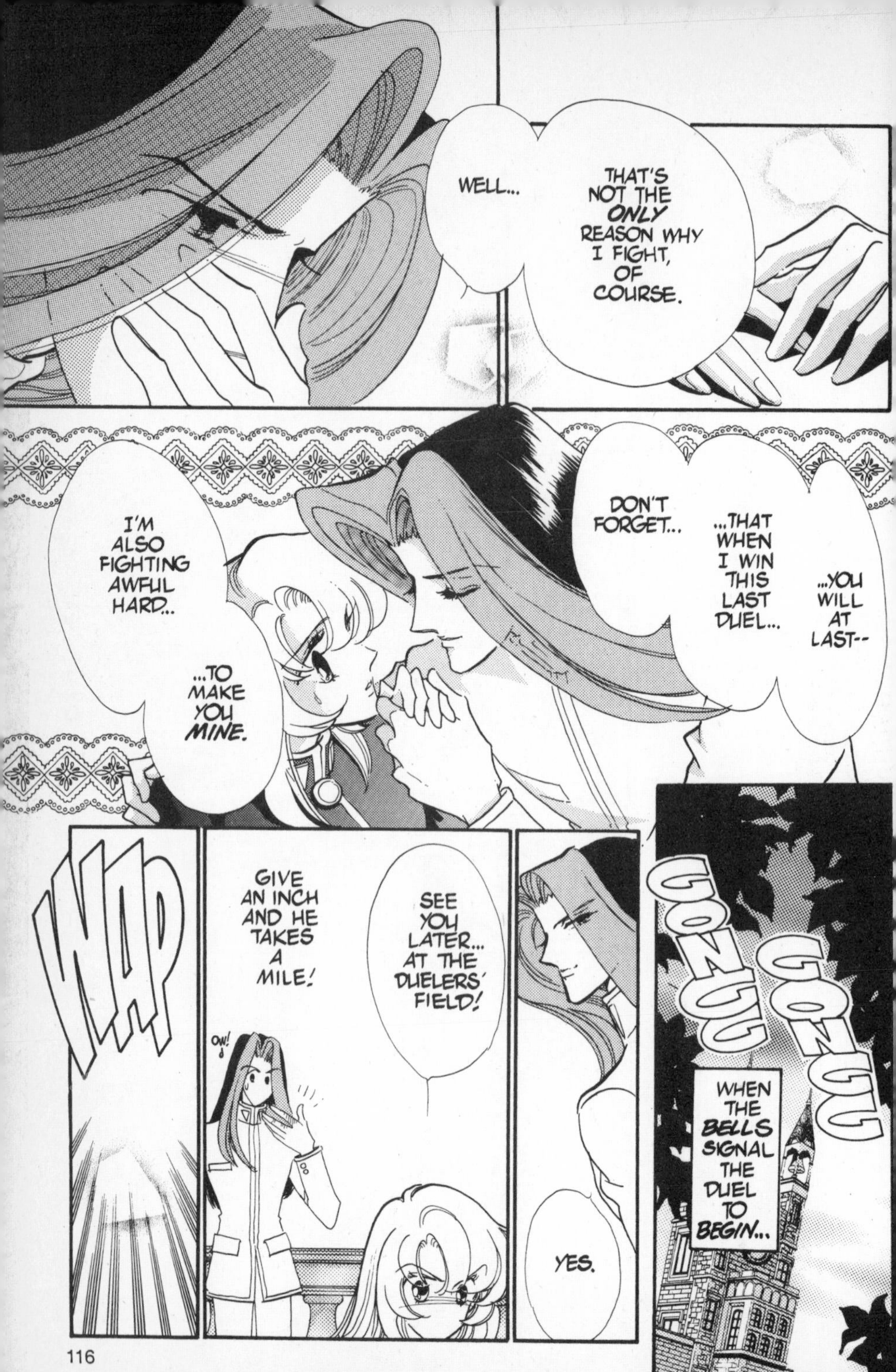
WELL...
THAT'S NOT THE ONLY REASON WHY I FIGHT, OF COURSE.
I'M ALSO FIGHTING AWFUL HARD...
...TO MAKE YOU MINE.
DON'T FORGET...
...THAT WHEN I WIN THIS LAST DUEL...
...YOU WILL AT LAST--
WAP
GIVE AN INCH AND HE TAKES A MILE!
SEE YOU LATER... AT THE DUELERS' FIELD!
OW!
YES.
GONG GONG
WHEN THE BELLS SIGNAL THE DUEL TO BEGIN...

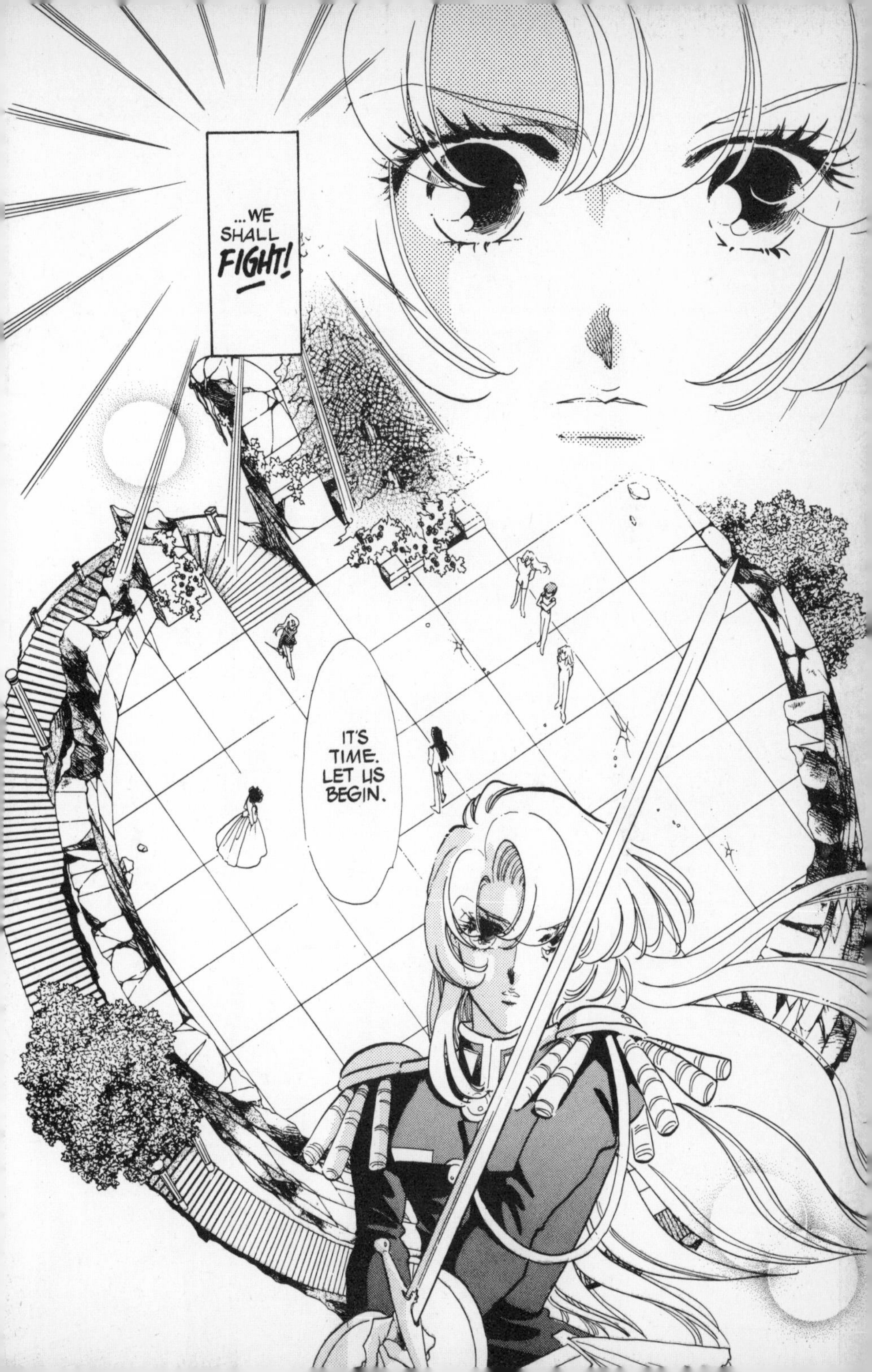
...WE SHALL FIGHT!
IT'S TIME. LET US BEGIN.

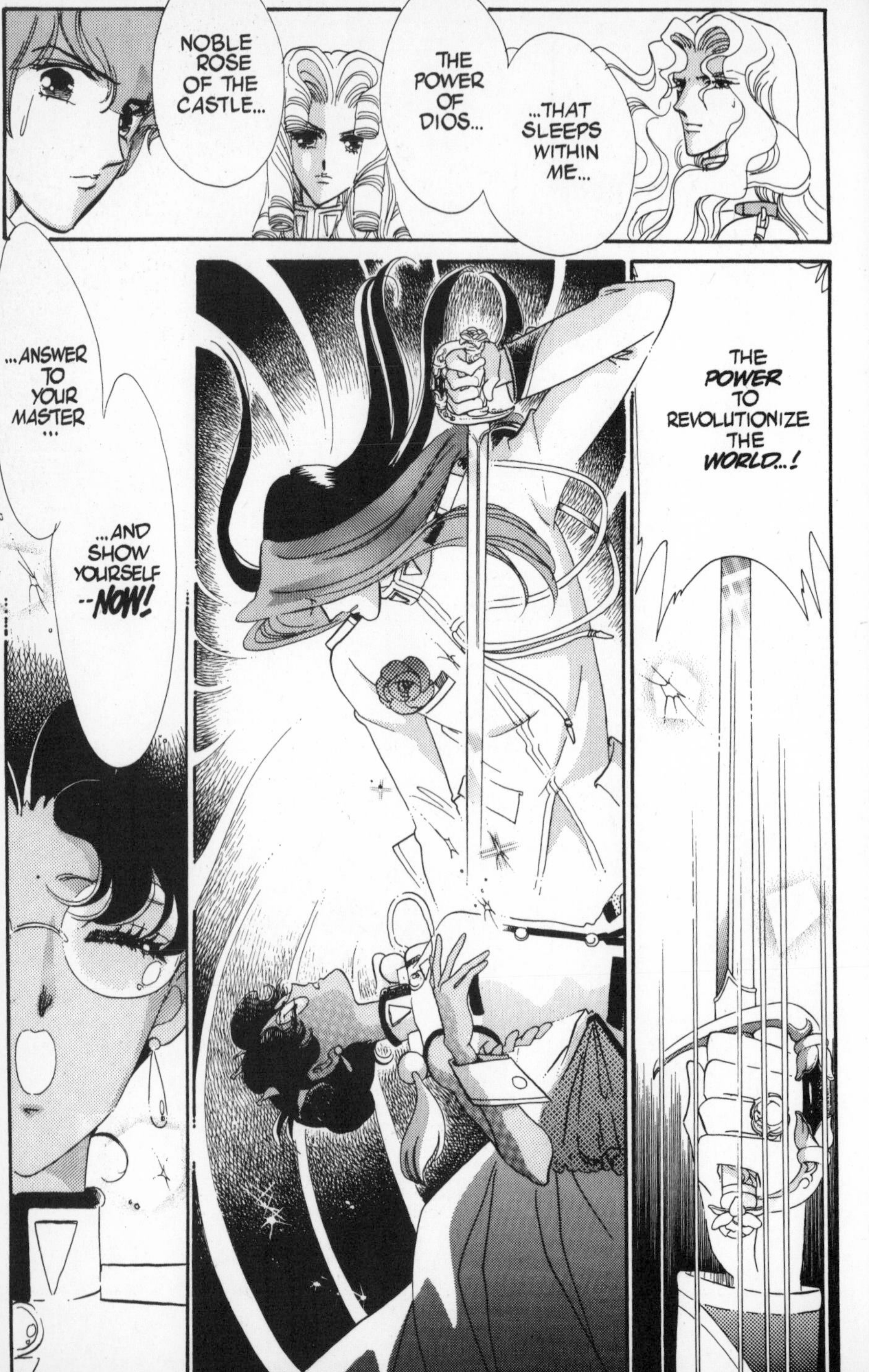
NOBLE ROSE OF THE CASTLE...
THE POWER OF DIOS...
...THAT SLEEPS WITHIN ME...
...ANSWER TO YOUR MASTER ...
...AND SHOW YOURSELF --NOW!
THE POWER TO REVOLUTIONIZE THE WORLD...!

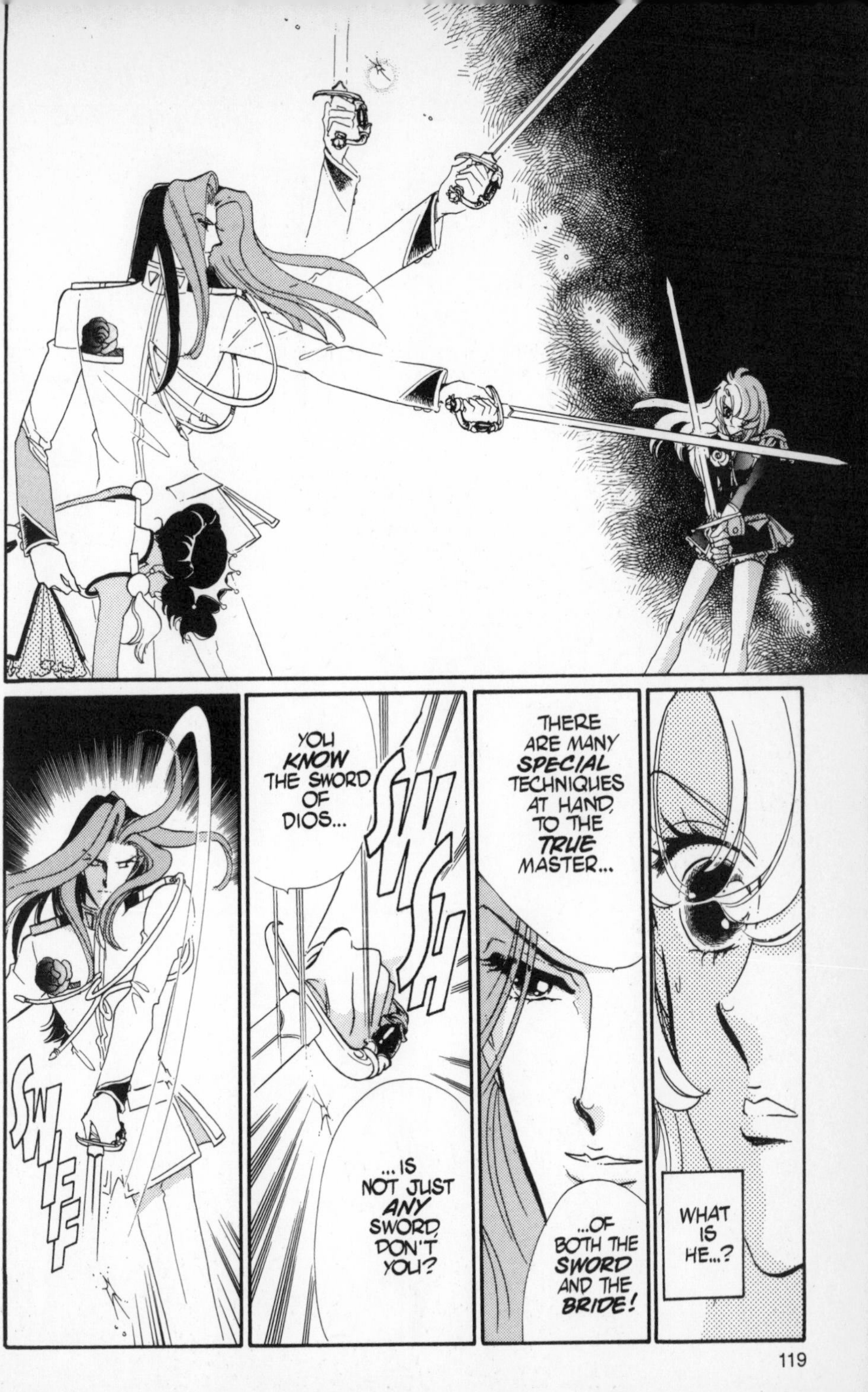
SWIFF
YOU KNOW THE SWORD OF DIOS...
SWISH
...IS NOT JUST ANY SWORD, DON'T YOU?
THERE ARE MANY SPECIAL TECHNIQUES AT HAND, TO THE TRUE MASTER...
...OF BOTH THE SWORD AND THE BRIDE!
WHAT IS HE...?

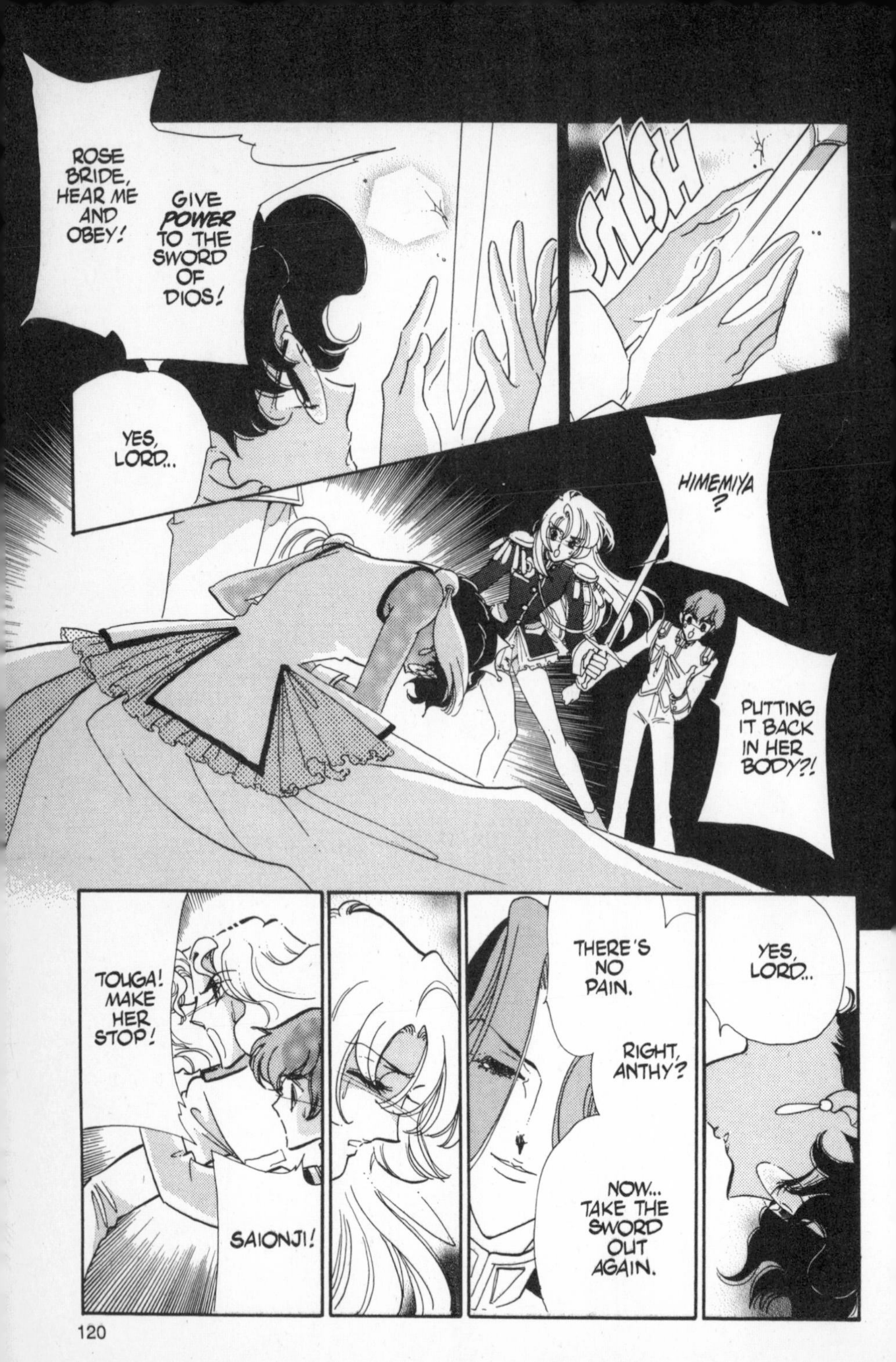
ROSE BRIDE, HEAR ME AND OBEY!
GIVE POWER TO THE SWORD OF DIOS!
SHLSH
YES, LORD...
HIMEMIYA?
PUTTING IT BACK IN HER BODY?!
TOUGA! MAKE HER STOP!
SAIONJI!
THERE'S NO PAIN.
RIGHT, ANTHY?
NOW... TAKE THE SWORD OUT AGAIN.
YES, LORD...

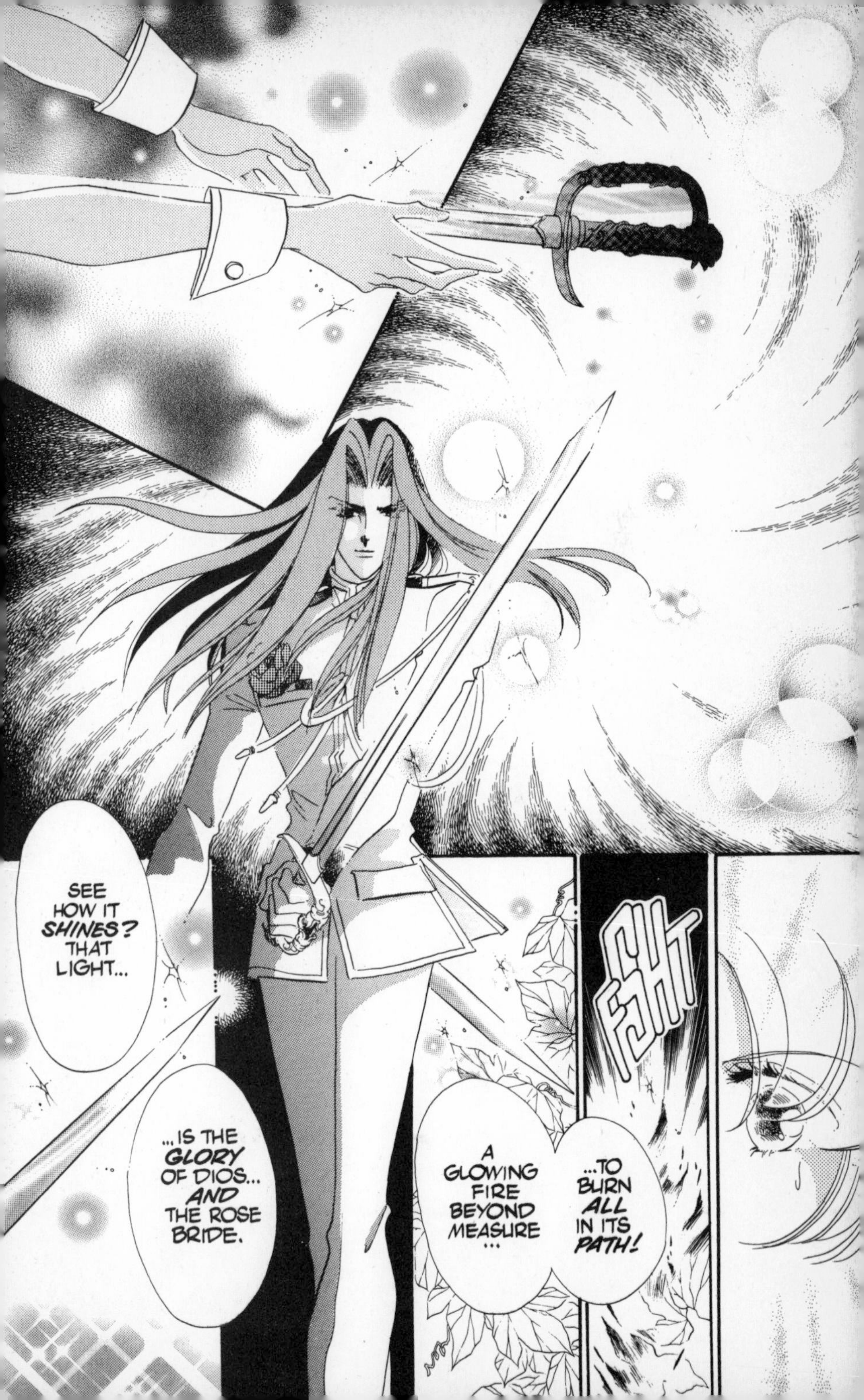
SEE HOW IT SHINES? THAT LIGHT...
...IS THE GLORY OF DIOS... AND THE ROSE BRIDE.
A GLOWING FIRE BEYOND MEASURE...
...TO BURN ALL IN ITS PATH!
FSHT

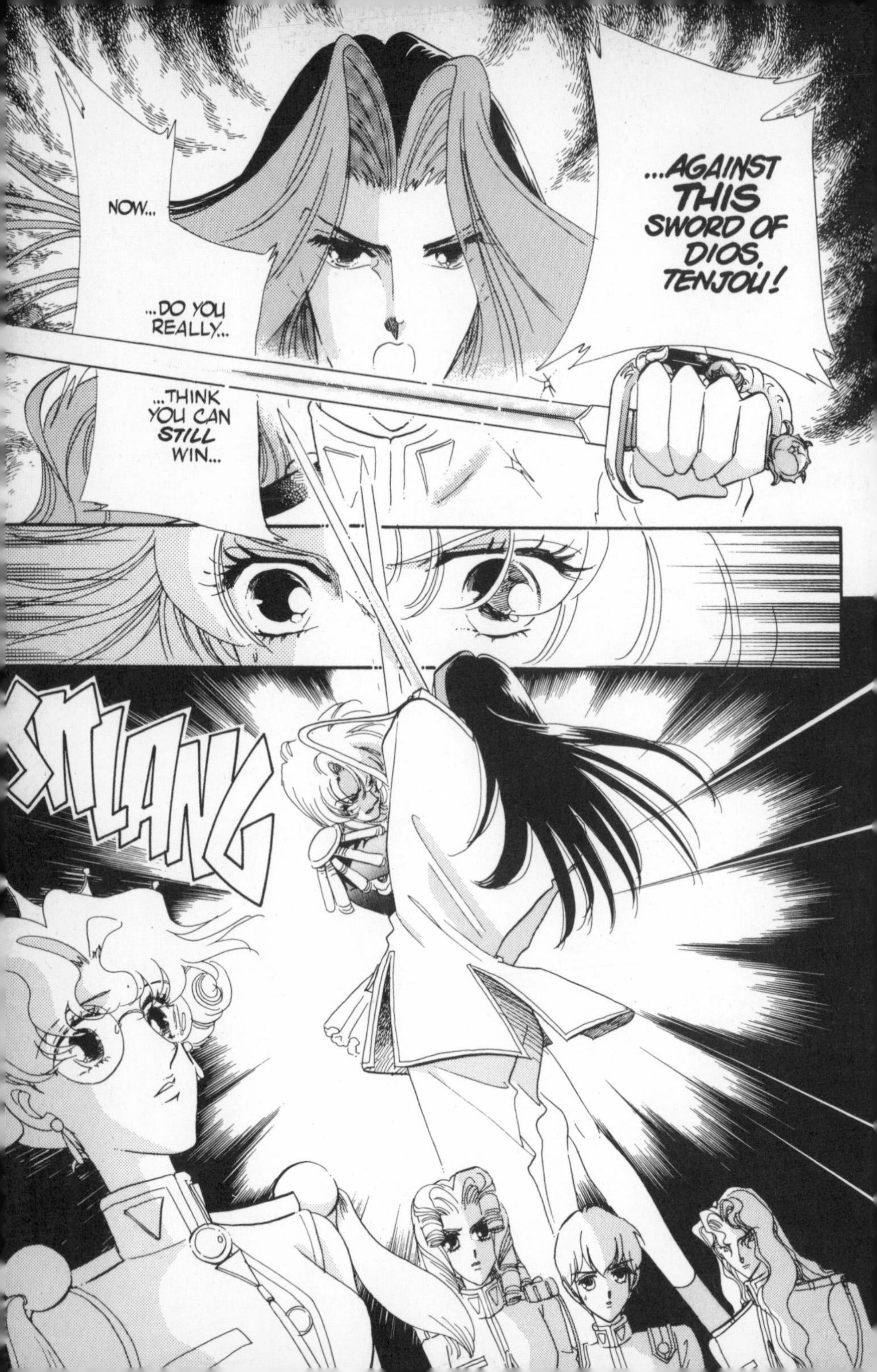
NOW...
...DO YOU REALLY...
...THINK YOU CAN STILL WIN...
...AGAINST THIS SWORD OF DIOS, TENJOU!
SHLANG

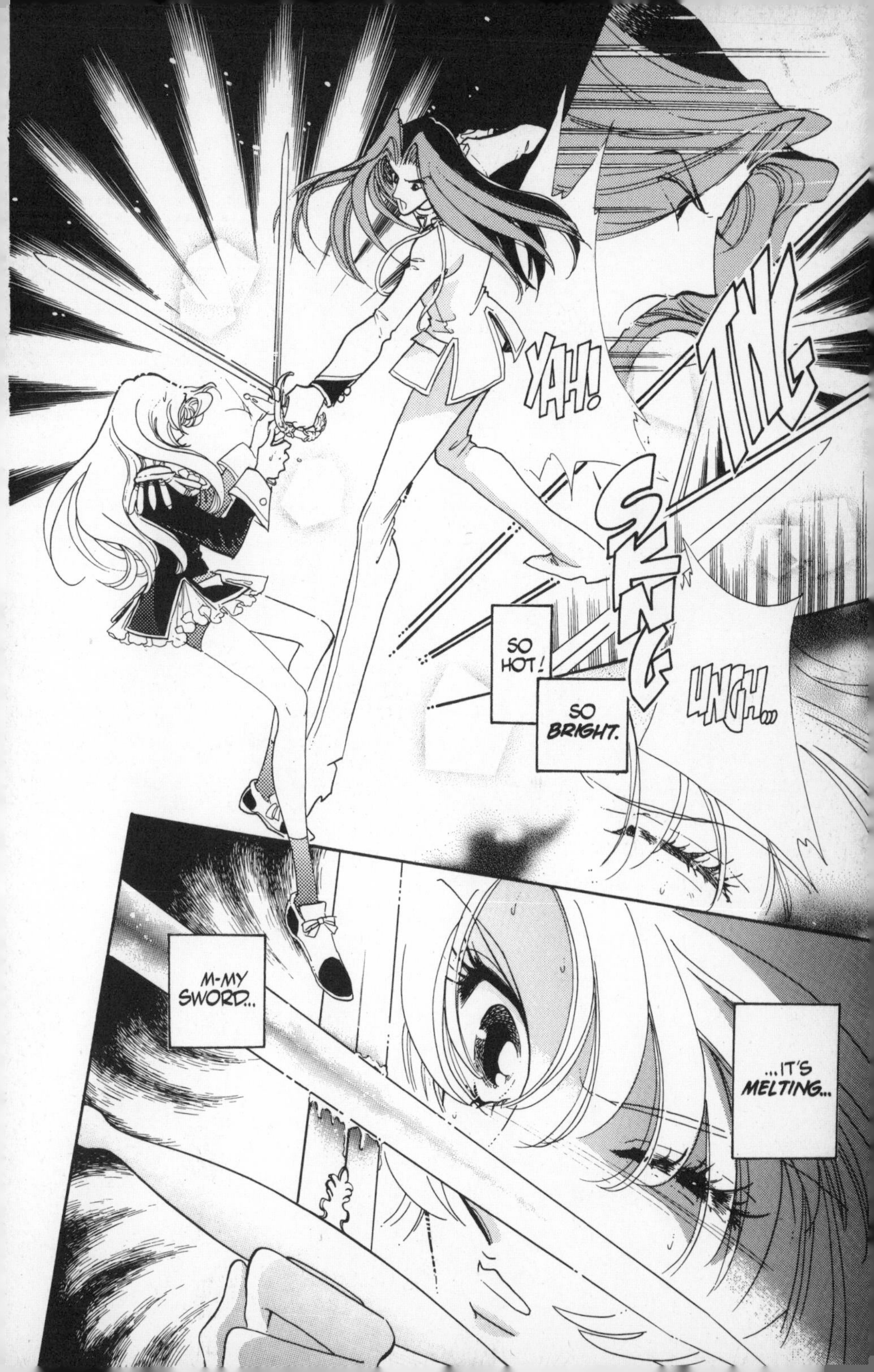
YAH!
TING
SHING
SO HOT!
SO BRIGHT.
UNGH...
M-MY SWORD...
...IT'S MELTING...

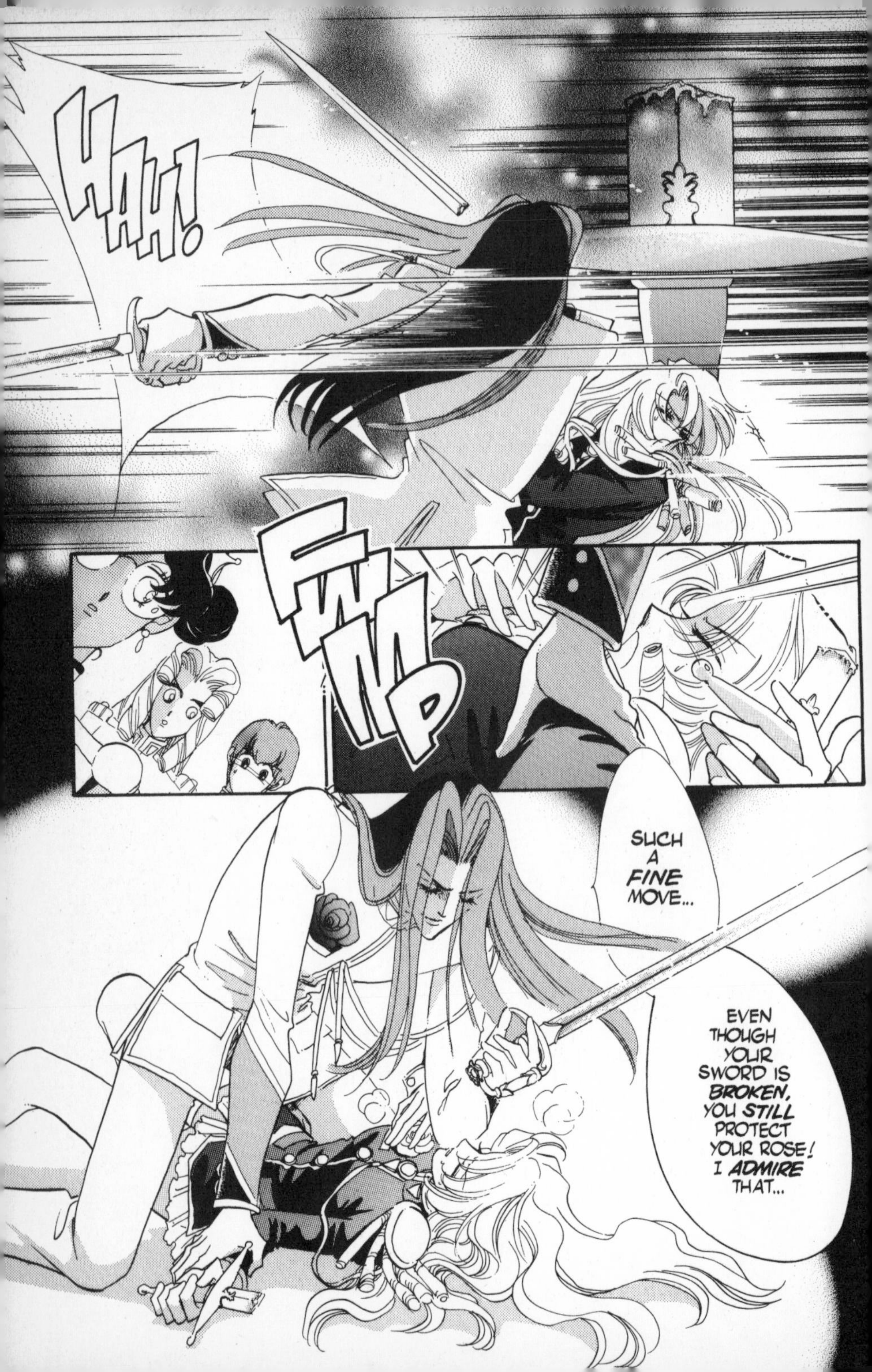

HAH!
FWMP
SUCH A FINE MOVE...
EVEN THOUGH YOUR SWORD IS BROKEN, YOU STILL PROTECT YOUR ROSE! I ADMIRE THAT...

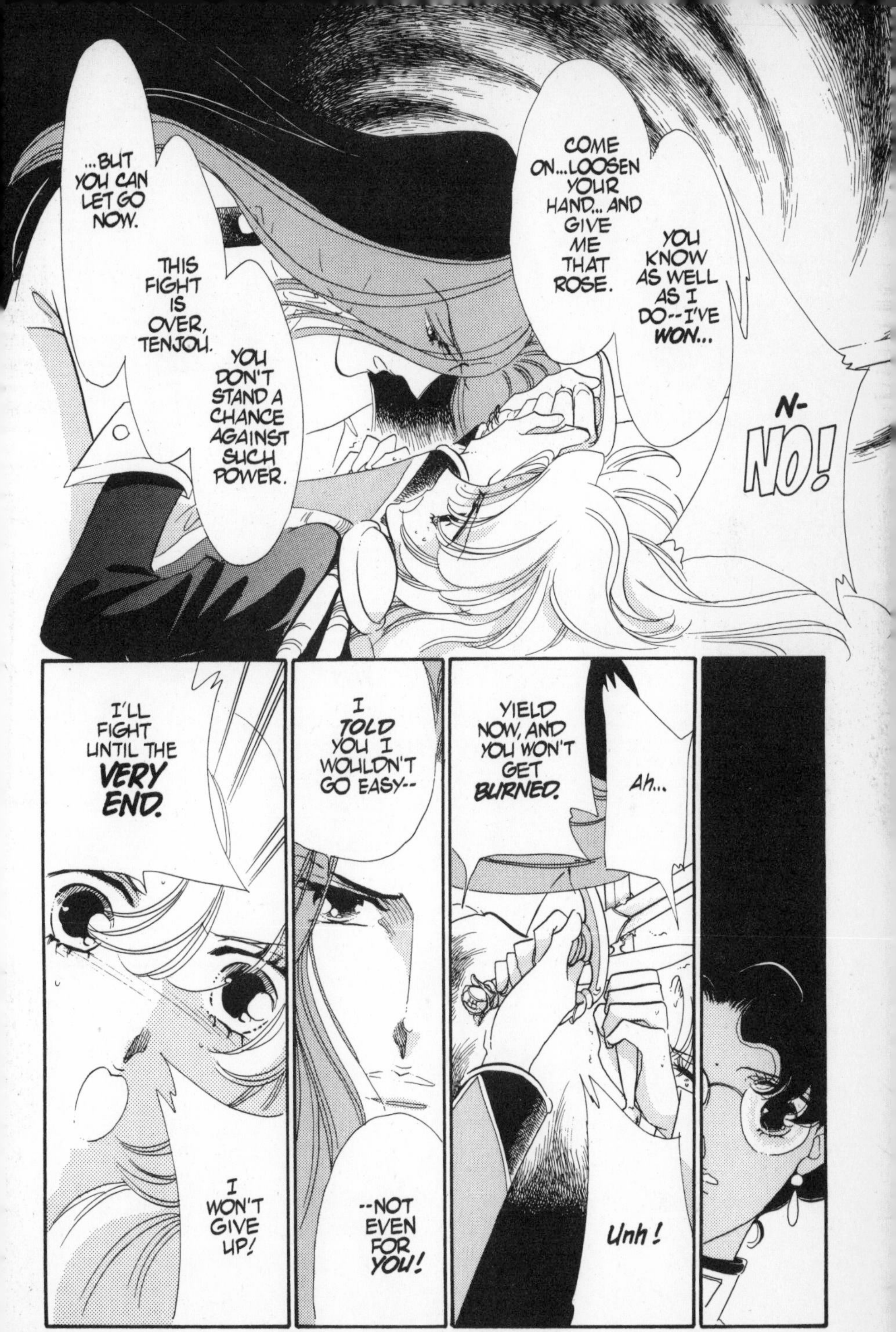
...BUT YOU CAN LET GO NOW.
THIS FIGHT IS OVER, TENJOU.
YOU DON'T STAND A CHANCE AGAINST SUCH POWER.
COME ON...LOOSEN YOUR HAND... AND GIVE ME THAT ROSE.
YOU KNOW AS WELL AS I DO--I'VE WON...
N-NO!
I'LL FIGHT UNTIL THE VERY END.
I WON'T GIVE UP!
I TOLD YOU I WOULDN'T GO EASY--
--NOT EVEN FOR YOU!
YIELD NOW, AND YOU WON'T GET BURNED.
Ah...
Unh!

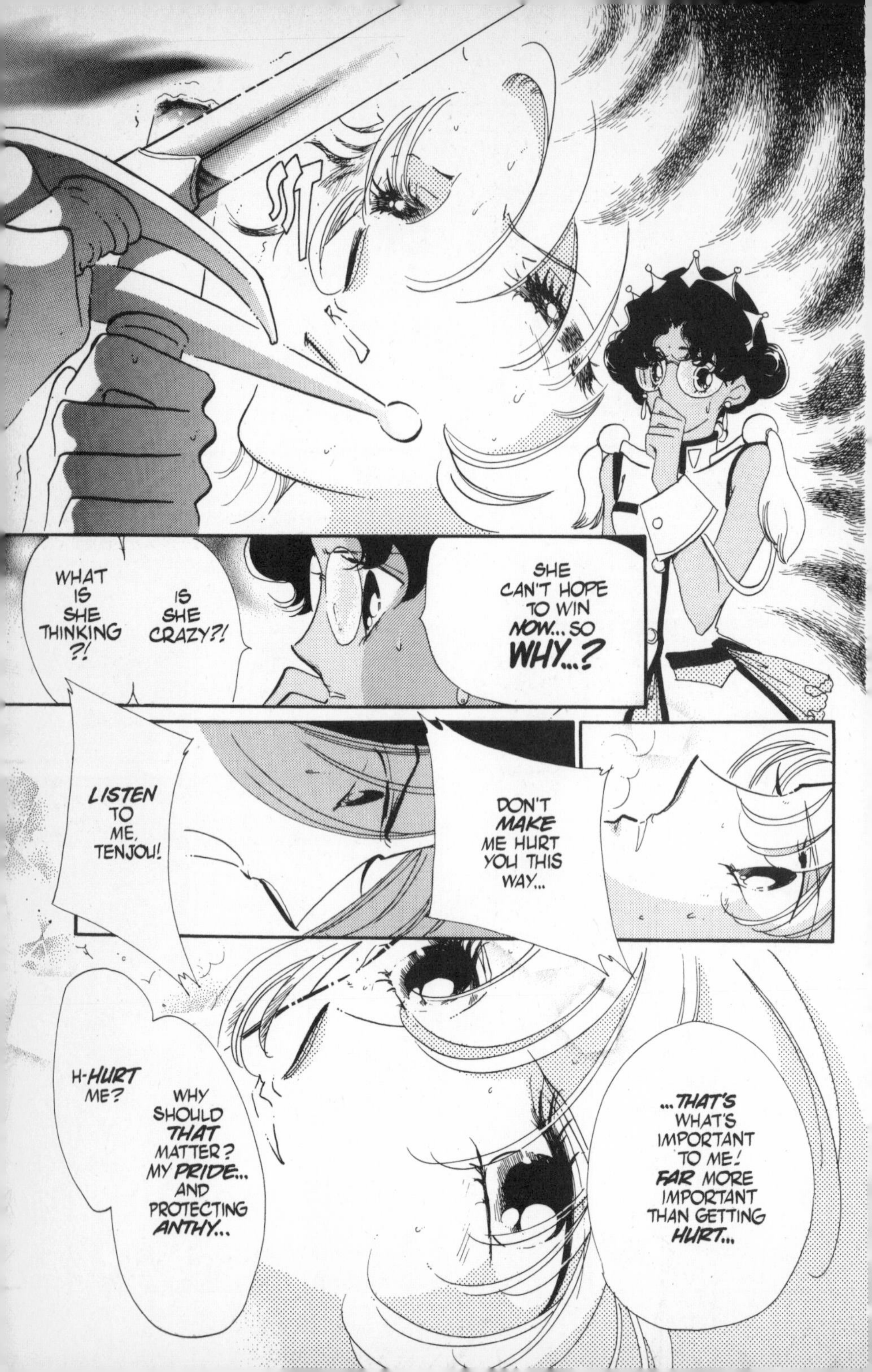
WHAT IS SHE THINKING ?!
IS SHE CRAZY?!
SHE CAN'T HOPE TO WIN NOW... SO WHY...?
LISTEN TO ME, TENJOU!
DON'T MAKE ME HURT YOU THIS WAY...
H-HURT ME?
WHY SHOULD THAT MATTER? MY PRIDE... AND PROTECTING ANTHY...
...THAT'S WHAT'S IMPORTANT TO ME! FAR MORE IMPORTANT THAN GETTING HURT...

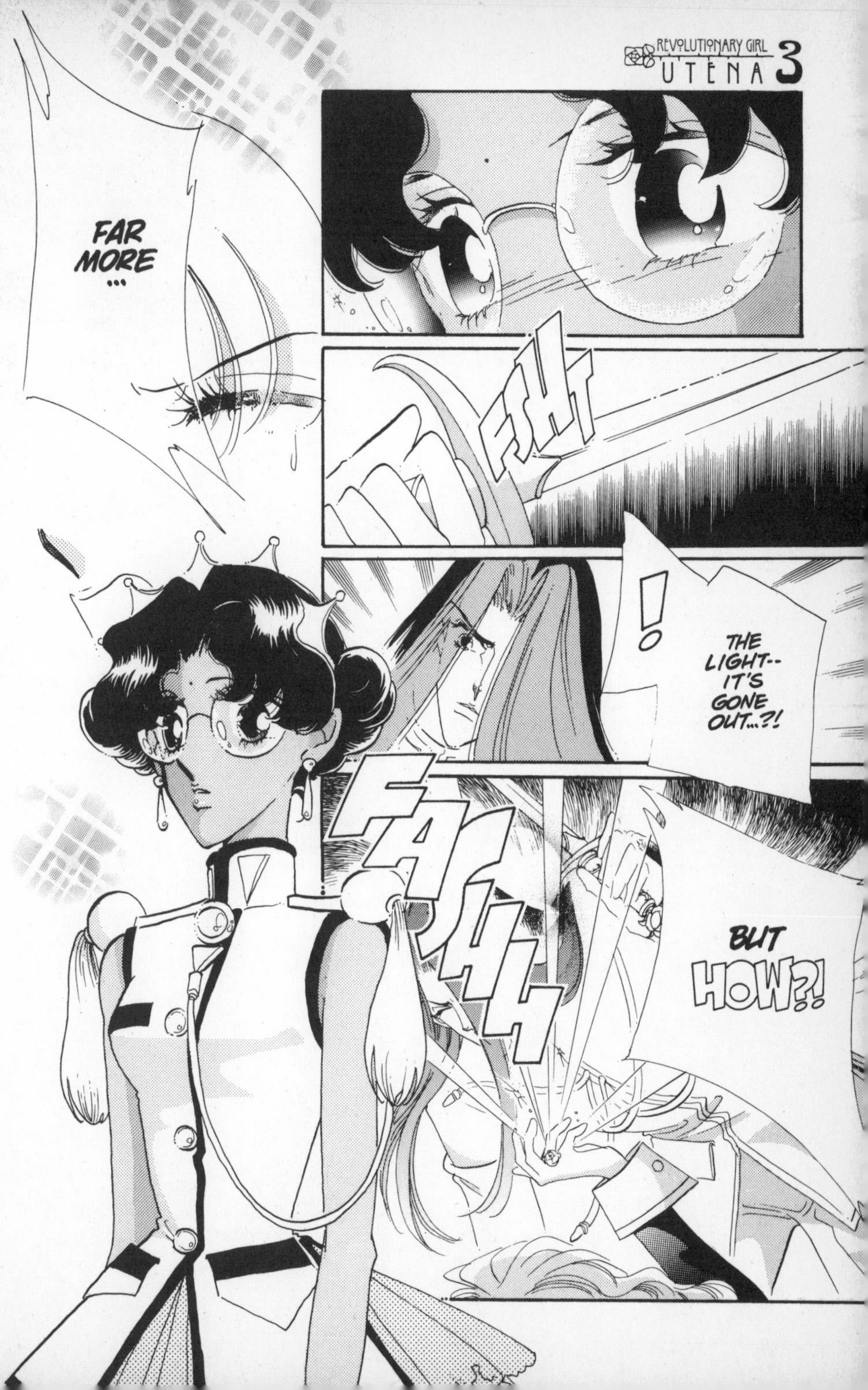
FAR MORE ...
FSHT
!
THE LIGHT-- IT'S GONE OUT...?!
FASHH
BUT HOW?!

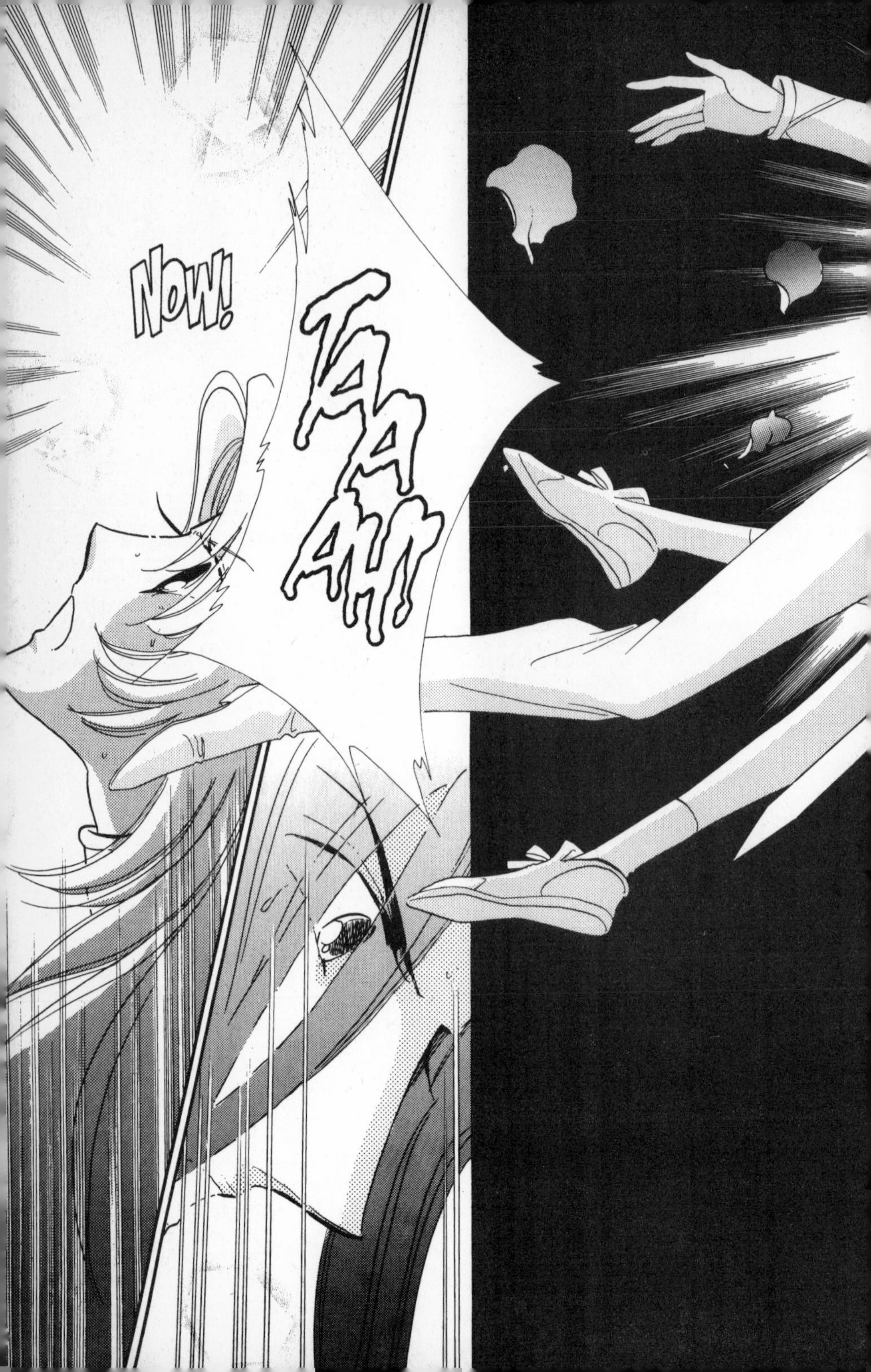
NOW!
TAAAH!

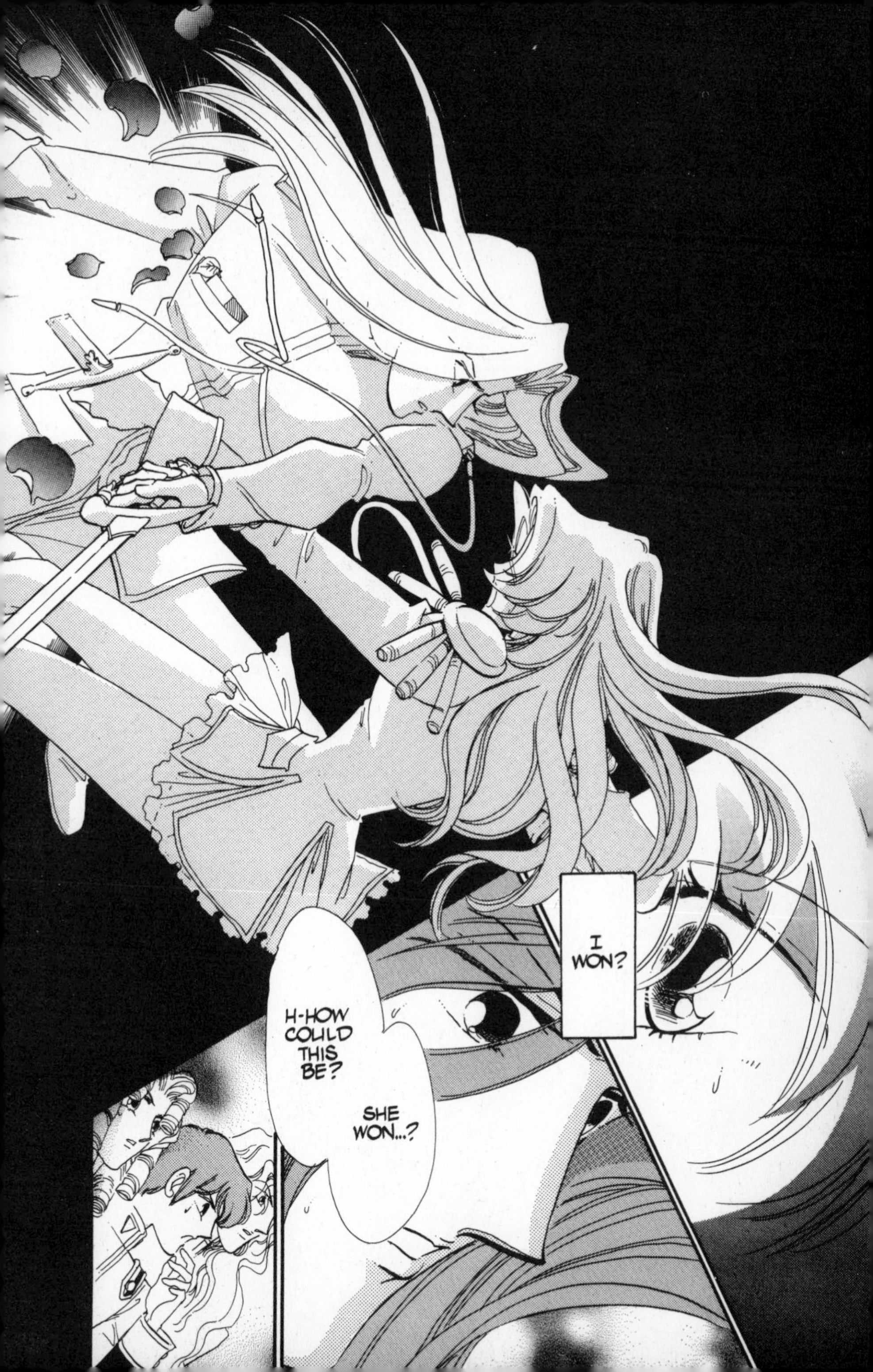
I WON?
H-HOW COULD THIS BE?
SHE WON...?

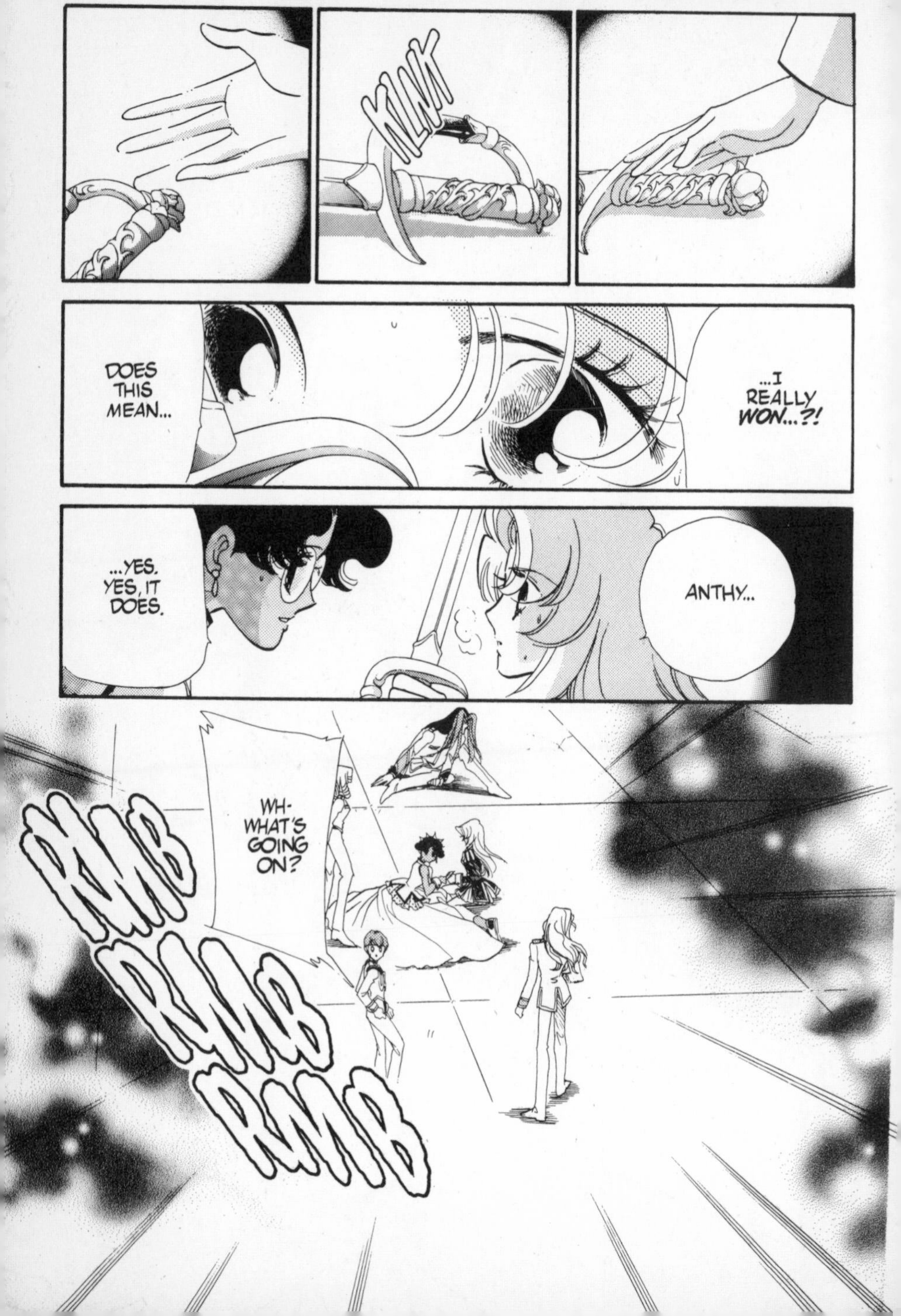
KLINK
DOES THIS MEAN...
...I REALLY WON...?!
...YES. YES, IT DOES.
ANTHY...
RMB RMB RMB
WH-WHAT'S GOING ON?

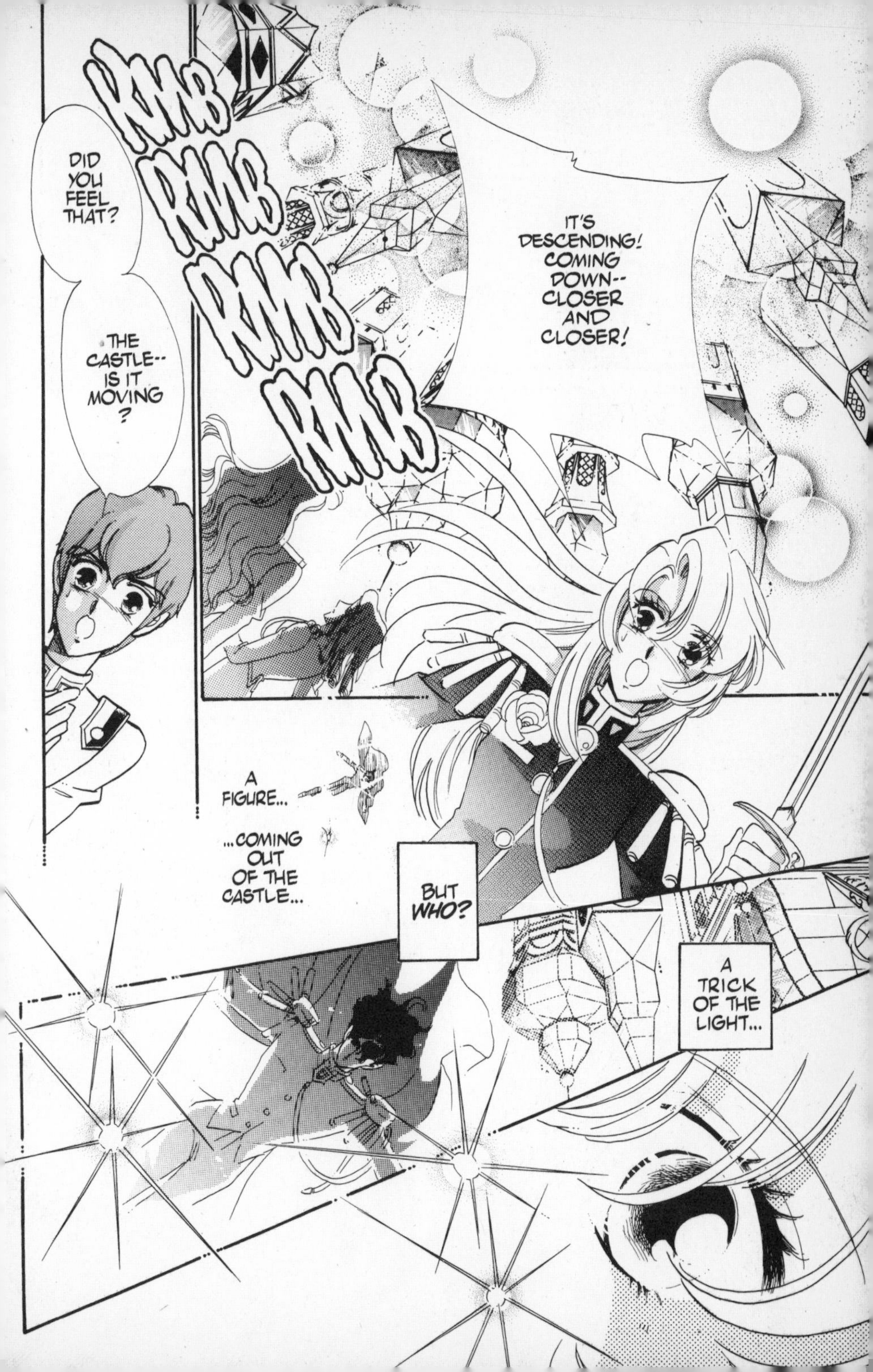
DID YOU FEEL THAT?
THE CASTLE-- IS IT MOVING ?
RMB
RMB
RMB
RMB
RMB
IT'S DESCENDING! COMING DOWN-- CLOSER AND CLOSER!
A FIGURE...
...COMING OUT OF THE CASTLE...
BUT WHO?
A TRICK OF THE LIGHT...

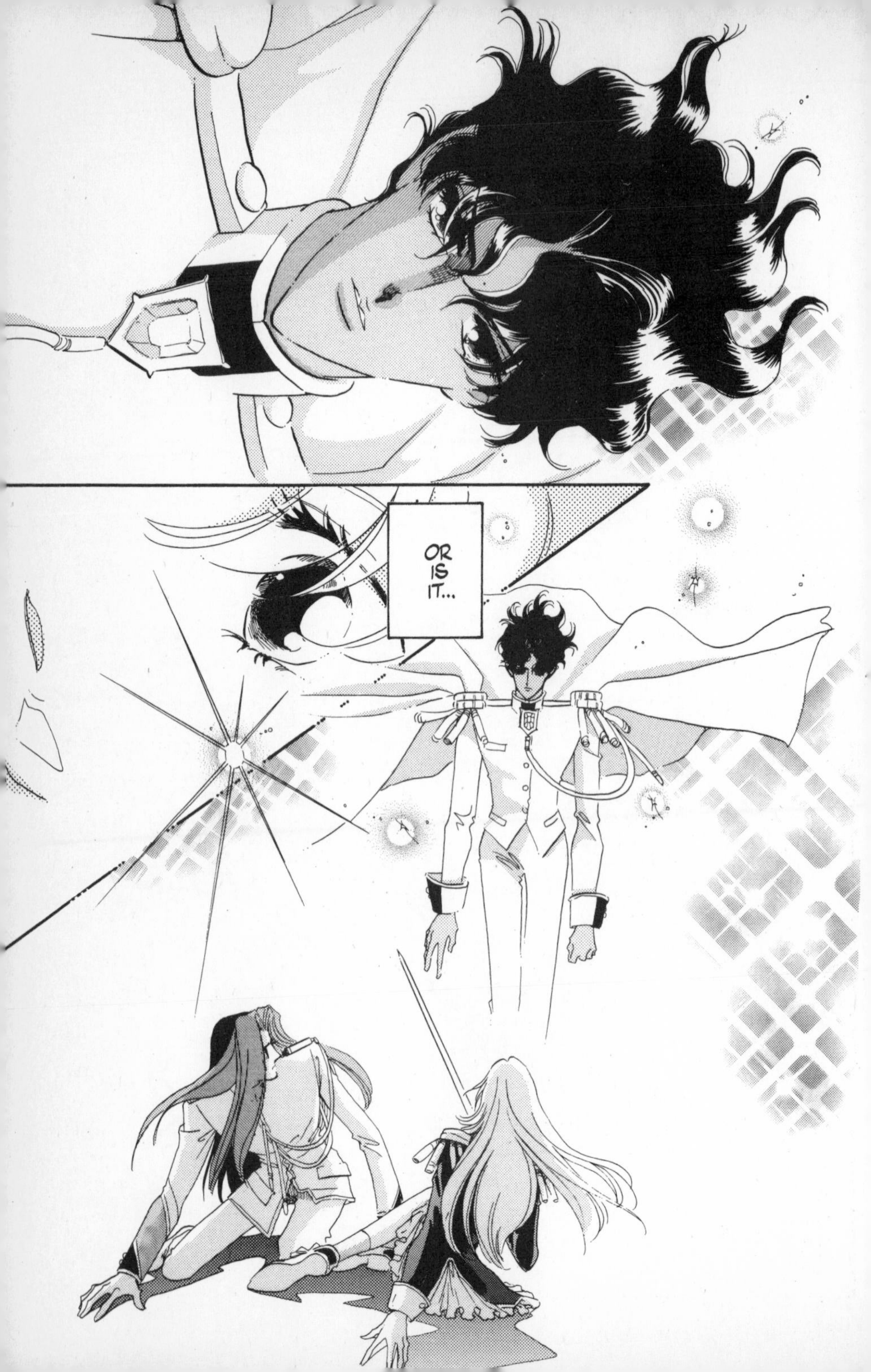
OR IS IT...

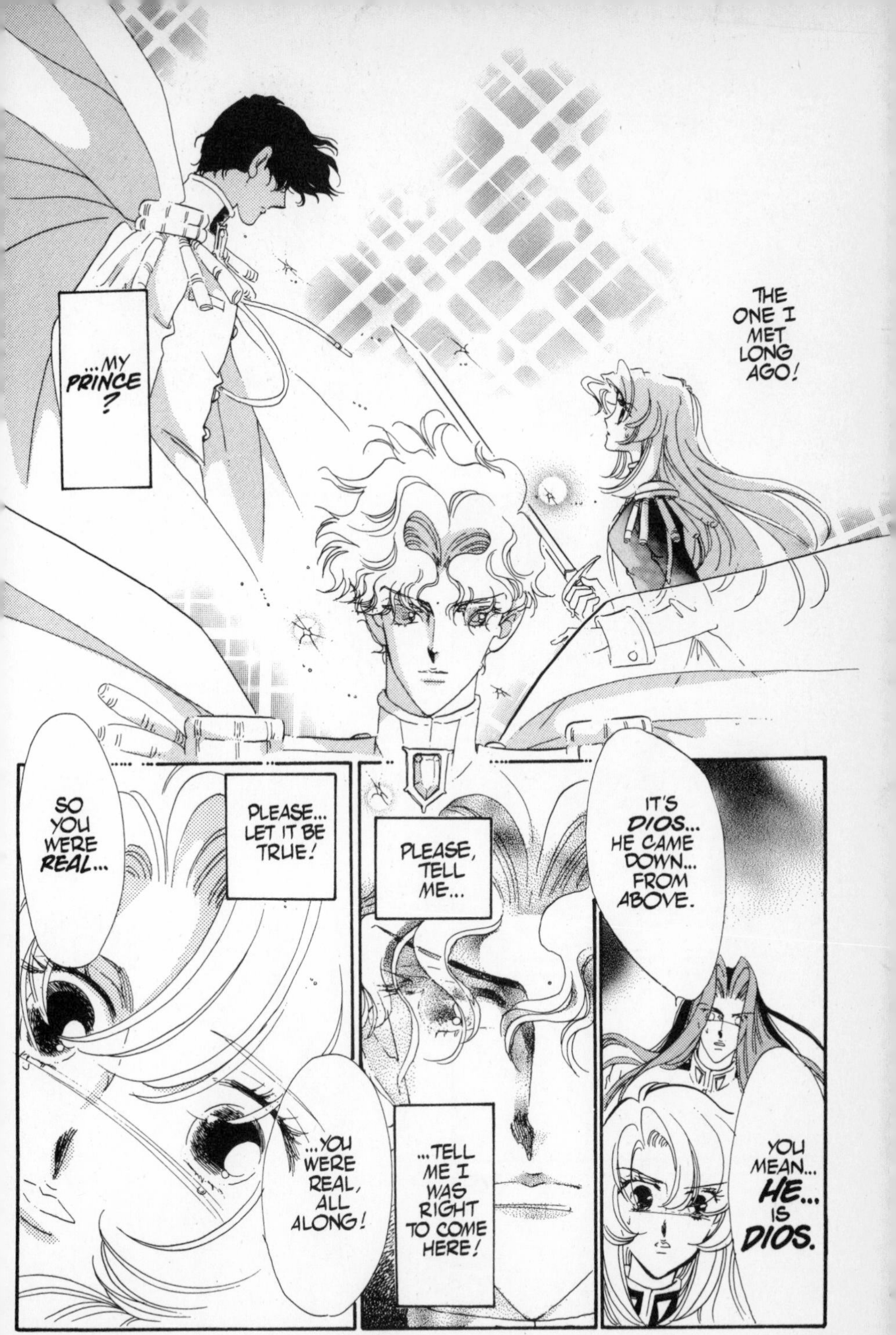

...MY PRINCE ?
THE ONE I MET LONG AGO!
SO YOU WERE REAL...
PLEASE... LET IT BE TRUE!
...YOU WERE REAL, ALL ALONG!
PLEASE, TELL ME...
...TELL ME I WAS RIGHT TO COME HERE!
IT'S DIOS... HE CAME DOWN... FROM ABOVE.
YOU MEAN... HE... IS DIOS.

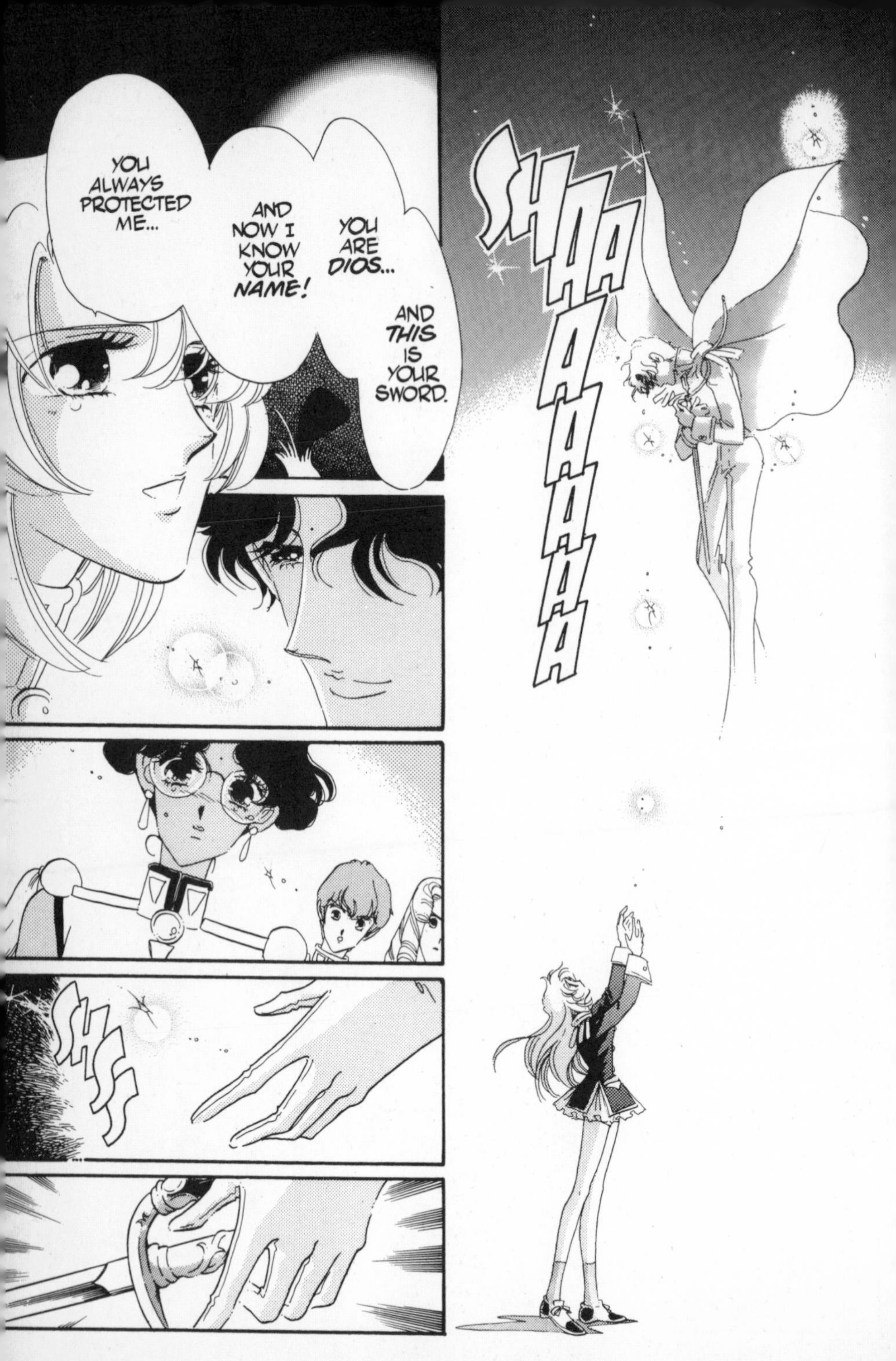
YOU ALWAYS PROTECTED ME...
AND NOW I KNOW YOUR NAME!
YOU ARE DIOS...
AND THIS IS YOUR SWORD.
SHAAAAAAAAAA
SHSS

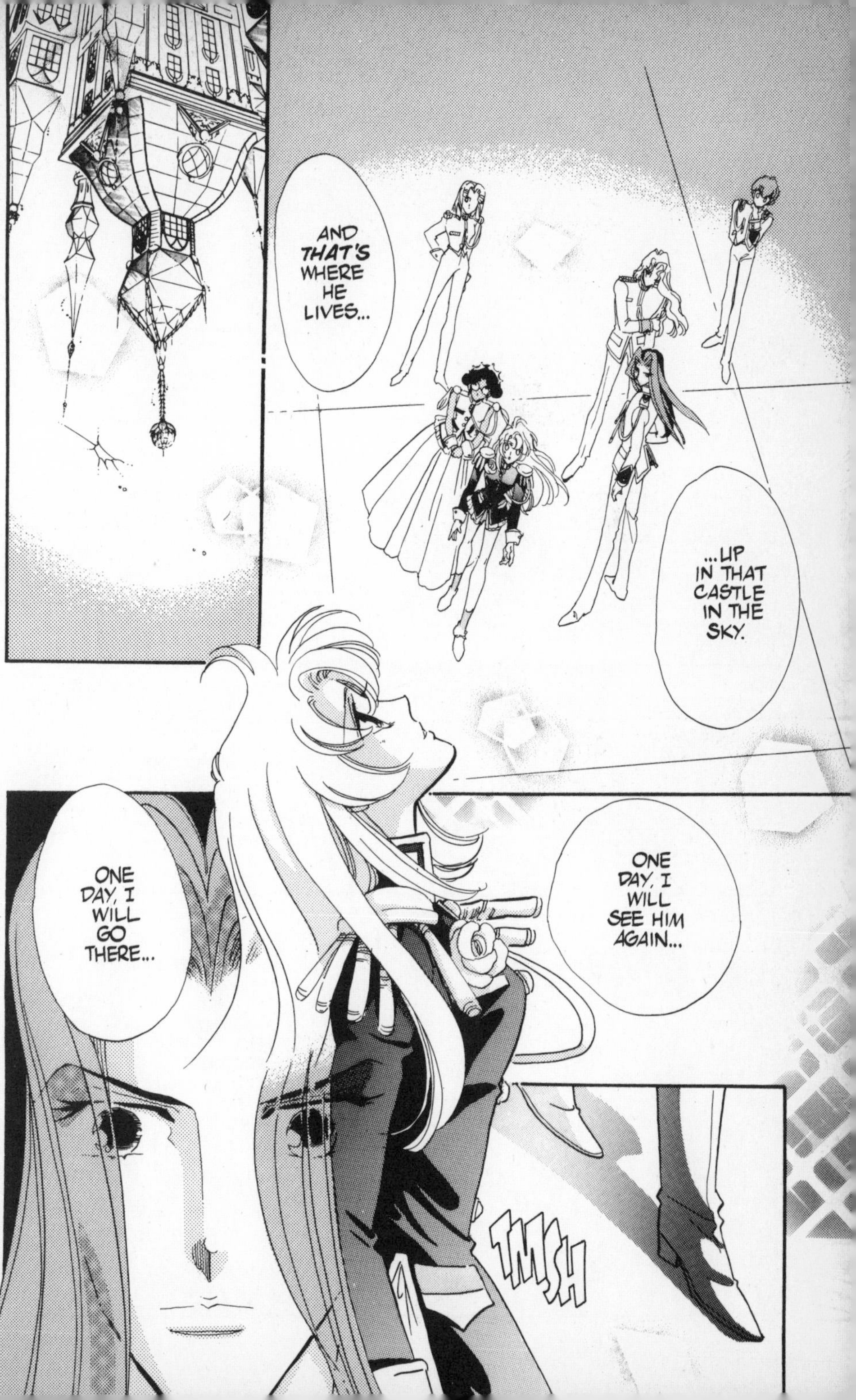
AND THAT'S WHERE HE LIVES...
...UP IN THAT CASTLE IN THE SKY.
ONE DAY, I WILL GO THERE...
ONE DAY, I WILL SEE HIM AGAIN...
TMSH

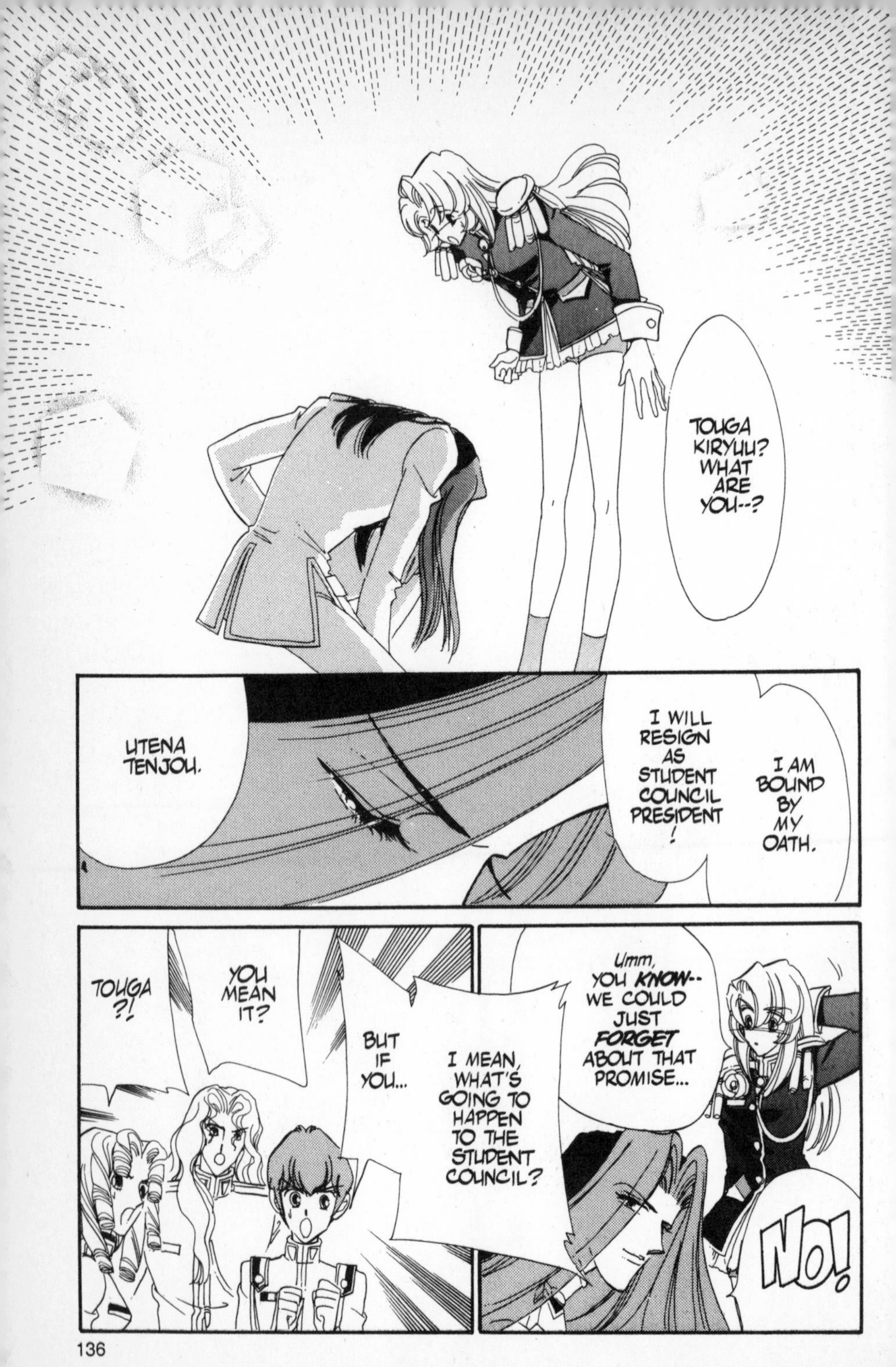
TOUGA KIRYUU? WHAT ARE YOU--?
UTENA TENJOU.
I WILL RESIGN AS STUDENT COUNCIL PRESIDENT!
I AM BOUND BY MY OATH.
TOUGA?!
YOU MEAN IT?
BUT IF YOU...
I MEAN, WHAT'S GOING TO HAPPEN TO THE STUDENT COUNCIL?
Umm, YOU KNOW-- WE COULD JUST FORGET ABOUT THAT PROMISE...
NO!

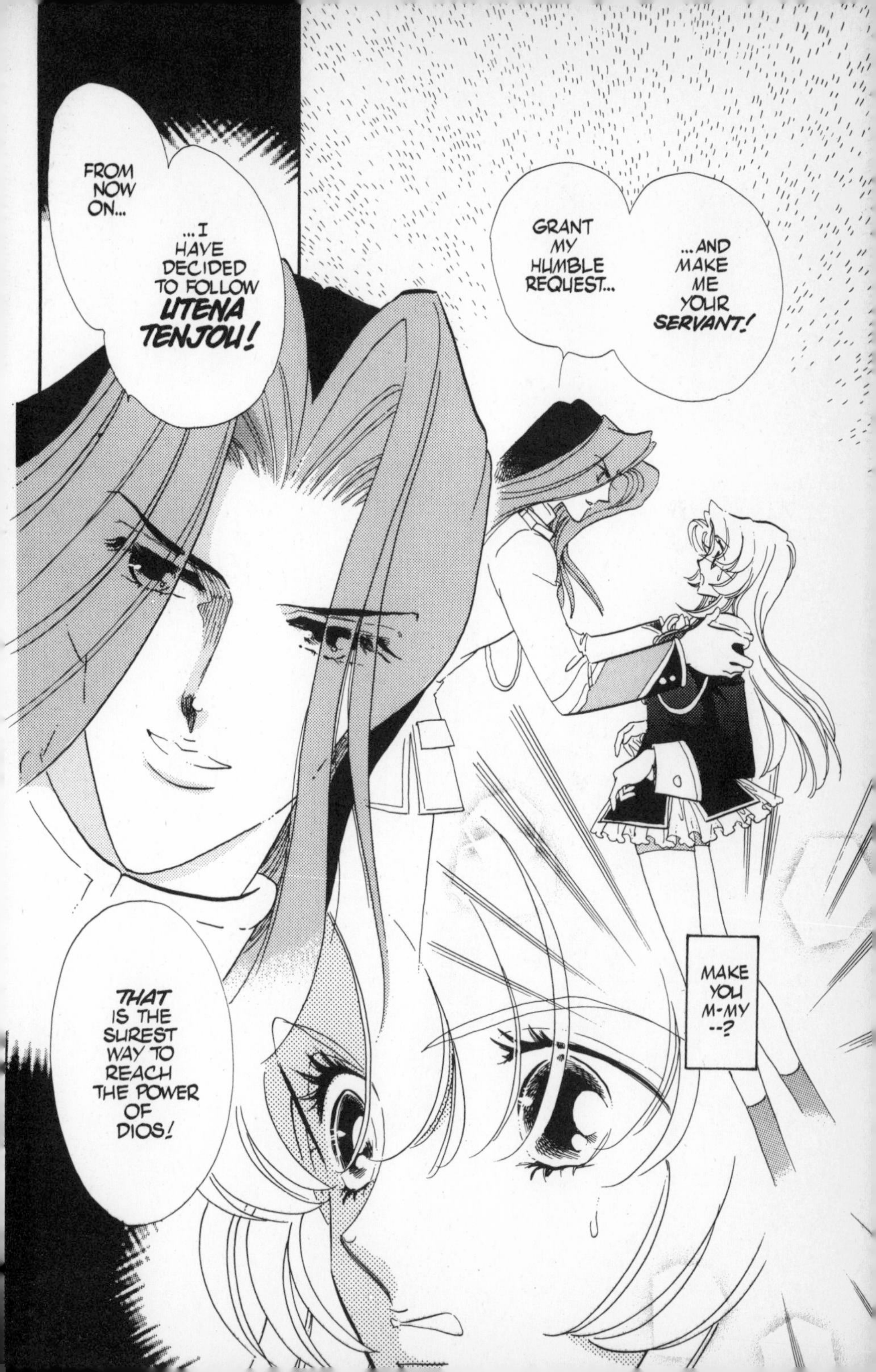
FROM NOW ON... ...I HAVE DECIDED TO FOLLOW UTENA TENJOU!
GRANT MY HUMBLE REQUEST... ...AND MAKE ME YOUR SERVANT!
THAT IS THE SUREST WAY TO REACH THE POWER OF DIOS!
MAKE YOU M-MY --?

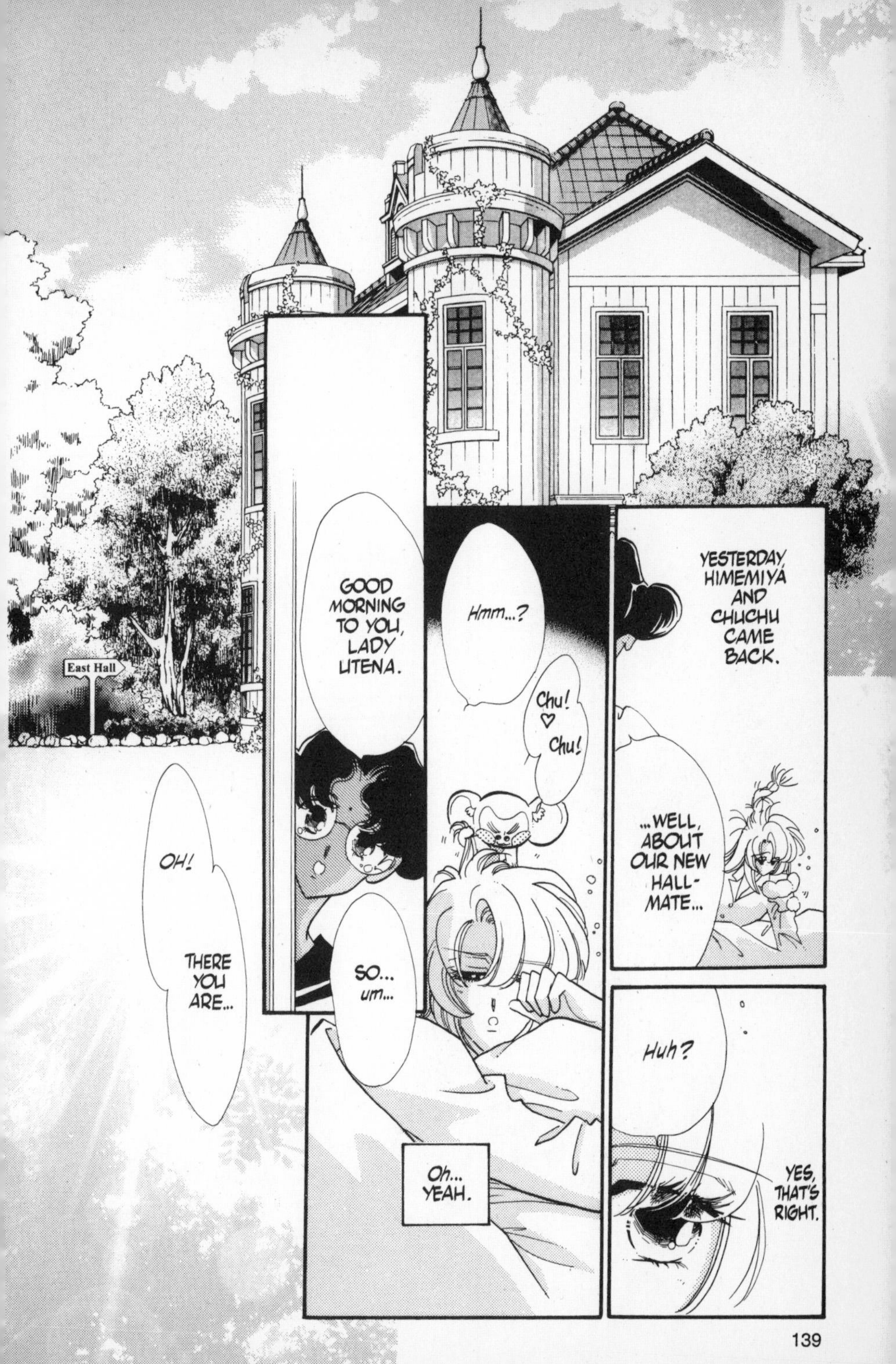
East Hall
OH!
THERE YOU ARE...
GOOD MORNING TO YOU, LADY UTENA.
Hmm...?
Chu! ♥ Chu!
SO... um...
Oh... YEAH.
YESTERDAY, HIMEMIYA AND CHUCHU CAME BACK.
...WELL, ABOUT OUR NEW HALL-MATE...
Huh?
YES, THAT'S RIGHT.

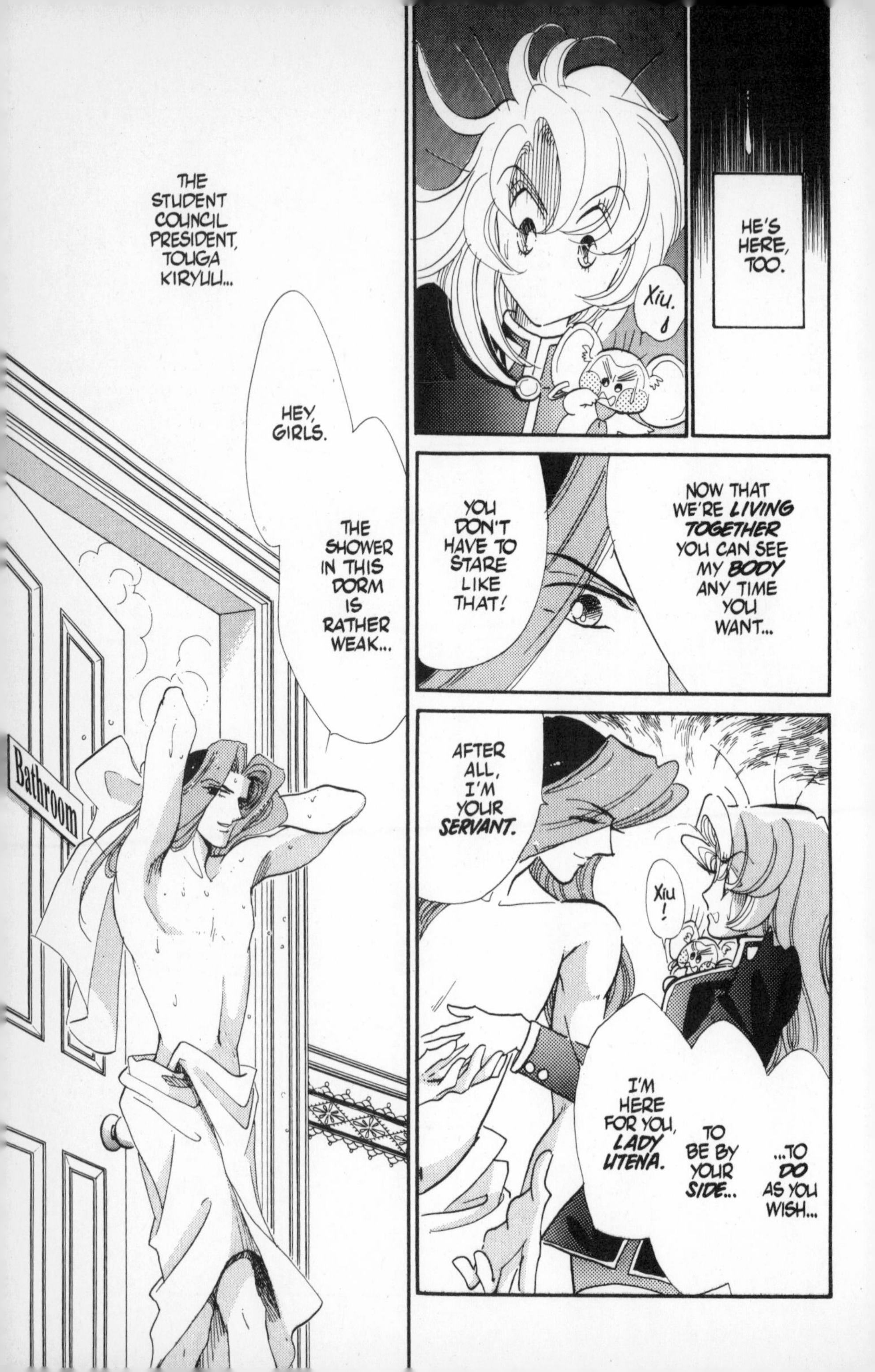
THE STUDENT COUNCIL PRESIDENT, TOUGA KIRYUU...
HEY, GIRLS.
THE SHOWER IN THIS DORM IS RATHER WEAK...
Bathroom
Xiu.
HE'S HERE, TOO.
YOU DON'T HAVE TO STARE LIKE THAT!
NOW THAT WE'RE **LIVING TOGETHER** YOU CAN SEE MY **BODY** ANY TIME YOU WANT...
AFTER ALL, I'M YOUR **SERVANT.**
Xiu!
I'M HERE FOR YOU, **LADY UTENA.**
TO BE BY YOUR **SIDE...**
...TO **DO** AS YOU WISH...

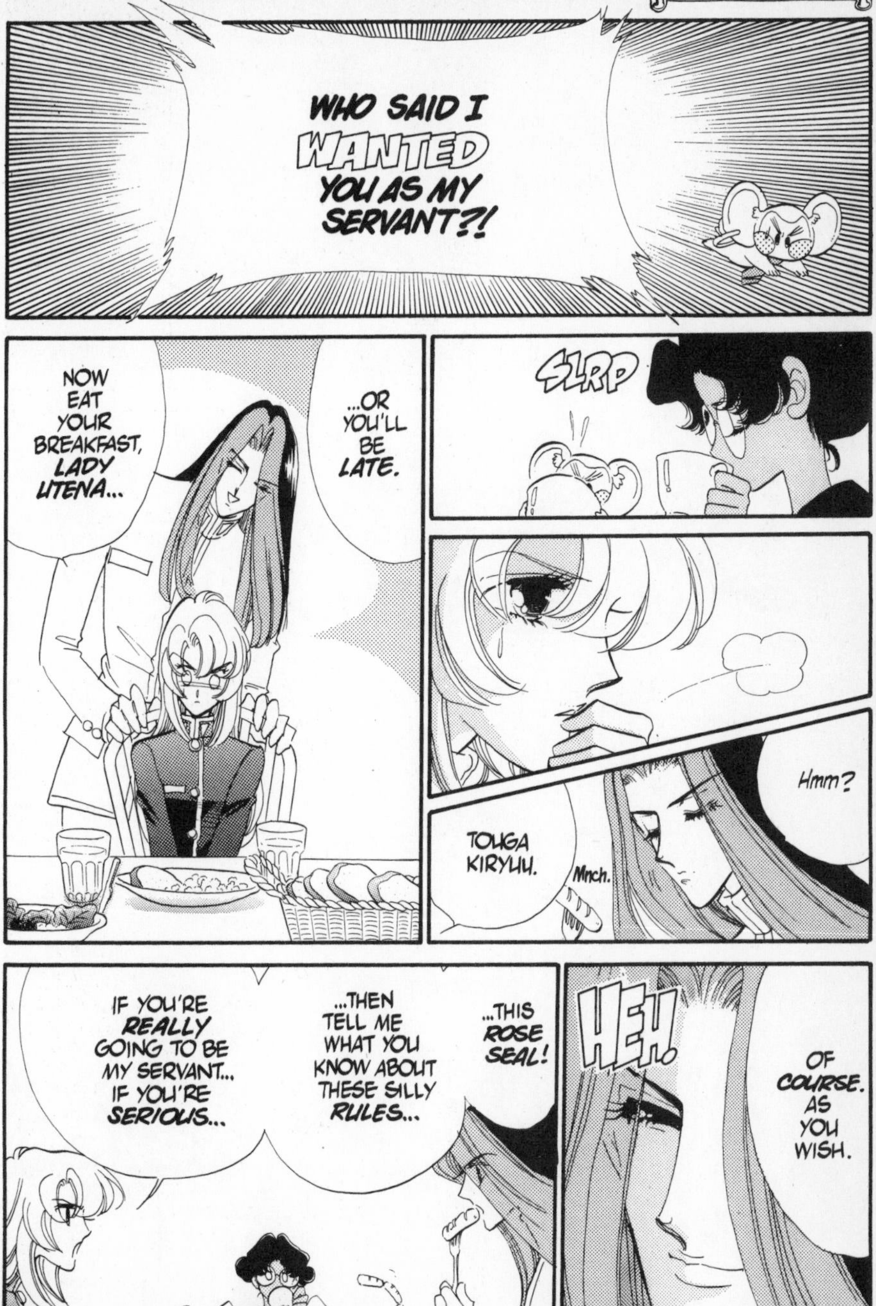
WHO SAID I WANTED YOU AS MY SERVANT?!
NOW EAT YOUR BREAKFAST, LADY UTENA...
...OR YOU'LL BE LATE.
SLRP
Hmm?
TOUGA KIRYUU.
Mnch.
IF YOU'RE REALLY GOING TO BE MY SERVANT... IF YOU'RE SERIOUS...
...THEN TELL ME WHAT YOU KNOW ABOUT THESE SILLY RULES...
...THIS ROSE SEAL!
HEH.
OF COURSE. AS YOU WISH.

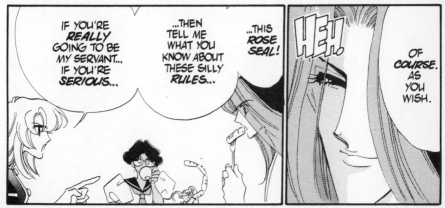

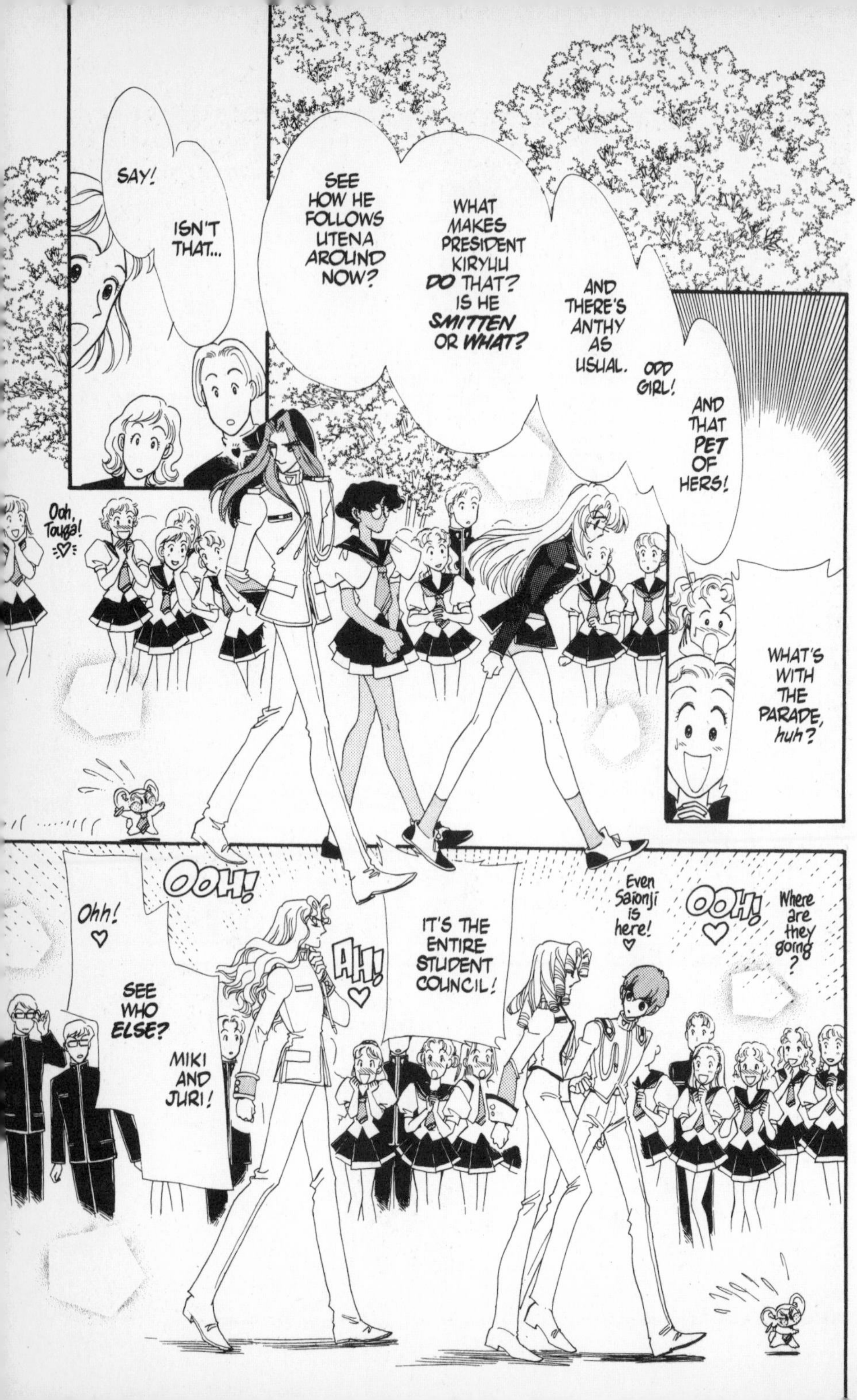
SAY!
ISN'T THAT...
SEE HOW HE FOLLOWS UTENA AROUND NOW?
WHAT MAKES PRESIDENT KIRYUU **DO** THAT? IS HE **SMITTEN** OR **WHAT?**
AND THERE'S ANTHY AS USUAL.
ODD GIRL!
AND THAT **PET** OF HERS!
Ooh, Touga!
WHAT'S WITH THE PARADE, huh?
OOH!
Ohh!
SEE WHO **ELSE?**
MIKI AND JURI!
AH!
IT'S THE ENTIRE STUDENT COUNCIL!
Even Saionji is here!
OOH!
Where are they going?

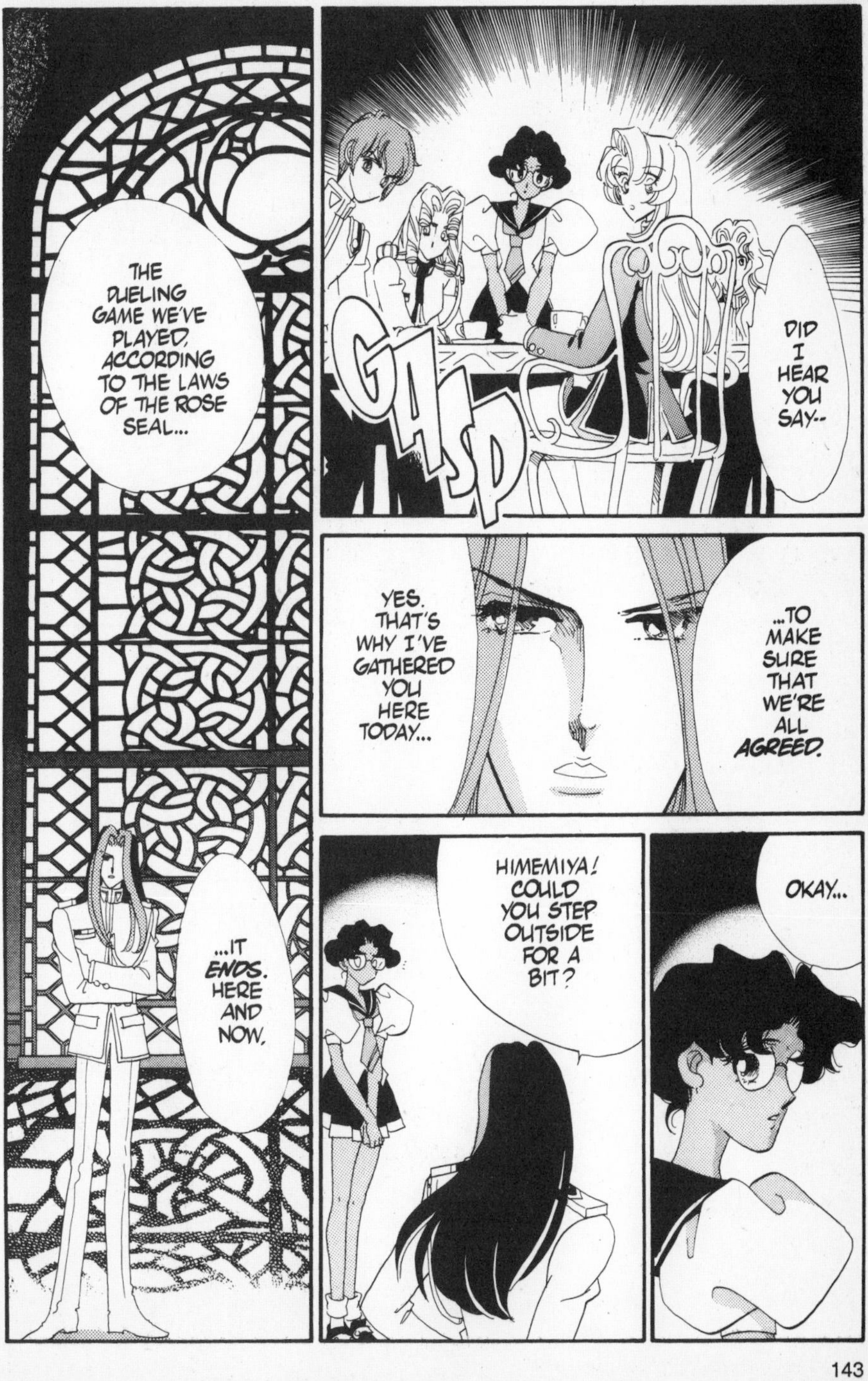
THE DUELING GAME WE'VE PLAYED, ACCORDING TO THE LAWS OF THE ROSE SEAL...
...IT ENDS. HERE AND NOW.
GASP
DID I HEAR YOU SAY--
YES. THAT'S WHY I'VE GATHERED YOU HERE TODAY...
...TO MAKE SURE THAT WE'RE ALL AGREED.
HIMEMIYA! COULD YOU STEP OUTSIDE FOR A BIT?
OKAY...

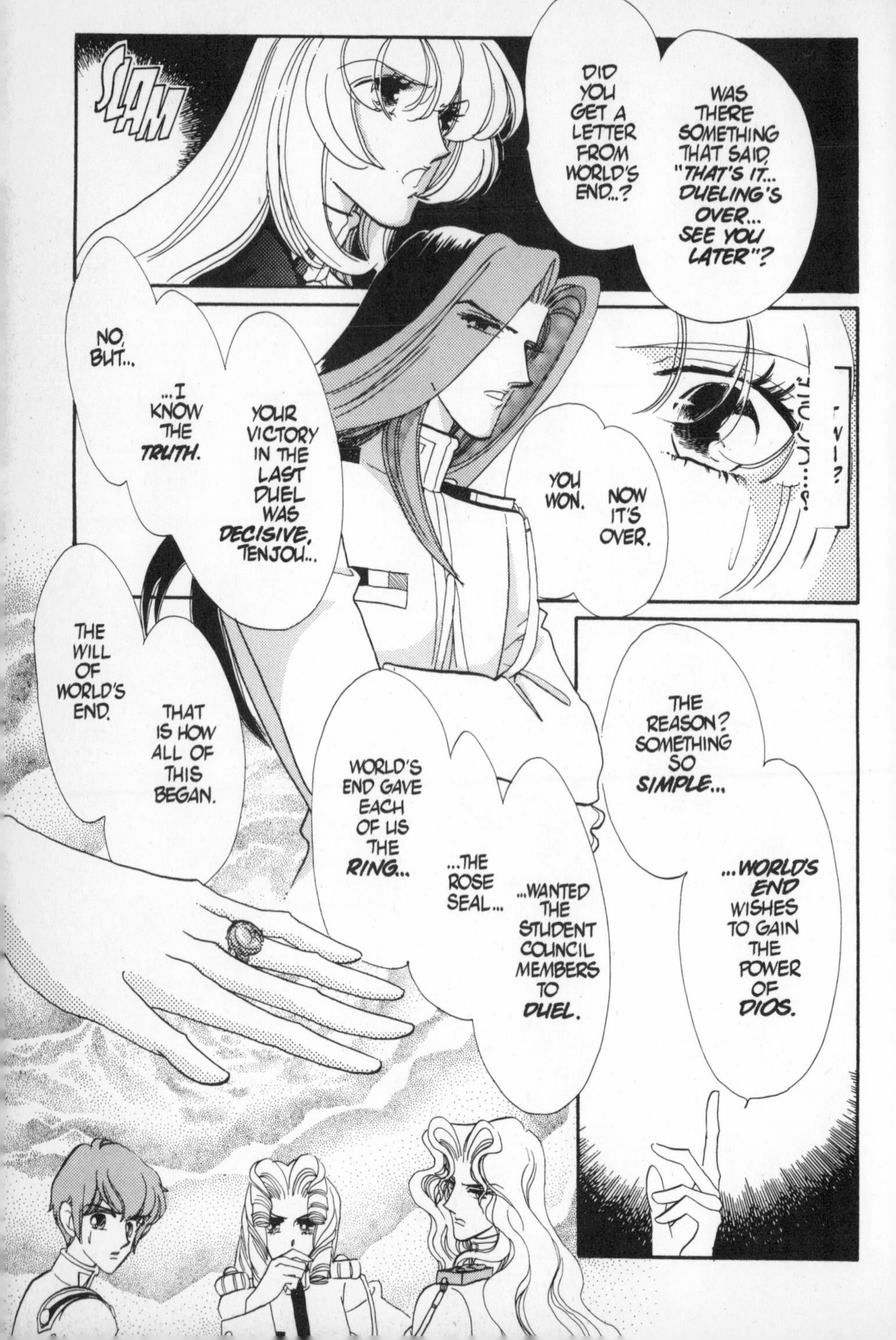

SLAM
DID YOU GET A LETTER FROM WORLD'S END..?
WAS THERE SOMETHING THAT SAID, "THAT'S IT... DUELING'S OVER... SEE YOU LATER"?
NO, BUT...
...I KNOW THE TRUTH.
YOUR VICTORY IN THE LAST DUEL WAS DECISIVE, TENJOU...
YOU WON.
NOW IT'S OVER.
THE WILL OF WORLD'S END.
THAT IS HOW ALL OF THIS BEGAN.
WORLD'S END GAVE EACH OF US THE RING...
...THE ROSE SEAL...
...WANTED THE STUDENT COUNCIL MEMBERS TO DUEL.
THE REASON? SOMETHING SO SIMPLE...
...WORLD'S END WISHES TO GAIN THE POWER OF DIOS.

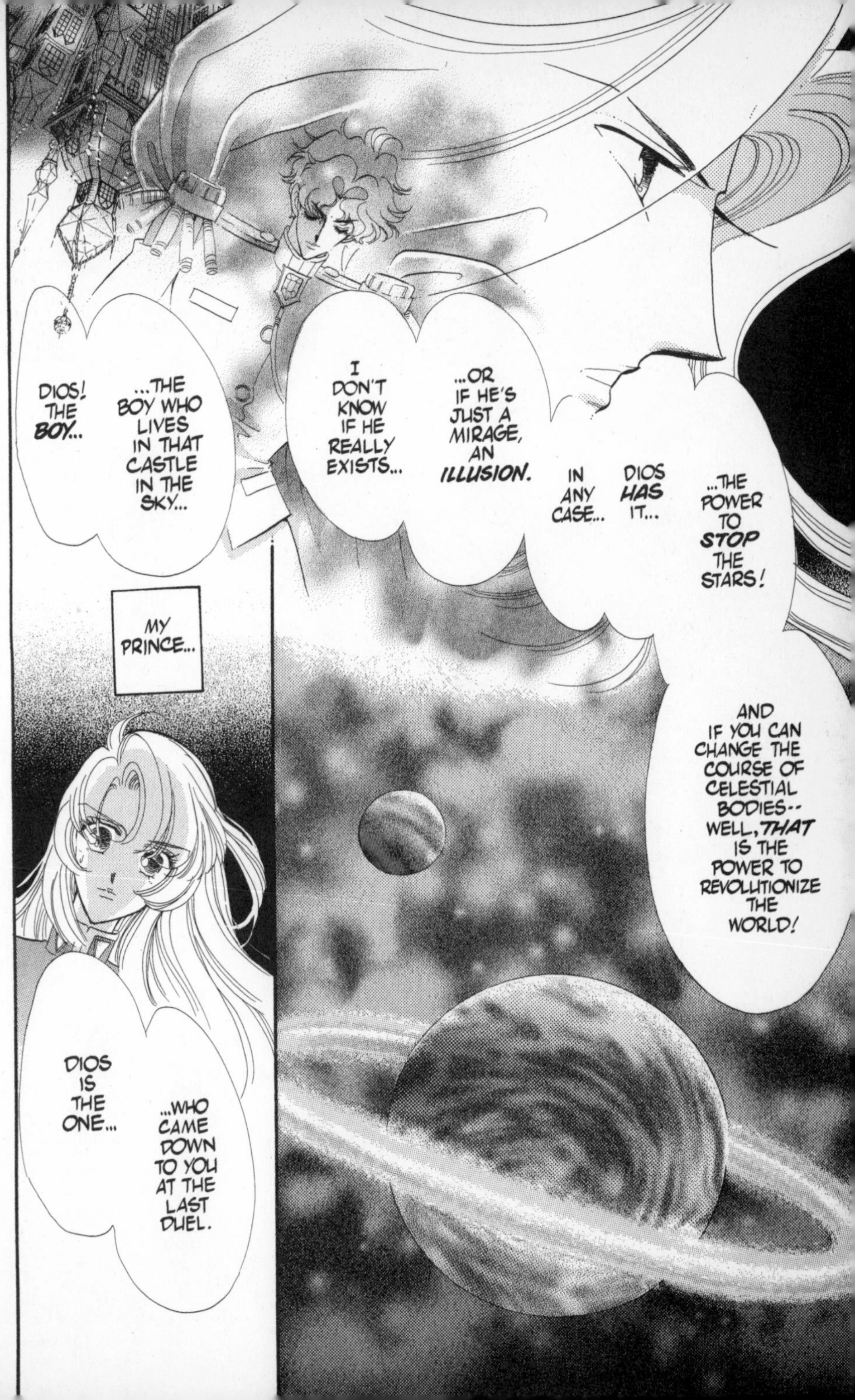
DIOS! THE *BOY*...
...THE BOY WHO LIVES IN THAT CASTLE IN THE SKY...
I DON'T KNOW IF HE REALLY EXISTS...
...OR IF HE'S JUST A MIRAGE, AN *ILLUSION*.
IN ANY CASE...
DIOS *HAS* IT...
...THE POWER TO *STOP* THE STARS!
MY PRINCE...
DIOS IS THE ONE...
...WHO CAME DOWN TO YOU AT THE LAST DUEL.
AND IF YOU CAN CHANGE THE COURSE OF CELESTIAL BODIES-- WELL, *THAT* IS THE POWER TO REVOLUTIONIZE THE WORLD!

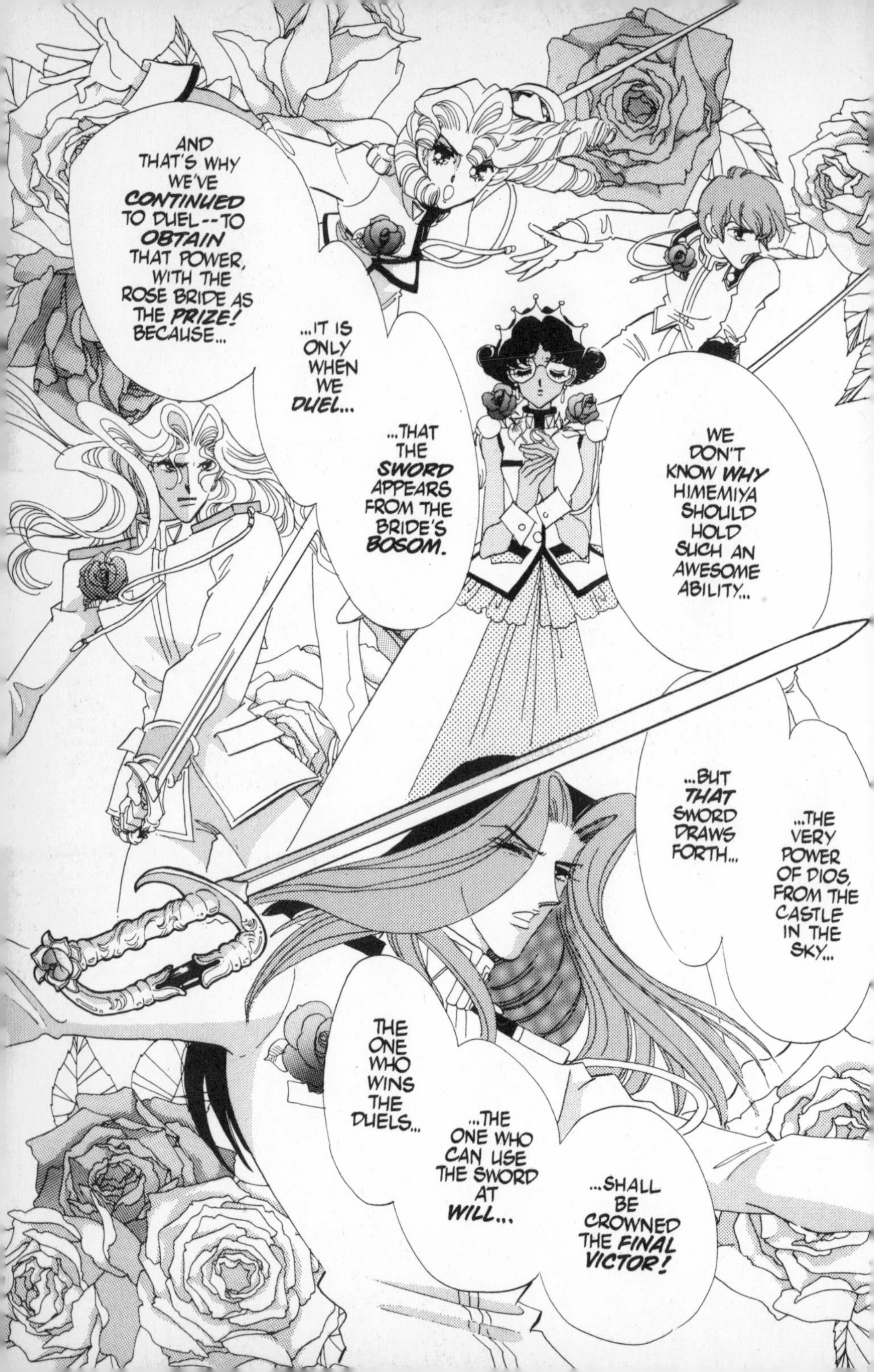
AND THAT'S WHY WE'VE CONTINUED TO DUEL--TO OBTAIN THAT POWER, WITH THE ROSE BRIDE AS THE PRIZE! BECAUSE...
...IT IS ONLY WHEN WE DUEL...
...THAT THE SWORD APPEARS FROM THE BRIDE'S BOSOM.
WE DON'T KNOW WHY HIMEMIYA SHOULD HOLD SUCH AN AWESOME ABILITY...
...BUT THAT SWORD DRAWS FORTH...
...THE VERY POWER OF DIOS, FROM THE CASTLE IN THE SKY...
THE ONE WHO WINS THE DUELS...
...THE ONE WHO CAN USE THE SWORD AT WILL...
...SHALL BE CROWNED THE FINAL VICTOR!

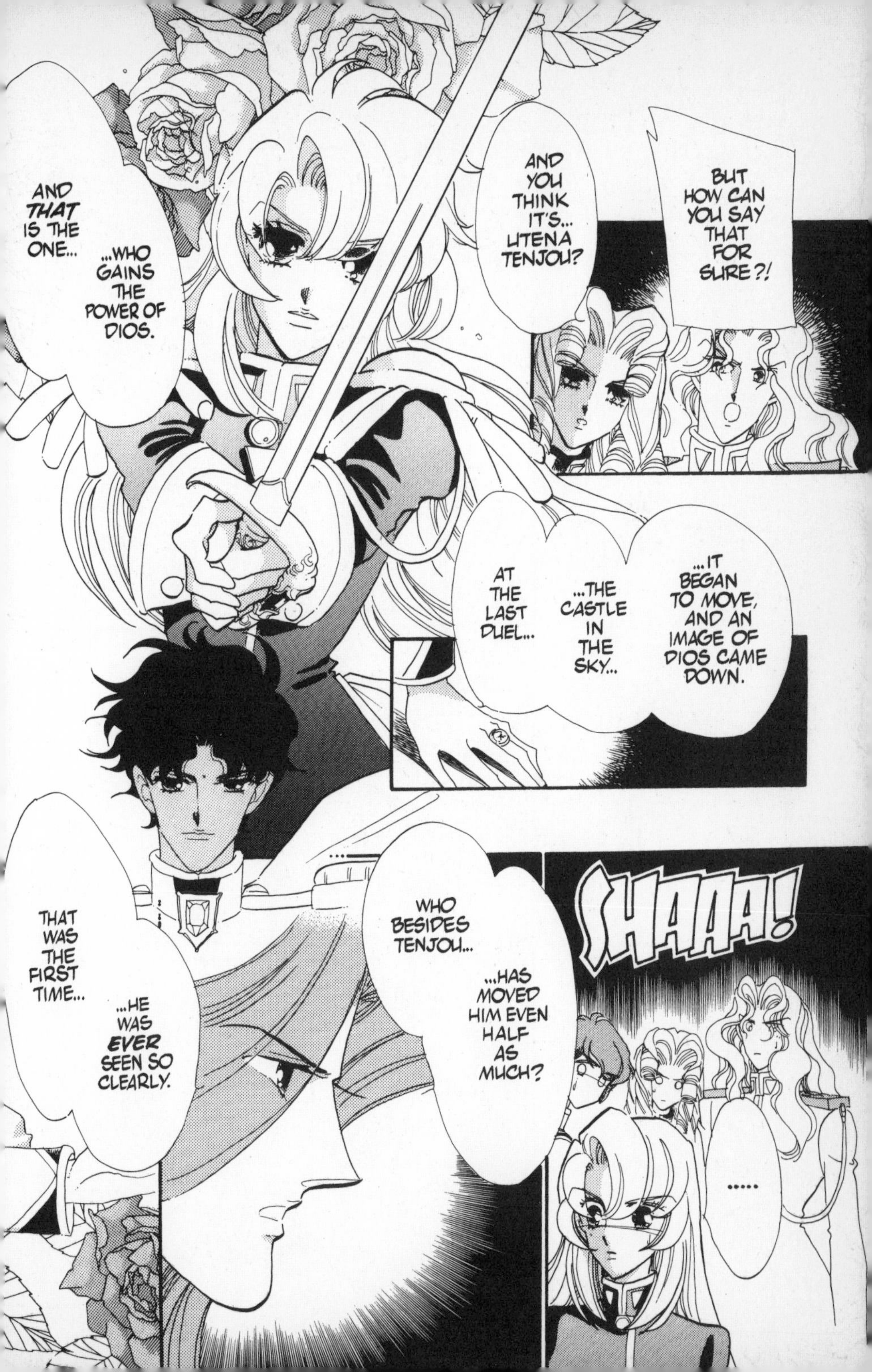
AND *THAT* IS THE ONE...
...WHO GAINS THE POWER OF DIOS.
AND YOU THINK IT'S... UTENA TENJOU?
BUT HOW CAN YOU SAY THAT FOR SURE?!
AT THE LAST DUEL...
...THE CASTLE IN THE SKY...
...IT BEGAN TO MOVE, AND AN IMAGE OF DIOS CAME DOWN.
THAT WAS THE FIRST TIME...
...HE WAS *EVER* SEEN SO CLEARLY.
WHO BESIDES TENJOU...
...HAS MOVED HIM EVEN HALF AS MUCH?
SHAAA!
.....

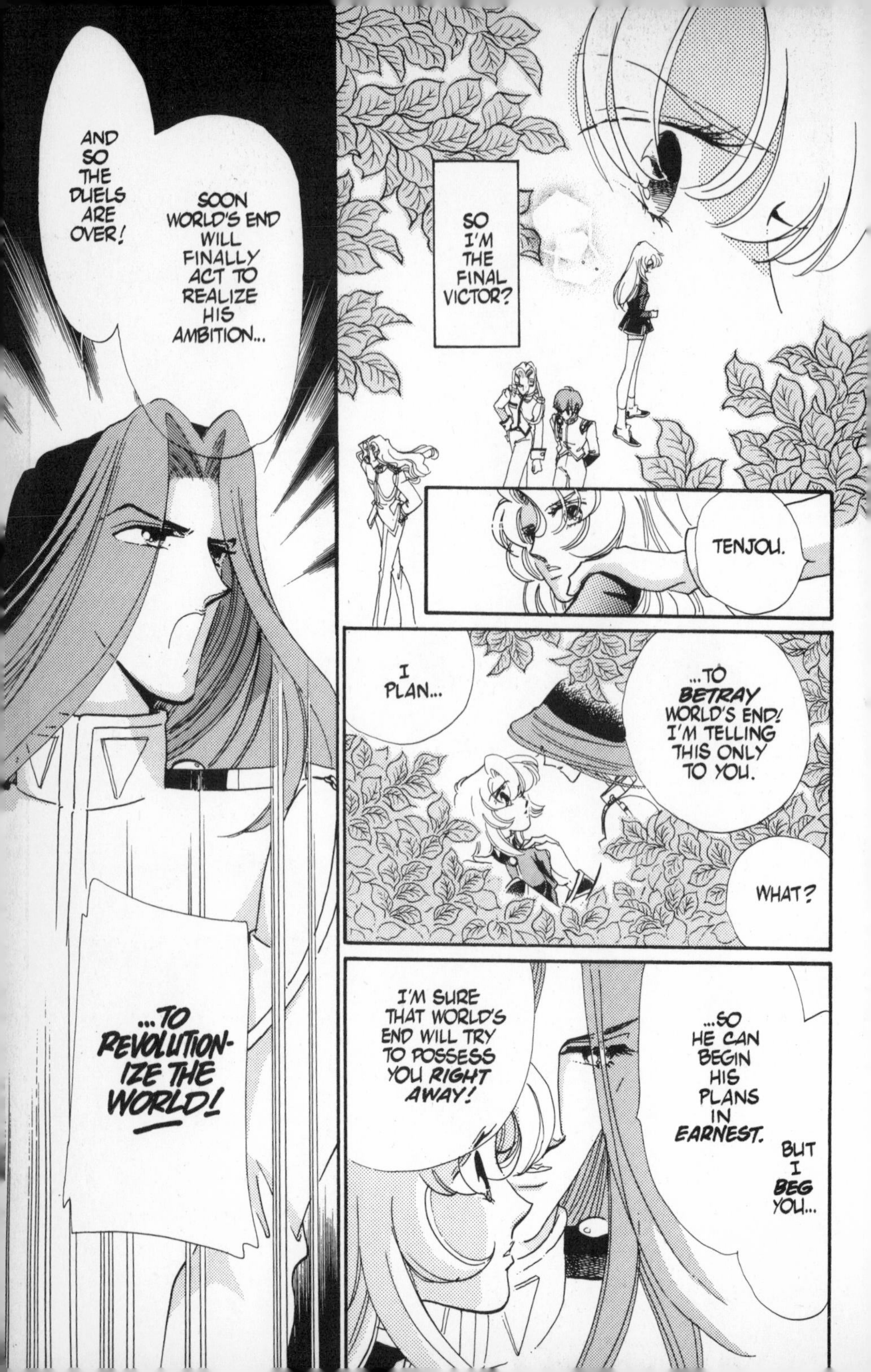
AND SO THE DUELS ARE OVER!
SOON WORLD'S END WILL FINALLY ACT TO REALIZE HIS AMBITION...
...TO REVOLUTION-IZE THE WORLD!
SO I'M THE FINAL VICTOR?
TENJOU.
I PLAN...
...TO BETRAY WORLD'S END! I'M TELLING THIS ONLY TO YOU.
WHAT?
I'M SURE THAT WORLD'S END WILL TRY TO POSSESS YOU RIGHT AWAY!
...SO HE CAN BEGIN HIS PLANS IN EARNEST.
BUT I BEG YOU...

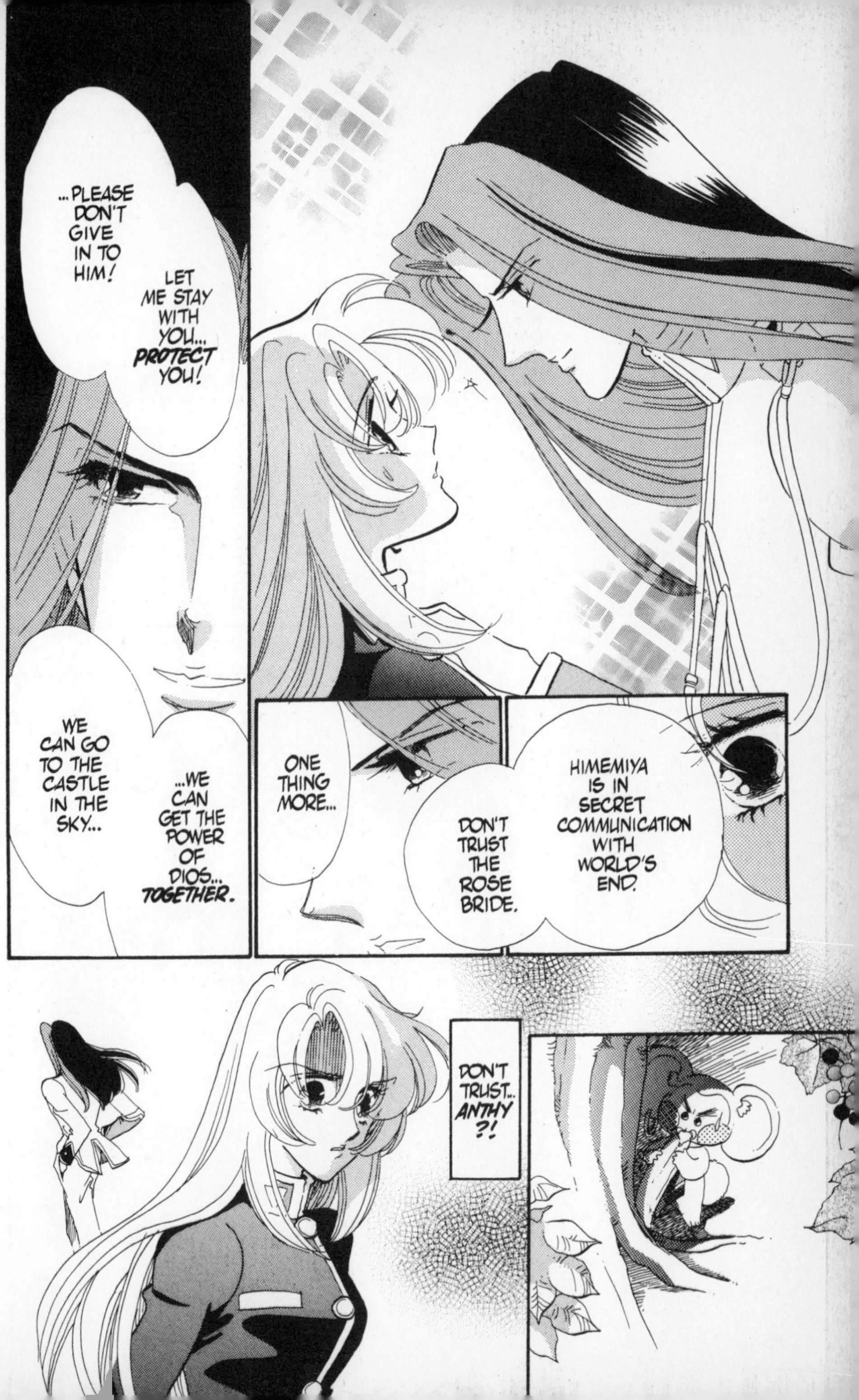
...PLEASE DON'T GIVE IN TO HIM!
LET ME STAY WITH YOU... PROTECT YOU!
WE CAN GO TO THE CASTLE IN THE SKY...
...WE CAN GET THE POWER OF DIOS... TOGETHER.
ONE THING MORE...
DON'T TRUST THE ROSE BRIDE.
HIMEMIYA IS IN SECRET COMMUNICATION WITH WORLD'S END.
DON'T TRUST.. ANTHY?!

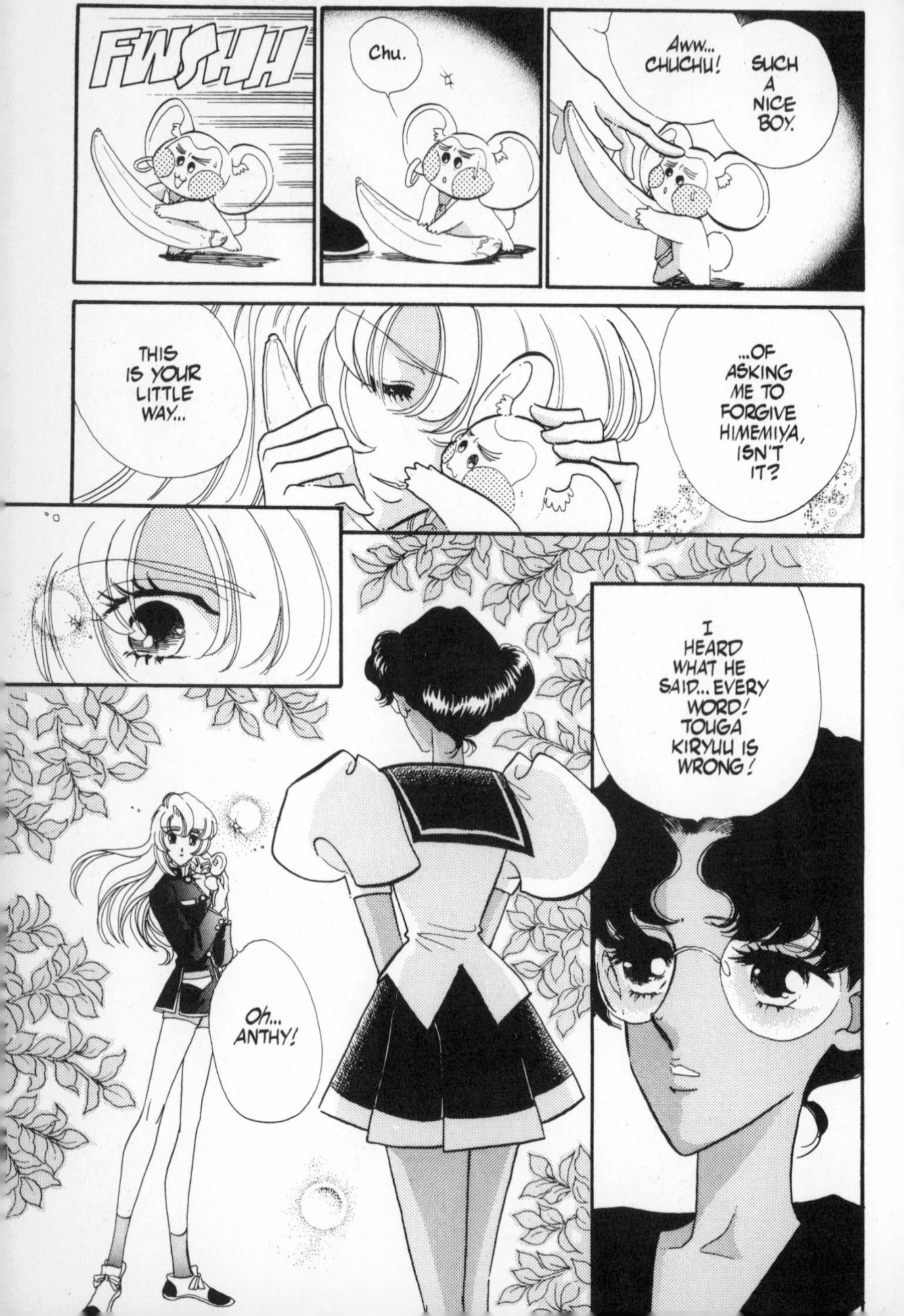
FWSHH
Chu.
Aww... CHUCHU!
SUCH A NICE BOY.
THIS IS YOUR LITTLE WAY...
...OF ASKING ME TO FORGIVE HIMEMIYA, ISN'T IT?
I HEARD WHAT HE SAID... EVERY WORD! TOUGA KIRYUU IS WRONG!
Oh... ANTHY!

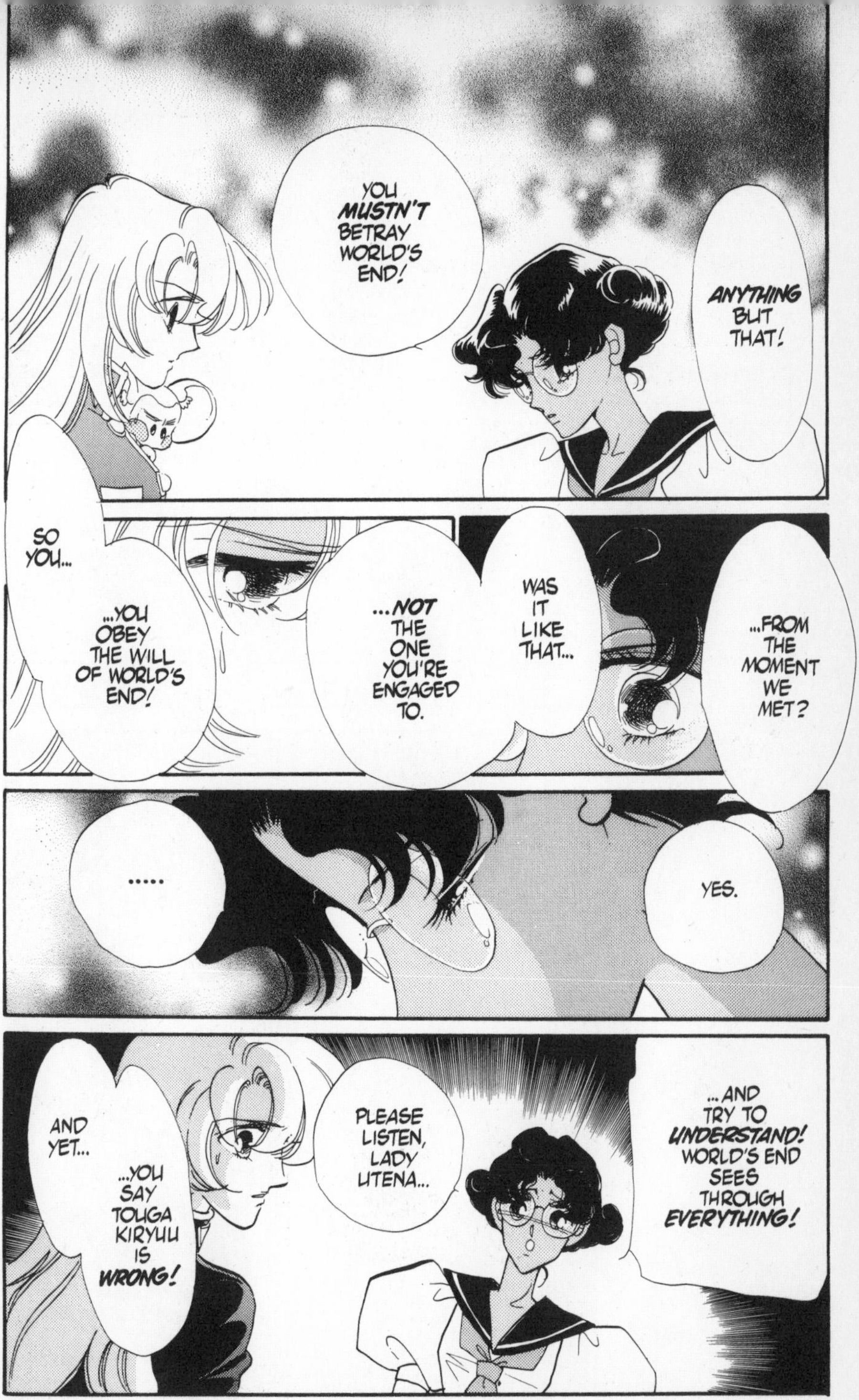

YOU MUSTN'T BETRAY WORLD'S END!
ANYTHING BUT THAT!
SO YOU...
...YOU OBEY THE WILL OF WORLD'S END!
...NOT THE ONE YOU'RE ENGAGED TO.
WAS IT LIKE THAT...
...FROM THE MOMENT WE MET?
.....
YES.
AND YET...
...YOU SAY TOUGA KIRYUU IS WRONG!
PLEASE LISTEN, LADY UTENA...
...AND TRY TO UNDERSTAND! WORLD'S END SEES THROUGH EVERYTHING!

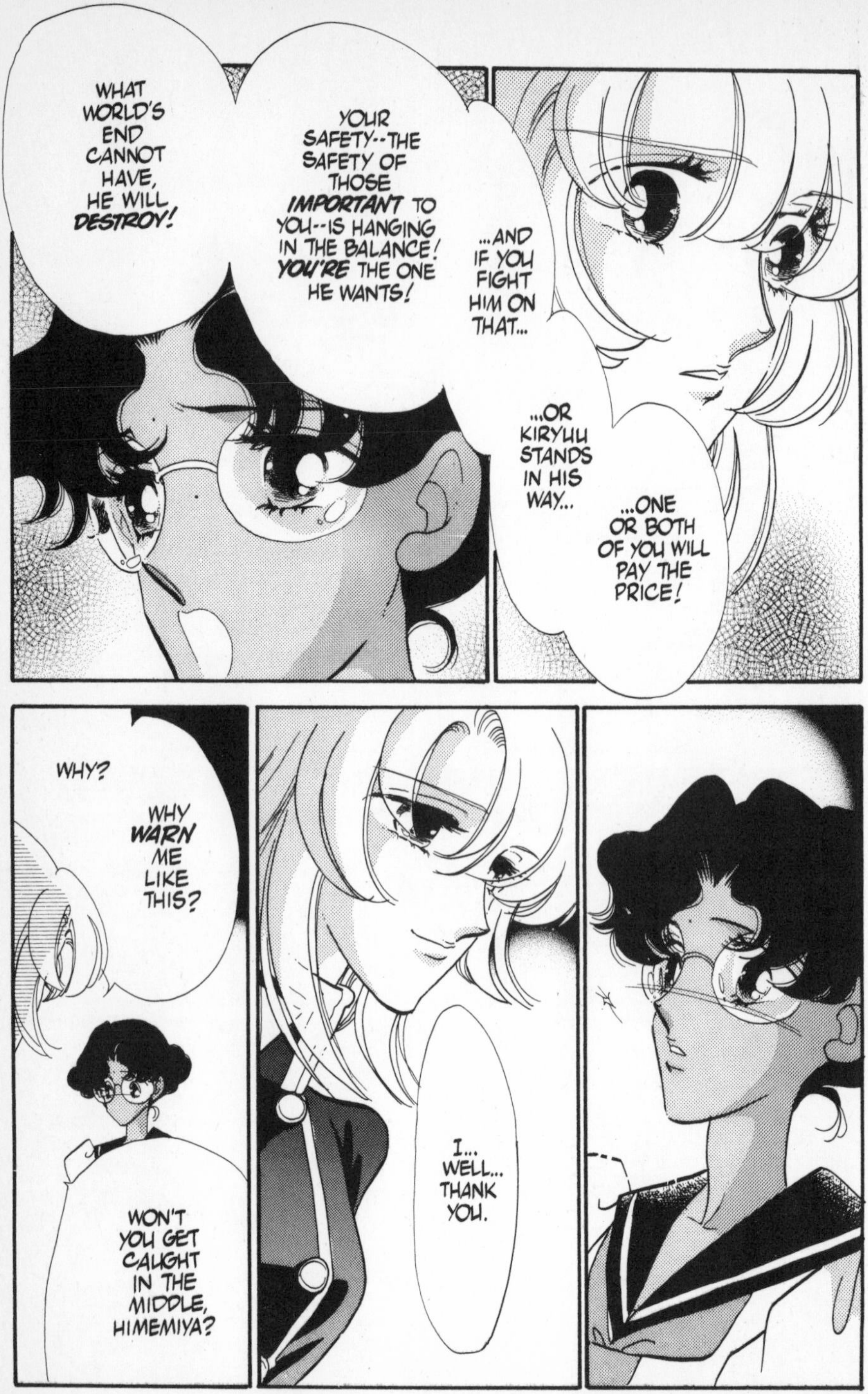
WHAT WORLD'S END CANNOT HAVE, HE WILL DESTROY!
YOUR SAFETY--THE SAFETY OF THOSE IMPORTANT TO YOU--IS HANGING IN THE BALANCE! YOU'RE THE ONE HE WANTS!
...AND IF YOU FIGHT HIM ON THAT...
...OR KIRYUU STANDS IN HIS WAY...
...ONE OR BOTH OF YOU WILL PAY THE PRICE!
WHY?
WHY WARN ME LIKE THIS?
WON'T YOU GET CAUGHT IN THE MIDDLE, HIMEMIYA?
I... WELL... THANK YOU.

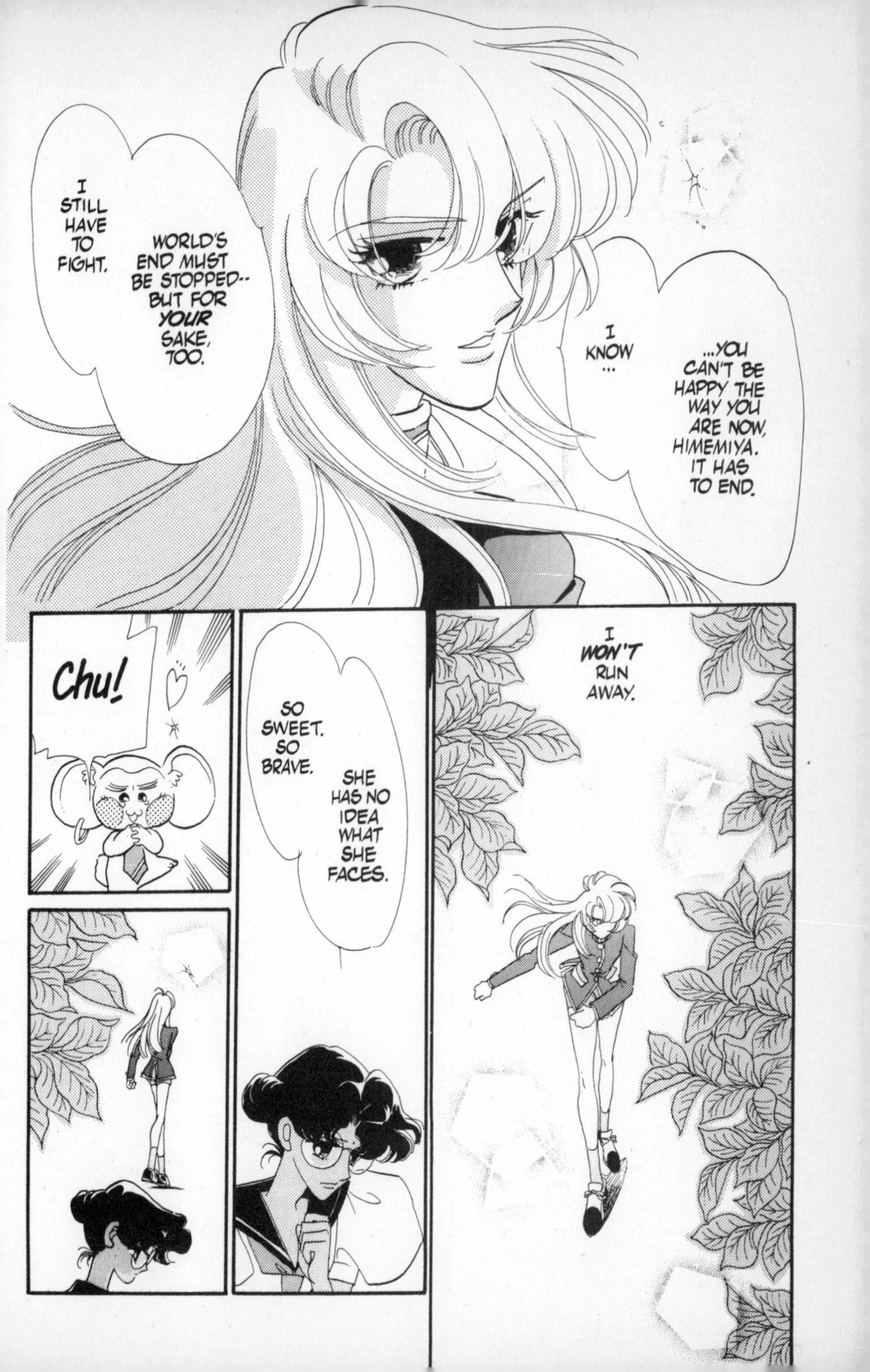
I STILL HAVE TO FIGHT.
WORLD'S END MUST BE STOPPED-- BUT FOR *YOUR* SAKE, TOO.
I KNOW ...
...YOU CAN'T BE HAPPY THE WAY YOU ARE NOW, HIMEMIYA. IT HAS TO END.
Chu!
SO SWEET. SO BRAVE.
SHE HAS NO IDEA WHAT SHE FACES.
I *WON'T* RUN AWAY.

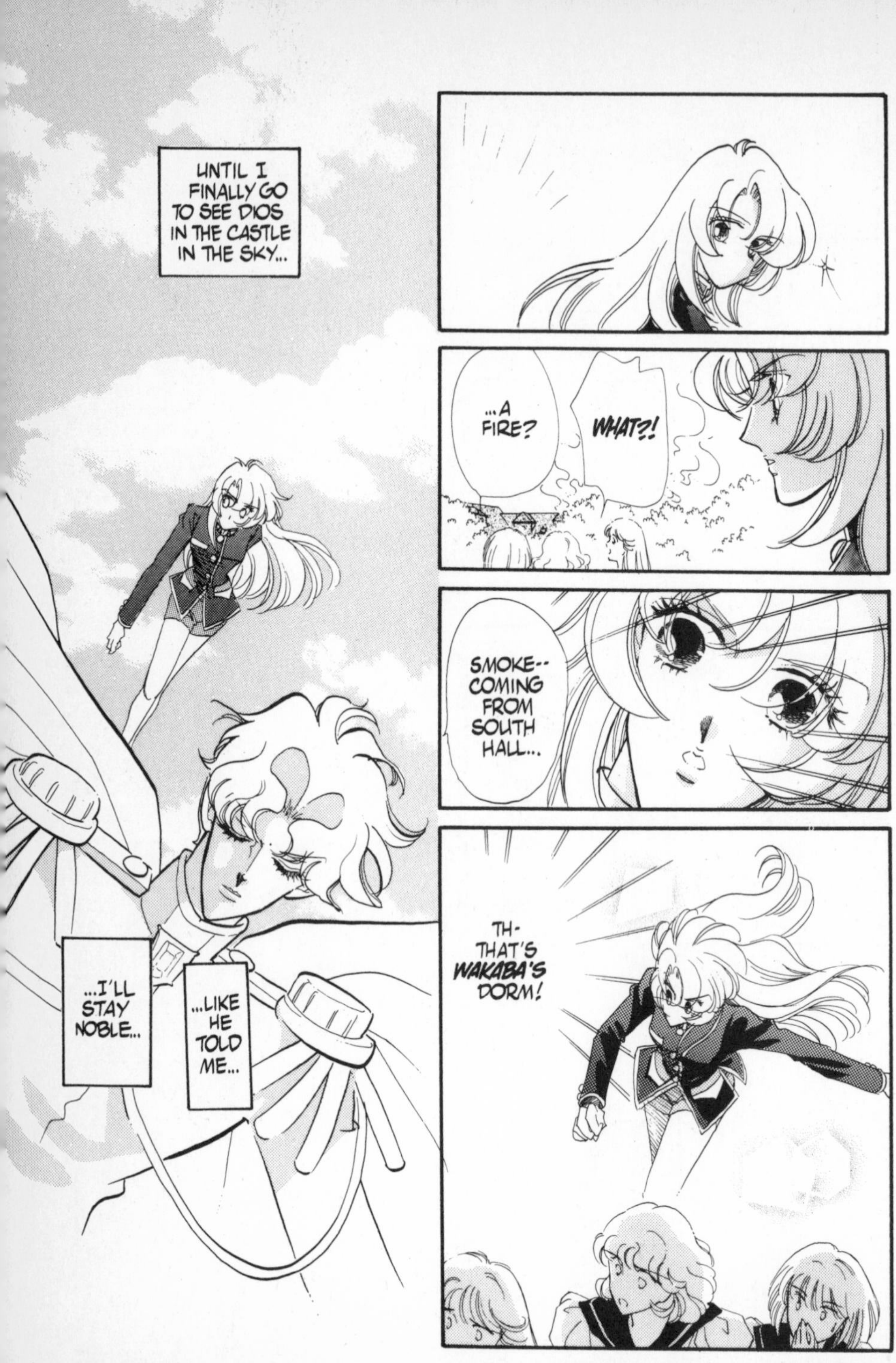
UNTIL I FINALLY GO TO SEE DIOS IN THE CASTLE IN THE SKY...
...I'LL STAY NOBLE...
...LIKE HE TOLD ME...
...A FIRE?
WHAT?!
SMOKE--COMING FROM SOUTH HALL...
TH-THAT'S WAKABA'S DORM!

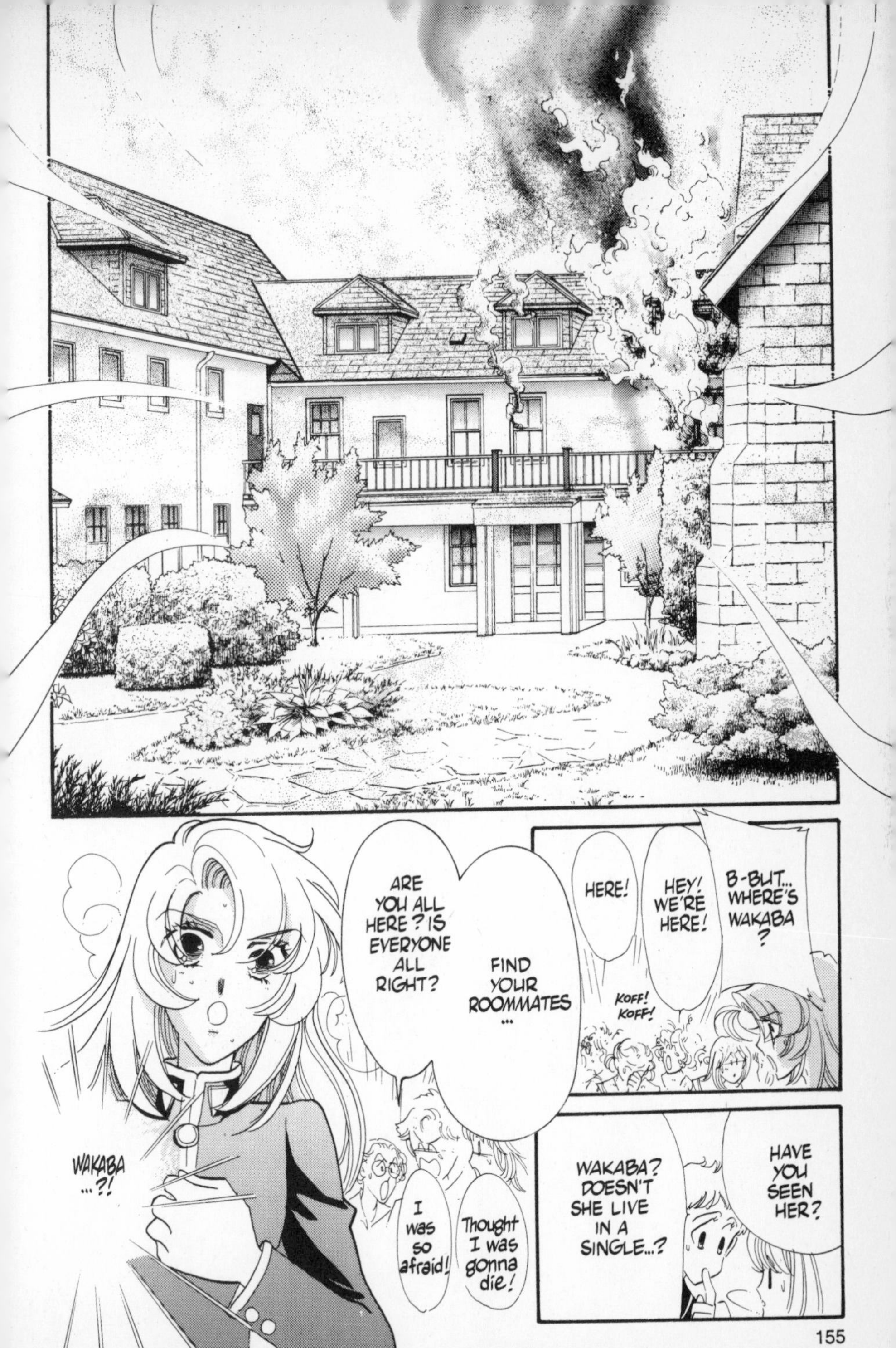
ARE YOU ALL HERE? IS EVERYONE ALL RIGHT?
FIND YOUR ROOMMATES...
WAKABA...?!
I was so afraid!
Thought I was gonna die!
HERE!
HEY! WE'RE HERE!
B-BUT... WHERE'S WAKABA?
KOFF! KOFF!
WAKABA? DOESN'T SHE LIVE IN A SINGLE...?
HAVE YOU SEEN HER?

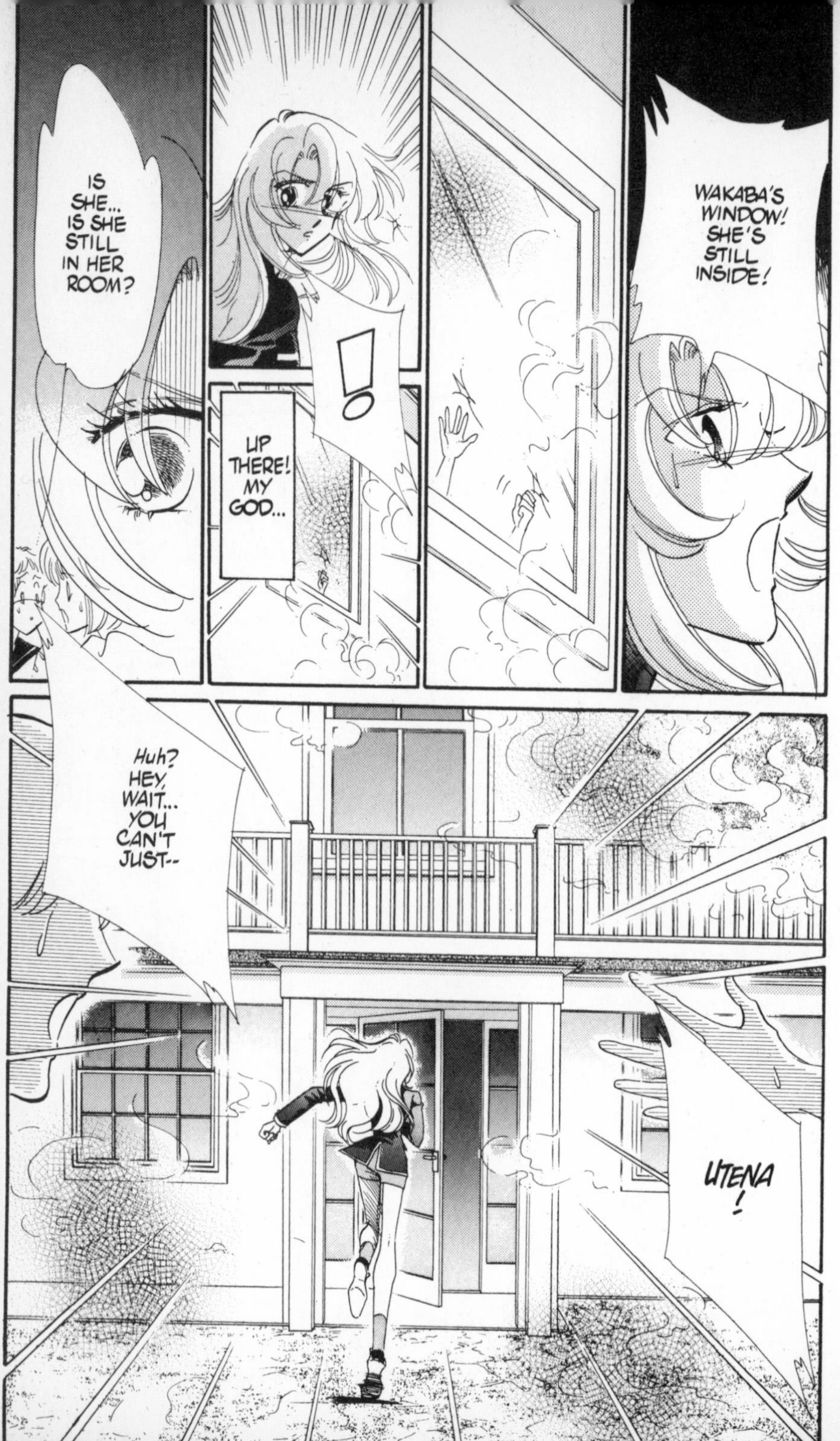
IS SHE... IS SHE STILL IN HER ROOM?
!
UP THERE! MY GOD...
WAKABA'S WINDOW! SHE'S STILL INSIDE!
Huh? HEY, WAIT... YOU CAN'T JUST--
UTENA!

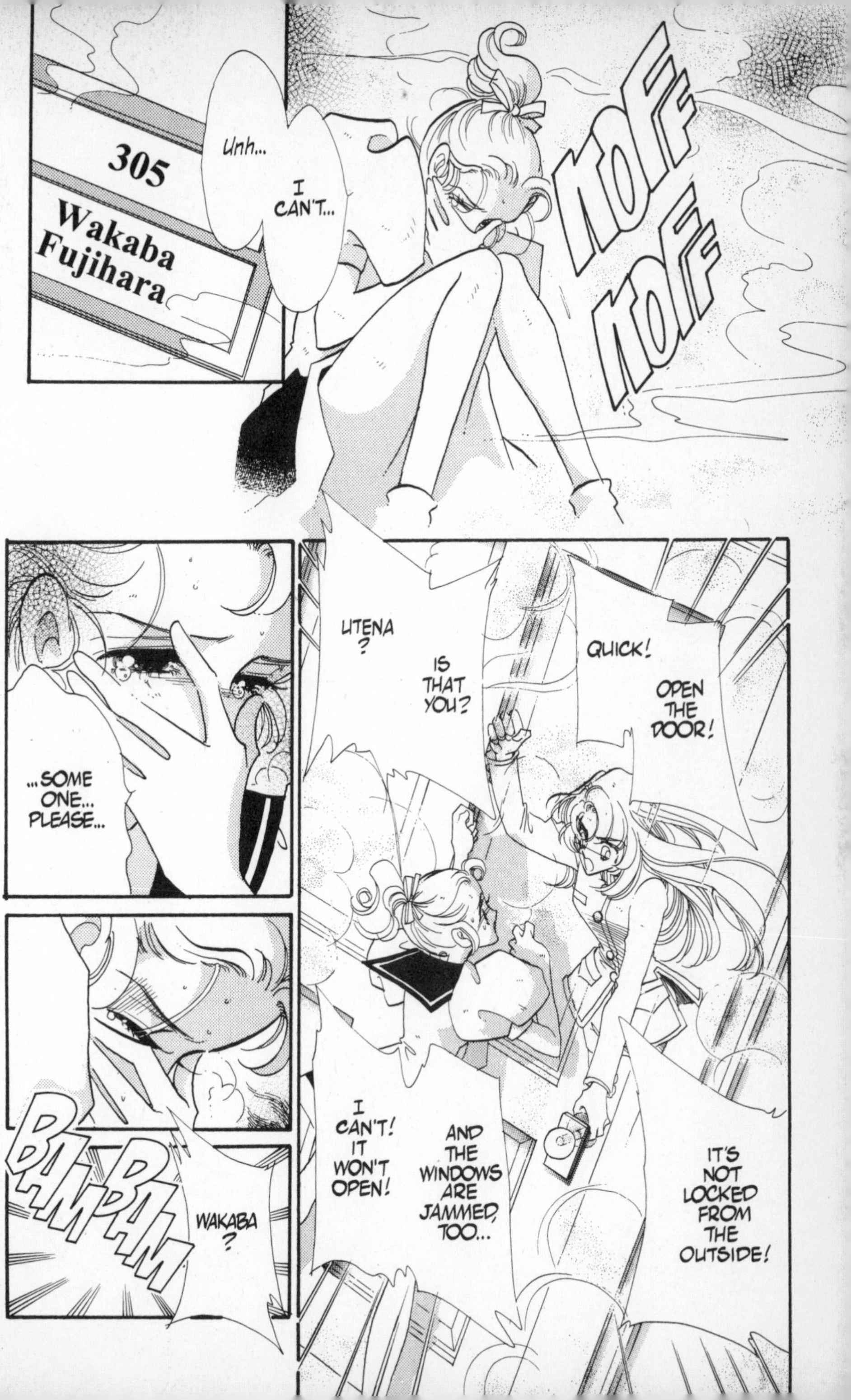
305
Wakaba Fujihara
Unh...
I CAN'T...
KOFF KOFF
...SOME ONE... PLEASE...
BAM BAM
WAKABA?
UTENA? IS THAT YOU?
QUICK! OPEN THE DOOR!
I CAN'T! IT WON'T OPEN!
AND THE WINDOWS ARE JAMMED, TOO...
IT'S NOT LOCKED FROM THE OUTSIDE!

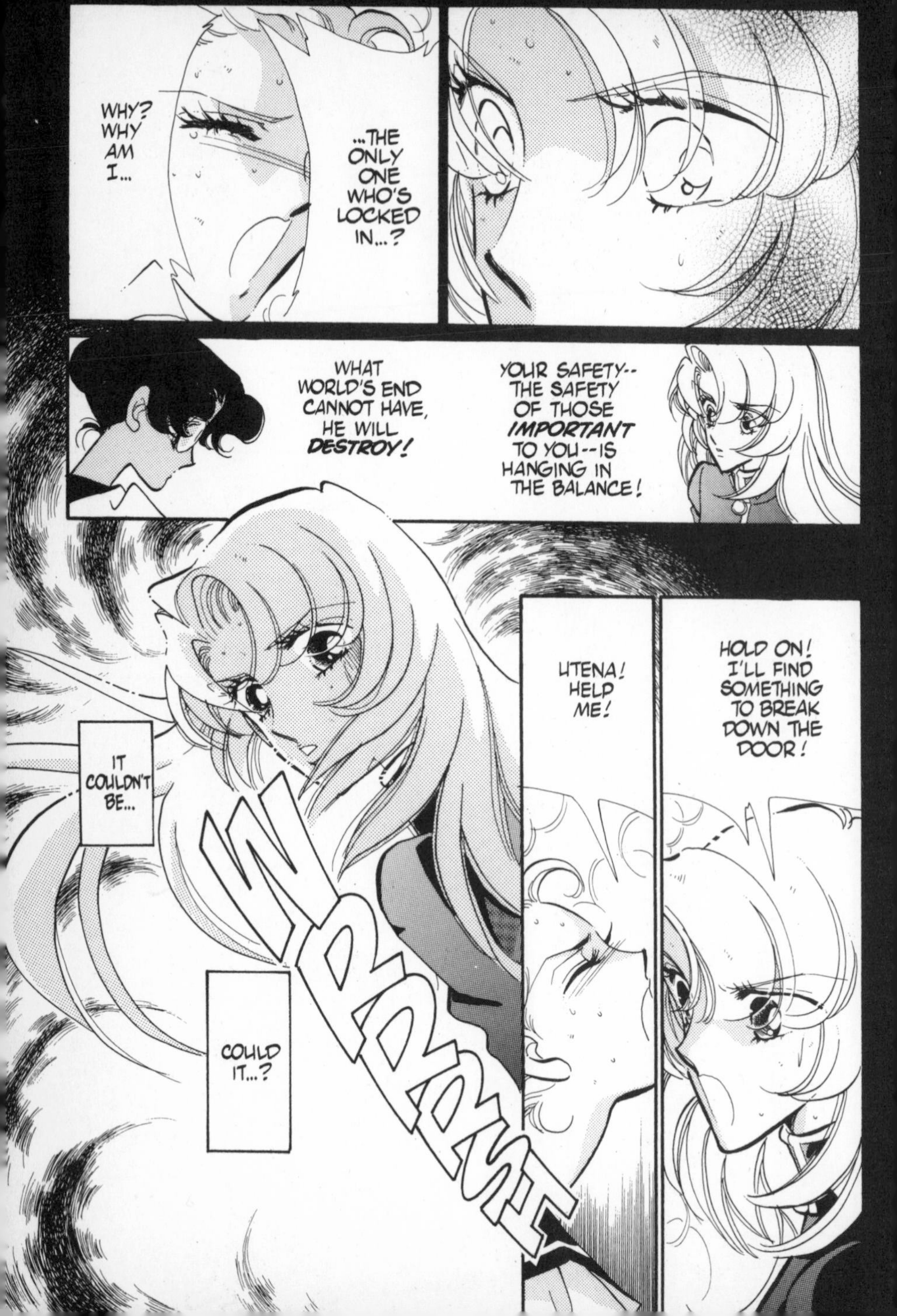
WHY? WHY AM I...
...THE ONLY ONE WHO'S LOCKED IN...?
WHAT WORLD'S END CANNOT HAVE, HE WILL **DESTROY!**
YOUR SAFETY-- THE SAFETY OF THOSE ***IMPORTANT*** TO YOU--IS HANGING IN THE BALANCE!
IT COULDN'T BE...
COULD IT...?
UTENA! HELP ME!
HOLD ON! I'LL FIND SOMETHING TO BREAK DOWN THE DOOR!

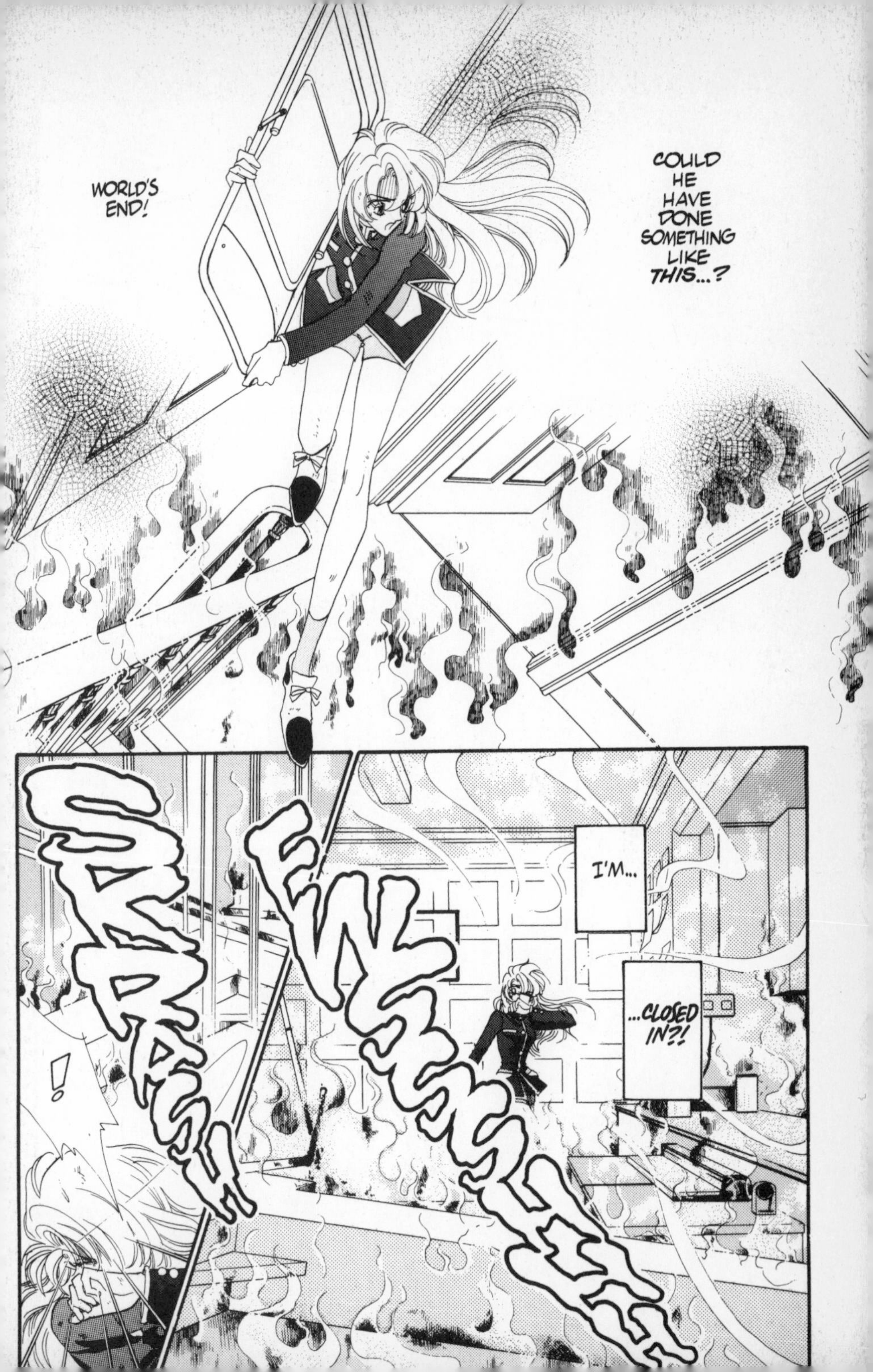
WORLD'S END!
COULD HE HAVE DONE SOMETHING LIKE THIS...?
I'M...
...CLOSED IN?!
!

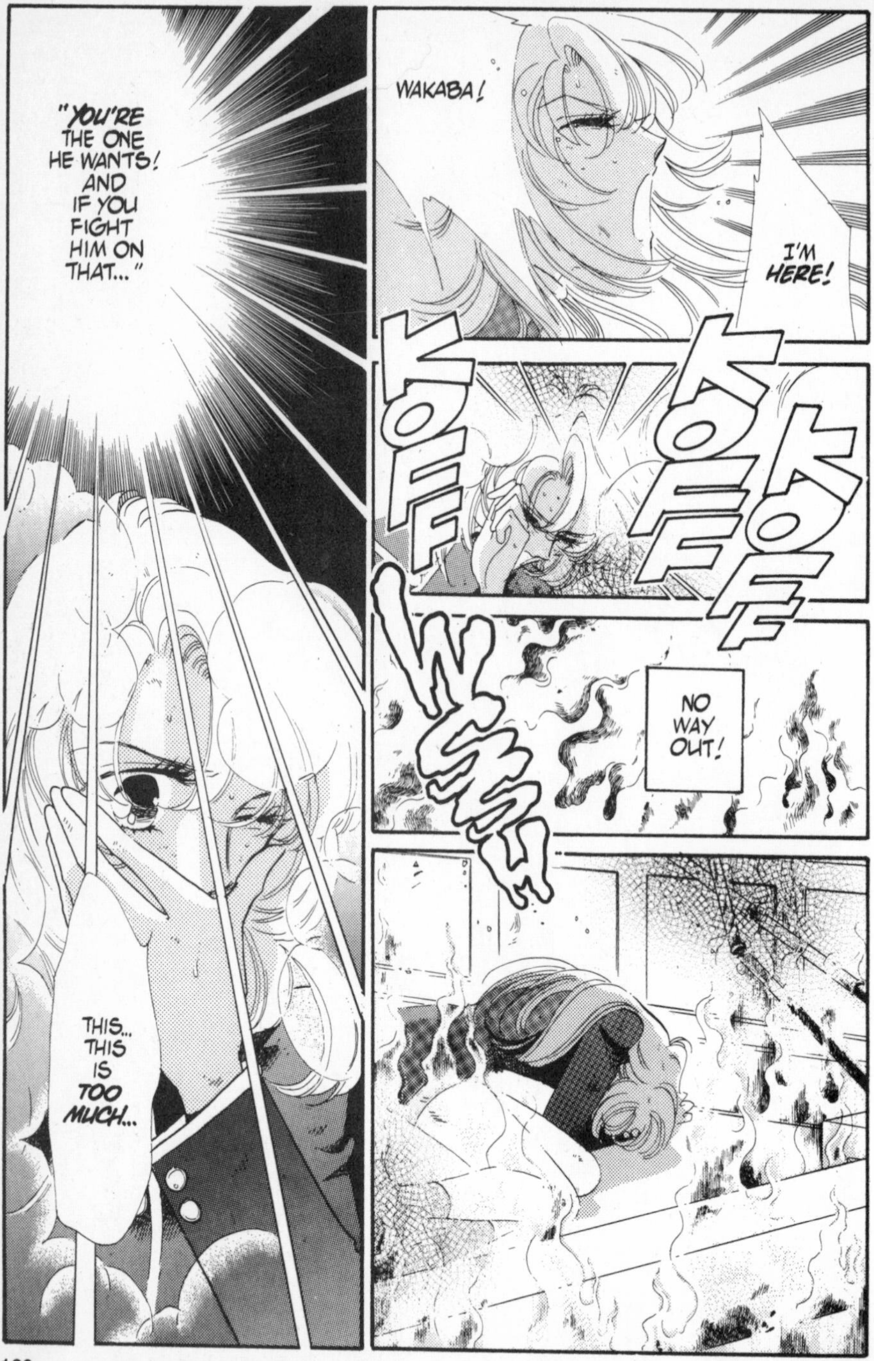
WAKABA!
I'M HERE!
KOFF
KOFF
KOFF
NO WAY OUT!
"YOU'RE THE ONE HE WANTS! AND IF YOU FIGHT HIM ON THAT..."
THIS... THIS IS TOO MUCH...

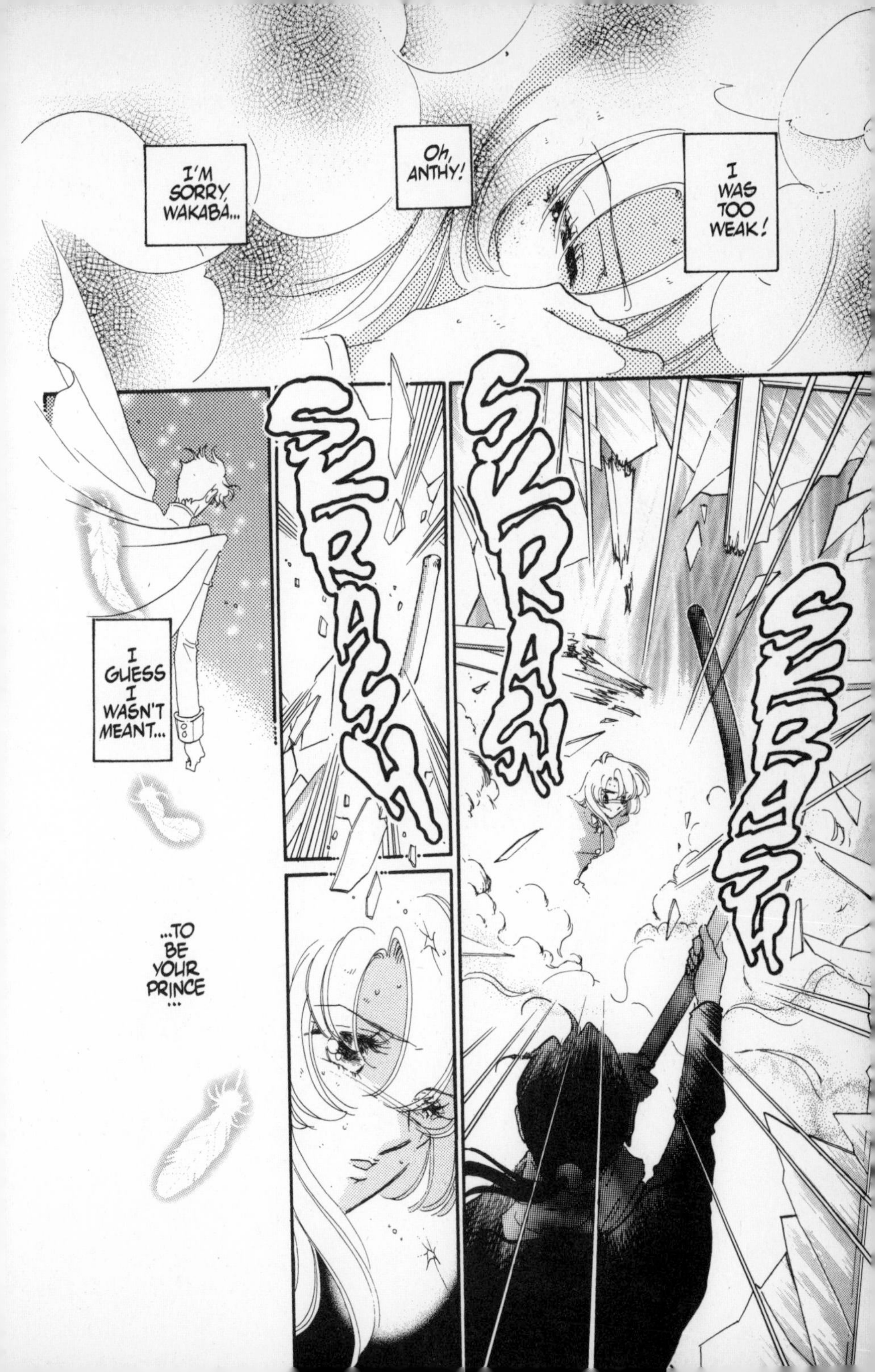
I'M SORRY, WAKABA...
Oh, ANTHY!
I WAS TOO WEAK!
I GUESS I WASN'T MEANT...
...TO BE YOUR PRINCE...
SKRASH
SKRASH
SKRASH

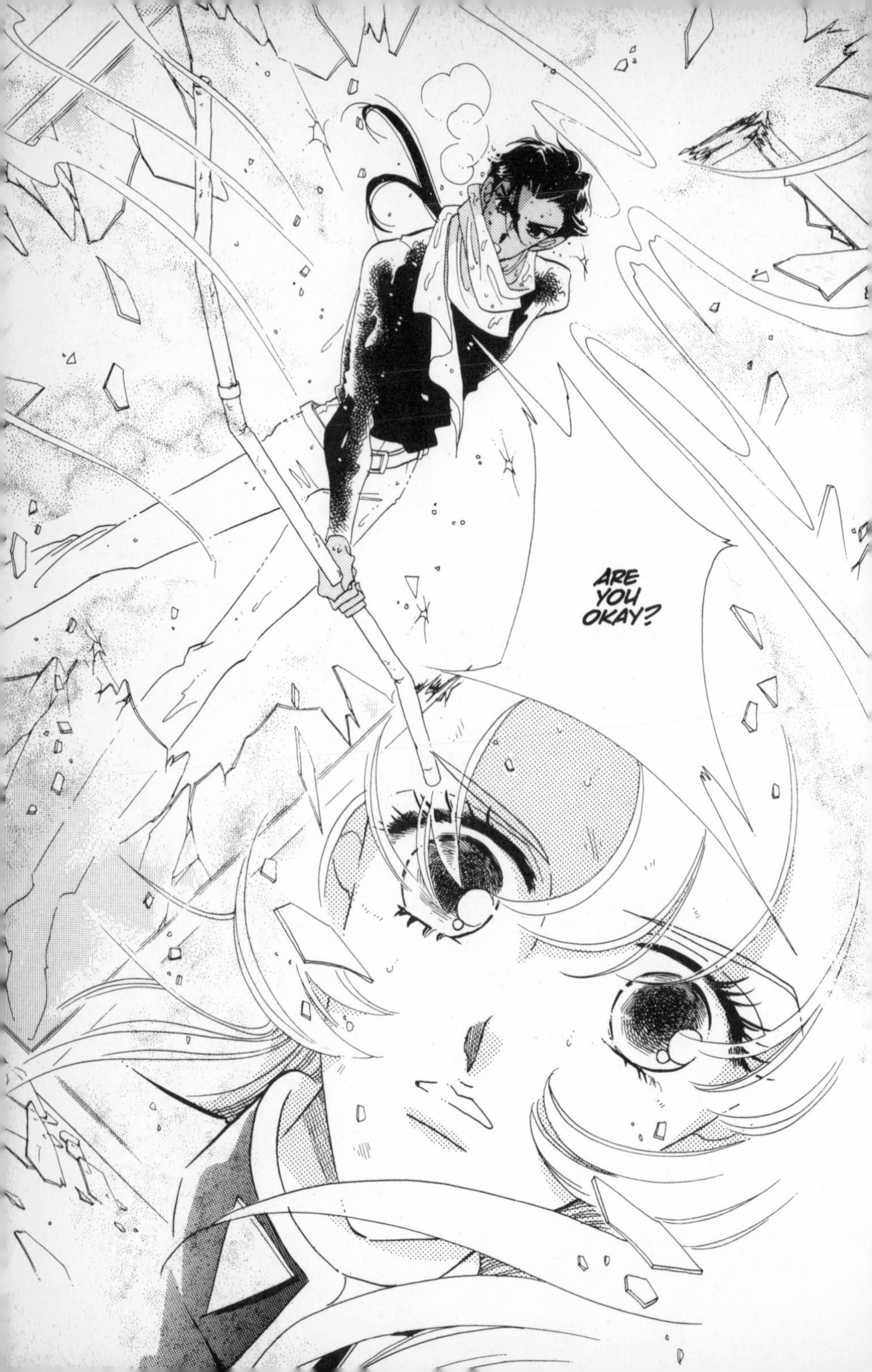
ARE YOU OKAY?

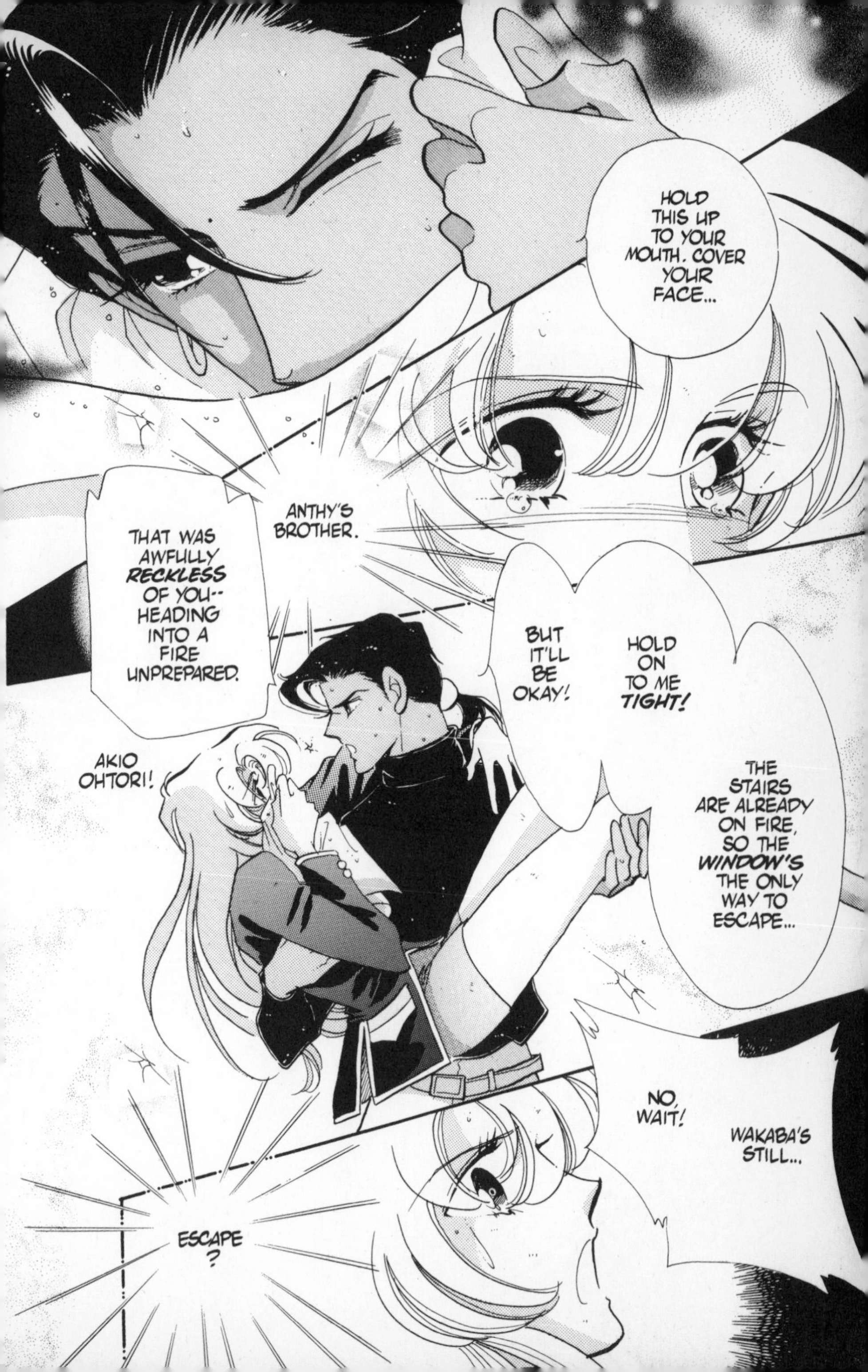
HOLD THIS UP TO YOUR MOUTH. COVER YOUR FACE...
THAT WAS AWFULLY ***RECKLESS*** OF YOU-- HEADING INTO A FIRE UNPREPARED.
ANTHY'S BROTHER.
AKIO OHTORI!
BUT IT'LL BE OKAY!
HOLD ON TO ME ***TIGHT!***
THE STAIRS ARE ALREADY ON FIRE, SO THE ***WINDOW'S*** THE ONLY WAY TO ESCAPE...
ESCAPE?
NO, WAIT!
WAKABA'S STILL...

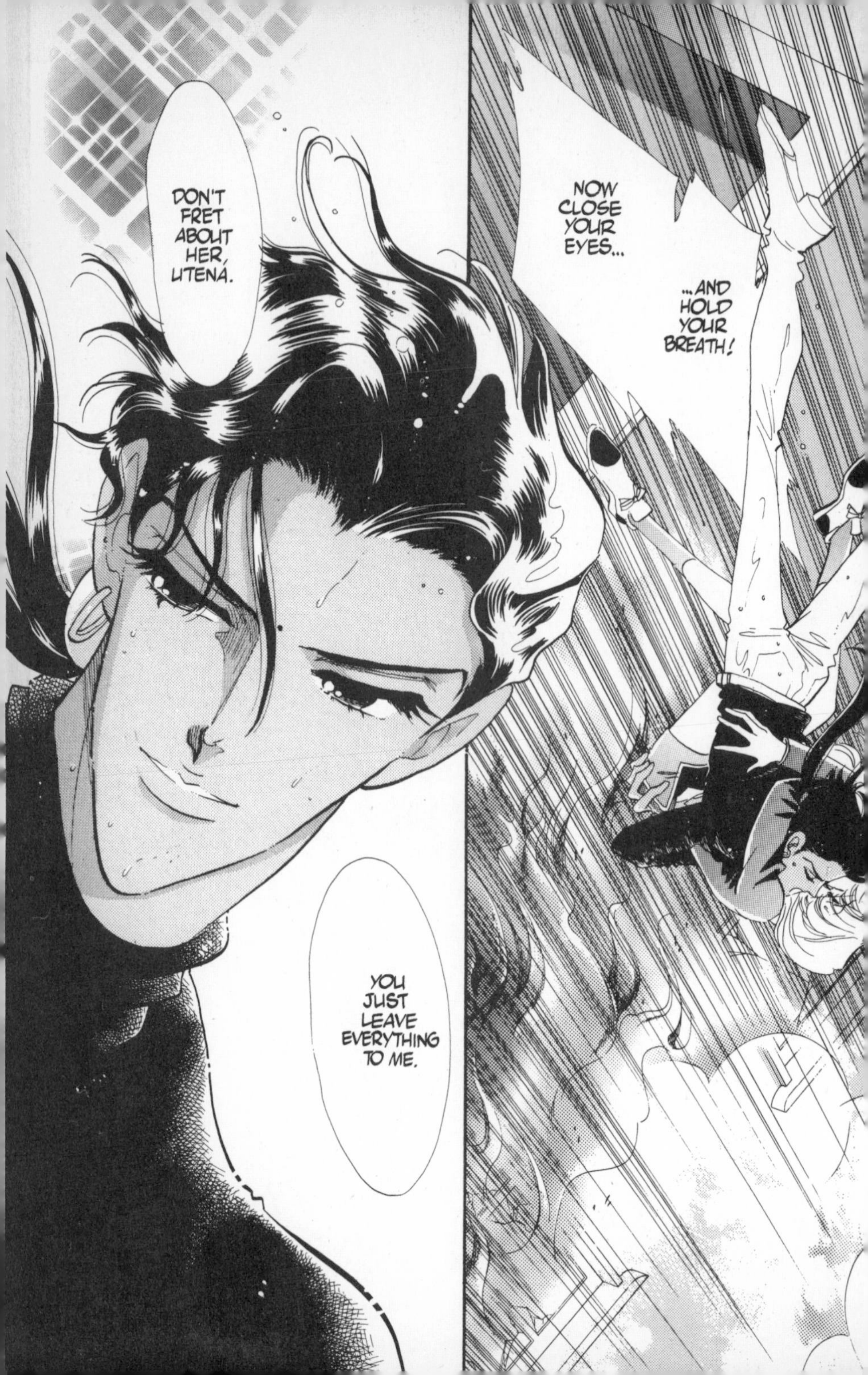
DON'T FRET ABOUT HER, UTENA.
YOU JUST LEAVE EVERYTHING TO ME.
NOW CLOSE YOUR EYES...
...AND HOLD YOUR BREATH!

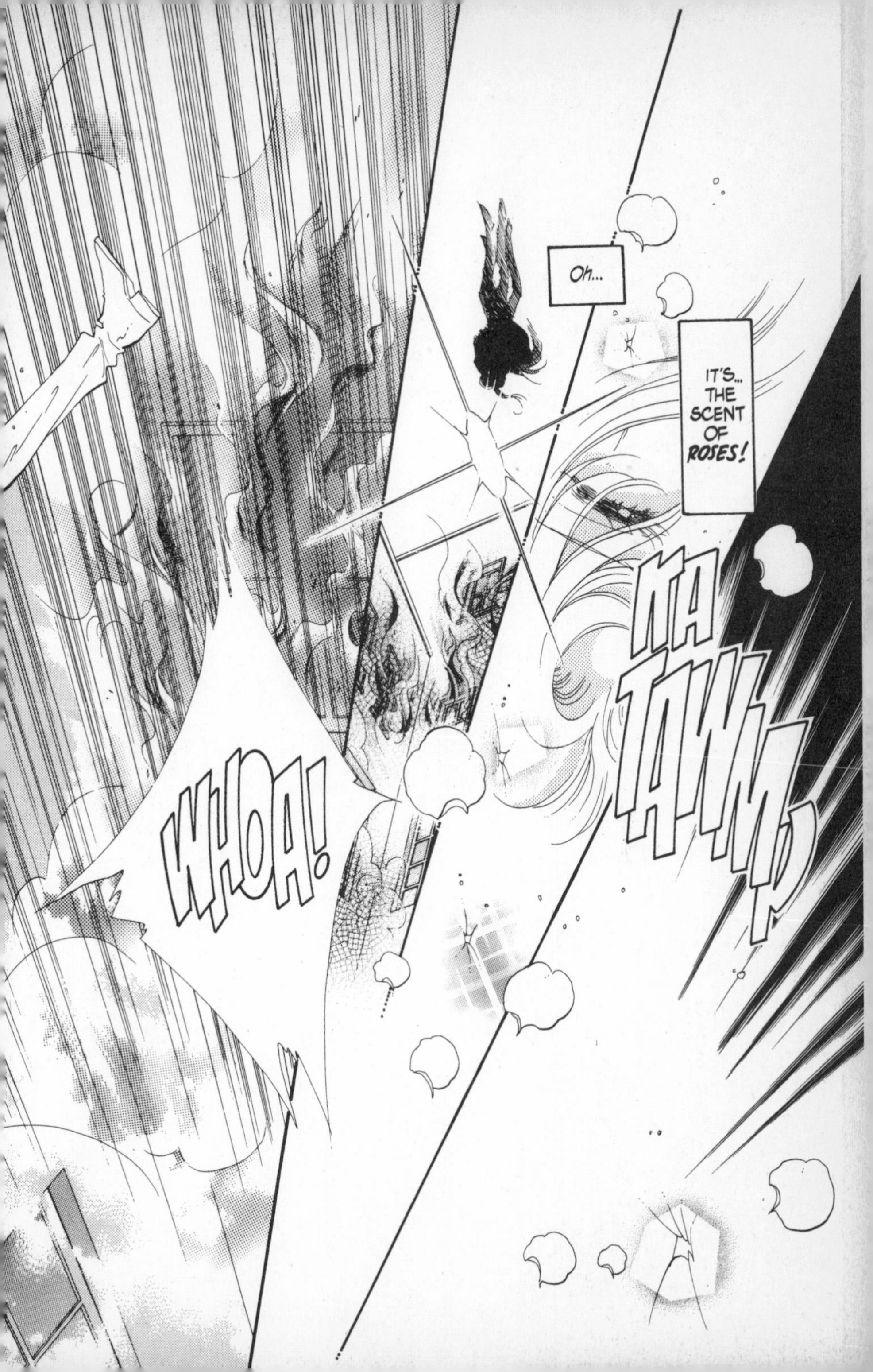
WHOA!
Oh...
IT'S... THE SCENT OF ROSES!
KA TAMP

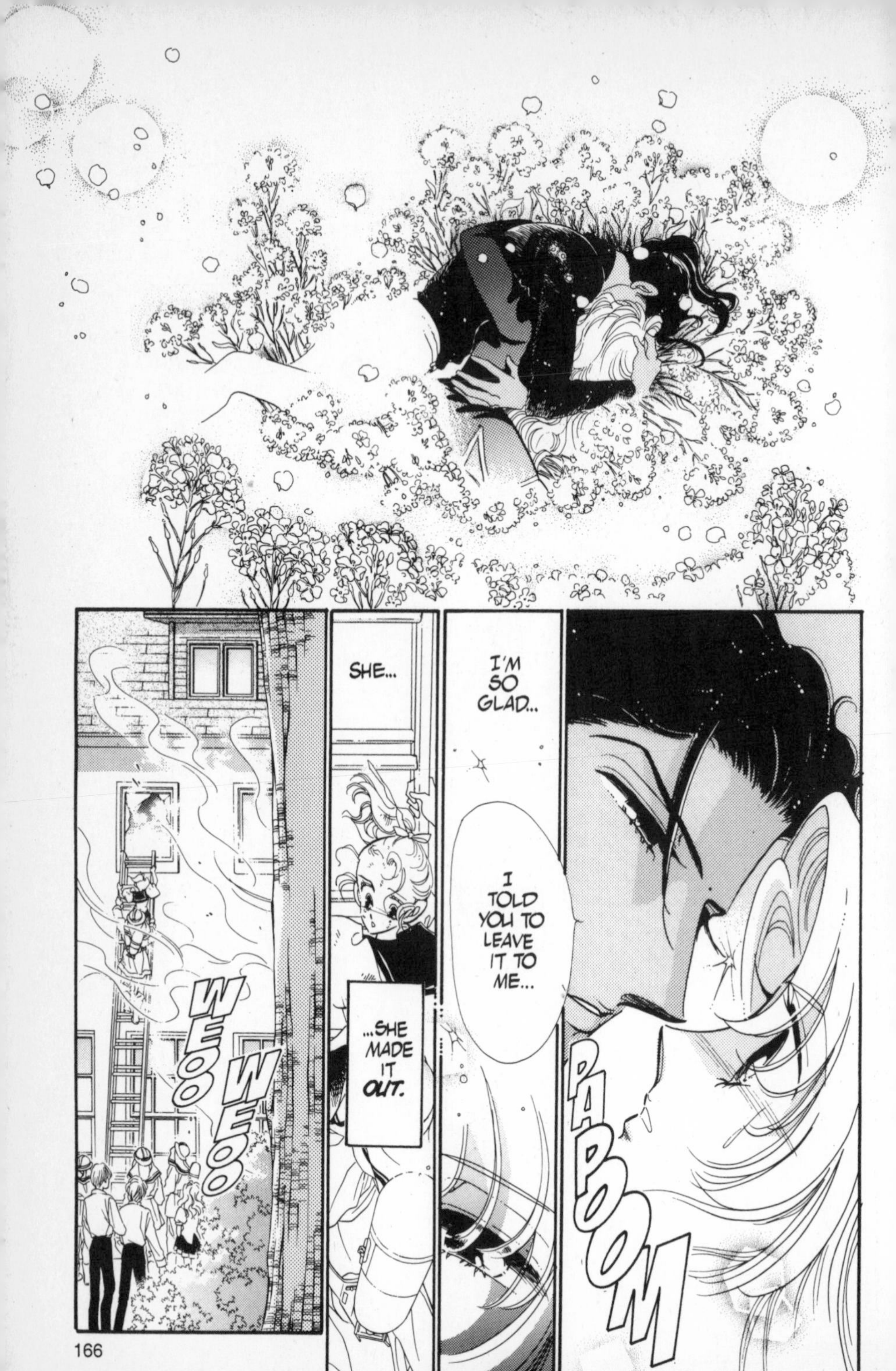

WEEOO
WEEOO
SHE...
...SHE MADE IT OUT.
I'M SO GLAD...
I TOLD YOU TO LEAVE IT TO ME...
PAPOOM

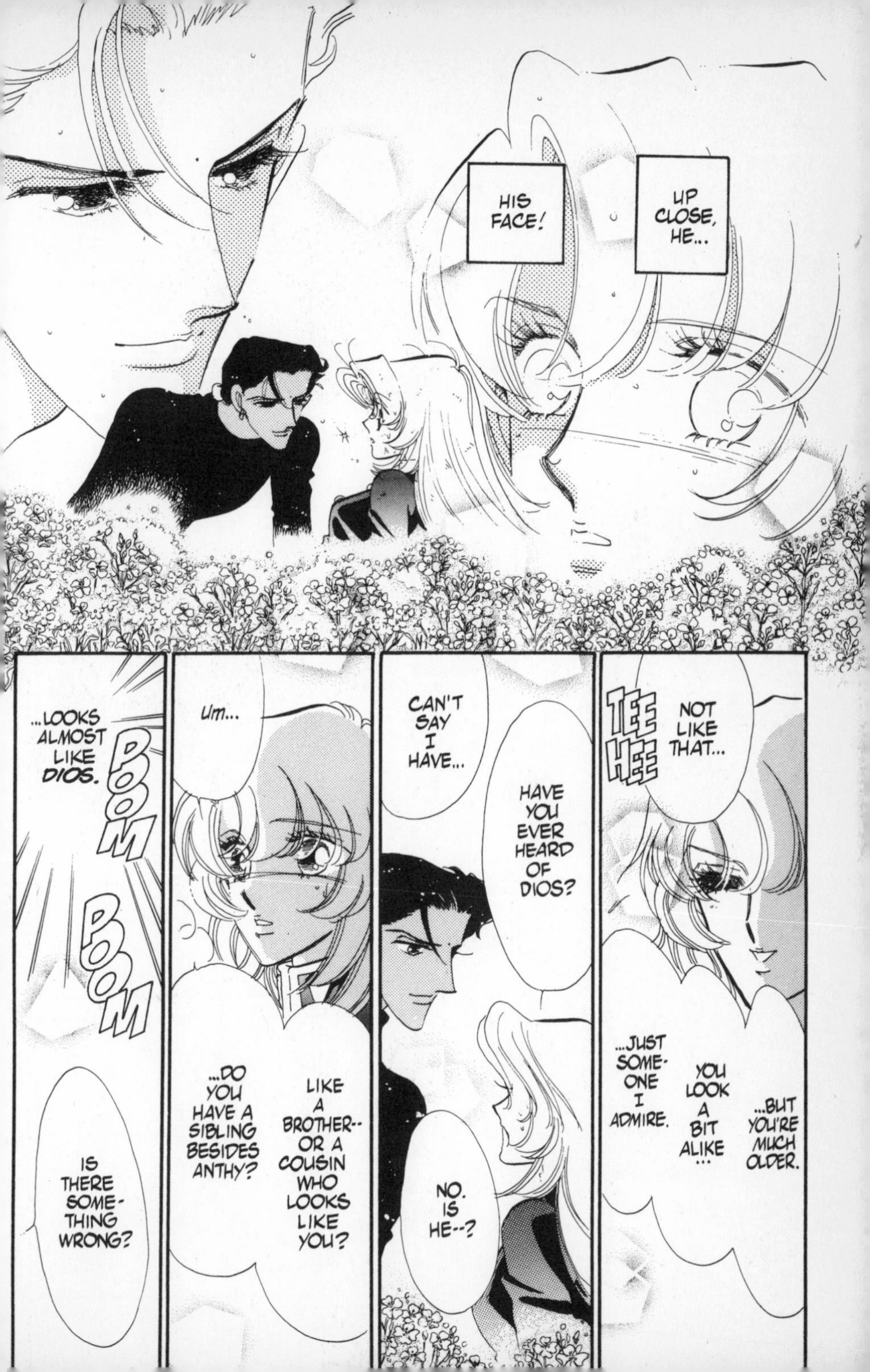
HIS FACE!
UP CLOSE, HE...
...LOOKS ALMOST LIKE DIOS.
POOM POOM
IS THERE SOME-THING WRONG?
Um...
...DO YOU HAVE A SIBLING BESIDES ANTHY?
LIKE A BROTHER-- OR A COUSIN WHO LOOKS LIKE YOU?
CAN'T SAY I HAVE...
HAVE YOU EVER HEARD OF DIOS?
NO. IS HE--?
TEE HEE
NOT LIKE THAT...
...JUST SOME-ONE I ADMIRE.
YOU LOOK A BIT ALIKE...
...BUT YOU'RE MUCH OLDER.

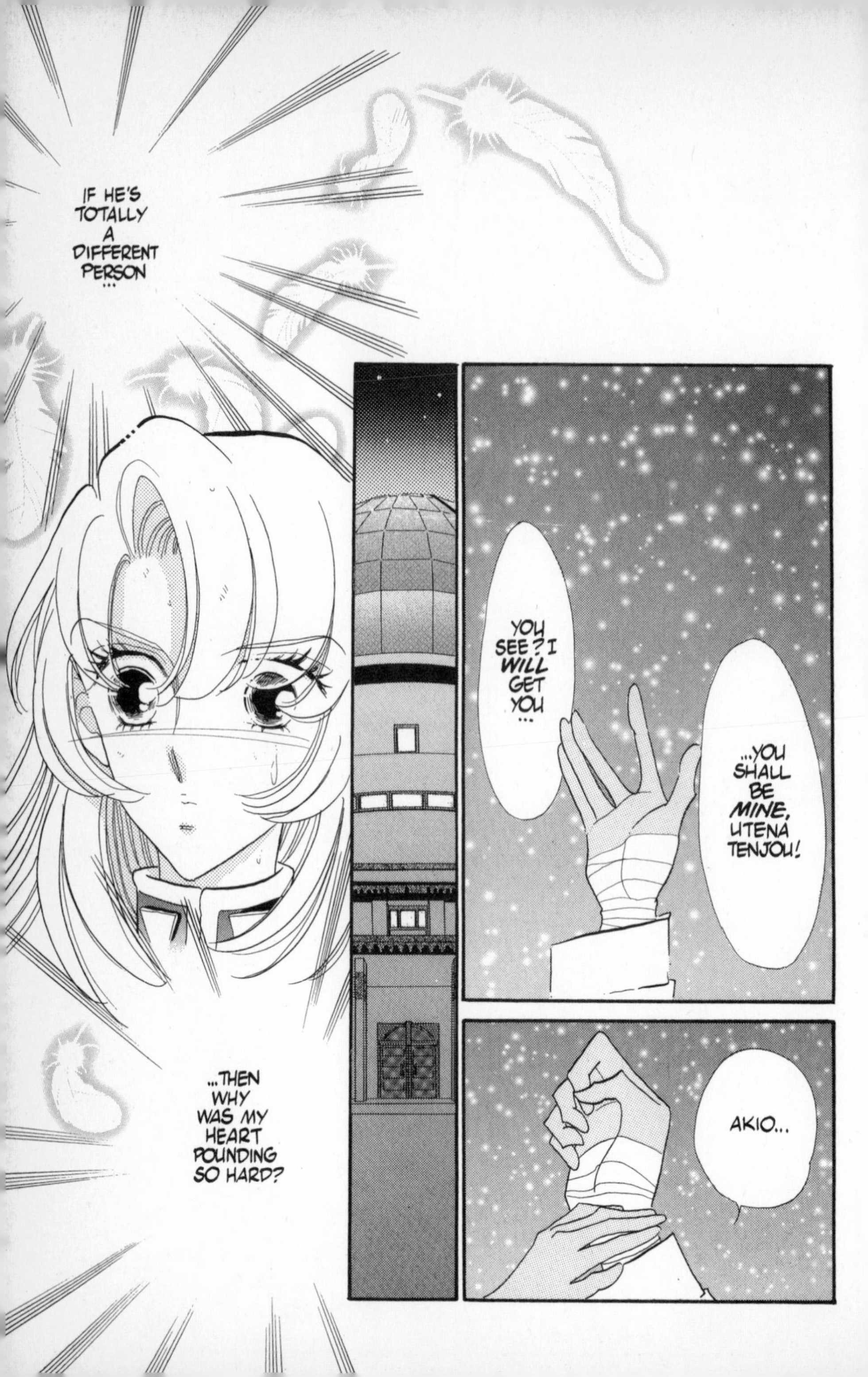
IF HE'S TOTALLY A DIFFERENT PERSON...
...THEN WHY WAS MY HEART POUNDING SO HARD?
YOU SEE? I *WILL* GET YOU...
...YOU SHALL BE *MINE*, UTENA TENJOU!
AKIO...

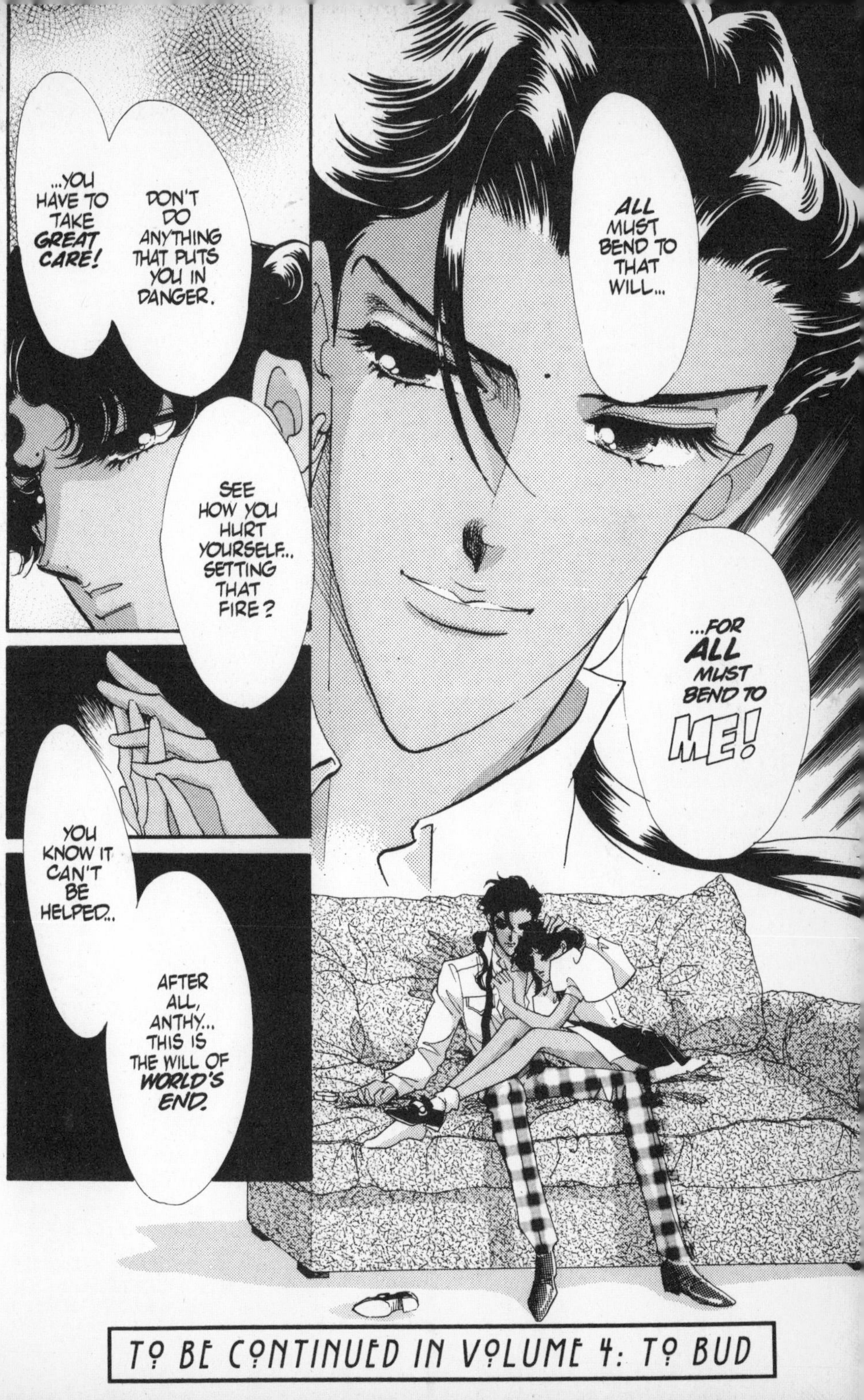
...YOU HAVE TO TAKE GREAT CARE!
DON'T DO ANYTHING THAT PUTS YOU IN DANGER.
SEE HOW YOU HURT YOURSELF... SETTING THAT FIRE?
YOU KNOW IT CAN'T BE HELPED...
AFTER ALL, ANTHY... THIS IS THE WILL OF WORLD'S END.
ALL MUST BEND TO THAT WILL...
...FOR ALL MUST BEND TO ME!
TO BE CONTINUED IN VOLUME 4: TO BUD

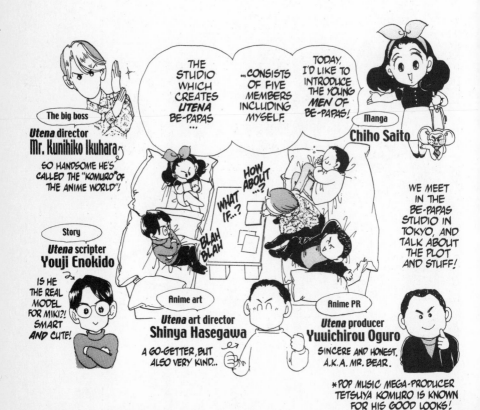

THE STUDIO WHICH CREATES *UTENA* BE-PAPAS...
...CONSISTS OF FIVE MEMBERS INCLUDING MYSELF.
TODAY, I'D LIKE TO INTRODUCE THE YOUNG *MEN* OF BE-PAPAS!
The big boss
Utena director
Mr. Kunihiko Ikuhara
SO HANDSOME HE'S CALLED THE "KOMURO* OF THE ANIME WORLD"!
Manga
Chiho Saito
HOW ABOUT...?
WHAT IF...?
BLAH BLAH
WE MEET IN THE BE-PAPAS STUDIO IN TOKYO, AND TALK ABOUT THE PLOT AND STUFF!
Story
Utena scripter
Youji Enokido
IS HE THE REAL MODEL FOR MIKI?! SMART *AND* CUTE!
Anime art
Utena art director
Shinya Hasegawa
A GO-GETTER, BUT ALSO VERY KIND...
Anime PR
Utena producer
Yuuichirou Oguro
SINCERE AND HONEST. A.K.A. MR. BEAR.
*POP MUSIC MEGA-PRODUCER TETSUYA KOMURO IS KNOWN FOR HIS GOOD LOOKS!

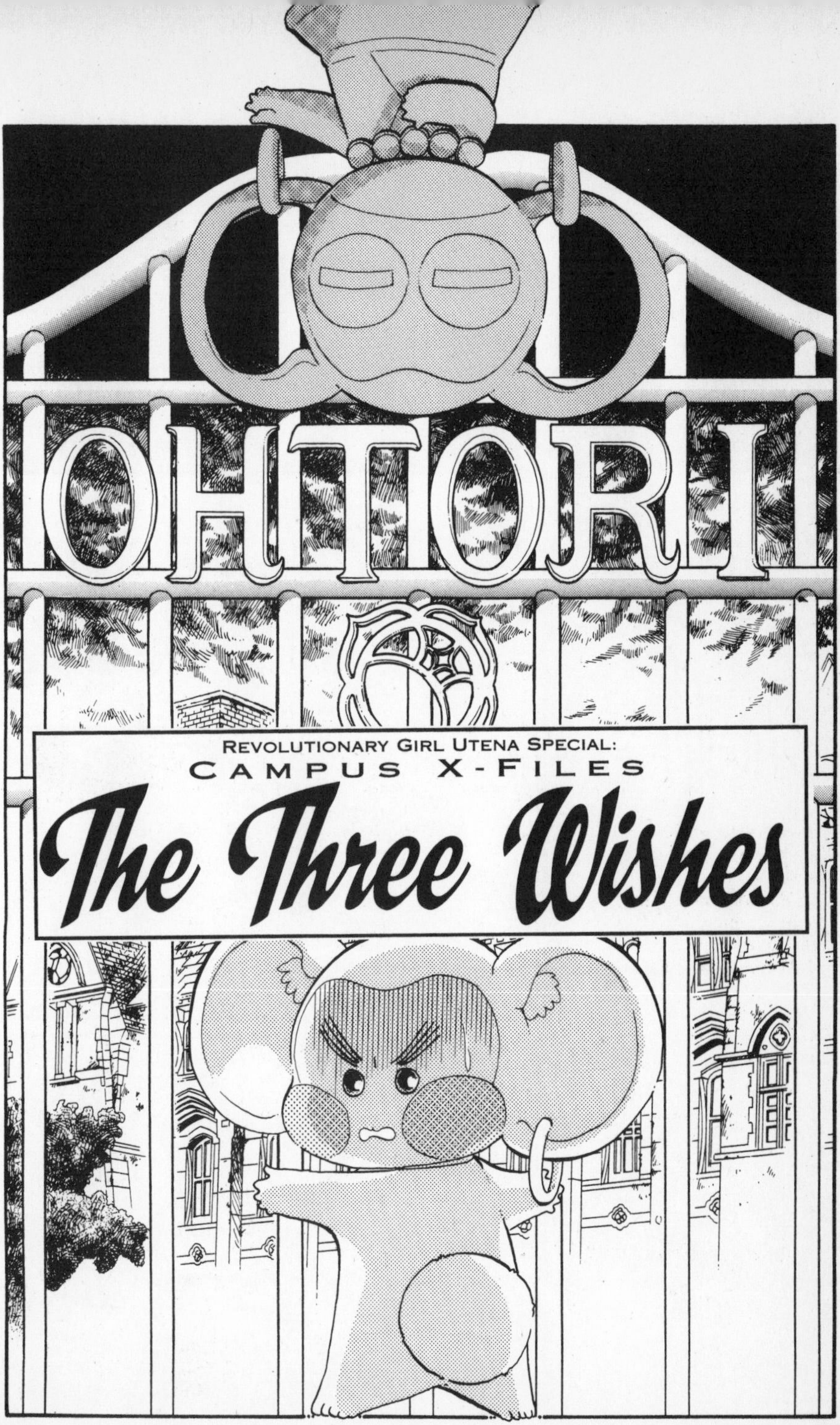
OHTORI
REVOLUTIONARY GIRL UTENA SPECIAL:
CAMPUS X-FILES
The Three Wishes

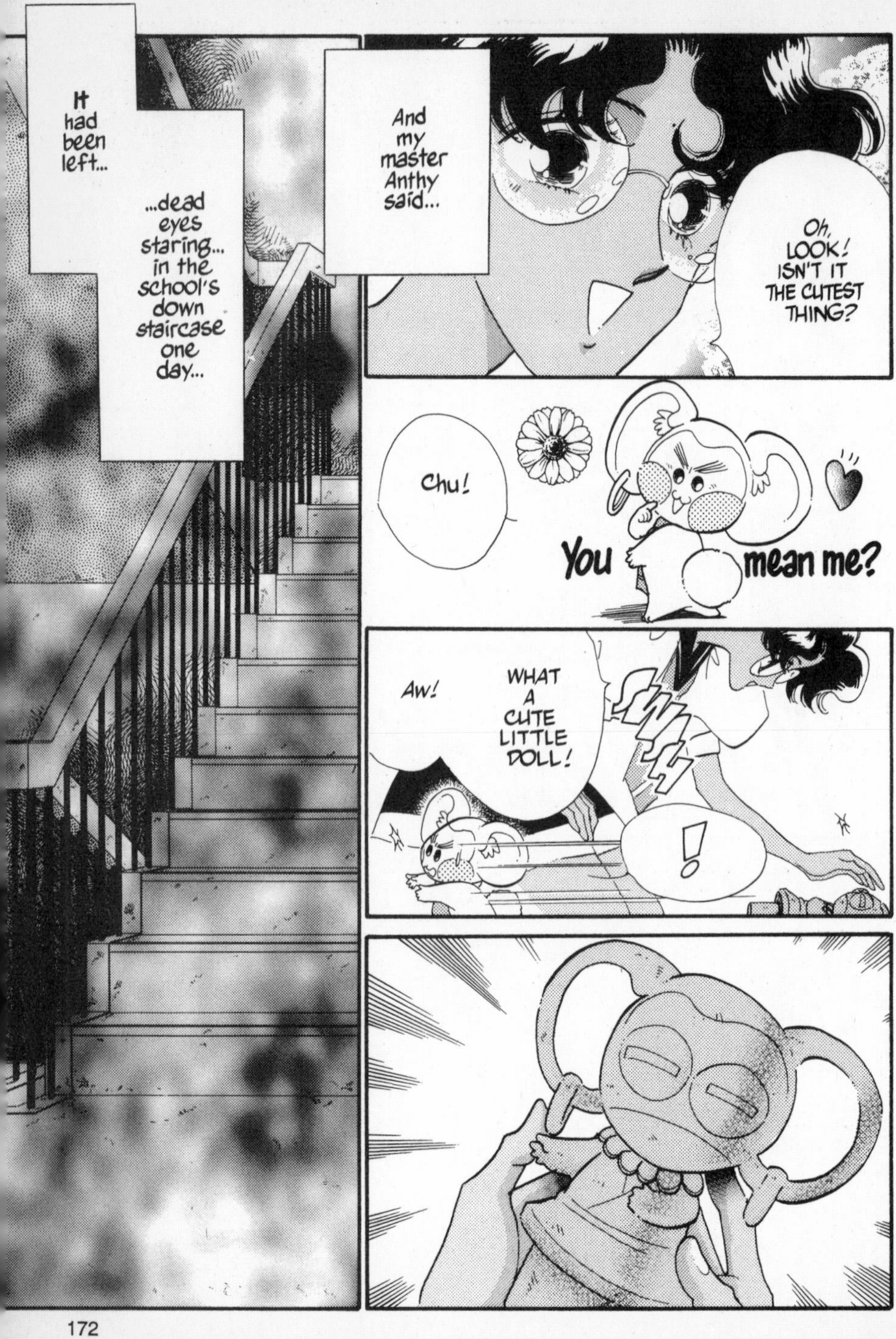
It had been left...
...dead eyes staring... in the school's down staircase one day...
And my master Anthy said...
Oh, LOOK! ISN'T IT THE CUTEST THING?
Chu!
You mean me?
Aw!
WHAT A CUTE LITTLE DOLL!
!

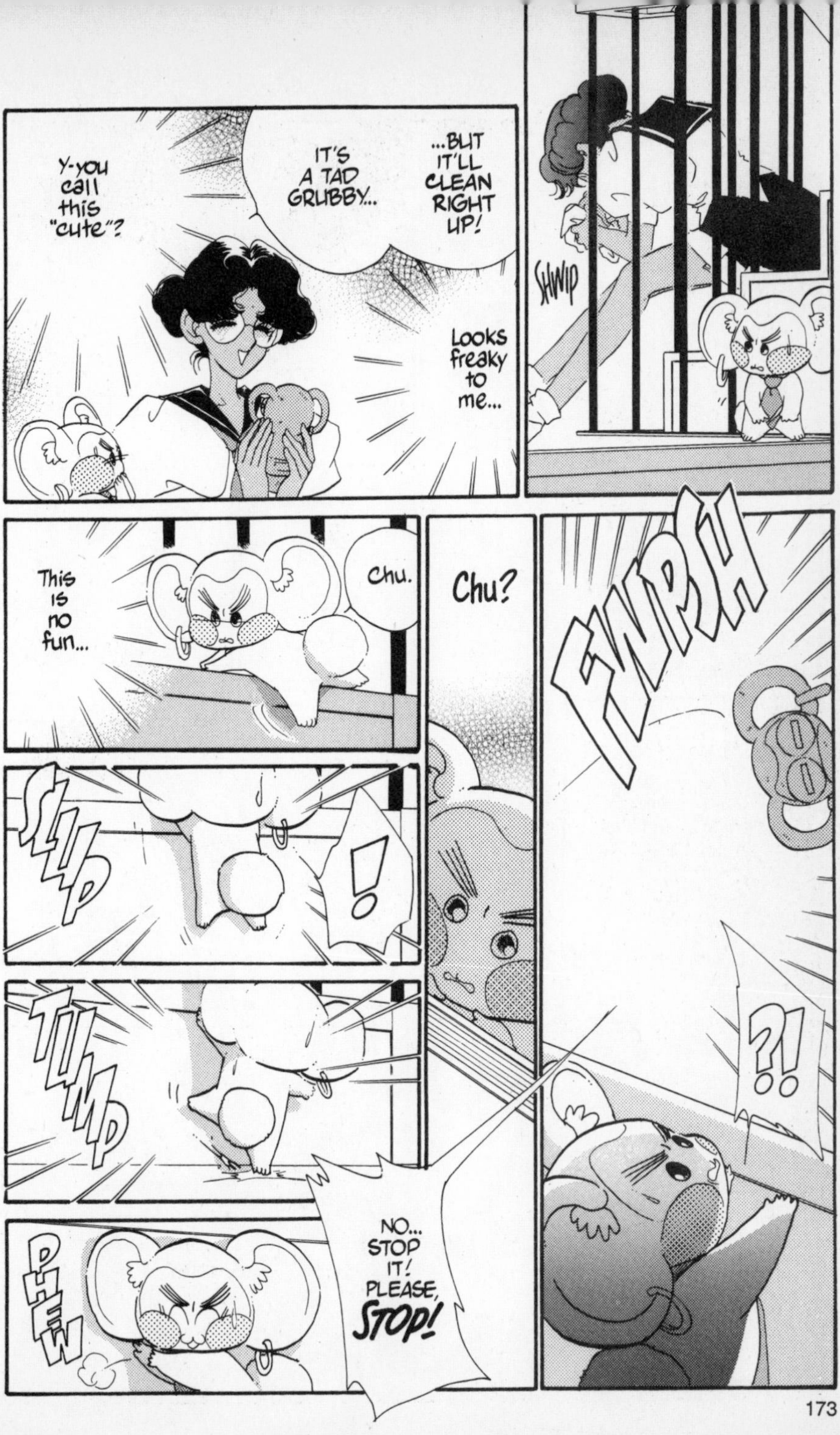
Y-you call this "cute"?
IT'S A TAD GRUBBY...
...BUT IT'LL CLEAN RIGHT UP!
Looks freaky to me...
SHWIP
This is no fun...
Chu.
SLUMP
!
THUMP
PHEW
NO... STOP IT! PLEASE, STOP!
Chu?
?!!

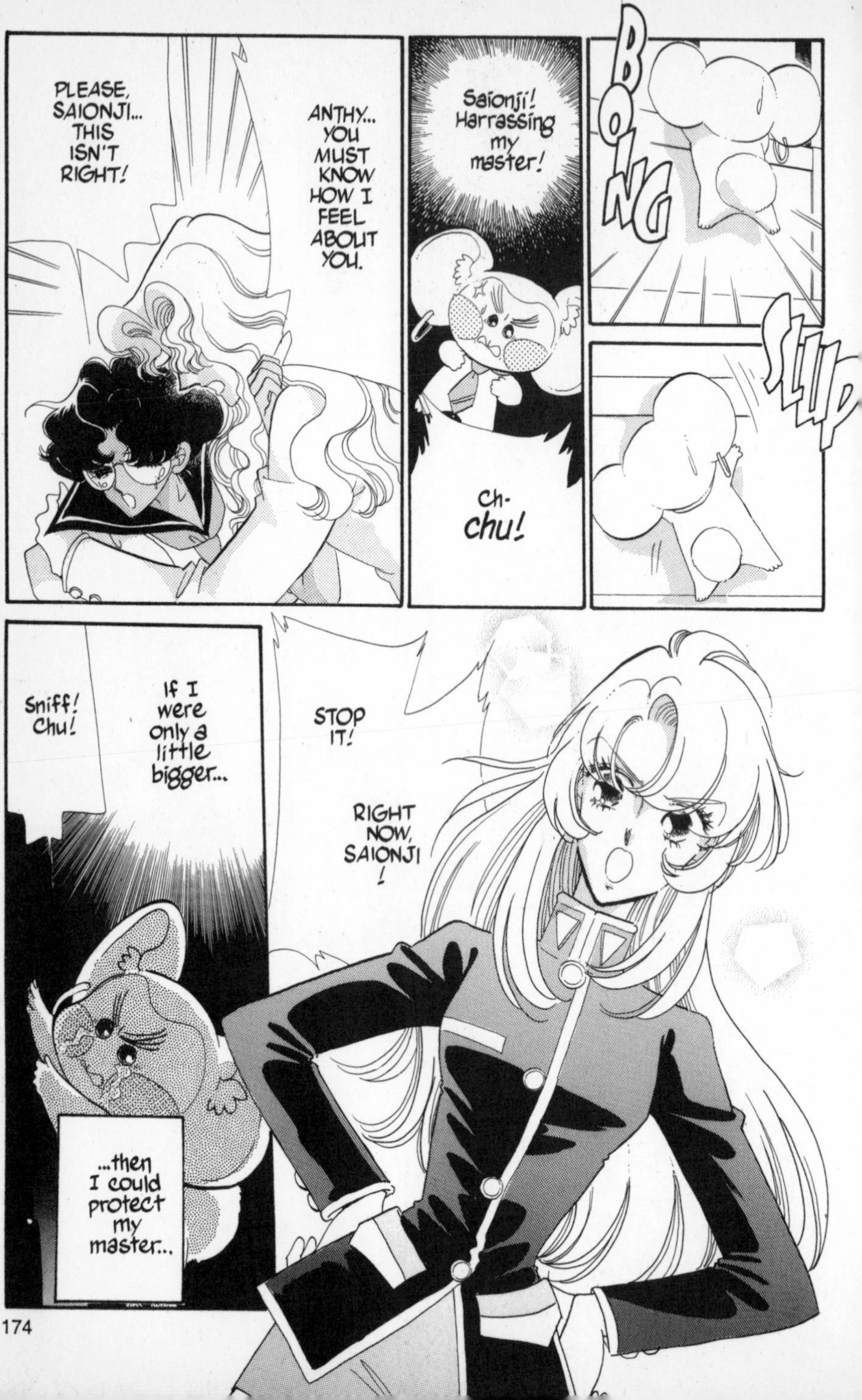
PLEASE, SAIONJI... THIS ISN'T RIGHT!
ANTHY... YOU MUST KNOW HOW I FEEL ABOUT YOU.
Saionji! Harrassing my master!
Ch-chu!
BOING
SLIP
Sniff! Chu!
If I were only a little bigger...
...then I could protect my master...
STOP IT!
RIGHT NOW, SAIONJI!

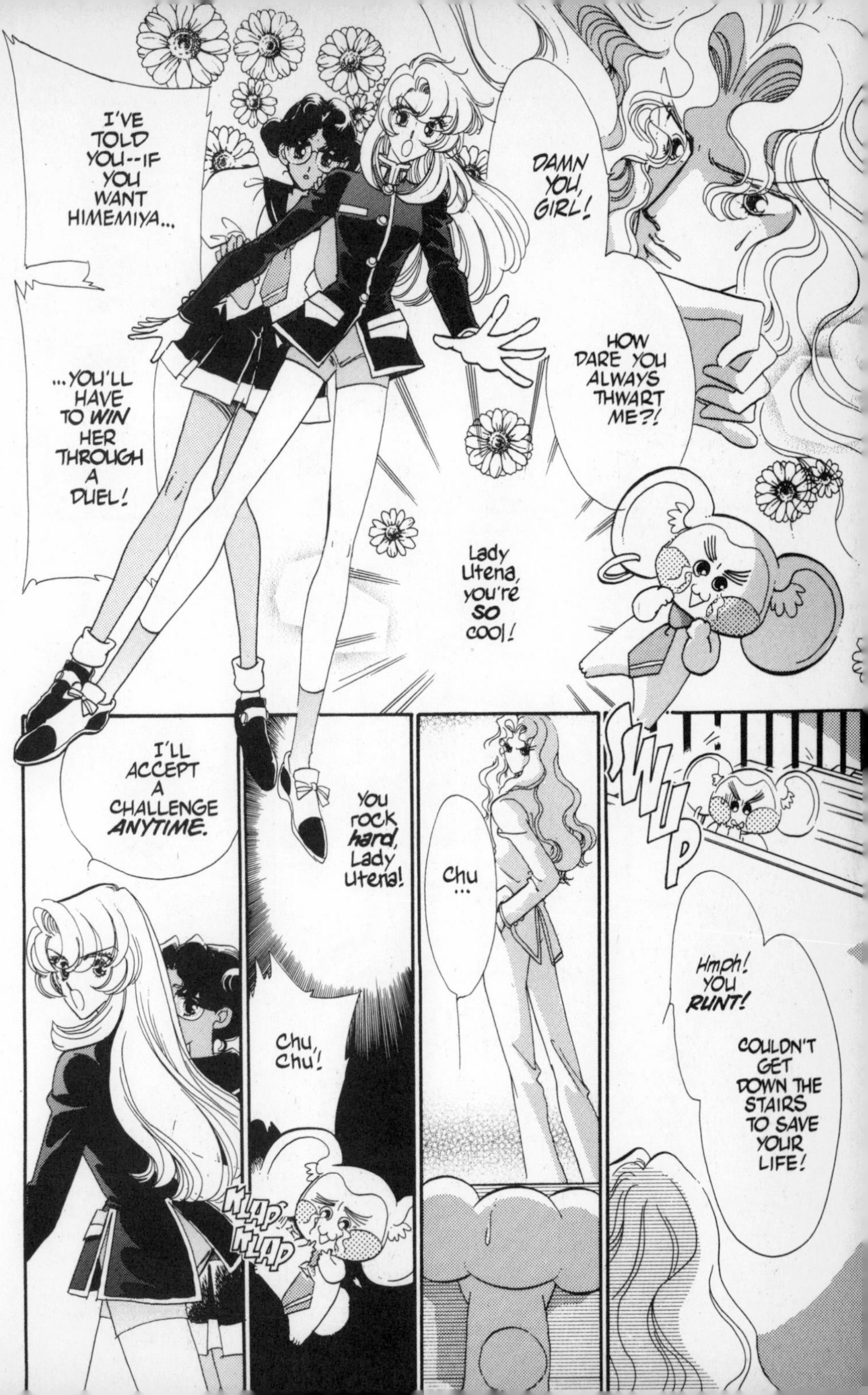
I'VE TOLD YOU--IF YOU WANT HIMEMIYA...
...YOU'LL HAVE TO *WIN* HER THROUGH A DUEL!
DAMN YOU, GIRL!
HOW DARE YOU ALWAYS THWART ME?!
Lady Utena, you're **SO** cool!
I'LL ACCEPT A CHALLENGE ***ANYTIME.***
You rock *hard*, Lady Utena!
Chu, Chu!
KLAP KLAP
Chu...
SWUP
Hmph! YOU ***RUNT!***
COULDN'T GET DOWN THE STAIRS TO SAVE YOUR LIFE!

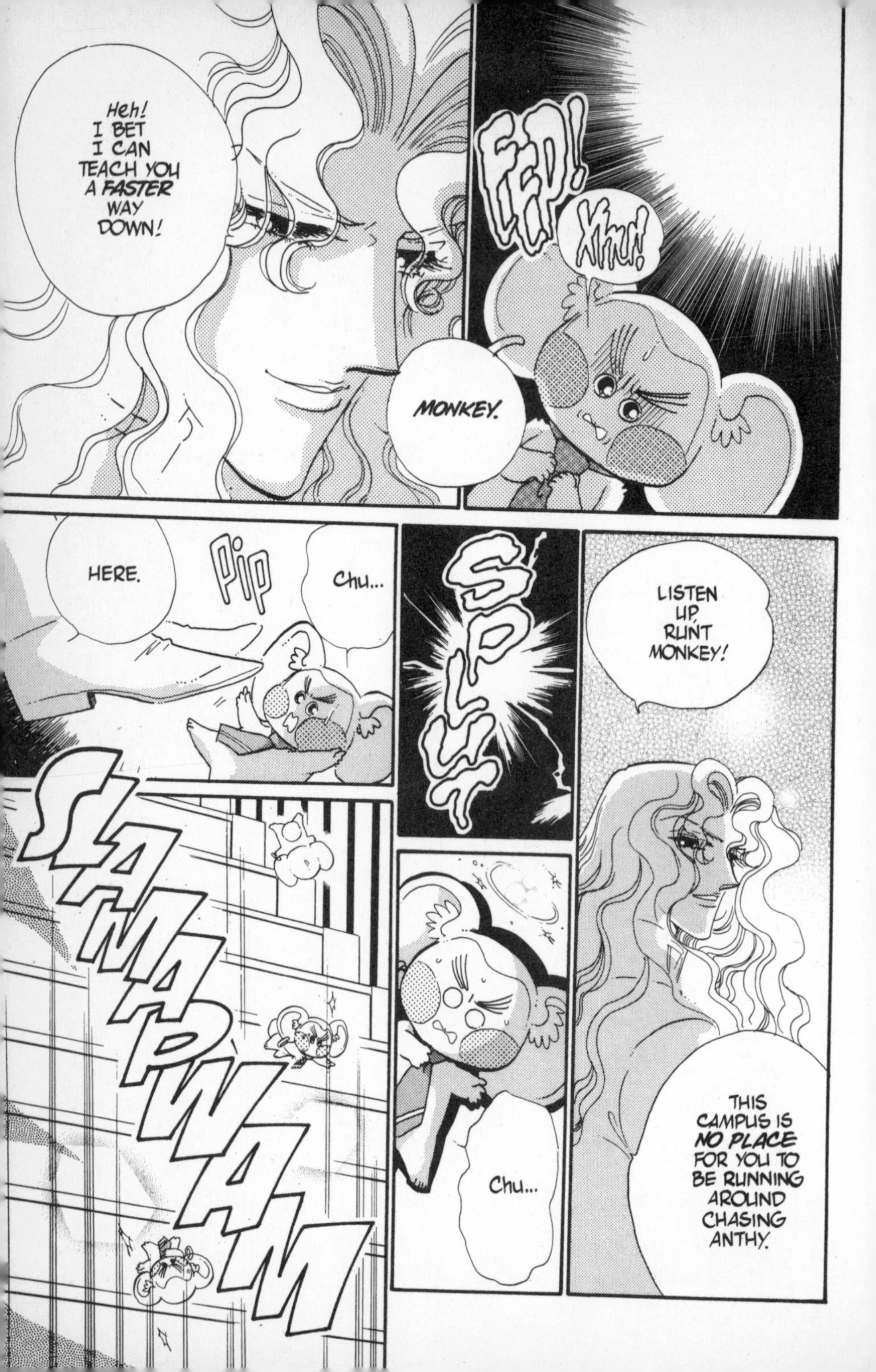
Heh! I BET I CAN TEACH YOU A *FASTER* WAY DOWN!
FEP!
Xhu!
MONKEY.
HERE.
Pip
Chu...
SLAMWAM
SPLT
LISTEN UP, RUNT MONKEY!
Chu...
THIS CAMPUS IS ***NO PLACE*** FOR YOU TO BE RUNNING AROUND CHASING ANTHY.

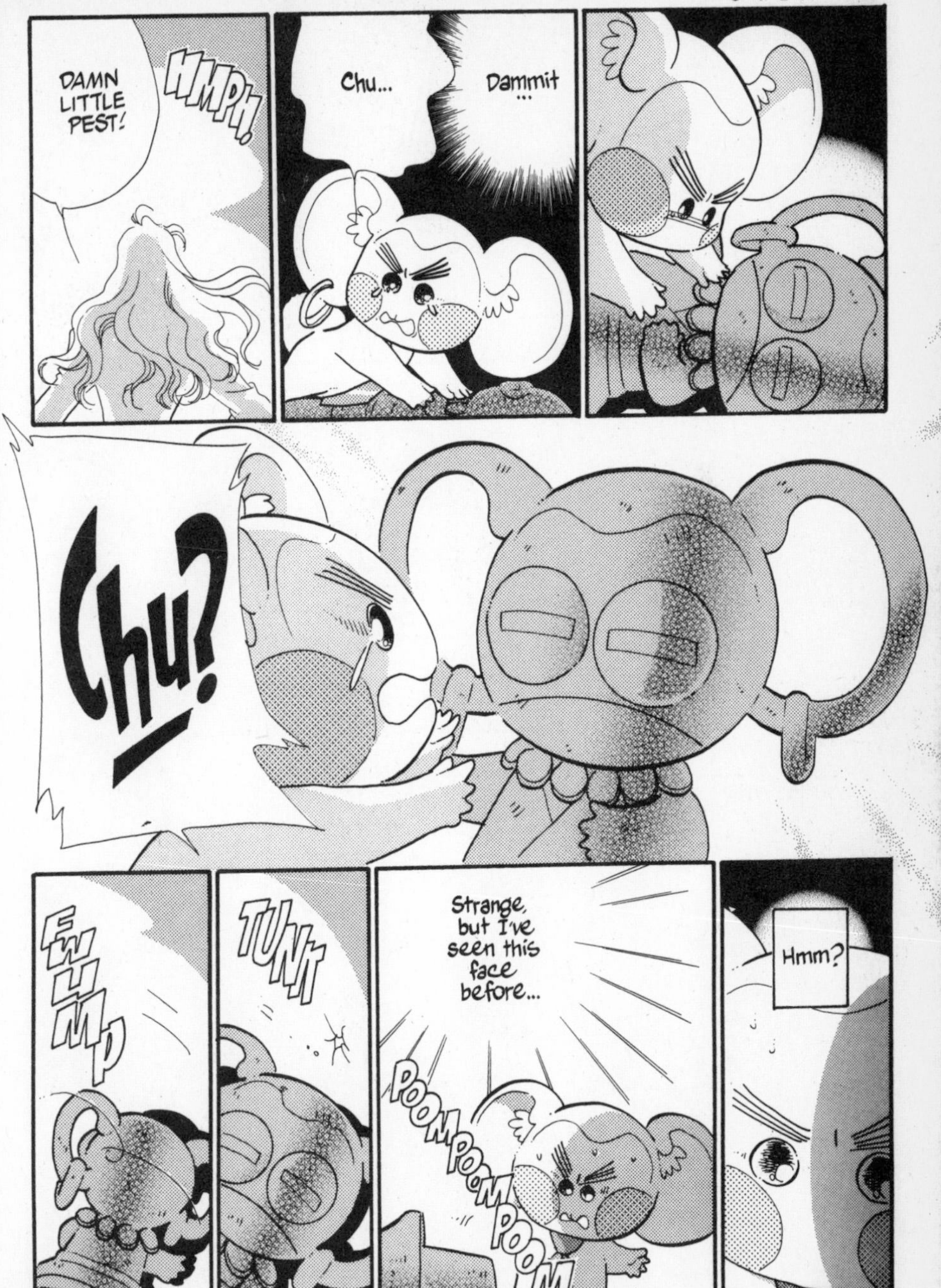
DAMN LITTLE PEST!
HMPH!
Chu...
Dammit ...
Chu?
FWUMP
TUNK
Strange, but I've seen this face before...
POOMPOOMPOOM
Hmm?

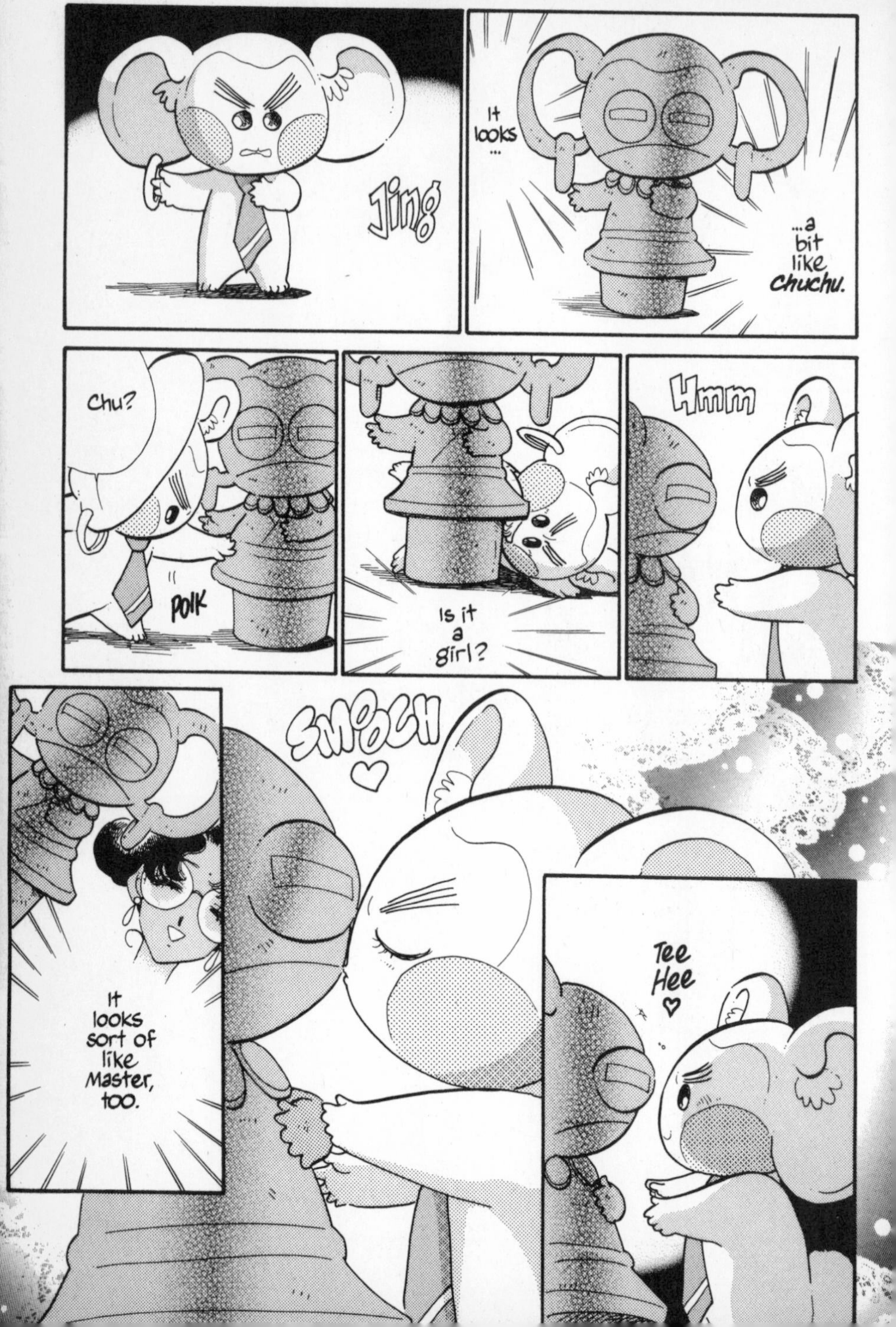
Jing
It looks ...
...a bit like Chuchu.
Chu?
POIK
Is it a girl?
Hmm
SMOOCH ♡
It looks sort of like Master, too.
Tee Hee ♡

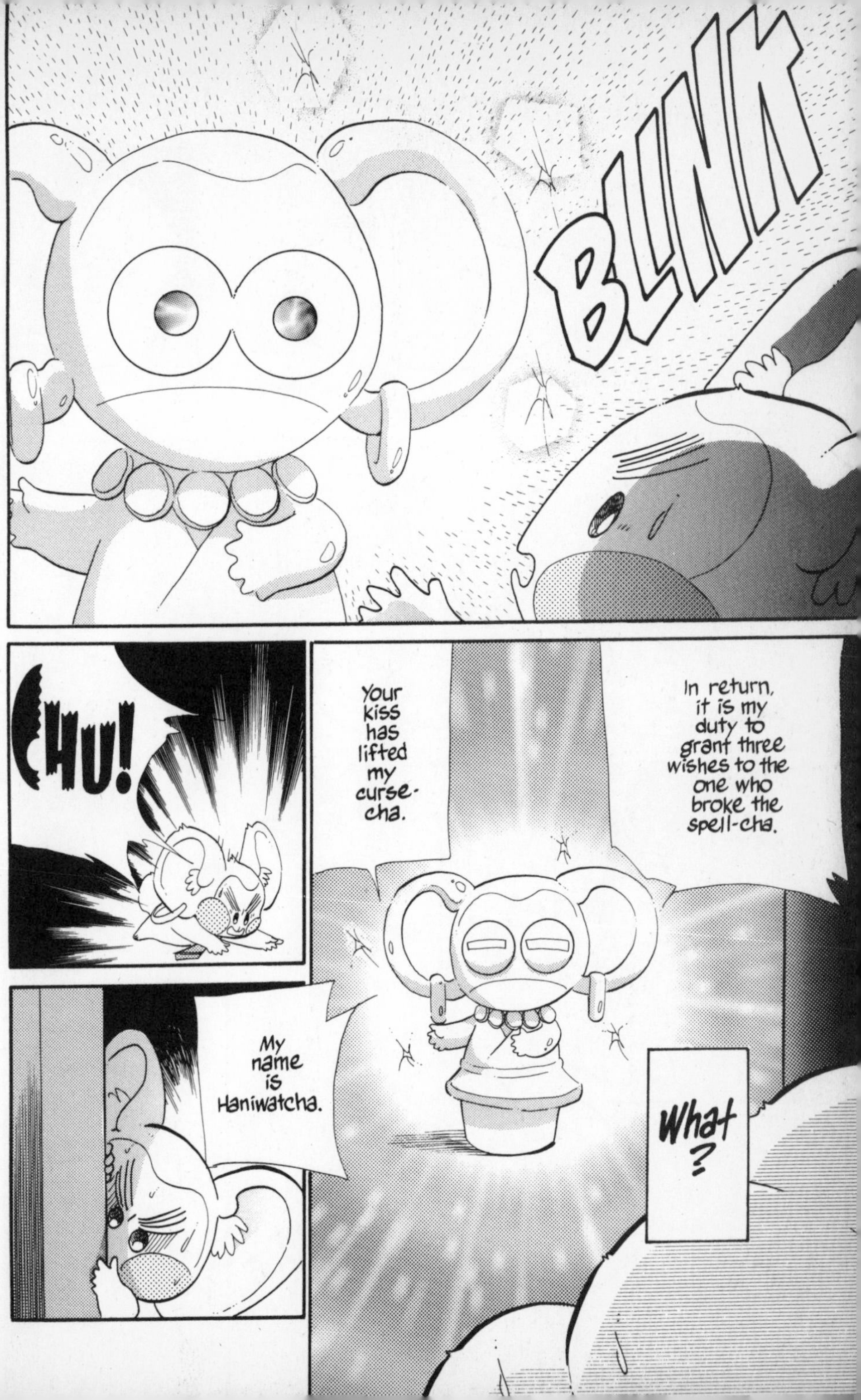
BLINK
CHU!
My name is Haniwatcha.
Your kiss has lifted my curse-cha.
In return, it is my duty to grant three wishes to the one who broke the spell-cha.
What?

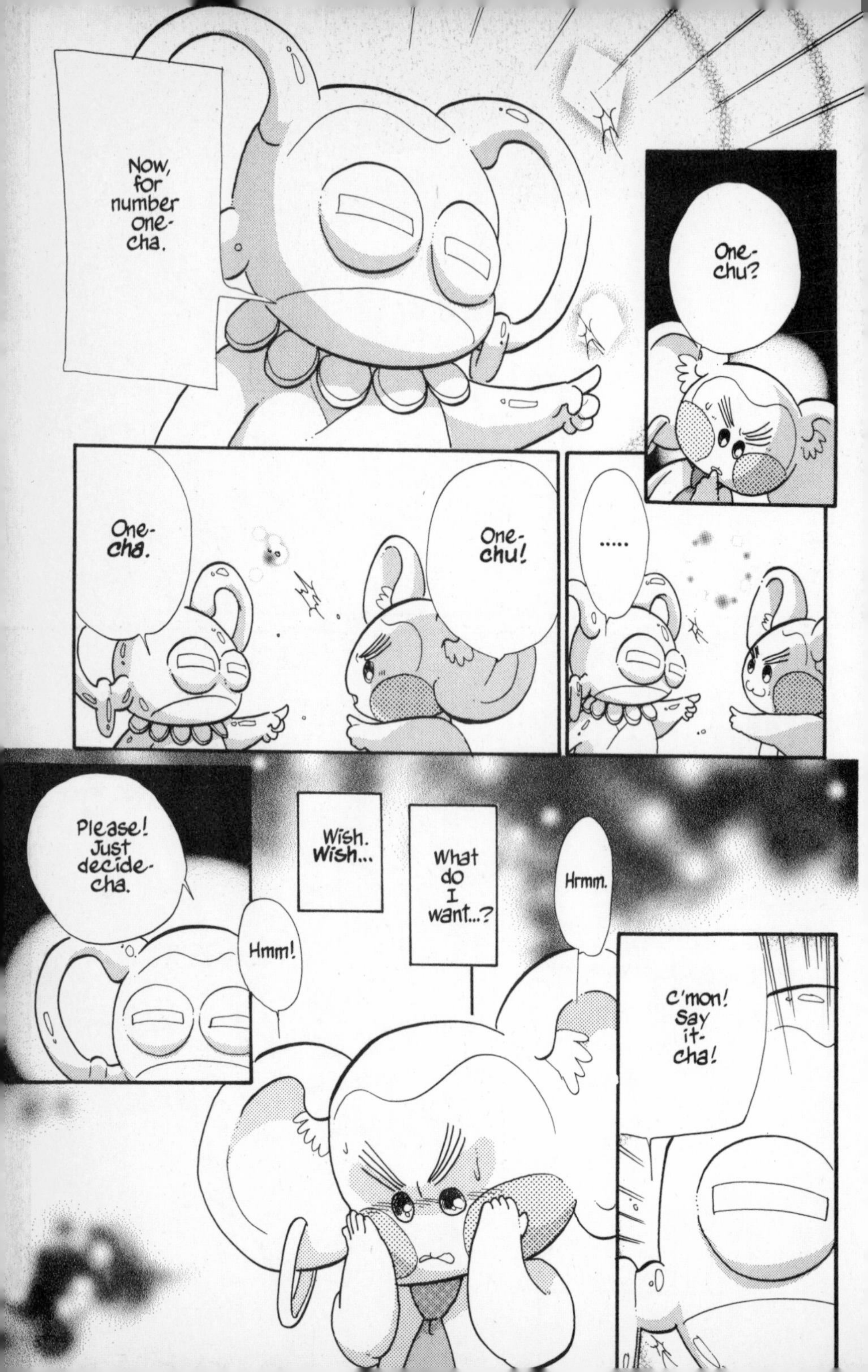
Now, for number one-cha.
One-chu?
One-cha.
One-chu!
.....
Please! Just decide-cha.
Hmm!
Wish. Wish...
What do I want...?
Hrmm.
C'mon! Say it-cha!

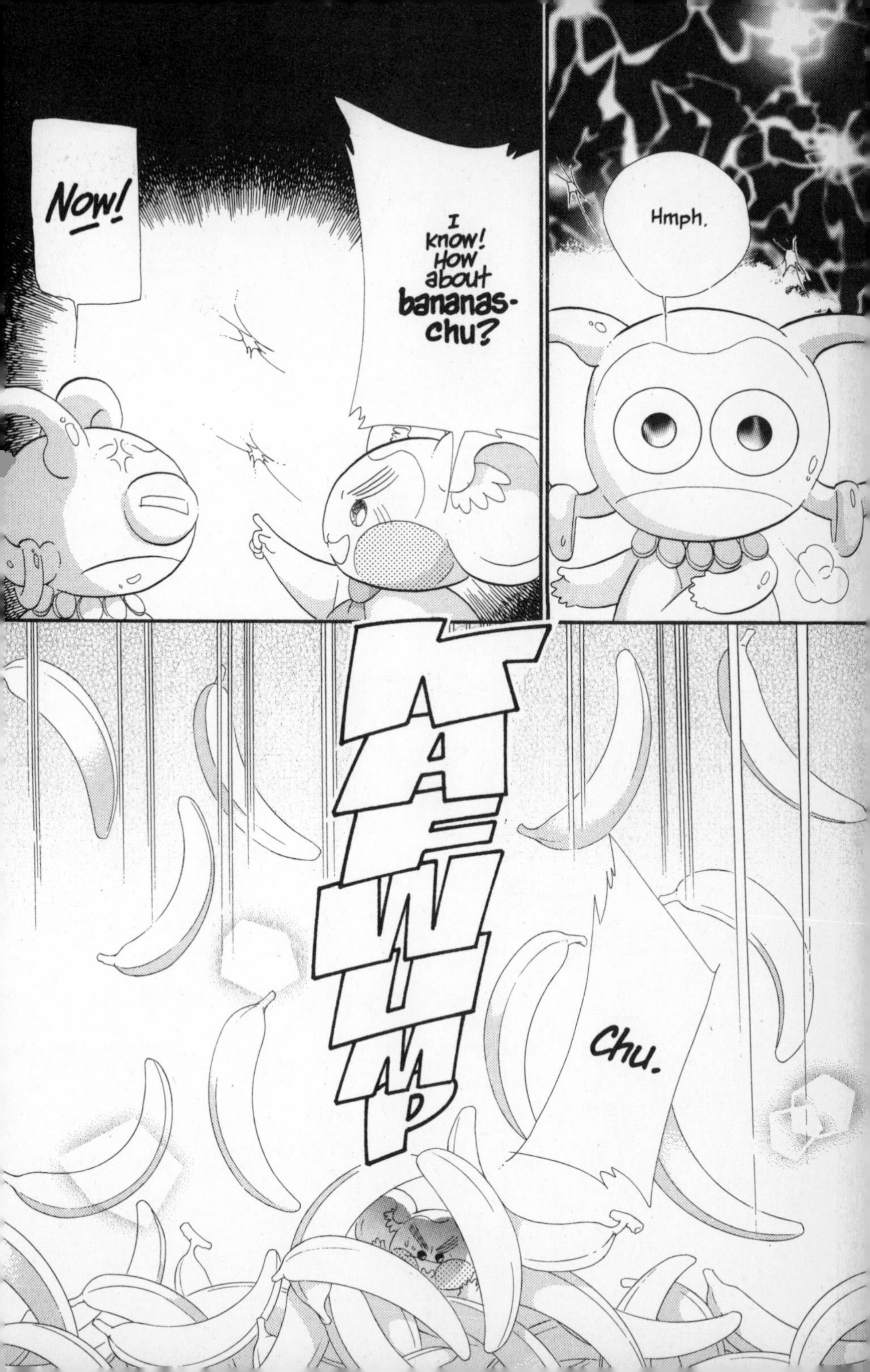
NOW!
I know! How about bananas-chu?
Hmph.
THWUMP
Chu.

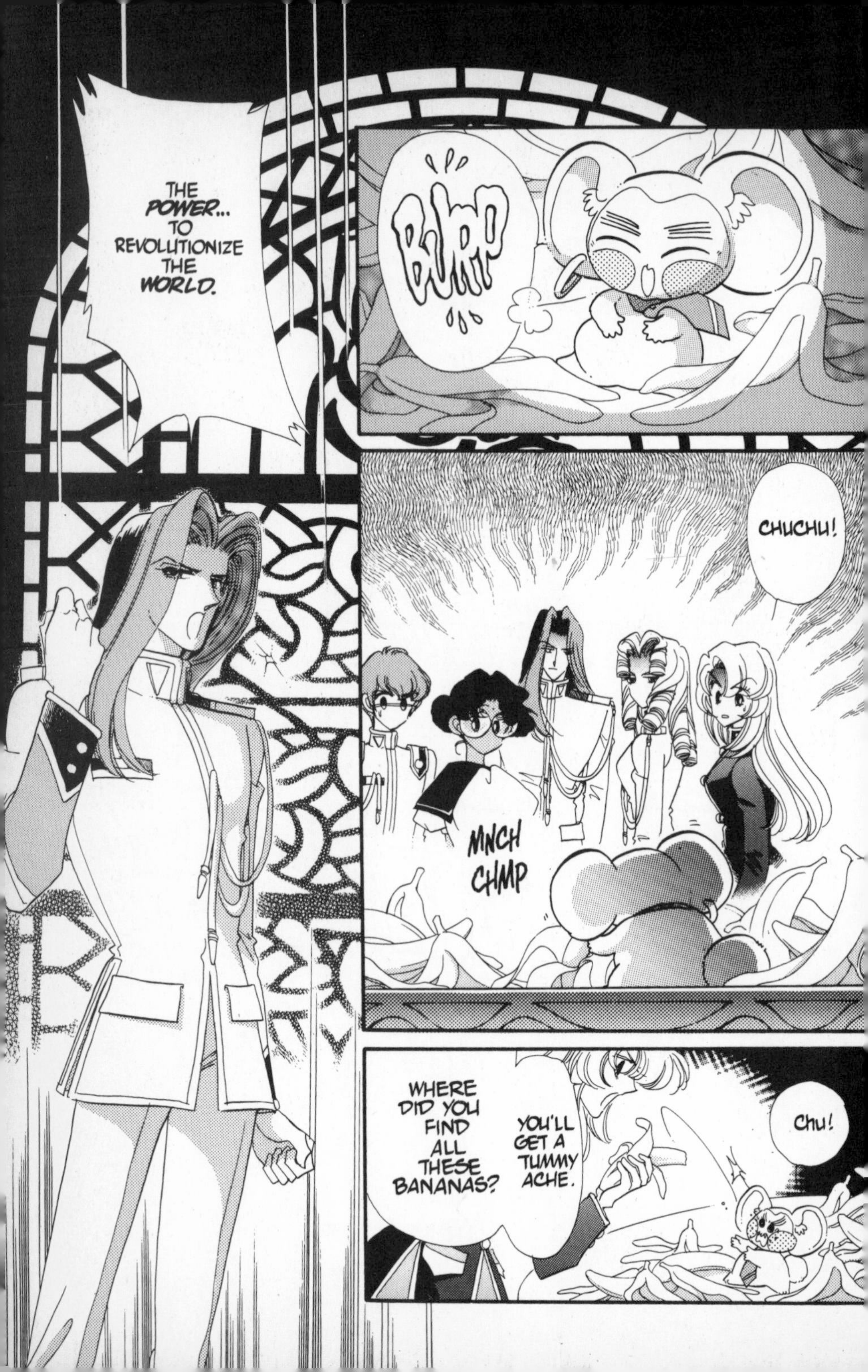
THE POWER... TO REVOLUTIONIZE THE WORLD.
BURP
CHUCHU!
MNCH CHMP
WHERE DID YOU FIND ALL THESE BANANAS?
YOU'LL GET A TUMMY ACHE.
Chu!

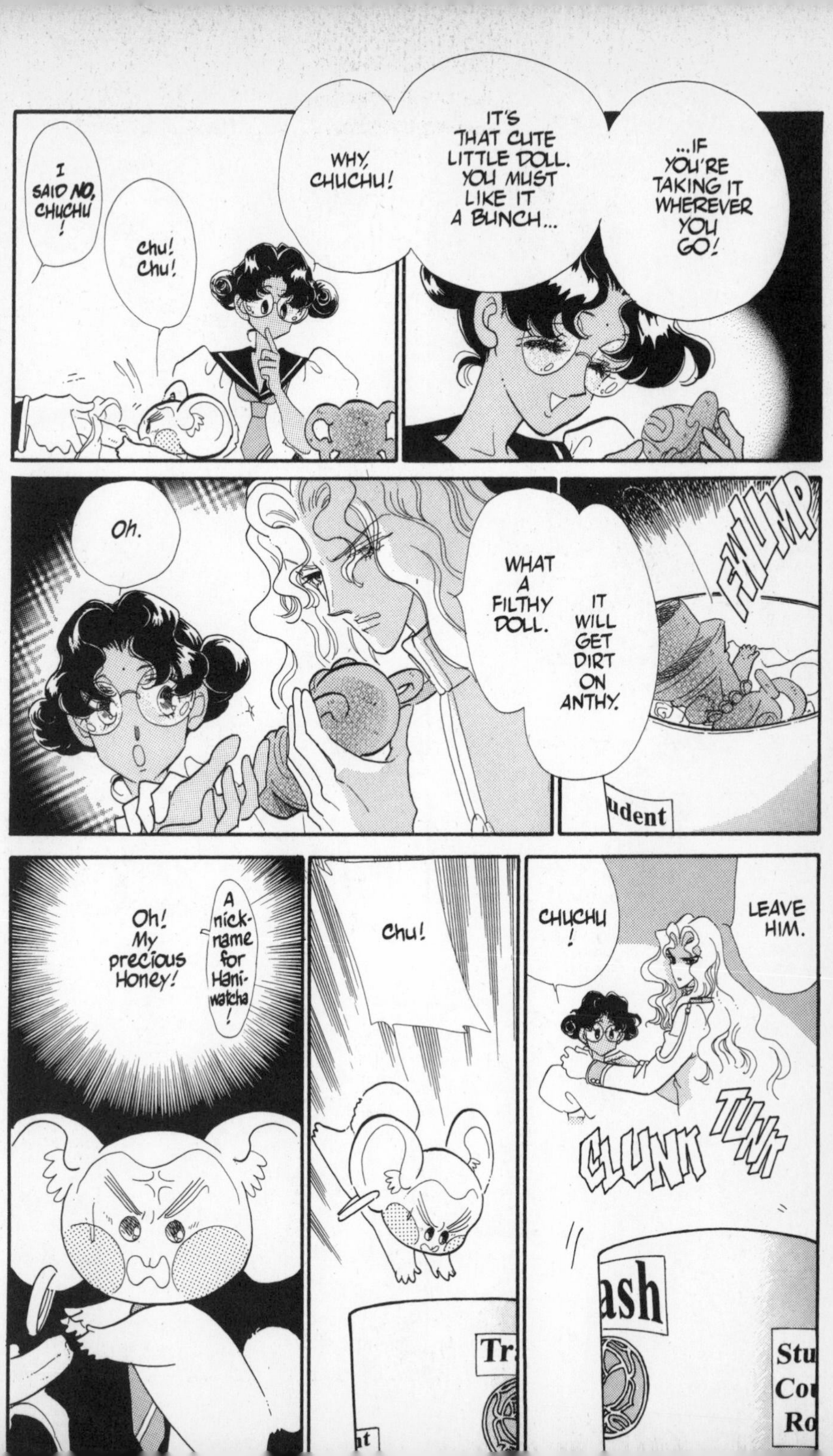
I SAID NO, CHUCHU!
Chu! Chu!
WHY, CHUCHU!
IT'S THAT CUTE LITTLE DOLL. YOU MUST LIKE IT A BUNCH...
...IF YOU'RE TAKING IT WHEREVER YOU GO!
Oh.
WHAT A FILTHY DOLL.
IT WILL GET DIRT ON ANTHY.
FWUMP
udent
Oh! My precious Honey!
A nick-name for Hani-watcha!
Chu!
Tra
CHUCHU!
LEAVE HIM.
CLUNK
TUNK
ash
Stu
Co
Ro

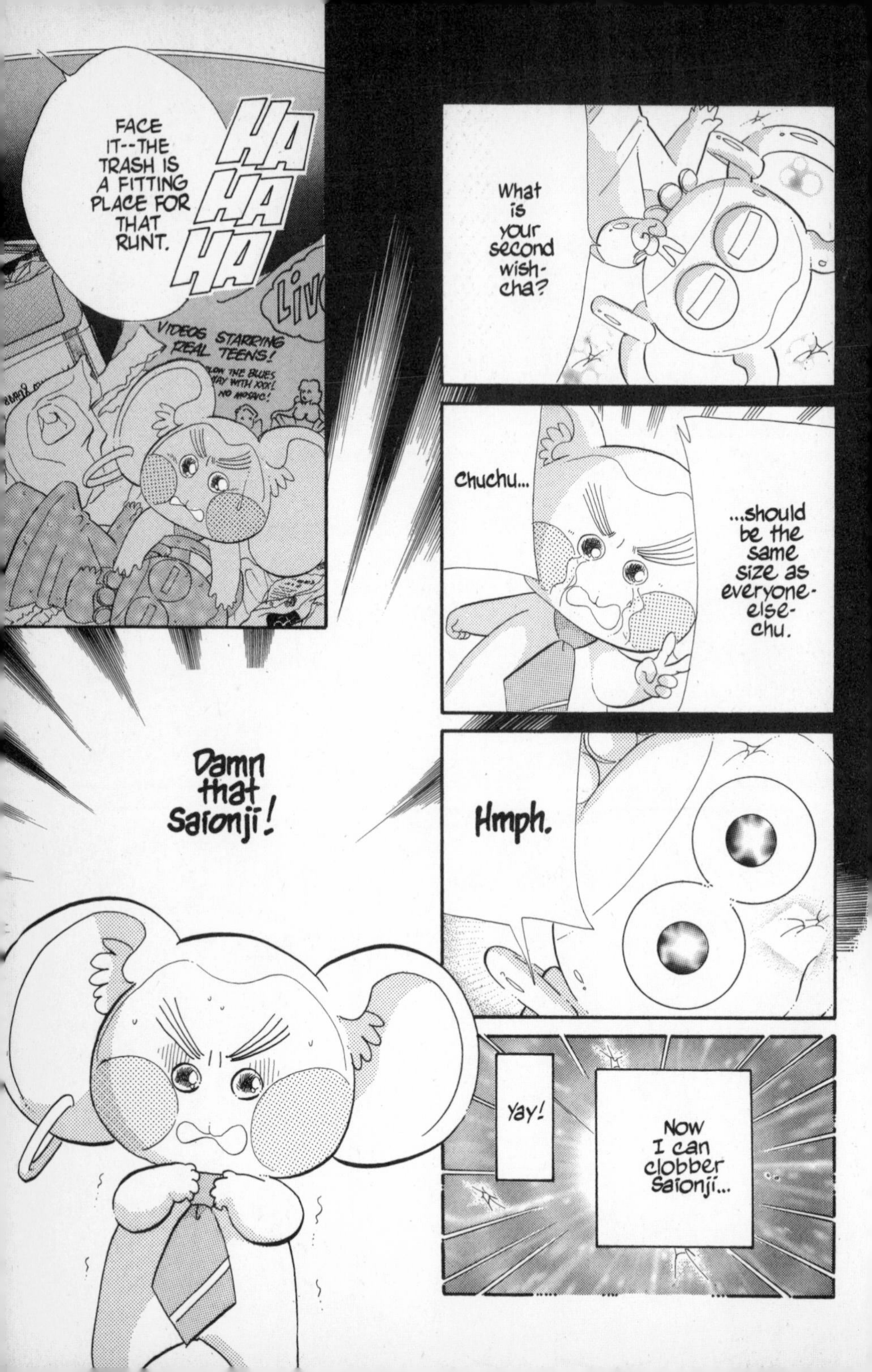
FACE IT--THE TRASH IS A FITTING PLACE FOR THAT RUNT.
HA HA HA
VIDEOS STARRING REAL TEENS!
Damn that Saionji!
What is your second wish-cha?
Chuchu...
...should be the same size as everyone-else-chu.
Hmph.
Yay!
Now I can clobber Saionji...

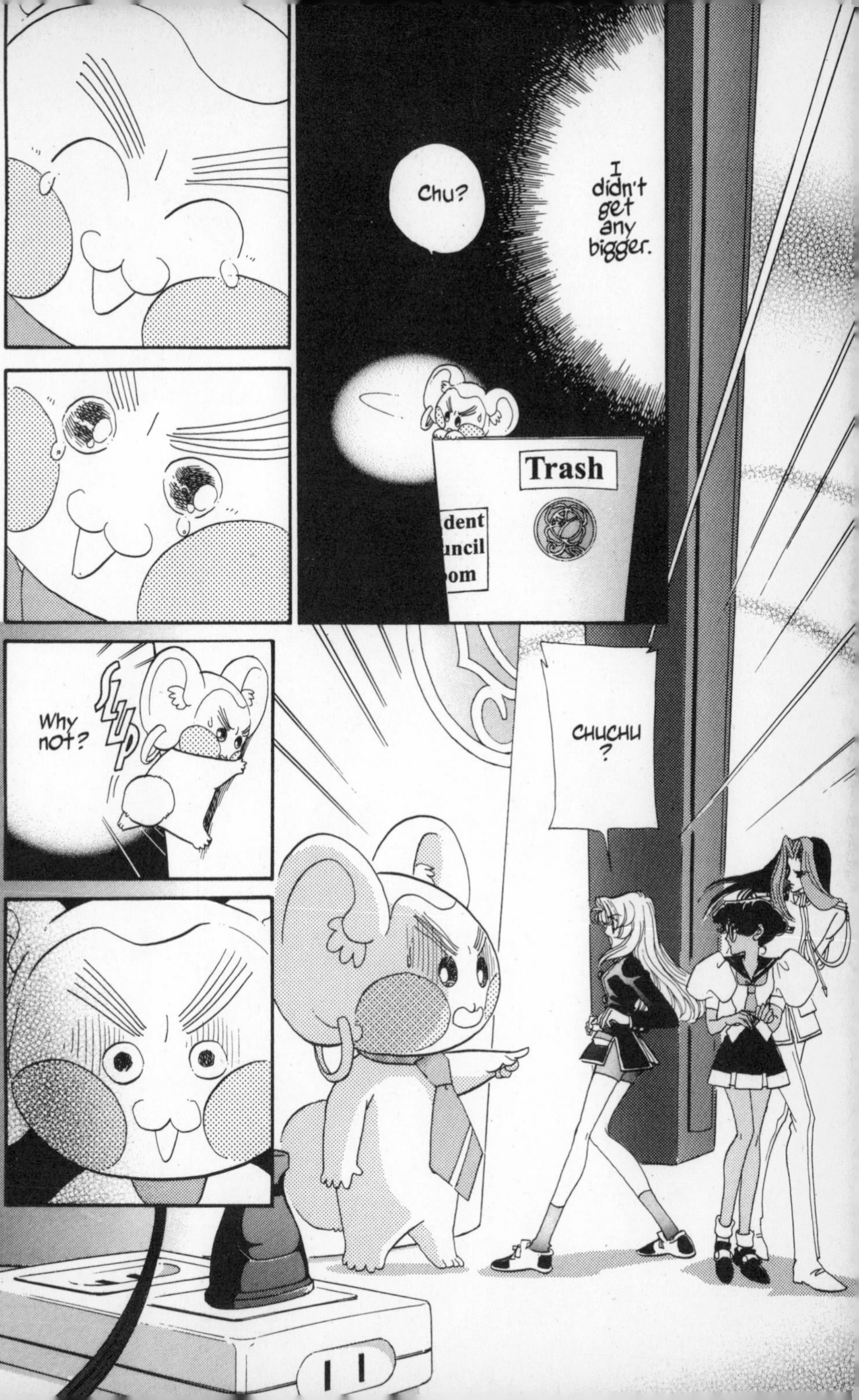
Chu?
I didn't get any bigger.
Trash
Why not?
SLUP
CHUCHU ?

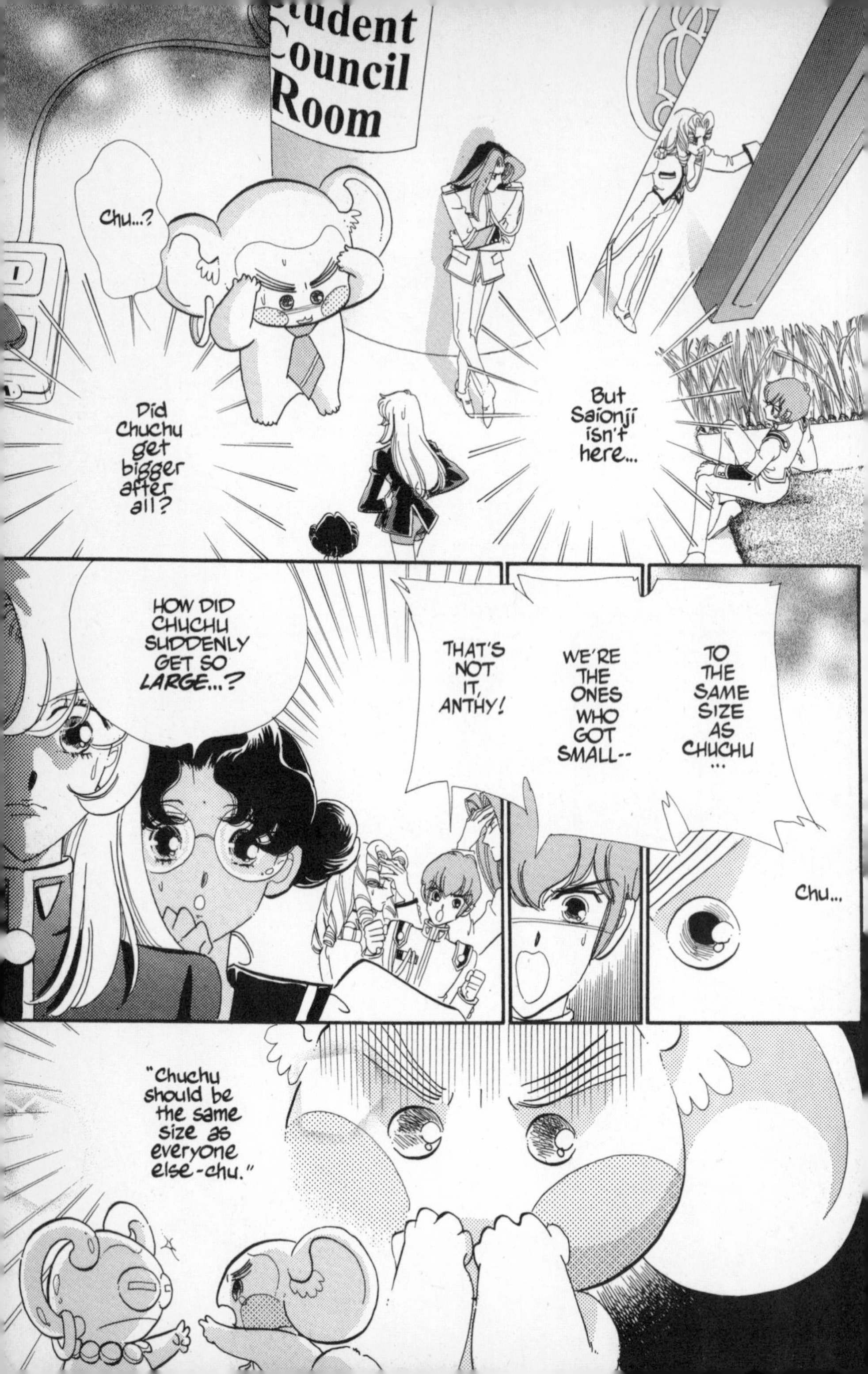

tudent Council Room
Chu...?
Did Chuchu get bigger after all?
But Saionji isn't here...
HOW DID CHUCHU SUDDENLY GET SO *LARGE*...?
THAT'S NOT IT, ANTHY!
WE'RE THE ONES WHO GOT SMALL--
TO THE SAME SIZE AS CHUCHU...
Chu...
"Chuchu should be the same size as everyone else-chu."

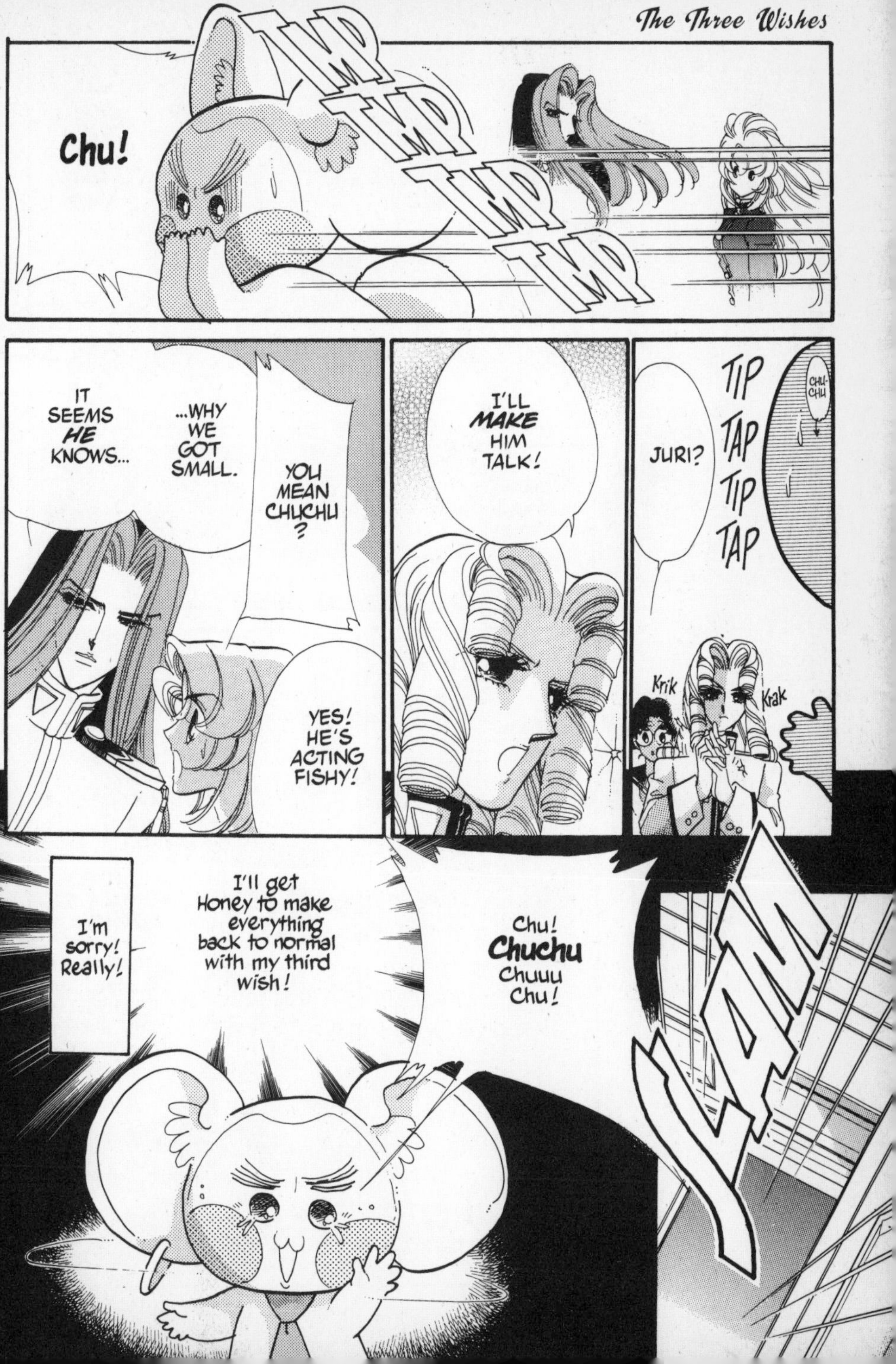
Chu!
TMP TMP TMP TMP
IT SEEMS HE KNOWS...
...WHY WE GOT SMALL.
YOU MEAN CHUCHU?
YES! HE'S ACTING FISHY!
I'LL MAKE HIM TALK!
JURI?
TIP TAP TIP TAP
CHU-CHU
Krik
Krak
I'm sorry! Really!
I'll get Honey to make everything back to normal with my third wish!
Chu! Chuchu Chuuu Chu!
SLAM

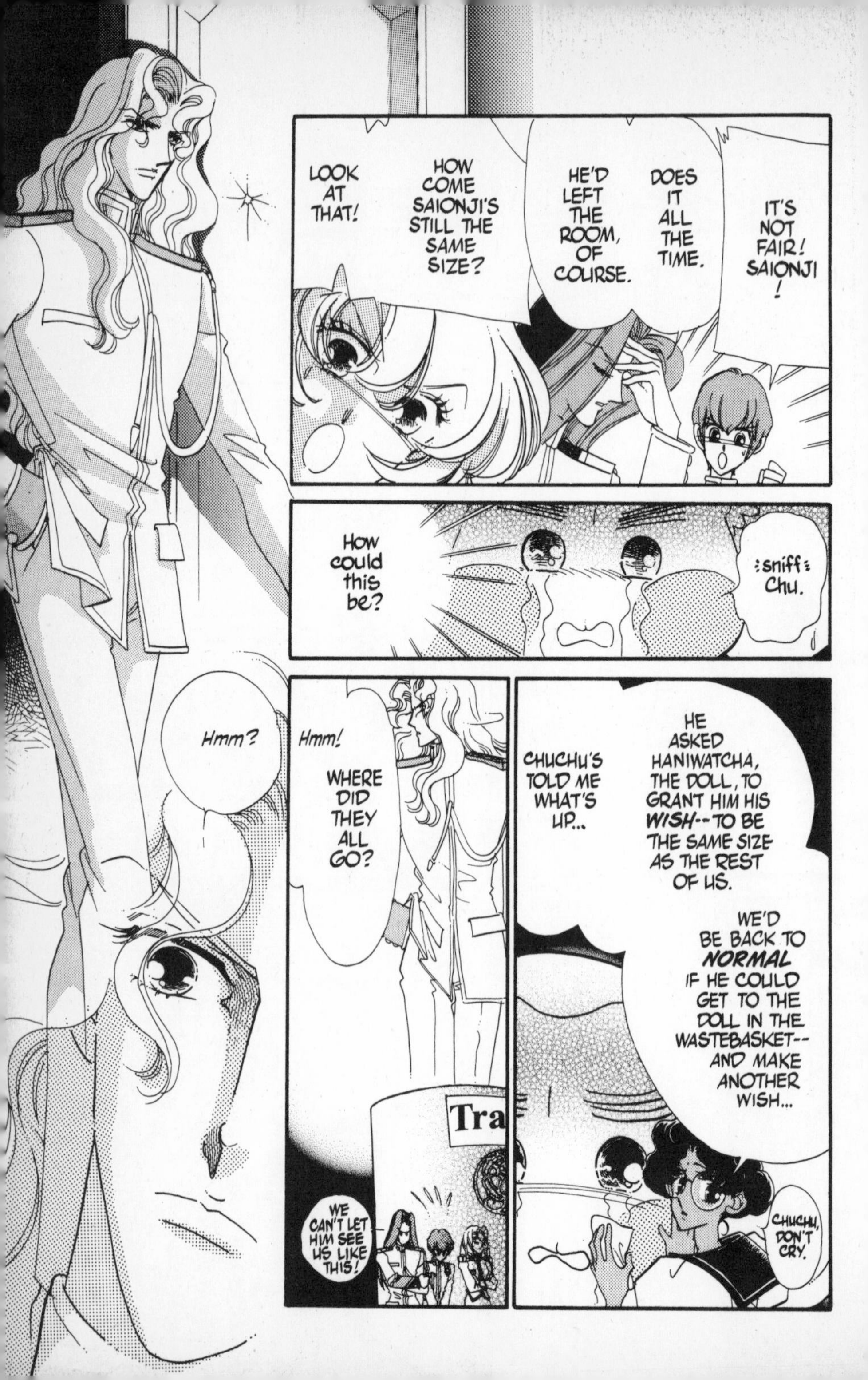

Hmm?
LOOK AT THAT!
HOW COME SAIONJI'S STILL THE SAME SIZE?
HE'D LEFT THE ROOM, OF COURSE.
DOES IT ALL THE TIME.
IT'S NOT FAIR! SAIONJI!
How could this be?
:sniff: Chu.
Hmm!
WHERE DID THEY ALL GO?
Tra
WE CAN'T LET HIM SEE US LIKE THIS!
CHUCHU'S TOLD ME WHAT'S UP...
HE ASKED HANIWATCHA, THE DOLL, TO GRANT HIM HIS WISH--TO BE THE SAME SIZE AS THE REST OF US.
WE'D BE BACK TO NORMAL IF HE COULD GET TO THE DOLL IN THE WASTEBASKET--AND MAKE ANOTHER WISH...
CHUCHU, DON'T CRY.

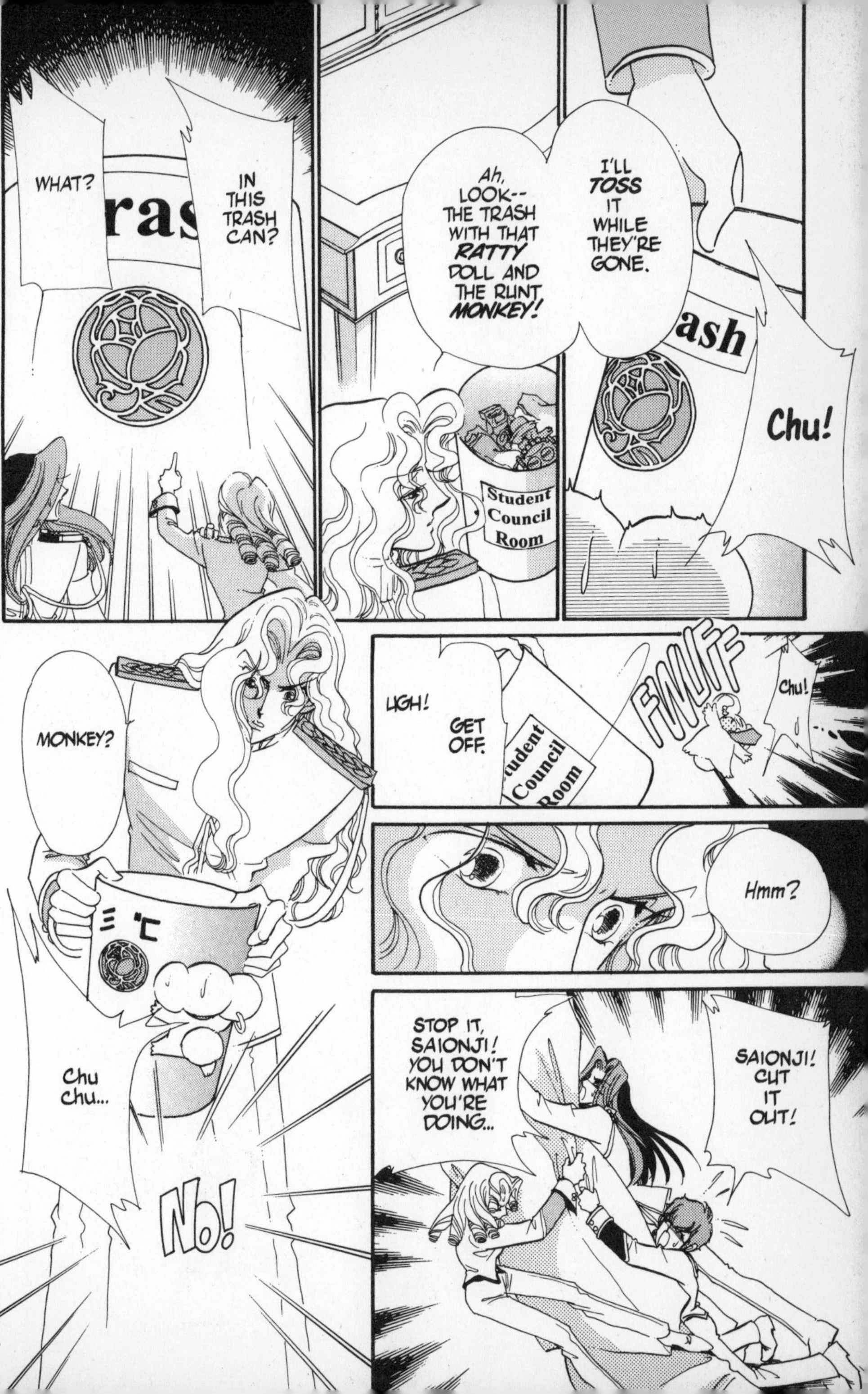

WHAT?
IN THIS TRASH CAN?
Ah, LOOK-- THE TRASH WITH THAT RATTY DOLL AND THE RUNT MONKEY!
I'LL TOSS IT WHILE THEY'RE GONE.
Student Council Room
Chu!
MONKEY?
Chu chu...
No!
UGH!
GET OFF.
Student Council Room
FWUFF
Chu!
Hmm?
STOP IT, SAIONJI! YOU DON'T KNOW WHAT YOU'RE DOING...
SAIONJI! CUT IT OUT!

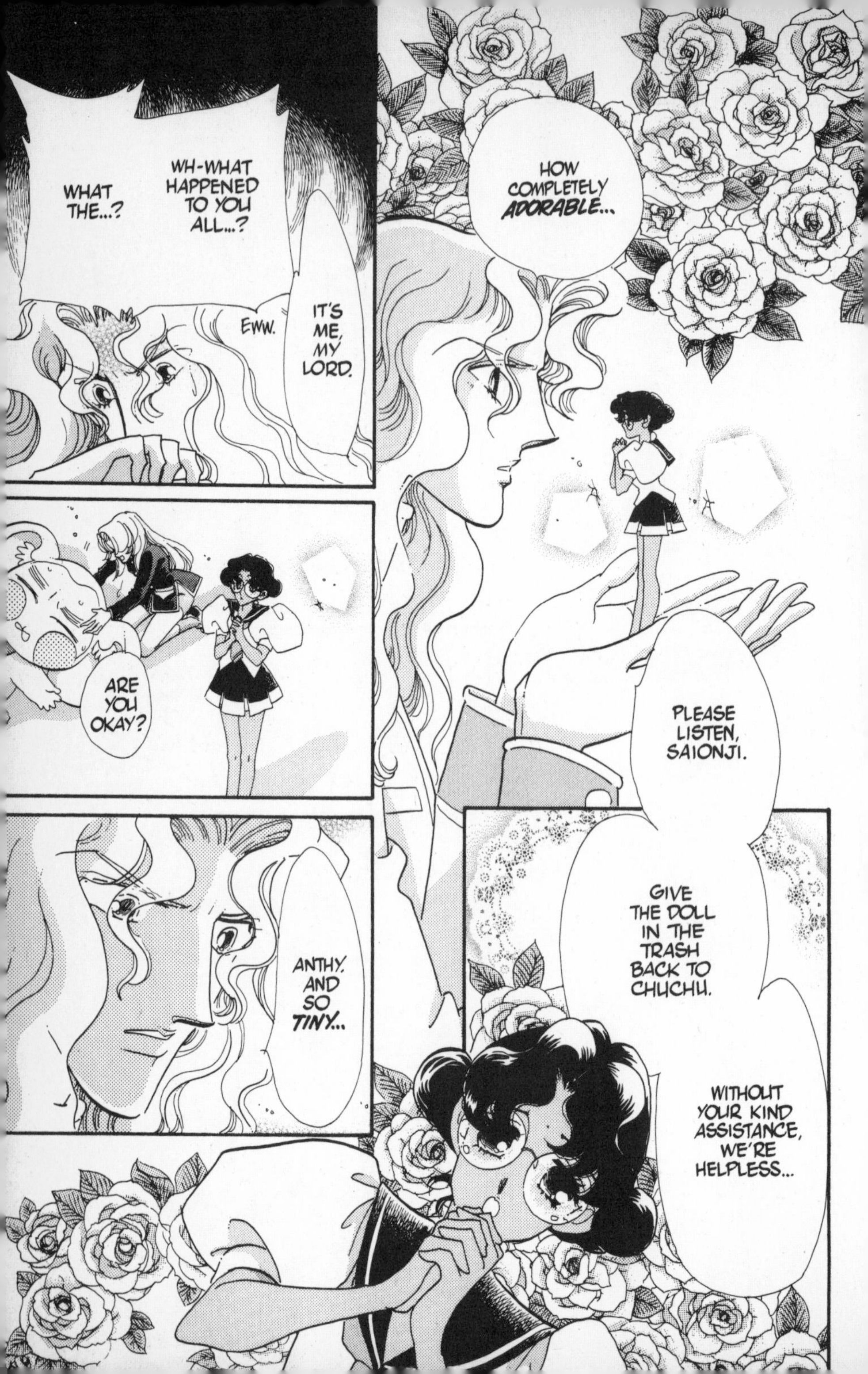
WHAT THE...?
WH-WHAT HAPPENED TO YOU ALL...?
EWW.
IT'S ME, MY LORD.
ARE YOU OKAY?
ANTHY. AND SO *TINY*...
HOW COMPLETELY *ADORABLE*...
PLEASE LISTEN, SAIONJI.
GIVE THE DOLL IN THE TRASH BACK TO CHUCHU.
WITHOUT YOUR KIND ASSISTANCE, WE'RE HELPLESS...

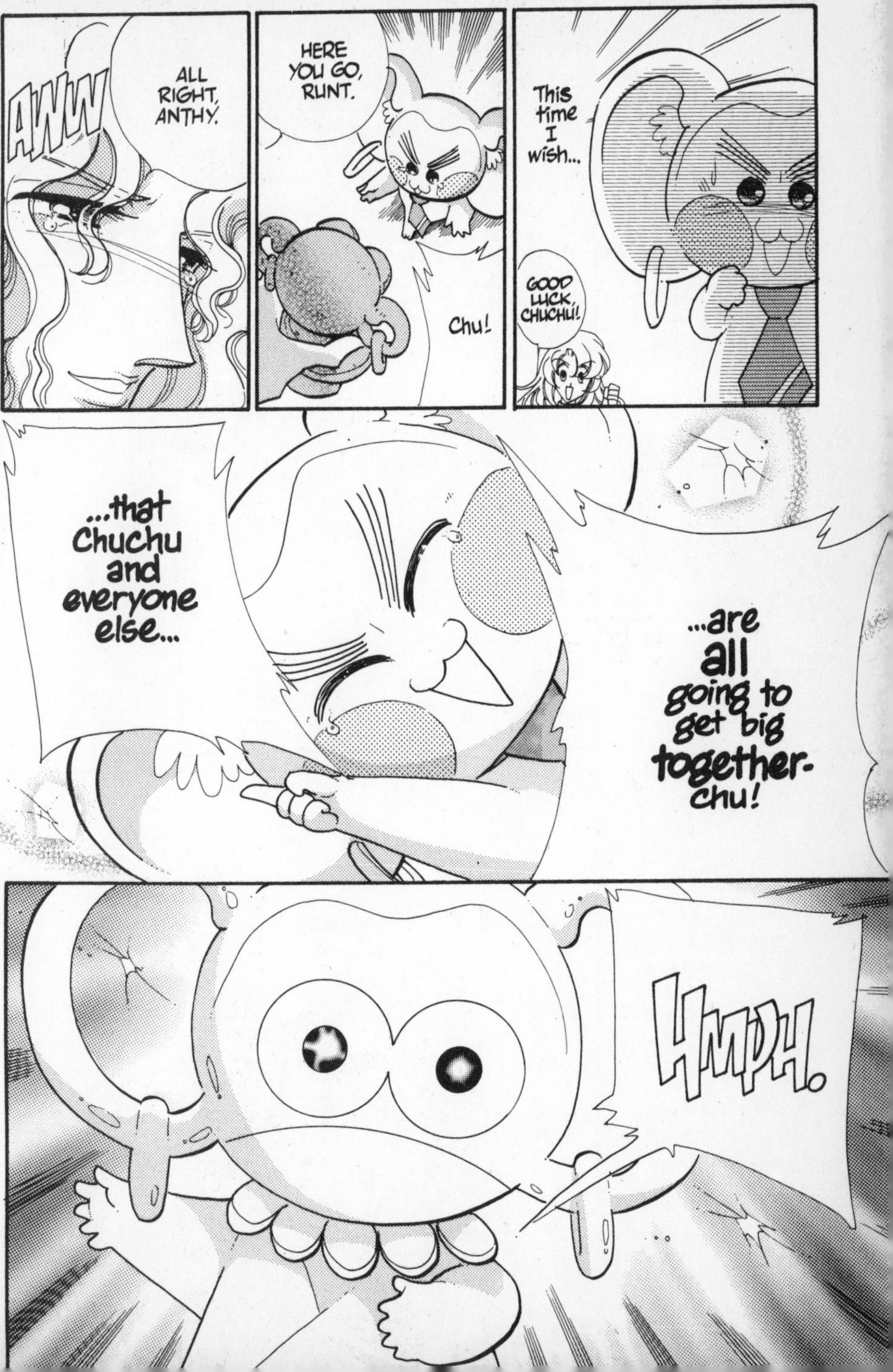
AWW
ALL RIGHT, ANTHY.
HERE YOU GO, RUNT.
Chu!
This time I wish...
GOOD LUCK, CHUCHU!
...that Chuchu and everyone else...
...are all going to get big together-chu!
HMPH.

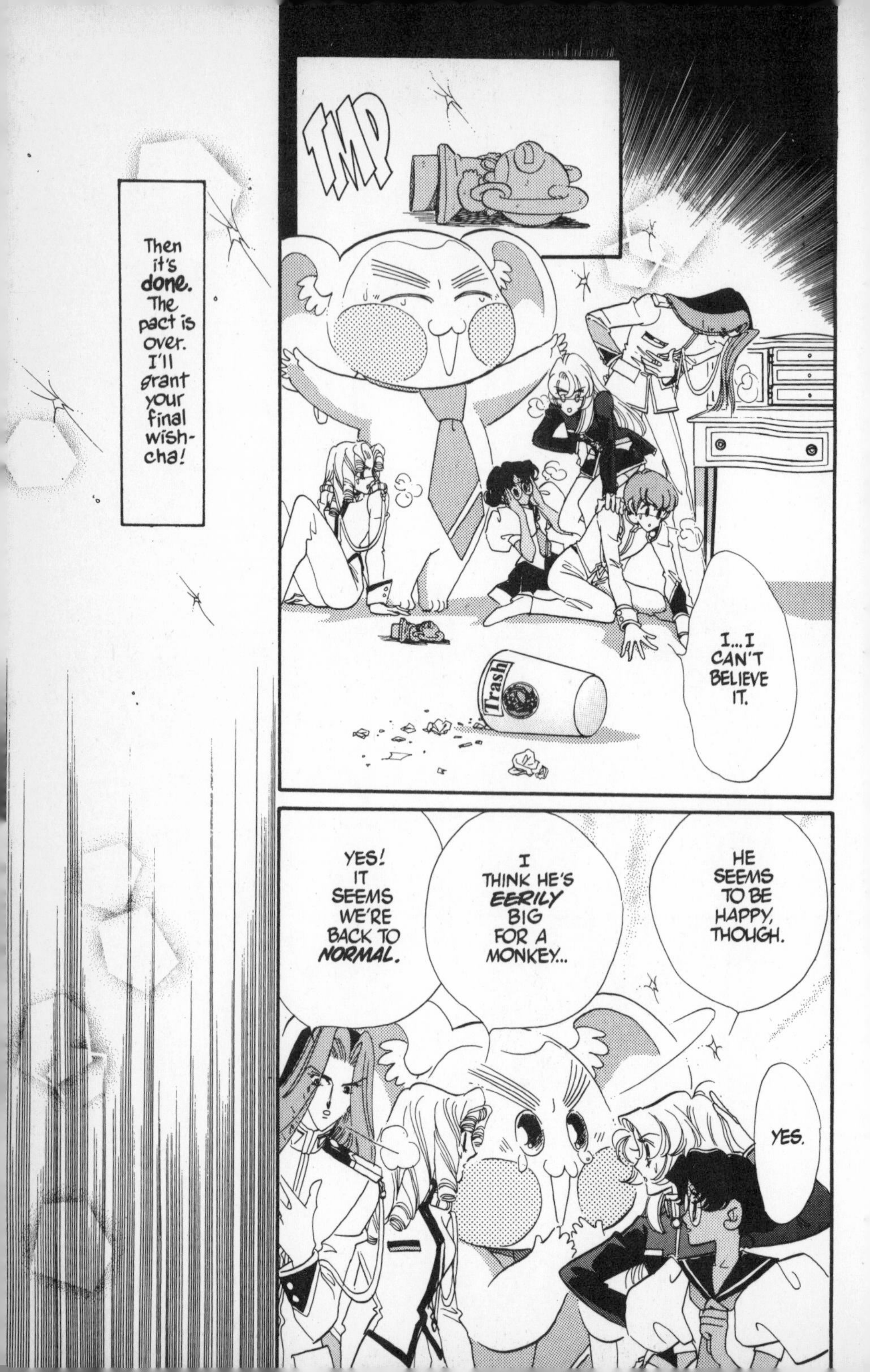
Then it's done. The pact is over. I'll grant your final wish-cha!
TMP
I... I CAN'T BELIEVE IT.
YES! IT SEEMS WE'RE BACK TO NORMAL.
I THINK HE'S EERILY BIG FOR A MONKEY...
HE SEEMS TO BE HAPPY, THOUGH.
YES.

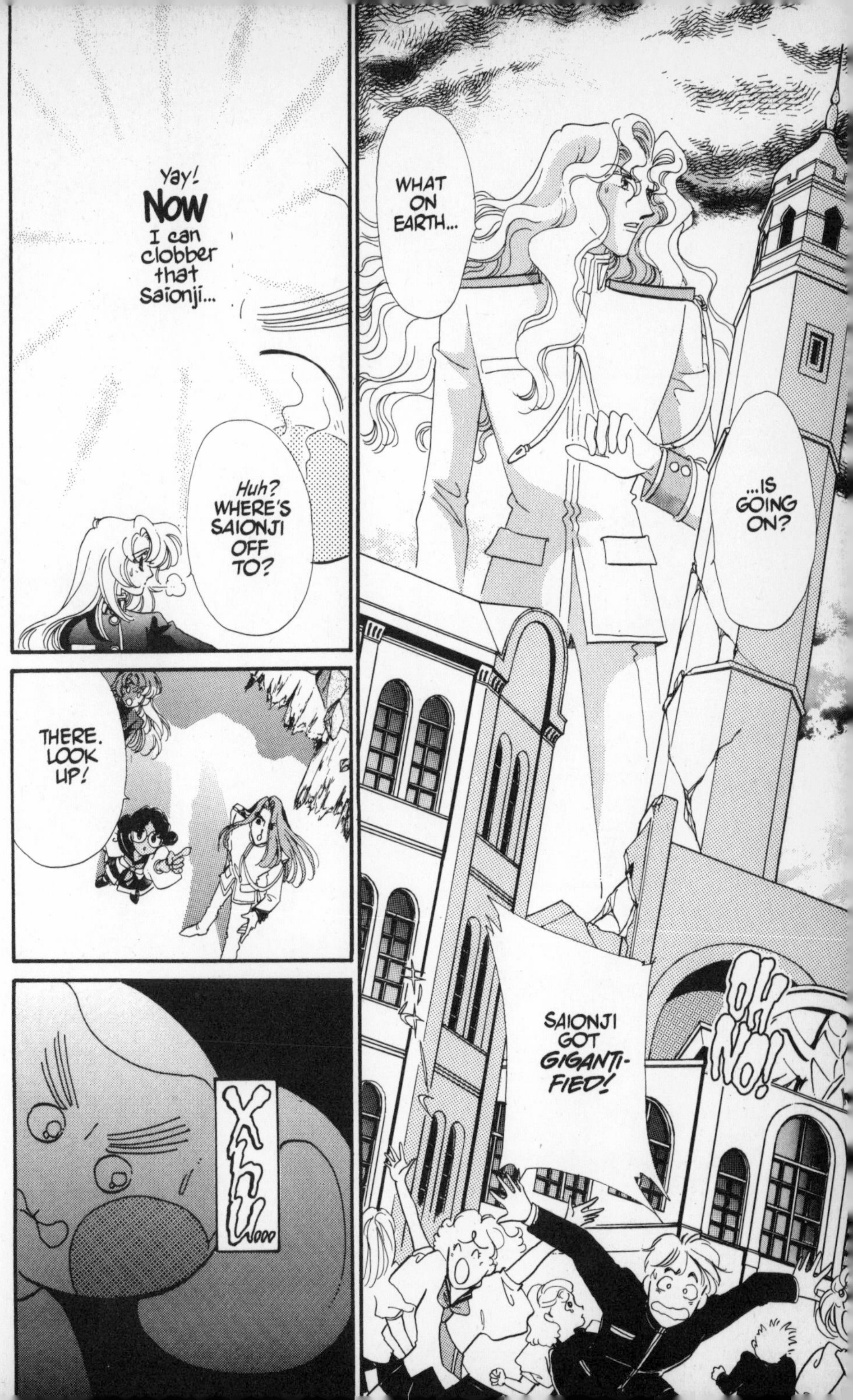
Yay! NOW I can clobber that Saionji...
Huh? WHERE'S SAIONJI OFF TO?
THERE. LOOK UP!
WHAT ON EARTH...
...IS GOING ON?
SAIONJI GOT GIGANTI-FIED!
OH NO!

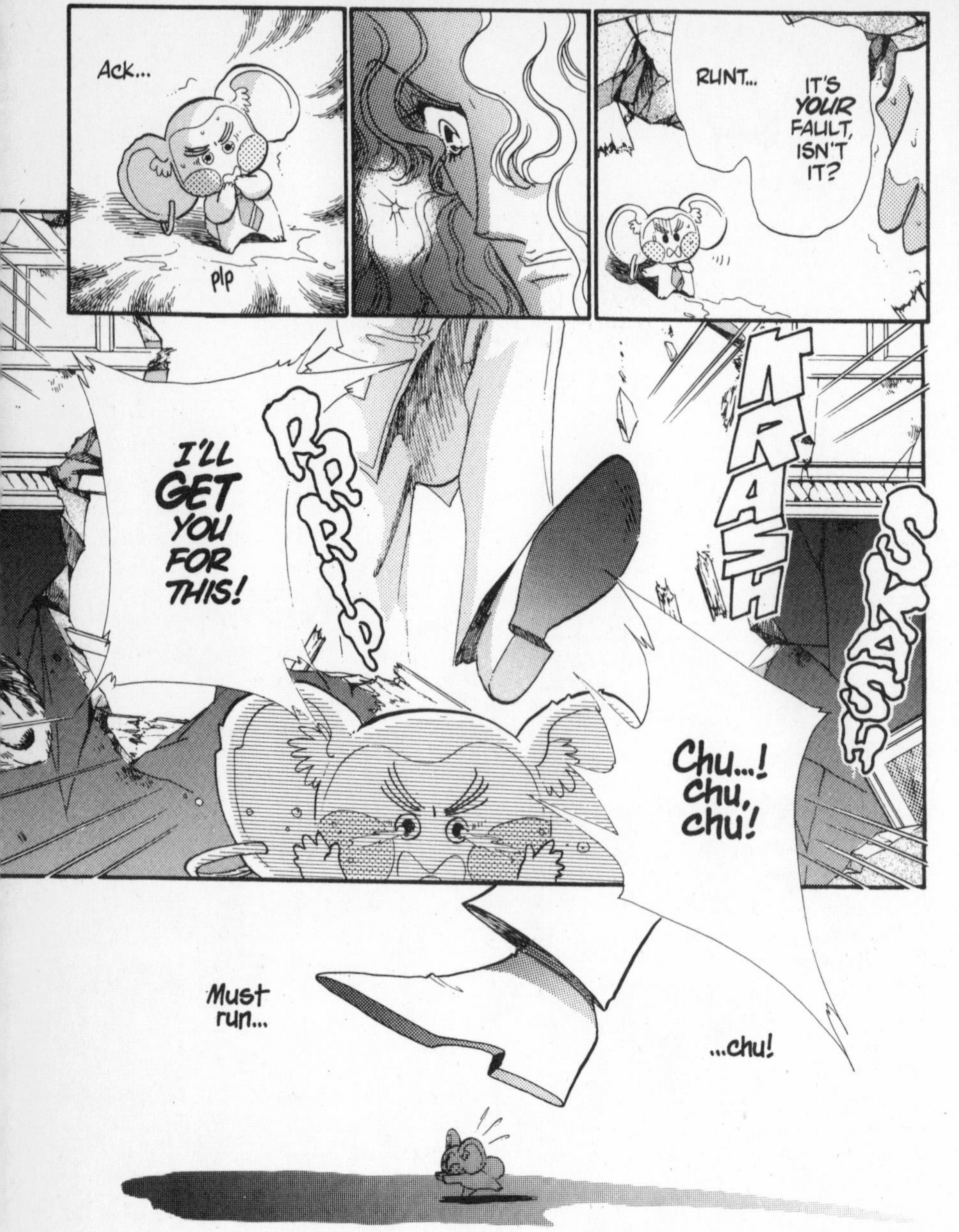
ACK...
PLP
RUNT...
IT'S YOUR FAULT, ISN'T IT?
I'LL GET YOU FOR THIS!
RRRIP
KRASH
SPLASH
Chu...! chu, chu!
Must run...
...chu!

The Three Wishes: The End

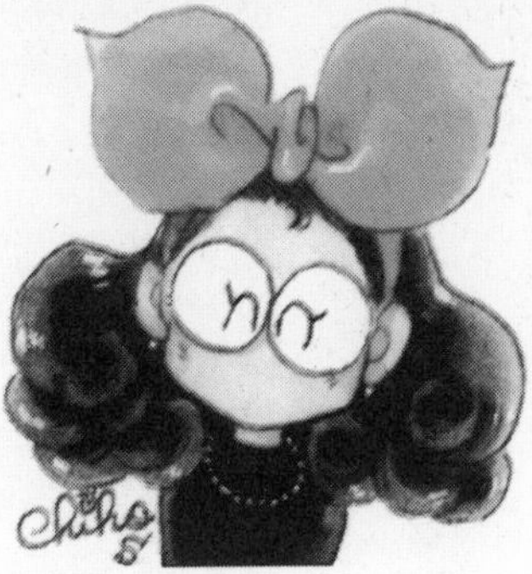
Chiho

The "Search for One's Prince" is probably a combination of the search for "that kind of parental-like love that would never betray you," and a feeling that you are, "the child waiting to be rescued." No matter how gallantly Utena battles on, deep in her heart is the oppressive yearning to have someone "take care of her," which sometimes finds its way onto her facial expressions. In my opinion, that's a very human failing and very sweet.

Chiho Saito

When I was in the art club in high school, I was very anxious to hear praise from a girl I admired, and I tried to draw pictures that would match her tastes. Looking on it now, they weren't pictures that I actually wanted to draw, and I can see that I was wasting my time...probably. But even so, at the time it really filled my heart. I guess you could call that the power of love.

Kunihiko Ikuhara

Be Papas:

A group of highly creative people founded by director Kunihiko Ikuhara (Sailor Moon, Schell Bullet) and including such storied members as master manga artist Chiho Saito (Kakan no Madonna, Lady Masquerade) and Animator Shinya Hasegawa (Evangelion). Their collaboration produced the Utena TV series and the movie, Revolutionary Girl Utena: The Adolescence of Utena, and recently they have produced a new work called The World of S&M.

THE POWER TO REVOLUTIONIZE THE WORLD

THE STORY OF UTENA TENJOU IS RIFE WITH SWORD FIGHTS, GENDER CONFUSION, SEXUAL SERVITUDE, HINTS OF INCEST AND HEAVY DOLLOPS OF SYMBOLIC IMAGERY. KINKY AND HIGHLY STYLIZED, IT'S THE STORY OF A TEENAGE GIRL WHO WANTS TO BE A PRINCE.

FIRST PUBLISHED IN 1996 AS **SHOUJO KAKUMEI UTENA**, **REVOLUTIONARY GIRL UTENA** WOULD EVENTUALLY POP UP ON JAPANESE TELEVISION AND IN MOVIE THEATERS. IT WOULD EVEN BE SERIALIZED A SECOND TIME IN PRINT. WITH EACH NEW INTERPRETATION, THE STORY WOULD CHANGE SLIGHTLY BUT REMAIN ESSENTIALLY THE SAME.

BUT IN 1996, THE STORY OF A SWORD-FIGHTING, CROSS-DRESSING HEROINE WAS NOTHING NEW TO JAPANESE MANGA READERS. OSAMU TEZUKA PIONEERED THE CONCEPT BACK IN 1953 WITH **PRINCESS KNIGHT**. AND NEARLY TWENTY YEARS LATER, RIYOKO IKEDA SPICED IT UP WITH A FRENCH HISTORICAL TWIST IN HER EPIC, **THE ROSE OF VERSAILLES**.

MORE THAN ANYTHING, HOWEVER, **REVOLUTIONARY GIRL UTENA** EXISTS AS A METAPHOR FOR A YOUNG GIRL'S PASSAGE INTO ADULTHOOD. YES, THERE IS SUB-TEXT AND SYMBOLIC OVERLOAD ON EVERY PAGE, BUT DON'T LET THAT STUFF DETRACT YOU FROM ENJOYING THIS TIMELESS STORY.

UTENA TENJOU GREW UP WANTING TO BE A PRINCE BUT ULTIMATELY BECAME A PRINCESS. IN THE END, SHE DISCOVERED WHO SHE REALLY WANTED TO BE AND IN THE PROCESS SHE REVOLUTIONIZED THE WORLD.

ERIC SEARLEMAN
EDITOR, **REVOLUTIONARY GIRL UTENA**

Like Revolutionary Girl Utena?

Here are three more books we think you'll enjoy:

X/1999:

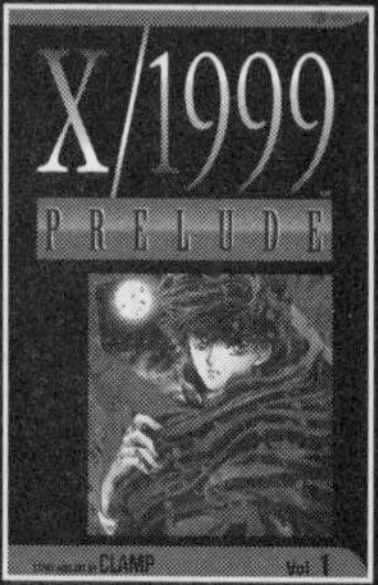
X/1999
PRELUDE
CLAMP
Vol. 1

Produced by the popular CLAMP creative team, here's the mother of all epic science fiction, occult and fantasy shôjo titles. If there's not enough girl power spizz energy in your life, look no further than the X.

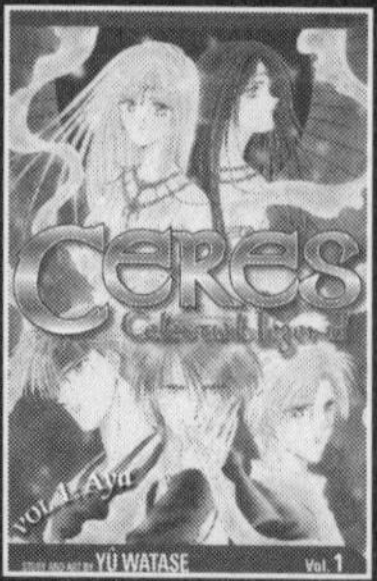
Ceres
YÛ WATASE
Vol. 1

CERES CELESTIAL LEGEND:

Aya Mikage is an average high school kid until her 16th birthday. That's the day she discovers her parents want to kill her. Yû Watase, the creator of **Fushigi Yûgi**, sharpens her wit with this funny and highly unusual horror story.

A, A' [A Prime]:

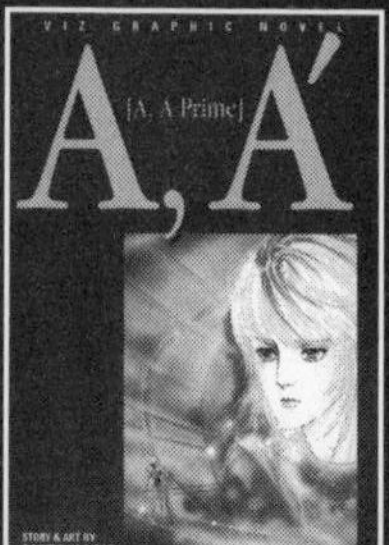
VIZ GRAPHIC NOVEL
A, A'
[A, A Prime]
STORY & ART BY
MOTO HAGIO

A prime example of science fiction shôjo. Artist Moto Hagio presents four separate (but thematically related) short stories exploring mankind's moral obligation to the future.

COMPLETE OUR SURVEY AND LET US KNOW WHAT YOU THINK!

☐ Please check here if you DO NOT wish to receive information or future offers from VIZ

Name: _____

Address: _____

City: _____ **State:** _____ **Zip:** _____

E-mail: _____

☐ Male ☐ Female **Date of Birth** (mm/dd/yyyy): ___/___/_____ (Under 13? Parental consent required)

What race/ethnicity do you consider yourself? (please check one)

☐ Asian/Pacific Islander ☐ Black/African American ☐ Hispanic/Latino

☐ Native American/Alaskan Native ☐ White/Caucasian ☐ Other: _____

What VIZ product did you purchase? (check all that apply and indicate title purchased)

☐ DVD/VHS _____

☐ Graphic Novel _____

☐ Magazines _____

☐ Merchandise _____

Reason for purchase: (check all that apply)

☐ Special offer ☐ Favorite title ☐ Gift

☐ Recommendation ☐ Other _____

Where did you make your purchase? (please check one)

☐ Comic store ☐ Bookstore ☐ Mass/Grocery Store

☐ Newsstand ☐ Video/Video Game Store ☐ Other: _____

☐ Online (site: _____)

What other VIZ properties have you purchased/own? _____

_____

How many anime and/or manga titles have you purchased in the last year? How many were VIZ titles? (please check one from each column)

ANIME	MANGA	VIZ
☐ None	☐ None	☐ None
☐ 1-4	☐ 1-4	☐ 1-4
☐ 5-10	☐ 5-10	☐ 5-10
☐ 11+	☐ 11+	☐ 11+

I find the pricing of VIZ products to be: (please check one)

☐ Cheap ☐ Reasonable ☐ Expensive

What genre of manga and anime would you like to see from VIZ? (please check two)

☐ Adventure ☐ Comic Strip ☐ Detective ☐ Fighting

☐ Horror ☐ Romance ☐ Sci-Fi/Fantasy ☐ Sports

What do you think of VIZ's new look?

☐ Love It ☐ It's OK ☐ Hate It ☐ Didn't Notice ☐ No Opinion

THANK YOU! Please send the completed form to:

NJW Research
42 Catharine St.
Poughkeepsie, NY 12601

All information provided will be used for internal purposes only. We promise not to sell or otherwise divulge your information.